MW01096302

MacArthur's Korean War Generals

MODERN WAR STUDIES

Theodore A. Wilson
General Editor

Raymond Callahan
Jacob W. Kipp
Allan R. Millett
Carol Reardon
Dennis Showalter
David R. Stone
James H. Willbanks
Series Editors

MacArthur's Korean War Generals

STEPHEN R. TAAFFE

 University Press of Kansas

© 2016 by the University Press of Kansas
All rights reserved

Published by the University Press of Kansas (Lawrence, Kansas 66045),
which was organized by the Kansas Board of Regents and is operated and
funded by Emporia State University, Fort Hays State University, Kansas
State University, Pittsburg State University, the University of Kansas, and
Wichita State University

Library of Congress Cataloging-in-Publication Data

Names: Taaffe, Stephen R., author.
Title: MacArthur's Korean War generals / Stephen R. Taaffe.
Description: Lawrence, Kansas : University Press of Kansas, 2016. |
Series: Modern war studies | Includes bibliographical references and
index.
Identifiers: LCCN 2015044258
ISBN 9780700622214 (cloth : alk. paper)
SBN 9780700622221 (ebook)
Subjects: LCSH: Korean War, 1950–1953—Campaigns. | United States.
Army. Army, 8th—History—Korean War, 1950–1953. | United States.
Army. Army, 8th—Biography. | Korean War, 1950–1953—Biography. |
Generals—United States—History—20th century. | Generals—United
States—Biography. | MacArthur, Douglas, 1880–1964.
Classification: LCC DS919 .T33 2016 | DDC 951.904/24092273—dc23 LC
record available at http://lccn.loc.gov/2015044258.

British Library Cataloguing-in-Publication Data is available.

Printed in the United States of America

10 9 8 7 6 5 4 3 2 1

The paper used in this publication is recycled and contains 30 percent
postconsumer waste. It is acid free and meets the minimum requirements
of the American National Standard for Permanence of Paper for Printed
Library Materials z39.48-1992.

Contents

Acknowledgments

Numerous people helped make this book possible. My department chair at Stephen F. Austin State University, Dr. Mark Barringer, secured an occasional course reduction for me so I could have more time to write. The university's Office of Research and Sponsored Programs funded some of my research. The staff at the United States Army Heritage and Education Center was accommodating during my two trips there. My friend and colleague, Dr. Philip Catton, read through the manuscript and offered his usual sound advice. Another old friend, Ken Arbogast-Wilson, created the book's maps. Finally, editor-in-chief Mike Briggs and the folks at the University Press of Kansas were as usual very supportive.

On the home front, my wife, Cynthia, rode herd over our four kids while I worked on the manuscript. I am thankful for a spouse who understands the demands and eccentricities of an academic's life.

In February 2015 I attended the History Graduate Student Association's conference at my alma mater at Ohio University in Athens, Ohio. There for the first time in years I saw many former classmates and professors. Reminiscing with old friends reminded me how much I learned from my professors. I am sure it was not apparent at the time, but they taught me how to formulate a workable thesis, conduct research, run a seminar, deliver a lecture, deal with the difficult people who populate academia, and a hundred other things big and small that are now part of my job. Some of them also wrote the scores of letters of recommendation necessary for me to secure a tenure-track job. Therefore, I dedicate this book to those Ohio University history professors who are responsible, for good or ill, for my presence in the profession: Dr. Marvin Fletcher, Dr. John Lewis Gaddis, Dr. Alonzo Hamby, Dr. Steven Miner, Dr. Chester Pach, and Dr. Bruce Steiner.

MacArthur's Korean War Generals

Introduction

On Saturday evening, 24 June 1950, Major General William Dean attended a costume party thrown for his headquarters staff in Kokura, Japan. Dean commanded the Twenty-fourth Division, one of four divisions in Lieutenant General Walton Walker's Eighth United States Army garrisoning occupied Japan. Leading an infantry division, even a skeletonized one like the Twenty-fourth, was hard work, so Dean looked forward to a rare relaxing night out. Like so many army officers of his generation, Dean had seen a good bit of the world during his twenty-seven years in the service, including a fifteen-month stint in neighboring Korea. Dean had not understood Korea's culture particularly well, but he had picked up enough information there to inspire the garb he selected for the evening's festivities. Dean arrived wearing the attire of a traditional Korean gentleman, complete with a black stovepipe hat and a long robe. Despite his outfit, Korea was just about the furthest thing on Dean's mind that night. Although he had found his time in Korea both interesting and troublesome, Dean was not inclined to dwell much on the past. Instead, he focused on enjoying what turned out to be the last pleasant social gathering he would experience in a very long time. After attending church next morning, Dean swung by the post office on his way to division headquarters to see if there was a letter waiting for him from either of his two children. On his way there, the duty officer hailed him to tell him that a few hours earlier, communist North Korea had invaded noncommunist South Korea. As he processed the news, Dean never guessed that within two weeks he and the men of his division would be fighting for their lives in a country he had never expected to see again, or that within two months he would become the highest-ranking American prisoner of war in one of the most frustrating conflicts in American history.[1]

Referring to the Korean War as America's forgotten conflict has become a hoary cliché, but there is still considerable truth to the assertion. Wedged chronologically between World War II and Vietnam, the Korean War possesses neither the virtuous triumphalism of the former nor the tragic pathos of the latter. Instead, it was a confusing, exasperating, and contradictory Cold War episode that is often relegated to the historical back burner. President Harry Truman justified American intervention as part of the Cold War struggle against international communism even though South Korea itself had little direct strategic, economic, or political value to the United States. Most Americans supported defending South Korea, but there was considerable controversy during the war as to the best means to do so. This debate reflected widespread dissatisfaction with the limited nature of the conflict. Unlike World War II, waging the Korean War did not require the full mobilization of American resources but instead the careful calibration of means and ends that was hard to explain and understand, let alone implement. Although the United States achieved its primary goal of preserving South Korea's independence, the North Koreans and their communist Chinese allies remained unbowed and defiant at the war's end. Such incongruities and frustrations became increasingly pronounced as the war dragged on, leading to a steady decline in Truman's popularity. By the time all sides reached a cease-fire agreement in July 1953, the United States had committed nearly 1.8 million men to Korea, of whom approximately 36,500 died and another 103,300 were wounded. Considering its high price and ambivalent conclusion, it was scarcely surprising that Secretary of State Dean Acheson famously said, "If the best minds in the world had set out to find us the worst possible location in the world to fight this damnable war, politically and militarily, the unanimous choice would have been Korea."[2]

The Korean War was just as exasperating for American army officers as it was for the general public. The army was woefully unprepared for the conflict, so its initial battlefield encounters with its North Korean counterpart were disastrous. Throughout the long, hot summer of 1950, the North Koreans drove the Eighth Army's ill-equipped and understrength units southward in disorderly retreat. Weapons malfunctioned, radios failed to work, air and artillery support were uncertain, and the poorly trained and confused soldiers broke and ran under fire on numerous occasions. Fortunately, the troops managed to hold out along the Pusan Perimeter in Korea's southeastern corner, and then the stunningly successful amphibious landing at Inchon in mid-September reversed the war's tide. The Eighth Army's subsequent invasion of North Korea, however, exposed it to a second calamity. When the Chinese intervened to aid their communist North Korean allies in October and November 1950, the Eighth Army repeated many of its previous mistakes. The Chinese inflicted heavy losses on American troops, who withdrew pell-mell back down the Korean peninsula in disarray. No sooner had the Eighth Army finally stopped the communist advance than Truman fired General Douglas MacArthur, the commander of American, South Korean, and United Nations forces in East Asia, because of their increasingly public disagreements over the best way to prosecute the war. In the ensuing public fallout, the Joint Chiefs of Staff (JCS) denounced MacArthur's ideas in congressional hearings. Whatever the merits of the controversy, the public airing of the army's dirty laundry did little to enhance its reputation and prestige. At the end of the war, the United States accepted a negotiated ceasefire more or less along the prewar 38th Parallel boundary between the two Koreas, which prompted some to observe—inaccurately—that this was the first time the army failed to achieve complete victory over its opponent. To many army officers, this stalemated outcome seemed like a weak return on their collective investment.

Such concerns and regrets are overdrawn. In fact, although the army's performance in Korea was often uneven in the war's first chaotic year, it fought creditably enough to win the conflict in a strictly military sense. Considering the prewar constraints under which it operated, the Eighth Army deployed to Korea from Japan with astonishing speed. Indeed, the first American ground troops entered combat only ten days after the North Korean invasion. If they did not fight with much skill at first, their dogged rearguard actions slowed the North Korean advance and bought time for help to arrive. The Eighth Army's stand in the Pusan Perimeter was mobile defense at its finest. Walker's ability to fend off repeated North Korean attacks while simultaneously coordinating with the South Koreans, working out organizational and doctrinal kinks, and absorbing reinforcements of varying quality was impressive. The marines may have spearheaded the Inchon landing, but the army supplied the follow-up units that contributed to the liberation of the South Korean capital at Seoul. Moreover, in breaking out of the Pusan Perimeter, the Eighth Army practically destroyed its North Korean counterpart. Pyongyang, North Korea's capital, fell a little more than a month after Inchon, bringing the Americans and South Koreans to the verge of victory. China's intervention led to one of the most painful and humiliating defeats in American military history, but the army's confused and panicky response was due in part to insufficient guidance from MacArthur and the Truman administration. Under Lieutenant General Matthew Ridgway's fresh leadership, the Eighth Army recovered its élan in a remarkably short time, enabling it to arrest the Chinese onslaught south of the 38th Parallel. In the spring of 1951, the Chinese and North Koreans launched an all-out offensive designed to win the war. The Eighth Army not only repulsed the assault but also inflicted so many casualties as to render the enemy combat ineffective. The Eighth Army's subsequent counterattack brought it above the 38th Parallel, and it probably could have continued its progression northward. At that point, though, Truman decided to negotiate an end to the war on the basis of a divided Korea because he did not believe that securing the entire peninsula was worth the casualties. It was therefore a political decision, not the immediate military situation, that stopped the Eighth Army. From then on, the Eighth Army suspended large-scale offensives and remained on the strategic defensive until the negotiators finished their work two long years later.

It is impossible to accurately evaluate the army's performance in the first, decisive year in Korea without examining its high-ranking combat commanders there. After all, an army is no better than its leadership. It was the army's field army, corps, and division commanders in Korea who implemented operational and tactical directives, administered their headquarters, coordinated with neighboring units, interacted with the rank and file, and selected their subordinates and staff. In that first year, the Eighth Army's leadership ran the gamut from impressive to lackluster. Because all the Eighth Army's high-ranking officers had been tested in the crucible of World War II combat only a few years earlier, this unevenness is surprising; those unable to fight effectively should have been weeded out back then. Although part of the reason for these leadership difficulties was the army's woefully unprepared state at the war's start, there was more to it than that. MacArthur's habit of manipulating and playing his subordinates off each other for his own purposes certainly did not encourage selfless teamwork; in fact, it inhibited efforts to find the best men for the important positions. Of equal import, the army faced a leadership dilemma that had plagued all armed forces since time immemorial: those leaders who excel in peacetime do not always possess the necessary attributes to deliver victory on the battlefield in wartime. The Eighth Army's prewar senior combat commanders often attained their positions for reasons other than combat prowess, such as bureaucratic politics, army personnel policy, administrative ability, personal connections, and seniority. These men, perfectly adequate in the serene prewar years, were sometimes found wanting leading large units under fire. Culling them and identifying more effective replacements became one of the army's biggest personnel challenges in 1950–1951. In the end, the army succeeded in appointing men to its important combat posts mostly, though not always, on the basis of their perceived combat skills. This does not mean that they always lived up to their billing, but enough of them did to enable the Eighth Army to defeat the Chinese and North Koreans until the Truman administration called a halt to its active large-scale offensive operations in the summer of 1951.

1

A Sudden and Unexpected Conflict

The Koreans

Korea is defined as much by its geography as anything else. Tacked onto northeast Asia, seemingly as a geological afterthought, the Idaho-sized Korean peninsula extends southward 600 miles into the sea toward Japan and is ninety to 120 miles wide. More than 80 percent of its 85,200 square miles is mountainous, and temperatures run the gamut from frigid cold in winter to stifling and oppressive summertime heat. To compound Korea's topographic and meteorological extremities, the bigger and more powerful countries of China, Japan, and Russia ring the peninsula, all of which have at one time or another sought to bully and subjugate the Koreans. After the Russo-Japanese War of 1904–1905, the Japanese occupied and then formally annexed Korea. Despite occasional violent resistance, the Japanese ruled over Korea for nearly forty years, during which time they tried to manipulate Korean culture for their own ends. Japanese power deflected much worldwide interest in or knowledge of Korea's plight, but all this changed when Japan declared war on the United States and Great Britain in December 1941. Even before World War II ended, the Allies started planning for the postwar world. Korea was not a high priority, but at the Cairo Conference in late 1943, the Allies pledged support for Korea's freedom and independence. Japan's sudden capitulation in August 1945, brought about by the dropping of the atomic bombs and Soviet intervention, caught the Allies flat-footed. To facilitate Japanese surrender throughout the region, the Americans and Soviets hurriedly agreed to temporarily divide Korea in two along the 38th Parallel, with the Soviets occupying the northern half and the Americans the southern half of the peninsula.

Unfortunately, increasing Cold War tensions between the Soviet Union and the United States rendered this temporary division permanent. After some sporadic attempts at formulating a unification plan failed, the Soviets and Americans focused on molding their halves of the peninsula in their own ideological images. In this the Soviets were far more successful than the Americans. To rule over the new Democratic Republic of Korea (North Korea), the Soviets selected thirty-three-year-old Kim Il Sung. Kim was virtually unknown inside Korea and in fact had scarcely stepped foot in his homeland since he was a boy, but he had served the Soviets loyally as a Red Army officer during World War II and was therefore a known quantity. With the Soviets' heavy-handed help, Kim established a brutal communist dictatorship through forced land reform, the nationalization of industry, and the suppression of civil liberties and dissent. When the Soviets withdrew most of their soldiers in 1948, they left behind a stalwart communist regime overseeing nine million people and led by a man determined to unite the entire peninsula under his unquestioned authority.

On the other hand, American efforts to build a nation out of the twenty-one million inhabitants in the southern part of the peninsula were far more confused and ad hoc. American army occupation officers had little understanding of Korean culture and even less of the baffling cacophony of political activity that Japan's surrender generated. In their desperate search for someone with sufficient anticommunist credentials who could bring some order to the prevailing political chaos, the Americans turned to Syngman Rhee. The seventy-year-old Rhee had as a young man been tortured by the Japanese and expelled from Korea for protesting Japanese domination of the peninsula. He spent most of his subsequent years in exile in the United States, during which he attained a doctorate from Princeton University in international law, befriended Woodrow Wilson, and developed a jaded view of American government promises and motives. Upon returning to Korea in October 1945, Rhee set about consolidating his power with American assistance. He was elected president of the Republic of Korea (South Korea, or ROK) in July 1948, but his new regime was plagued by economic problems, a domestic communist insurgency, internal divisions within the ruling political party, and uncertainty about American intentions and support. Behind his democratic facade, Rhee used repression and manipulation to maintain his power. South Korea's manifest instability did not prevent him from calling for the forced reunification of the peninsula under his auspices.

Unhappily for Rhee, the Korean peninsula was not a high priority for the United States. In the late 1940s the Truman administration lacked the necessary resources to easily fulfill American postwar international responsibilities. In an effort to square this geostrategic circle, the United States relied on its atomic bomb monopoly to keep military spending to a minimum and limit the Soviet threat to the political, economic, and ideological arenas. The Soviet detonation of their own atomic bomb in 1949, however, upset such delicate calculations and underscored the fact that the Truman administration had to choose carefully which parts of the globe were worth protecting from international communism and which were not. Remote South Korea, with its seemingly inherent political insta-

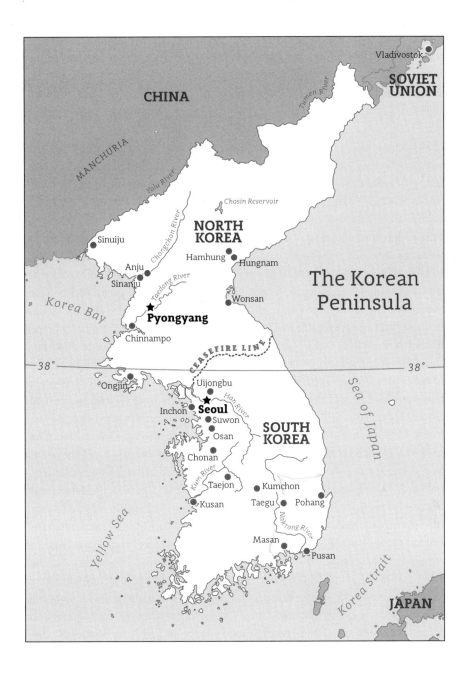

The Korean Peninsula

CHINA

MANCHURIA

Yalu River

SOVIET UNION

Vladivostok

Tumen River

NORTH KOREA

Chosin Reservoir

Chongchon River

Sinuiju

Anju

Sinanju

Taedong River

Hamhung

Hungnam

Korea Bay

Pyongyang

Wonsan

Chinnampo

38°

CEASEFIRE LINE

Ongjin

Uijongbu

Han River

Inchon

Seoul

Suwon

SOUTH KOREA

The Korean Peninsula

Sea of Japan

38°

Osan

Chonan

Kum River

Taejon

Kumchon

Kusan

Taegu

Pohang

Naktong River

Masan

Pusan

Yellow Sea

Korea Strait

JAPAN

bility, was a clear candidate for the latter category. It certainly could not be compared to Western Europe's or Japan's strategic importance.

Still, the Truman administration, after interminable and confused bureaucratic bickering, tried to have it both ways. Although it made no overt commitment to South Korea's defense, it undertook efforts to support Rhee's regime. Most obviously, it left behind a 500-man-strong Korean Military Advisory Group (KMAG) to train the nascent South Korean army after the last American combat troops withdrew from the peninsula in the summer of 1949. American officials, though, feared that Rhee might start a war with North Korea, so they refused to supply the ROK army with heavy weapons. On the eve of the Korean War, South Korea's army mustered 98,000 partially trained men organized in eight combat divisions, half of which were scattered throughout the country engaged in counterinsurgency operations. It possessed no armor, no effective antitank or antiaircraft weapons, fewer than a hundred artillery pieces, and only enough ammunition for two weeks of hard fighting. Its officer corps contained some veterans of the Japanese army but was not especially efficient. South Korea's navy was equally rudimentary, and there was scarcely any air force to speak of. As a result, the South Korean military was more of a constabulary for maintaining internal order than an organization capable of waging modern war.

Like Rhee, Kim also harbored ambitions to reunite the Korean peninsula. In his case, however, the army at his disposal was formidable enough to make his dream seem attainable. With the decline of the communist insurgency in the south, Kim concluded that the only way to destroy Rhee's regime was through direct military action. Acquiring Soviet permission was not easy, but Kim assured Soviet dictator Joseph Stalin that the North Koreans would conquer South Korea before the Americans could effectively intervene. Stalin okayed the invasion on the condition that communist Chinese dictator Mao Zedong also approved. Mao did, on the assumption that the North Koreans required little Chinese assistance beyond the transfer to Kim's army of two veteran Chinese divisions composed of ethnic Koreans. Happily for Kim, the Soviets were more forthcoming. They not only sent plenty of modern military equipment, including tanks and aircraft, to bolster the North Korean military, but also reinforced their military mission to Pyongyang so it could do much of the operational planning for the attack. By June 1950, the North Korean army was superior to its South Korean counterpart in almost every respect and was ready for a short and violent conflict. Its 135,000 well-equipped and well-trained soldiers possessed 150 T-34 tanks against which the South Koreans had no defense and had 300 artillery pieces that could outshoot and outrange anything in South Korea's slim arsenal.

North Korea invaded South Korea at 4 AM on 25 June 1950. The attack caught almost everyone from Seoul to Washington by surprise. As is often the case, in retrospect there was plenty of evidence pointing to North Korea's intentions—most obviously, the removal of North Korean civilians along the border and the rapid buildup of North Korean armored units there—but flawed assumptions and business as usual drowned out such portents. The North Koreans crashed across the 38th Parallel with 90,000 men organized into seven divisions and a tank brigade. Because many South Korean troops were on leave helping in the rice paddies, there were only around 15,000 men available to oppose the assault. The ancient capital of Kaesong fell within hours, as did the isolated Ongjin peninsula to the west. The main North Korean thrust, however, came down the Uijongbu corridor straight toward Seoul. Although the outnumbered and outgunned South Koreans fought surprisingly well, considering the circumstances, they could not stop the enemy. In particular, they had nothing with which to combat the terrifying T-34 tanks. Over the next few days South Korean generals frantically fed reinforcements into the battle without much rhyme or reason, but North Korean firepower scattered them like chaff in the wind. With the enemy approaching the Han River and Seoul, Rhee fled the capital on 27 June. South Korean morale there began to crack as the surviving soldiers retreated southward. American officials in Tokyo and Washington, blinded by overly optimistic reports about the South Korean army's abilities, may have been initially confident that South Korea could hold, but KMAG officers on the ground soon realized that without help the country was doomed. Then, on 29 June, a C-54 command plane flew through the overcast and oily smoke and landed at an airfield at Suwon, twenty miles south of Seoul, carrying the embodiment of American power in East Asia: General Douglas MacArthur had arrived for a firsthand look at the deteriorating situation.[1]

Douglas MacArthur's World

By the time his plane touched down at Suwon, MacArthur was already a military legend. He was born on a Little Rock, Arkansas, army post in 1880, the son of Arthur MacArthur, a famous general in his own right who had seen action in the Civil War and the Philippines insurrection. Douglas's mother, Pinky, ferociously looked after her son's interests and even lived near him when he attended the United States Military Academy in West Point, New York. Despite the severe hazing to which he was subjected because of his pedigree, MacArthur graduated at the top of his 1903 class. He subsequently served as an aide first to his father in East Asia, then to President Theodore Roosevelt in Washington. Various staffing and engineering postings followed, and in 1914 he participated in the Veracruz expedition. It was World War I, though, that thrust MacArthur into the military spotlight for the first time. In France he fought bravely and flamboyantly as chief of staff and a brigade commander in the Forty-second "Rainbow" Division. Scouring the front in distinctly unmilitary apparel—turtleneck sweater, long purple scarf, and a flat cap—he repeatedly exposed himself to enemy fire and emerged from the conflict with a fistful of medals and a promotion to brigadier general. The war's end did not stop his upward career trajectory. He became superintendent of West Point in 1919 and tried with marginal success to reform the institution by emphasizing liberal arts. He thereafter filled numerous jobs stateside and in the Philippines, gaining his second star along the way. In 1930 President Herbert Hoover appointed him chief of staff, making him, at age fifty, the commander of the entire army. MacArthur played a prominent and controversial role in dispersing the Bonus Army in 1932, and he later clashed with President Franklin Roosevelt over the army's Depression-era budget.

MacArthur's personal life was equally turbulent. His 1922 marriage to socialite Louise Cromwell Brooks ended in divorce seven years later, after which he took up with a young Filipino woman until they got bored with each other. In 1937 he married Jean Marie Faircloth, a Southern belle who referred to him as "general" and bore him a son. He retired from the army when his tenure as chief of staff ended, but he chose not to settle down and run out his last years. Instead, he accepted an offer from Philippines president Manuel Quezon to prepare the archipelago's army for independence. Both MacArthur and Quezon had big egos, and this, as well as budgetary issues, gradually undermined their relationship. As war clouds gathered over the Pacific, in 1941 Roosevelt recalled MacArthur to active duty and put him in charge of all American and Filipino forces in East Asia with orders to prepare them for possible conflict with Japan.

World War II made MacArthur famous, but only after a series of humiliating defeats belied his assertion that his Filipino and American troops were combat ready. Despite plenty of warning, the Japanese destroyed the bulk of MacArthur's air force on the ground eight hours after their raid on Pearl Harbor. Several weeks later, the Japanese invaded the main Philippines island of Luzon and drove MacArthur's ill-trained and underequipped army southward in disarray to the Bataan peninsula near Manila. President Roosevelt thwarted MacArthur's plan to stay there and share the fate of his 80,000 soldiers by ordering him, his family, and selected staff members to leave, so MacArthur was not on hand to see his men surrender on 10 April 1942. Instead, he was in Australia, from where he promised to return to the Philippines to free the archipelago from Japanese control. As commander of the newly organized Southwest Pacific Area theater, he pursued the Philippines liberation with a single-minded determination bordering on obsession. While doing so, he monopolized all the limelight in his theater and subverted American grand strategy. Although the Joint Chiefs of Staff initially planned for the navy to lead the counterattack toward Japan through the central

Pacific from Hawaii, MacArthur strong-armed them into permitting him to undertake his own offensive from Australia toward the China–Formosa–Luzon region. In a brilliant and cost-effective campaign, he streaked across New Guinea's north coast in six months, which put him in position to persuade the JCS to authorize an assault on the Philippines starting in October 1944. Wresting the Philippines from the Japanese required considerable resources and was still a work in progress when Japan surrendered in September 1945. At that point MacArthur assumed responsibility for governing occupied Japan as supreme commander for the Allied powers. In his new job he displayed the right combination of tact, majesty, and austerity necessary to disarm Japan and eventually help resurrect it as a peaceful, prosperous, and democratic nation.

As his record indicated, there was much to admire about MacArthur. His forceful personality, winning charisma, raw intelligence, physical courage, and gentlemanly manner made him one of the great generals in American history. Erudite and possessing a phenomenal memory, he could expound knowledgeably on a wide variety of topics, ranging from atomic warfare to Oriental philosophy. One person remembered, "There's nobody in our age who had more stuff stored away up there that he could use from the English language to football statistics; information would come out of that head like an encyclopedia."[2] He combined this analytical prowess with a personal magnetism and persuasive skills that enchanted even those predisposed to dislike him and his ideas. Visitors to his office invariably received a firm handshake, a warm smile, and his undivided attention. "Oh, he was charming with them," recalled one officer. "I never saw any of them who came out of his office who weren't smiling and just tickled to death. Oh, my, he could charm the birds out of the trees."[3] One caller put it more bluntly: "I walked out of there like I had just talked to God."[4] Pacing while he made his points and using Shakespearian language, he often seemed to speak beyond his immediate audience, as if trying to rally future generations to his posthumous banner. He possessed a mystique rare among American army officers, one that differentiated him from equally capable and talented men. As a strategist, MacArthur was ruthless in the execution of his plans and rarely took counsel of his fears. Not surprisingly, he inspired intense loyalty among those drawn into his orbit and willing to do his bidding. These qualities, combined with his rigid self-assuredness and an absolute certainty in whatever cause he advocated, made him a formidable leader.[5]

Unfortunately, there was also a dark side to MacArthur that ultimately doomed his career. His total commitment to his causes often degenerated into self-righteousness, pomposity, self-delusion, and egomania. For all his undoubted intelligence, he lacked the necessary introspection to admit mistakes and acknowledge shortcomings. His sycophantic staff officers enabled his failings by frequently telling him what he wanted to hear. Although he was invariably polite to visitors, he transformed conversations into long-winded monologues that denied listeners the opportunity to express their views, ask questions, and raise important concerns. To achieve his goals, which he all too often confused with his country's, he lied to and manipulated those around him. His unhealthy craving for the spotlight led him to withhold from subordinates the credit they deserved and to play them off against each other for his own benefit. He sincerely believed that he knew better than everyone else, and he expressed disdain for superiors who issued orders to him with which he did not agree. Indeed, he was fully capable of intense hatred toward generals and politicians whose opinions and worldviews differed from his own, spitting out words such as "treasonous," "malevolent," "horrendous," and "infamous" to characterize their motives. Predictably, he could not separate civil and military issues, and his clumsy and amateurish forays into the political arena often backfired and embarrassed him. For all his strategic acumen, by the Korean War, he had lost touch with the nitty-gritty of the battlefield, and his occasional whirlwind tours of the combat zone deceived him into thinking he was more knowledgeable about operations than was the case. He also cared little about enemy intentions, leading to a carelessness that cost his army dearly in Korea. A British officer who observed him during World War II probably described MacArthur best: "He is shrewd, proud, remote, highly strung and vastly vain. He has imagination, self-confidence, physical courage and charm, but no humor about himself, no regard to truth, and is unaware of these defects. He mistakes his emotions and ambitions for principles. With moral depth he would be a great man; as it is he is a near miss which may be worse than a mile."[6]

MacArthur and his headquarters oversaw American interests in Japan and much of the surrounding region—but not Korea, which was primarily the State Department's bailiwick—from the Dai Ichi building in Tokyo. There MacArthur led a regimented, austere, and insulated life. He did so partly to conserve energy, partly to maintain the proper image for the Japanese people, and partly out of personal preference. His Spartan fifth-floor office contained little more than a clean desk, sofa, some chairs, a large rug, and a solitary picture on the wall, entitled *A Roman General's Creed*, given to him by a former classmate. The absence of an office telephone enhanced his staff's gatekeeper role and reinforced his remoteness. Although most of his staff had arrived since the end of World War II, some of them traced their association to MacArthur back to their desperate Bataan days. Among the most important staffers were generals Edward Almond, Charles Willoughby, and Courtney Whitney. Almond was MacArthur's hard-driving chief of staff and Willoughby his arrogant intelligence officer. As for Whitney, he was technically MacArthur's director of public relations and Japanese civil affairs, but his main task was serving as MacArthur's confidante, alter ego, and sounding board. As a group, these men shared MacArthur's worldview, jockeyed to bask in his reflected glory, and often told him what he wanted to hear. The lower-ranking staff officers compensated for some of their seniors' intellectual and character deficiencies. MacArthur's headquarters skimmed off the best and brightest young officers that the army dispatched to Japan, leaving the remainder for the Eighth Army. Many of these talented men were willing to speak their minds, but they rarely had the opportunity to do so, and their purview typically fell short of policy issues and grand strategy anyway.

In the rarified atmosphere of MacArthur's headquarters, the Eighth Army and its command structure were secondary concerns to reforming Japan and overseeing American interests in the region. MacArthur once admitted that he did not know much about the minutiae of soldiering, so he usually gave his combat leaders wide latitude to fulfill his directives as long as they did not interfere with his prerogatives and stayed out of his spotlight. During World War II, MacArthur looked for aggressive combat leaders who had proven themselves in independent missions within his theater. He was reluctant to assign officers to command his large units until he had an opportunity to observe them in action first. In occupied Japan, however, he paid less attention to his division and regimental commanders and was content to accept the ones the army sent him.[7]

MacArthur learned of the North Korean invasion the morning it began. After he hung up the phone in his personal residence, he recalled a similar incident nine years earlier when he was informed of the Japanese raid on Pearl Harbor: "It couldn't be, I told myself. Not again!"[8] Tellingly, his second response was to assess—and deflect—blame for this unforeseen conflict by wondering how the Truman administration could have let such a thing happen. Initial reports accurately relayed the gravity of the situation, but calm pervaded MacArthur's headquarters as the staff monitored conditions and facilitated the evacuation of foreign nationals from Seoul. While the Truman administration weighed its options and pondered its response, MacArthur, after several days, decided to fly to South Korea for a firsthand look. He left on the morning of 29 June with key members of his staff—including Almond, Whitney, and Willoughby—and landed a few hours later at the airfield at Suwon. Emerging from the plane wielding his long-stemmed corncob pipe between his fingers like a weapon, he surveyed the scene with the eagerness of a man grateful to be back in his element.

At the airfield he met with Rhee, American ambassador John Muccio, and Brigadier General John Church, the head of a survey group dispatched to the peninsula two days earlier to gather information and coordinate American actions there. In response to MacArthur's and Almond's questions, Church emphasized the dire straits the South Koreans faced. After the briefing ended, MacArthur announced that he wanted to go to the front—"The only way to judge a war is to see the troops in action," he intoned. Several people tried to talk him out of it, but to no avail. Instead, they commandeered some vehicles and drove through cheering locals north to Yongdungpo, on the Han River's south bank. From there MacArthur surveyed the scene while Seoul burned and artillery rumbled in the distance, taking particular notice of the South Korean refugees and soldiers streaming by. Many of the troops, he noticed, were smiling and unhurt, and they still possessed their weapons. On his way back to Suwon, North Korean aircraft appeared overhead. Most of the party scrambled out of their vehicles and raced for cover in a big ditch behind a tree, but MacArthur remained seated in his sedan. When one of his staffers suggested that he join them, MacArthur said, "Aw, no. These things aren't going to hit me." Once back at Suwon, MacArthur held another meeting with Rhee before returning to Japan. Whatever the wisdom of his trip, it convinced MacArthur that only the commitment of American ground troops could save South Korea, a conclusion he conveyed to Washington the next day. He also started to formulate in his mind the plan that ultimately turned the war around.[9]

As far as President Harry Truman and his advisers were concerned, the North Korean invasion was more than just an isolated case of aggression in a remote part of the globe. Instead, they viewed it within the context of the Cold War struggle with the communist Soviet Union for world supremacy. Truman administration officials quickly concluded that the Soviets ordered the attack to test American resolve and as a possible precursor for further communist actions against American interests. As they saw things, failure to respond vigorously to the North Korean offensive might dishearten noncommunist allies, ruin American credibility as defender of the free world, and encourage the Soviets to challenge the United States elsewhere. Moreover, Truman was already under political siege for China's recent fall to Mao Zedong's communists, so letting another nation enter the communist orbit could have serious consequences for the Democratic Party in upcoming elections. For these reasons, Truman concluded that the United States could not stand by while North Korea forcibly reunited the peninsula. He thus made the momentous decision to reverse previous policy and commit the United States to South Korea's survival. On 27 June he ordered American air and naval units to intervene in the conflict, and three days later, when it became clear that that was not enough to save South Korea, he directed MacArthur to send in ground troops as well. He did so with the United Nations' approval but without securing explicit congressional authorization. To fight the war, and just in case the Soviets intended to engage the United States elsewhere, Truman also persuaded Congress to allocate money for a major military buildup. And so, less than five years after the end of World War II, the United States was again at war.

A Ramshackle Army

The army emerged from World War II as the greatest military force that had ever existed. When Japan surrendered in September 1945, the army contained more than eight million personnel organized into eighty-nine combat divisions deployed throughout the globe. In nearly four grueling years of war, American soldiers fought successfully in environments as harsh and diverse as the North African deserts, the rugged Italian mountains, the hedgerows of Normandy, the Belgium forests, the Ruhr's urban sprawl, and the Pacific Ocean's jungle-filled islands and atolls. Army officers applied a doctrine of annihilation against the Germans and Japanese to win the conflict. Through the total mobilization of American resources, the army used matériel superiority, skillful logistics, mechanization and maneuver, and overwhelming and well-coordinated firepower to destroy German and Japanese forces. The idea was to substitute metal for blood to inflict maximum damage on the enemy while keeping American casualties to a reasonable minimum. To be sure, the doctrine did not always survive the realities of World War II combat, and oftentimes the army's battles degenerated into brutal attrition. Even under these circumstances, though, the army's abundant advantages enabled it to prevail, albeit in a bloodier and messier manner than anyone wanted. As a result, once the army brought its weight to bear, it won its war in a timely manner and with substantially fewer losses than those sustained by other major combatants.

To lead the army's regiments, divisions, corps, and field armies during the war, chief of staff General George Marshall appointed a cadre of capable combat commanders, most of whom had been educated in the Command and General Staff School in Leavenworth, Kansas, and the Army War College at Washington Barracks in the nation's capital. The former school trained promising midlevel officers to serve as division and corps staffers, while the latter taught the best and brightest majors and colonels to command large units. As a group, they were not brilliant, but they did not need to be. Instead, the army required competent and professional officers who could apply American matériel superiority in an orderly and logical way. If this made many of them cautious and systematic, it was because they could afford such a methodical and safe approach to war. Their steadfastness, can-do attitudes, and confidence were the culmination of a decades-long effort to professionalize the officer corps that paid big dividends in World War II.

By 1950, however, the army was in deplorable shape. A slapdash postwar demobilization, the popular belief that future conflicts would be decided by atomic bombs dropped from air force bombers, and the Truman administration's commitment to fiscal austerity all led to severe cutbacks in the army's budget in the late 1940s. This resulted in the army's qualitative and quantitative decline. On the eve of the Korean War, the army contained 592,000 personnel organized into ten combat divisions and a number of unattached regiments. Even this figure was deceptive because the army skeletonized many of its units to preserve them. It reduced most of its regiments from three battalions to two, and it removed one artillery battery from each artillery battalion. Without sufficient funding, the army could not buy new equipment or maintain the old. Everything from vehicles to weapons to radios went unserviced. Draft calls were minimal, and the quality of recruits was disturbingly low. The officer corps was better, especially at the higher echelons. Although many World War II–era field army and corps commanders had retired, those who served at the regimental and division levels remained. Perhaps the biggest problem, though, was the army's—and the public's, for that matter—complete lack of urgency that fed its unpreparedness. For all the Cold War tension in the late 1940s, there seemed little chance that the army would be called upon to fight a ground war anytime soon, and certainly not one on the remote and unimportant Korean peninsula.

There were around 108,000 American soldiers in East Asia when the Korean War began, the vast majority of them in Lieutenant General Walton Walker's Eighth Army in occupied Japan. Like the army as a whole, the Eighth Army was in no condition to fight anyone in June 1950. MacArthur had inactivated its two corps—the First and Ninth—the previous March as a cost-cutting measure, leading to the dispersal of valuable personnel and units. As a result, Walker directly oversaw its four divisions: the First Cavalry (an infantry division despite its name), the Seventh, the Twenty-fourth, and the Twenty-fifth. All four were seriously understrength, and their combat readiness ranged from an overly generous 84 percent for the First Cav Division to 65 percent for the Twenty-fourth. Walker estimated the Eighth Army's overall readiness at only 40 percent. Despite attempts to reclaim and refurbish weapons and equipment from World War II battlefields, there were persistent shortages in most everything. Of the Eighth Army's 14,000 jeeps, for example, a mere 10,000 were operative. Similarly, only 4,441 of its 13,780 two-and-a-half-ton trucks were serviceable, and there were no more than forty-five-day stocks of ammunition and perishable food. Ninety percent of the Eighth Army's weapons and 75 percent of its vehicles had been salvaged from Pacific War battlefields and were therefore hardly top of the line.

As for the troops themselves, many people complained that they did not take their jobs as soldiers seriously because of the easy living conditions in Japan. "Living was too lush," one officer remembered. "Nobody really thought anything was going to occur, and they were there to enjoy a two year vacation."[10] These criticisms, though, were somewhat overstated. Walker, his staffers, and his senior commanders all recognized the Eighth Army's sorry condition. In fact, when Walker took over the Eighth Army in the summer of 1948, he persuaded MacArthur to release most of its soldiers from occupation duties so he could implement a training program to bring it up to snuff. Unfortunately, a high turnover rate in personnel, the large number of men on detached duty, poor facilities, the scattered location of units, inadequate weapons and equipment, and a lack of space in the congested country all hindered such efforts. Moreover, by the time the war broke out, the training had progressed only to the battalion level. So although the Eighth Army was by no means as unprepared for combat as some later claimed, it was far from ready to meet the challenges it soon faced.[11]

The quality of the Eighth Army's senior combat leaders at the beginning of the Korean War was one final question mark. Although all the division and regimental chiefs had served in World War II in one capacity or another, very few of them—two of the regimental and one of the division commanders—had much experience leading these units in action. Many of them had attended the Command and General Staff School, the War College, or both, and several had distinguished World War II records as senior staff officers, but there was a big difference between supporting the man in charge and making the big decisions oneself. Some of these officers successfully made the transition and provided good service in Korea, but others did not. The pity was that the army had plenty of officers who had successfully run regiments and divisions and were therefore familiar and comfortable with the responsibilities such jobs entailed, but they were not on hand in Japan at the war's start. After World War II, the army tended to assign high-ranking officers to positions not on the basis of proven combat prowess but rather in an effort to give staffers a chance at command. There was a logic to this because a well-rounded and versatile officer corps is a distinct advantage to an army. Also, it seemed only fair to give those hardworking and worthy officers denied the chance at troop command in World War II the opportunity to do so later. Sometimes, however, this practice degenerated into turning some posts into sinecures for senior officers who wanted a major combat command on their records before they retired. Besides, these men often had the extensive administrative know-how necessary to operate these outfits, and there seemed little chance that they would have to go to war with them anyway. As one officer later explained, "In peacetime they try to take . . . guys who were staff officers and give them divisions so that they have command on their records. Now the timing can well be off so that you just happen to finish up with a guy who is primarily a staff officer in a command position when the crap hits the fan."[12] As a result, it was not surprising that another officer lamented, "I thought some of the leadership of some of the American units in the early stages of Korea was not good."[13]

2

Stand or Die

William Dean's Last Stand

Harry Truman may have made the decision to intervene in Korea, but it was MacArthur's responsibility to implement it. He had to hurry; the North Koreans seized Seoul on 28 June and crossed the Han River the next day. Inchon and Yongdungpo both fell on 3 July, opening the way for a North Korean advance down the comparatively open west coast. To the east, North Korean progress was slower as a result of the difficult terrain and South Korean resistance. Even so, KMAG personnel estimated that the exhausted ROKs were down to approximately 25,000 men, so saving the country was clearly a race against time. Although American air and naval power could and did make important contributions to the war effort, only American ground forces could really stem the North Korean tide. On 30 June, MacArthur ordered the Twenty-fourth Division deployed to Korea. At first glance this seemed an unlikely choice because the Twenty-fourth was the weakest of the four divisions available in Japan. In fact, it had to be fleshed out with 2,600 men from the other divisions to bring it anywhere near acceptable strength. However, two of its three regiments were on Kyushu, nearest to Korea, and one of its battalions was just then undergoing air transportability training and could therefore be airlifted quickly to the peninsula. For all its flaws, the Twenty-fourth Division could get into action faster than any other infantry unit.

Whatever its problems, the Twenty-fourth Division was fortunate in having at its helm the most experienced of the Eighth Army's division chiefs: Major General William Dean. At age five, Dean decided on a military vocation after watching some soldiers and West Point cadets drill at the 1904 St. Louis exposition. He was deeply disappointed when he was not accepted into West Point, but he secured a commission in 1923 because he had participated in the Student Army Training Corps while enrolled at the University of California at Berkeley. In the interwar years, he was stationed in the Canal Zone, Utah, California, and Hawaii. He also attended the Infantry School from 1930 to 1931, the Command and General Staff School from 1934 to 1936, the Army Industrial College from 1938 to 1939, and the Army War College from 1939 to 1940. Much to his frustration, he rode a desk during the first part of World War II, and it appeared that his career had reached a standstill. He was therefore elated when he was appointed assistant commander of the Forty-fourth Division in February 1944. However, he almost missed out on the division's overseas deployment because he badly burned his leg during an errant flamethrower demonstration. Having come this close to seeing action, Dean was not about to be sidelined, so he sailed with the Forty-fourth to France in August 1944 even though he was still on crutches. He took over the division in December when its commander was invalided home and led it in the fighting in the Vosges Mountains and across the Rhine River into Germany. After the conflict ended, he returned to the Command and General Staff School, first as an instructor and then as assistant commandant. From there he went to East Asia to serve as South Korea's military governor. He redeployed the Seventh Division from Korea to Japan in January 1949, and, after a short stint as Eighth Army chief of staff, he persuaded Walker to lobby the army to put him in charge of the Twenty-fourth Division in October 1949.

Dean learned that he was returning to Korea to command the American ground forces there late on 30 June. As a result of a series of aeronautical snafus, he did not actually reach the peninsula until 3 July, two days after the first Twenty-fourth Division combat team—part of Colonel Brad Smith's First Battalion from the 21st Regiment, plus some attached units—was airlifted to Pusan. At Taejon, Dean discovered lots of refugees and ROK troops streaming southward— but precious little information. John Church, still leading the American survey group, was there, though, and he told Dean that he had dispatched Smith's demi-battalion northward to confront the charging North Koreans. Dean approved and flew back to Pusan to hurry Colonel Jay Lovless's newly arrived 34th Regiment forward. Dean's staffers were optimistic that their division could stop the enemy advance, perhaps because Dean radiated confidence in everything he did. Indeed, Dean was an impressive-looking man—tall and rugged, with a ruddy face and a bristling crew cut. He was highly respected throughout the army as a good soldier and fighter. As one person put it, "Determination and leadership seemed to flow from him and envelop everyone in the room."[1] He also possessed a disproportionate amount of introspection that gave him a certain perspective that his colleagues often lacked. Finally, his disarming modesty, cordiality, good nature, and kindness enabled him to get along with both civilian and military officials.

For all of Dean's superficial positivity, though, he was deeply concerned about the way events were unfolding. He understood perfectly well that his mission called for him to fight a delaying action until reinforcements arrived, one that meant buying time with the lives of his men. Moreover, because his division was arriving in driblets, he could not safely wait until it had all reached the peninsula before deploying it for a set-piece battle with the advancing North Koreans. Doing so would require surrendering too much time and good defensible ground to the north, and anyway there was no guarantee his understrength and underequipped division would be ready for that kind of engagement. As a result, he felt obligated to throw his men into battle as soon as they arrived in Korea to slow the North Korean offensive, even though this violated the sound tactics by which good officers tried to live. It was an unenviable mission. As one journalist remembered: "Few generals have ever been handed a more bleak and thankless job than was given Dean—to fight a delaying action with outnumbered, unseasoned, illtrained troops until reinforcements could arrive."[2]

Dean committed his division to battle piecemeal as it reached Korea, and as such, it was mauled by the advancing enemy. Smith's 540-man demibattalion encountered the North Koreans first, on 5 July, at Osan. North Korean armor sliced through Smith's thin line, followed by an infantry assault that chopped up and scattered the remainder of the outfit. Jay Lovless's two 34th Regiment battalions, containing fewer than 2,000 men, came up next. The 34th was the weakest of the Eighth Army regiments in almost every respect. Lovless had led a regiment in World War II, but he had taken over the 34th only a short time earlier and was therefore unfamiliar with it and with Dean. Lovless wanted to keep his two battalions together, but Dean insisted, over Lovless's strident objections, that he send one to Pyongtaek and the other to Anson, eleven miles away. Once each battalion had settled in, Brigadier General George Barth, a Twenty-fifth Division artillery officer serving temporarily as Dean's roving troubleshooter, on his own authority ordered Lovless's men to fall back to Chonan to avoid Smith's fate. Barth expected a fighting retreat, but instead the two battalions withdrew under fire in a disorderly fashion, giving up valuable ground in the process. Dean was furious when he found out, but shipping Barth back to his division and replacing Lovless with an old Forty-fourth Division comrade, Colonel Robert Martin, did not compensate for all the lost terrain. Martin arrived in Korea still in his street shoes, but determined and resolute. Unhappily, he had little chance to justify Dean's confidence in him because a North Korean tank round cut him in two on 8 July while he and his new regiment tried unsuccessfully to defend Chonan. To support the reeling 34th, Dean pushed forward the rest of Colonel Richard Stephens's 21st Regiment, but the North Koreans threw it out of Chochiwon on 10–11 July after two days of hard fighting. Although the 34th Regiment was receiving replacements to make up for some of its losses, the 21st was not, so Dean pulled it out of the line and dispatched his last regiment, Colonel Stan Meloy's newly arrived 19th, to help the 34th guard the Kum River. On 14–16 July, a North Korean assault across the river smashed the luckless 34th first, then the 19th. Meloy was among the casualties, wounded in the calf. Having breached the Kum, the North Koreans now headed for Taejon, a road and rail hub and the last major South Korean city northwest of the Sobaek Mountains.

There were plenty of explanations for the Twenty-fourth Division's substandard performance. Most obviously, the troops lacked all kinds of weapons and equipment necessary for them to fight successfully, including vehicles, mortars, trip flares, tripods, medicines, mines, and machine gun barrels. For example, until the army rushed a supply of 3.5-inch rocket launchers to the peninsula, there was no easy way to stop the formidable North Korean T-34 tanks. The shortage of communications gear—radios, batteries, telephone wire, and so forth—was especially problematic because it made it difficult for officers to call in the air and artillery support upon which the infantry relied, or to coordinate with higher headquarters and adjoining units. Even when the necessary matériel was available, it frequently did not work as a result of improper maintenance or a lack of spare parts. Moreover, the enlisted men were often poorly trained and unmotivated, so they did not possess the high morale, teamwork skills, stamina, and confidence of good soldiers. Scared and confused by their abrupt transition from the plush life in occupied Japan to the Korean rice paddies, it was not surprising that they did not perform well at first. As for the line officers, too many of them failed to exhibit much leadership. They did not show initiative, look after their men, inspire confidence, or demonstrate poise under fire. The fact that the North Koreans fought more skillfully than anyone anticipated merely exacerbated these unfortunate tendencies. Finally, the skeletonized condition of the units hindered tactical effectiveness. Because each regiment was short a battalion and each artillery battalion short a battery, commanders were deprived of the firepower and flexibility their outfits needed to accomplish their missions. As one officer exclaimed, "What can you do with a damn two-battalion regiment? You have no base to deploy around, no reserve—and no tactics, because all our tactics are founded on the assumption that you have three full battalions to maneuver with."[3] Dean was trying to wage war against a proficient opponent with a division that was simply not up to par.

Dean understood these problems as well as anyone, and he was under no illusions about the Twenty-fourth Division's liabilities. He was frustrated that his troops were unable to do more to retard the North Korean advance, and he worried about the heavy losses his division was suffering in the process, especially among the line officers. The pressure took a toll on him; he lost sleep, did not eat right, and suffered from dysentery. As his soldiers retreated from one position to another, he became convinced that they were not fighting as well as they could; he complained that they always seemed to be looking over their shoulders for the quickest escape route instead of concentrating on holding their ground. This was particularly true, he felt, of the hapless 34th Regiment, which had borne the brunt of the combat so far. On the other hand, he was impressed with the 34th's latest commander, Colonel Charles Beauchamp, who had led a Seventh Division regiment until Walker sent him to Korea to replace the unfortunate Martin. Moreover, he was buoyed by news that Walker and his Eighth Army headquarters were on their way to Korea to run the war and that the First Cavalry Division would soon be up to relieve his beleaguered men and help shoulder the burden. Through it all, he remembered that his mission was to slow the North Koreans as much as possible until this promised assistance arrived, even if it cost him a good part of his division. Even so, sacrificing the lives of his green and inexperienced soldiers weighed heavily on him. Years later, he recalled, "Any infantry officer must at times be ruthless. Part of the job is to send men into places from which you know they are not likely to come out again. This is never easy, but it's an especially soul-searing business when the only thing you can buy with other men's lives is a little more time."[4]

Fortunately for Dean, he maintained the support of his superiors. The Twenty-fourth Division's ordeal had convinced MacArthur that the North Koreans were more formidable than he initially believed and that they outnumbered and outgunned Dean's men. This being the case, he said that Dean was doing as well as could be expected. Army chief of staff General J. Lawton Collins was more circumspect. On 13 July, the same day the Twenty-fourth Division was digging in behind the Kum River, Dean took a jeep to Taegu to meet with Walker and Collins, both of whom had just flown in from Japan for a quick assessment of the situation. Everyone was calm and confident, but Dean expressed concern about his division's casualty rate. After Dean and his staff had finished their presentations, Collins asked if anyone had been to the front recently to verify all the reports coming in. When an embarrassed Dean said no, Collins turned to Walker and said slowly and clearly, "I think it would be a good idea if someone went up to the front to find out just what is the situation rather than depending on reports coming back."[5] Collins's implied rebuke, however, did nothing to diminish Walker's respect for Dean. In fact, the two men admired and respected one another. Walker asked Dean to try to hold onto Taejon for two days so he could bring up the First Cavalry Division, but he gave Dean the latitude to act as he saw best. As Walker later explained it, "Dean is a fighter, he won't give an inch if he can help it. I told him that I had every confidence in his judgement [sic], and that if it became necessary for him to abandon Taejon earlier, to make his own decision and that I would sustain him."[6] Having been reproached by Collins, albeit indirectly, Dean was determined not only to give Walker the two days he requested but also to be at the front lines in Taejon to make sure he got them.[7]

Taejon's strategic importance was obvious because it was the last city between the enemy and the Sobaek Mountains, through which the North Koreans needed to march to reach the vital communications hub at Taegu. Although he ordered his command post to Yongdong, about ten miles to the southeast, Dean stayed behind in Taejon to oversee the troubled and tired 34th Regiment and keep an eye on its new chief, Charles Beauchamp, who had limited combat experience. His assistant division commander and staff thought it was a bad idea for a high-ranking officer to operate so close to the front, but Dean shrugged and said that this was how he fought in Europe in the last war. When the North Koreans attacked on 19 July, they used their usual tactics of infiltration and flanking to leverage the jittery Americans out of their positions. Maneuvering to the southwest, the enemy established roadblocks to cut off the Americans in Taejon while hammering the weakened 34th Regiment in the city itself. By the morning of 20 July, North Korean troops were in Taejon and engaging the Americans in house-to-house fighting. With his communications collapsing around him, a discouraged Dean abdicated his primary responsibility of running his division and instead led several bazooka teams through the streets looking for North Korean armor. At one point he even fired at a tank with his pistol out of frustration and anger. In late afternoon, Dean finally gave the order to retreat to Yongdong, and the Americans scurried out of Taejon any way they could. Dean took one contingent across the Kum River into the mountains to the west. There he got separated from the group and wandered the countryside for thirty-six days until the North Koreans captured him on 25 August. He spent the rest of the war in a prison camp and did not come home until September 1953, a shell of his former self. By way of compensation, he received the Medal of Honor for his sacrifices.[8]

Walker got his two days, but at a price. Of the approximately 4,000 Americans defending Taejon, 1,150 became casualties. Indeed, the battle rendered the Twenty-fourth Division practically combat ineffective by the time its survivors regrouped at Yongdong. In two weeks of continuous combat, the Twenty-fourth Division retreated seventy-five miles and lost, for one reason or another, almost half of the 16,000 men it contained during this period. In addition to Dean, eight regimental and battalion commanders were killed, wounded, evacuated, or replaced. The North Koreans also captured enough matériel to equip an entire American division. In return, the Twenty-fourth Division inflicted substantial casualties on the North Koreans and slowed down their advance, though how many and by how much were debatable. As for Dean's performance, with typical modesty, he later downplayed his generalship and acknowledged mistakes:

There were heroes in Korea, but I was not one of them. There were brilliant commanders, but I was a general captured because he took the wrong road. I am an infantry officer and presumably was fitted for my fighting job. I don't want to alibi that job, but a couple of things about it should be made clear. In the fighting I made some mistakes and I've kicked myself a thousand times for them. I lost ground I should not have lost. I lost trained officers and fine men. I'm not proud of that record, and I'm under no delusions that my weeks in command constituted any masterly campaign.[9]

Some officers, then and later, were especially critical of Dean's decision to join the street fighting in Taejon instead of overseeing his division. Dean admitted that these charges had merit, but he chalked them up to frustration and an inability to contribute in any other way to the chaotic battle.[10]

Indeed, it is easy to identify Dean's mistakes during his two weeks leading the Twenty-fourth Division in action, especially at Taejon. For all his battle experience and exertions, he never controlled and maneuvered his units the way a successful officer should. Once he deployed them, they were often on their own, with little support from Dean and his headquarters. Some of the reasons for this were beyond Dean's control—poor communications equipment that hindered good air and artillery support, for example—but a more methodical approach and mutually supportive positioning might have enabled the Twenty-fourth Division to fight more effectively. On the other hand, Dean never lost sight of his mission, remained in contact with the enemy, and maintained the confidence of his immediate superior. For all the punishment the Twenty-fourth Division sustained and the errors it made, it stayed in the campaign and forced the North Koreans to repeatedly stop and deploy. Each instance they did so, they lost time they could not afford—time that the Americans used to bring in reinforcements, refurbish the ROKs, and bomb enemy military and economic targets. For this, Bill Dean deserved a good bit of the credit.

With Dean missing—the Americans did not learn conclusively that the North Koreans had captured him until December 1951—MacArthur and Walker needed to find a new Twenty-fourth Division commander as soon as possible to reorganize the bled-down and exhausted outfit. Time being of the essence, they took the path of least resistance and gave the post to John Church. Church, a relatively elderly brigadier general who had not graduated from the Army War College and who had never before led a division in combat, seemed an unlikely choice for the job. However, he was already in Korea, and he was also conveniently unemployed now that the Eighth Army's deployment to the peninsula had rendered his survey group redundant and unnecessary. Born in 1892 in Pennsylvania, Church matriculated at New York University in 1915. He joined the army when the United States entered World War I in 1917, earned a commission, and fought in France. There he was wounded twice and received the Distinguished Service Cross. He stayed in the service after the conflict and spent much of the interwar years training national guard officers. He also did a tour of duty in the Philippines and attended the Command and General Staff School from 1936 to 1937. During World War II, he saw action with the Forty-fifth Division in Sicily, southern Italy, Anzio, and southern France. He rose to become the unit's assistant divisional commander and later served in the same capacity with the Eighty-fourth Division. After Germany surrendered, Church ran first the Infantry Training Center and then the Fifth Division before becoming deputy chief of Army Field Forces from 1948 to 1949. He was working at MacArthur's headquarters when the Korean War began, from where MacArthur dispatched him to the peninsula to lead the survey group.

Opinions about Church varied. He was a spare, small-boned, and wiry man with a leathery face and an arthritic stoop. Some of those who encountered him when he took the survey group to Korea at the war's start were not impressed. He seemed tentative, confused, and officious. Thrust into a bewildering situation in an alien country, he was overwhelmed trying to separate truth from fiction in those rumor-charged early days. He was, however, sufficiently chauvinistic to denigrate South Korean troops, underrate the North Koreans, and project far more confidence in the American army than was warranted. If his grasp of the facts was faulty, he articulated what little he knew—or assumed he knew—very well when he briefed MacArthur and his staff at Suwon on 29 June. It was probably for this reason that MacArthur raised no objections to Walker's decision to put Church in charge of the Twenty-fourth Division.

Church struck a more positive note once he settled into a purely military role. Although he impressed some as peculiar, his quiet and calm demeanor was reassuring in the first stressful and chaotic months of the conflict. During his time as one of Church's regimental commanders, Charles Beauchamp observed that Church was "a solid enough citizen" with the right ideas about running a division with poor communications and more ground to cover than men to do so. Another officer noted that Church had a knack for discerning enemy intentions, and if this was because Eighth Army headquarters often had access to North Korean radio intercepts, Church was smart enough to take advantage of this information. He also gave his subordinates plenty of autonomy to fulfill their missions. Even so, his arthritis prevented him from getting out of his headquarters much to see his men at the front, so he did not have as firm a grasp of the situation as a more hands-on officer. Indeed, he was in constant pain during his time in Korea. Nor did his frail constitution inspire the kind of confidence that soldiers need in their leaders to fight well. There was nothing wrong with Church's professionalism and commitment, but the army contained healthier and more dynamic officers who could have run the Twenty-fourth Division better.[11]

Johnny Walker's Fighting Retreat

MacArthur's calls for additional resources for the war grew in direct proportion to his appreciation of North Korean power. He originally believed he could stop the North Korean invasion with a couple of divisions, but on 7 July he upped the ante considerably by requesting from the Joint Chiefs of Staff an additional four and a half divisions to augment the four already in his theater. To lead all the troops in and destined for Korea, MacArthur sent Walton Walker and his Eighth Army headquarters. On 9 July Walker established an advanced command post in Taegu, a communications hub in the southeastern part of the peninsula, about sixty miles northwest from the vital port of Pusan. Walker was well aware of the Twenty-fourth Division's ongoing ordeal; in fact, he and Dean had watched the 34th Regiment's helter-skelter withdrawal from Chonan on 8 July. Despite the discouraging stream of reports he received from Dean, Walker had reasons for optimism. Not only were the Twenty-fourth Division and American airpower slowing the North Korean advance but also the outgunned South Koreans were fighting hard in the Taebaek Mountains to the east. On 14 July, Rhee placed ROK forces under American command, enabling Walker to more effectively control and coordinate his war effort. Moreover, American reinforcements were arriving. The first regiment from Major General William Kean's Twenty-fifth Division landed at Pusan on 10 July, and eight days later, the lead elements of Major General Hobart Gay's First Cavalry Division came ashore at Pohang on South Korea's east coast. Both divisions were understrength, but the army was undertaking frantic efforts to bring its regiments in Korea up to three battalions apiece, and to add more artillery and armor.

The medium-term outlook was equally promising. MacArthur had persuaded the Joint Chiefs to dispatch the Second Division, a marine brigade, an airborne regiment, and a couple of independent regiments to Korea. Doing so stripped the army's strategic reserve bare and convinced the Truman administration to initiate the partial mobilization of the national guards and reserves, but this was not MacArthur's or Walker's concern. For all the punishment the ROK army had sustained, it remained extant and could therefore be expanded and improved with American money, weapons, advisers, and equipment. Finally, although it was hard to remember amid the daily travails Walker faced, the fact was that North Korea was a small, preindustrial nation with a population of only nine million. The United States, on the other hand, was the most powerful country that had ever existed, containing over 152 million people. As long as the American people possessed the necessary will, they could, one way or another, prevent North Korea from conquering South Korea. From this perspective, all Walker had to do was hold on until the United States mustered sufficient resources to bend North Korea to its will.

Walton Walker certainly possessed the résumé for the job. Born in Texas in 1889—both his grandfathers had been Confederate Army officers—Walker attended the Virginia Military Institute for a year before transferring to West Point, from which he graduated in 1912. He participated in the Veracruz expedition and patrolled the Mexican border before going overseas to fight in World War I. In France, he led a machine gun battalion at St. Mihiel and in the Argonne, winning a Silver Star in the process. He spent most of the interwar years in the classroom, punching his ticket at the Field Artillery School in 1920, the Infantry School in 1923, the Command and General Staff School in 1926, and the Army War College in 1936. He also taught at the Infantry School, the Coast Guard Artillery School, and West Point. These were all important postings that advanced Walker's career, but undoubtedly his most profitable tour of duty was his three years in China in the 1920s. There he gained a valuable patron by serving as George Marshall's executive officer.

Walker's relationship with Marshall paid big career dividends when Marshall became army chief of staff in 1939 and the United States entered World War II two years later. Marshall kept a sharp eye out for promising young officers such as Walker, and he used his power to move them through the army's hierarchy to increasingly responsible positions. After working in the War Plans Division, Walker served successively as commander of an armored brigade, division, and corps. He also set up the army's Desert Training Center in California. In February 1944, Walker took his Twentieth Corps to Britain and became part of Lieutenant General George Patton's Third Army. Although Patton initially had doubts about Walker because of his corpulence, he came to respect him for his combativeness and initiative. Walker led his corps across France, through some of the war's hardest fighting in Lorraine, and then over the Rhine River into Germany. At the end of the conflict, Patton rated Walker as his best combat soldier—or, as he colorfully put it, "my toughest son of a bitch." Generals Dwight Eisenhower and Omar Bradley, Walker's supreme commander and army group commander, respectively, were less effusive, each placing Walker somewhere in the middle of their rankings of their chief subordinates. Even so, Walker emerged from the war as one of the army's high flyers. After Germany surrendered, he became head of first the Eighth Service Command and then the stateside Fifth Army. In September 1948, Omar Bradley, now army chief of staff, put Walker in charge of the Eighth Army in Japan; therefore, he was the man on the spot when the Korean War began.

Walker was nicknamed "Johnny" after his favorite Scotch whisky. Most people, however, compared him to a bulldog. He certainly looked the part; he was a short, stubby, jowly, and barrel-chested man with thinning gray hair. Despite a bad back that accentuated the grimace on his lined face and kept him in constant pain, he was always on the move, roaring down rutted Korean roads in a trim and shiny jeep or flying over the lines in a small plane. Also like a stereotypical bulldog, he was stubborn, energetic, forceful, and so aggressive that he rarely needed prodding to take the initiative and get things done. One regimental commander remembered that during his first meeting with Walker, Walker asked him if his unit could fight, then pointed out his office window and said in his Texas twang, "Do you see those trains? Get on them and go that way."[12] Not surprisingly, his directness, impatience, and abruptness made him unpopular in some circles. He tried to model himself after his mentor and hero, George Patton, but lacked the personality to pull it off. He possessed Patton's love of spit and polish—reporters noted his lacquered helmet, immaculate jeep, and shiny boots—but not his charisma. Although affable in small groups, Walker tended to strut and pose in larger settings, projecting an off-putting pomposity. He neither understood nor liked journalists, so he suffered from poor press in Korea. He much preferred hunting and fishing to socializing anyway. Whatever his faults, no one doubted his courage, loyalty, and devotion. If he occasionally had worries about his ability to hold onto the peninsula, he rarely let anyone see them. Soon after he reached Korea, he bluntly stated, "There is no question whatever about the outcome of this struggle. We shall win."[13] His stout-hearted certainty in ultimate victory inspired and reassured those around him, and it played no small part in American and South Korean successes in late summer 1950.[14]

Unhappily for Walker—and, as things turned out, for the American war effort in general and the Eighth Army in particular—he failed to establish a fruitful relationship with MacArthur and his headquarters. MacArthur viewed Walker as a cantankerous and independent-minded outsider and never really warmed to him. As far as MacArthur was concerned, Walker was part of the Marshall–Eisenhower–Bradley European war clique he disliked and distrusted. During the war, he rarely expressed much affection for or confidence in Walker. MacArthur's reserved view of Walker was no doubt colored by his hard-driving and abrasive chief of staff, Ned Almond. Almond and Walker did not get along for several reasons. For one thing, their wives detested each other. More importantly, Walker resented Almond's attempts to run the Eighth Army from MacArthur's headquarters. Almond was a know-it-all who tried to boss everyone with whom he came into contact. Walker was not the kind of officer to disobey or question orders, but only if they came through proper channels, so he refused to let Almond steamroller him. One officer recalled listening to Almond issue Walker a directive over the phone. Walker responded, "Is this Ned Almond talking, or is this Ned Almond for MacArthur?"[15] Walker's knowledge that he did not possess MacArthur's full backing hindered his efforts to fight the war. He never felt at ease raising uncomfortable questions or expressing unpopular opinions because doing so might give MacArthur an excuse to relieve him of his command. This was especially problematic because, as the man

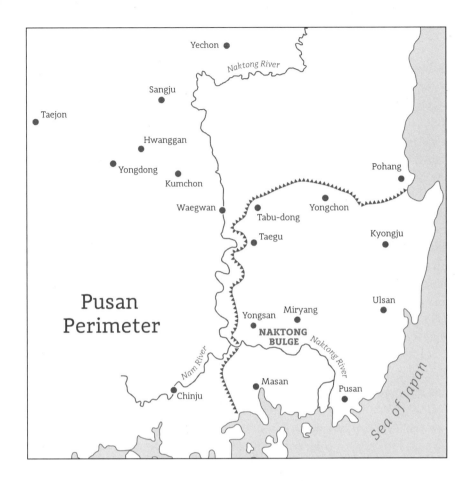

Pusan
Perimeter

Yechon

Naktong River

Sangju

Taejon

Hwanggan

Yongdong

Kumchon

Pohang

Waegwan

Yongchon

Tabu-dong

Taegu

Kyongju

Ulsan

Yongsan Miryang

**NAKTONG
BULGE** *Naktong River*

Nam River

Masan

Chinju

Pusan

Sea of Japan

on the scene, Walker often knew more about the immediate tactical and operational situations than MacArthur. As a result, Walker was always looking over his shoulder and wondering if his next mistake or misstep would end his career.[16]

Walker's other professional relationships were somewhat better. His steadfastness and professionalism made a good impression on Rhee, and he was always careful and correct in his dealings with ROK officers during his visits to their lines. Similarly, he cooperated well with the air force, on whose close air support the army relied. Although Walker's corps, division, and regimental commanders respected him as a soldier's soldier, Walker could be hurtfully abrupt and blunt with them, and he had little patience for even their legitimate complaints and excuses. He also rode herd over them and limited their battlefield autonomy by interfering down to the battalion level. Nor was he especially effusive with compliments. One subordinate remembered, "He wasn't one to praise you—you knew you were getting along with him because he just wasn't eatin' you out. If he left you alone, that was about the best that you could hope for."[17] However, he only relieved his subordinates when it was clear that they had failed, which led some to argue that he tolerated more mediocrity than he should have.[18]

On the basis of his careful study of terrain and an understanding of the forces at his disposal, Walker believed he could fulfill his mission to save South Korea. Dean's Twenty-fourth Division and the ROK units to the east had bought Walker enough time to deploy the First Cavalry and Twenty-fifth divisions in the Yong-dong region, from where he hoped to stop the North Koreans. If that did not work, he was prepared to fall back behind the Naktong River and make his stand there. Fighting defensively went against Walker's grain—he said, "This is the first time in my forty-three years of military experience that I have had to do anything else but attack"[19]—but he understood the necessity. Even so, he wanted his officers to do it in an aggressive manner that took advantage of any enemy mistakes or shortcomings. He was careful, though, to differentiate between aggressiveness and foolhardiness. When one gung-ho 34th Regiment officer told Walker that he planned to assail the North Koreans at the first opportunity, Walker corrected him: "Now, our idea is to stop those people. We don't go there and charge and slug it out. We take positions where we have the advantage, where we can fire the first shots and still manage a delaying action."[20] With a growing amount of firepower and manpower at his disposal, as well as decoded radio intercepts that revealed an increasing amount of information on enemy intentions and whereabouts, Walker was confident that he could halt the North Korean attacks. Once that happened, he hoped to launch a counteroffensive that would free South Korea and win the war. His intentions were clear enough but were complicated by two issues. One was Ned Almond, who annoyed Walker by phoning him daily from Tokyo to try to tell him how to use the Eighth Army. The other, more serious, problem was the quality of the American troops, about whom Walker had grave concerns. He lamented that his soldiers were now paying the price for his interrupted training program in occupied Japan. That, however, was all water under the bridge, so Walker had to wage war with the army he had.[21]

The newest big American unit in Walker's quiver was William Kean's Twenty-fifth Division. Born in New York in 1897, Kean entered West Point in 1917 and graduated in an accelerated program. He did not participate in World War I, but he served in the occupation army after the conflict. His interwar actions gave little indication of future success. Although he attended the Command and General Staff School from 1938 to 1939, he did not go to the Army War College. He jump-started his career during World War II by attaching himself to a general going places: Omar Bradley. Bradley recruited Kean as his chief of staff for the fighting in North Africa, Sicily, and Northwest Europe. When Bradley moved up to command the Twelfth Army Group in August 1944, he left Kean behind as First Army chief of staff. He did so not because he lacked confidence in Kean but rather because he hoped that Kean could instill some energy and resolve in his successor as First Army commander, the retiring and reticent Lieutenant General Courtney Hodges. With Kean's help, Hodges's First Army inflicted more casualties and gained more ground than any of Eisenhower's field armies. Kean's presence paid especially big dividends during the Battle of the Bulge, when Kean ran the First Army for a few crucial days while Hodges recovered from a serious illness. After the war ended, Kean led first the Fifth Division, and then, in September 1948, he became head of the Twenty-fifth Division in Japan.

Bill Kean was an intimidating man. Curt, humorless, tireless, and tough as nails, he ran Bradley's and Hodges's headquarters with such an iron fist that staffers referred to him behind his back as "Captain Bligh." However, Kean also possessed great personal courage, unswerving determination, and sound judgment. For all his abilities as a chief of staff, he had disliked the job and yearned for a combat post. Once he had it, he intended to make the most of it. Despite his authoritarian streak, he gave his subordinates considerable autonomy to achieve their missions, replacing them if they failed to do so. Although some considered him the Eighth Army's best division commander, others criticized him on several accounts. He never shook the aura of a staff officer, and his severe attitude alienated some of those who worked with him. He also was not the most articulate person in the army, and consequently he shunned the press. In addition, some said he did not oversee his battalions as well as he should have. As for Walker, he admired and respected Kean's attributes, but he complained that Kean sometimes questioned his orders and the Eighth Army headquarters' understanding of tactical situations. Kean's most obvious weakness, though, was his lack of experience in leading men into action. No doubt he had the potential to do so, but the fact was that there were plenty of available officers in the army who had already proven themselves at the division level.[22]

After a hasty and unorganized departure from Japan, the Twenty-fifth Division's lead elements landed at Pusan on 10 July. Walker initially used the division to backstop ROK units fighting in the Taebaek Mountains, but it soon became clear to him that he could more productively employ it around Sangju, northwest of Taegu. The interval, however, gave the Twenty-fifth Division's soldiers time to acclimate to the new environment into which they were so abruptly thrust. The division's weakest link was Colonel Horton White's all-black 24th Regiment, a relic from the army's fading segregationist past. The 24th was the only Eighth Army regiment with three battalions, but it faced the same equipment and weapons difficulties as everyone else. It also had some problems uniquely its own. Some white officers denigrated the outfit because they did not believe that blacks made good soldiers, while others damned it as the unfortunate consequence of segregation. Either way, a lot of white officers wanted nothing to do with it. As for Horton White, he was a long way from an efficient officer. He had no experience leading men in battle, and in fact after a few days in Korea he confessed, "Korea has so many damn mountains. It's really rough on an old man like me. War's a game for the young."[23] Although the 24th succeeded in taking the town of Yechon on 21 July, an all-out North Korean attack the next day routed it. Happily, the Twenty-fifth Division's other two regiments, while understrength, were both led by competent men who had commanded regiments during World War II. Colonel Henry Fisher's 35th Regiment had only one battalion in line, but it fought a solid rearguard action as it fell back. Colonel John "Mike" Michaelis's 27th Regiment did even better; it showed what well-led American soldiers could accomplish. Around Hwanggan on 24–25 July, the 27th gutted a North Korean assault and inflicted more heavy casualties as it withdrew through the skillful use of terrain, maneuver, and air and artillery support. Kean and Walker could be proud of most of the Twenty-fifth Division's performance in its baptism of fire, but they both knew that a retreat, even a well-conducted one, would not win the war.

On the left of Kean's Twenty-fifth Division, Hobart "Hap" Gay's First Cavalry Division was also undergoing a traumatic battlefield introduction. Gay's career paralleled Kean's in several important ways. Born in Illinois in 1894, Gay graduated from Knox College before securing a commission in the cavalry. Like Kean, he missed out on World War I and instead spent the conflict patrolling the Mexican border. In the 1920s, he worked at the Cavalry School as both a student and instructor, during which time he lost the use of an eye in a polo match accident. He later transferred to the Quartermaster Corps and served in that capacity at various posts throughout the 1930s. He attended the Quartermaster School in 1939 and the Army Industrial College a year later. Under normal circumstances, he would have spent World War II as a high-ranking logistics officer, especially because he had not gone to the Command and General Staff School or the Army War College. However, again like Kean, he changed the odds by hitching his wagon to another general's star. George Patton recruited his old friend Gay as his chief of staff for the North African and Sicily campaigns. Although Patton was happy with Gay's performance, his supreme commander, Dwight Eisenhower, was not. Eisenhower believed that Gay was not sufficiently forceful, and in February 1944, he successfully pressured Patton to replace him before the invasion of France. Patton did so but eventually brought him back to the position later in the year. Gay was with Patton when he suffered his fatal injuries in a car crash in December 1945, but Patton's death did not stop Gay's upward career trajectory. He commanded in succession the Fifteenth Army, the 2nd Constabulary Brigade, and the Washington Military District. Finally, in September 1949, Walker's good offices brought him to Japan to lead the First Cavalry Division.

As with Kean, Gay's climb through the army's postwar hierarchy to become head of one of its ten combat divisions served as evidence that the army's personnel assignments were based on more than mere combat prowess. With characteristic modesty, Gay once attributed his professional success to never overestimating his ability, but there was in fact much about him to admire. Small and wiry, and carrying a swagger stick Patton gave him years earlier, he looked like the cavalryman he once was. Considering his background as a quartermaster and chief of staff, it was not surprising that he was methodical, disciplined, reliable, and loyal, as well as a good administrator. Although he was chary with compliments, most found him easy to work with. Journalists appreciated his accessibility. MacArthur was happy to have him because he wanted a cavalryman to lead his favorite division. As for Walker, Gay was the only Eighth Army division commander of whom he was personally fond. For all his admitted talents, though, the fact was that Gay was not a combat general and had never led men into action. Moreover, because he had attended neither the Command and General Staff College nor the Army War College, he was not trained to do so. During World War II, when there were lots of divisions available and a limited number of qualified men to lead them, someone like Gay might have gotten one. After the conflict, however, the opposite was true. Gay's success in securing the First Cavalry Division was probably the result of then chief of staff Omar Bradley's desire to give him a combat post before he retired, as well as the belief that he would never have to take the outfit to war. Gay himself later acknowledged that he had expected his two or three years with the First Cavalry Division to be quiet and uneventful. Now, Gay suddenly found himself in a starring role in Korea. In the end, he performed creditably enough, but some observers argued that he was never quite up to the job. As one put it, "You say that Gay was Patton's Chief of Staff, yeah, but he wasn't Patton."[24]

Before the war, Walker's headquarters had rated the First Cavalry Division the best division in Japan. By the time it reached Korea, however, 750 of its noncommissioned officers had been transferred to other outfits to bring them up to strength, greatly reducing its size and quality. Two of its regiments, Colonel Carl Rohsenberger's 5th Cav and Colonel Raymond Palmer's 8th Cav, arrived at Pohang on 18 July. It was fortunate that they faced no opposition when they came ashore because both units had been loaded hurriedly and without much rhyme or reason. The next day, the two regiments moved to Yongdong while Gay traveled to Taegu to get his orders from Walker. Walker told him to protect Yongdong, but he warned him that there were no friendly troops available to guard his division's rear. Gay found the entire situation unnerving. He had no experience waging defensive warfare, but he knew enough about it to question Walker's insistence that he separate his two 8th Regiment battalions. Moreover, his green and weak regiments were led by older officers who thought more like cavalrymen than infantrymen.

Gay's initial hope that his outfit would fight well quickly disintegrated under North Korean pressure. When the North Koreans attacked on 23 July, the First Cavalry Division's experience was depressingly similar to the Twenty-fourth Division's. Equipment and weapons failed, officers and men panicked, companies were mauled and surrounded, and coordination among units was inadequate. Although Gay threw Colonel Cecil Nist's 7th Cav Regiment into the fight when it arrived on 25 July, the North Koreans chewed it up as well. Deeply concerned that the North Koreans might cut off his entire division, Gay ordered a withdrawal from Yongdong the same day. One journalist reported seeing Gay standing ankle deep in the dust of a Yongdong street, absentmindedly slapping his riding crop against his thigh, while his division pulled back around him to Kumchon, having lost over a thousand men. Later Gay wondered whether the retreat was really necessary, but he rationalized that maintaining a battleworthy division was more important than holding one South Korean town. Walker did not believe that the two options were mutually exclusive, so he expressed his unhappiness with Gay's first performance in Korea to him in his usual direct and coarse manner.[25]

While the First Cav and Twenty-fifth divisions struggled northwest of Taegu, the North Koreans were reaching around both of the Eighth Army's flanks to get to Pusan. Along the east coast, a North Korean offensive pushed toward Pohang, which was sixty-five miles north of Pusan. On the other side of the peninsula, two North Korean divisions sidestepped American positions screening Taegu, overran southwestern Korea, and advanced parallel along the southern coast toward Masan, just thirty miles west from Pusan. Because ROK troops were already in the vicinity of Pohang, Walker left its defense to them. The road to Masan, on the other hand, was wide open. To deal with this threat, on 24 July Walker turned to his only available reserve, John Church's bloodied and blown Twenty-fourth Division. Walker hated to send the outfit back into action so soon after its ordeal at Taejon but felt he had little choice. "I'm sorry to have to do this," he explained to Church. "But the whole south flank is open."[26]

To augment Church's depleted ranks, Walker attached to his division the two recently arrived 29th Regiment battalions. MacArthur had summoned the 29th Regiment from garrison duty on Okinawa, but it was even less prepared for combat than those units in Japan. In fact, some of the men had not fired their rifles since boot camp. Although Walker had hoped to give the regiment some last-minute refresher training before committing it, the critical military situation prevented that. Church deployed his division in the Chinju region and went in search of the enemy. In a series of engagements in late July, the North Koreans battered the exhausted Twenty-fourth Division and pushed it back. One of the 29th Regiment's battalions suffered especially heavy casualties at an ambush at Hadong Pass on 27 July, losing more than half its personnel. Chinju fell on 31 July, and the next day, Walker ordered the Twenty-fourth Division to withdraw behind the Naktong River. In his first time as a division commander, Church had not performed any better than Dean, Gay, or Kean. The experience had, however, compelled him to reevaluate his opinion of the North Korean army's prowess. As his men retreated, Church choked back his rage and disappointment and acknowledged that the North Koreans had beaten up his division. "You have to hand it to them," Church admitted. "They're good, that's all. They know how to handle their tanks, their artillery fire is accurate and their infantry attacks as well. In brief, we had hell kicked out of us."[27]

For Walker, late July was an extremely anxious time. He was deeply concerned about the quality of his American soldiers. Despite their growing numerical strength and overwhelming air and artillery support, they seemed unable to hold their ground when the North Koreans attacked in earnest. He was especially distressed by the Twenty-fourth Division's inability to stop the North Korean drive on Masan because deploying them there deprived him of his only reserves. As he explained it, "They would say you were crazy to fight a war without reserves. But that's what we are doing—because we have to."[28] He was so worried by the deteriorating state of affairs that he advised John Muccio, the American ambassador to South Korea, to move his operations from Taegu to Pusan. Walker, however, was nothing if not combative and resolute. He had seen his share of desperate situations in his career, and he was not about to quit on this one. Aggressive as ever, he scanned his maps and searched for ways to hit back at the enemy. He hated giving up ground, but if he had to, he intended to do so to his advantage. Walker decided to fall back behind the Naktong River and dig in there. This would shorten his lines, thus freeing up units and creating reserves he planned to dispatch to the Masan region to bolster the ineffective Twenty-fourth Division and arrest the North Korean threat to Pusan from that direction. Doing so would take advantage of his interior lines and his army's abundant mobility. It would also give Gay's First Cavalry Division time to get its act together. To undertake the shift to Masan, Walker initially turned to Mike Michaelis's 27th Regiment, but then he expanded the order to include the rest of Kean's Twenty-fifth Division. Kean had so far performed better than any other American division commander—or, more accurately, he had not done any worse—and was therefore the obvious candidate for the job.[29]

On 26 July, Walker asked MacArthur's headquarters for permission to move his bulky and valuable communications equipment from Taegu to Pusan. Perhaps because of a poor connection, Almond concluded from the phone conversation that Walker planned to transfer his advanced command post to Pusan preparatory to a general retreat to the port. A misunderstanding between the two men was hardly surprising. Although Walker and Almond had talked almost daily since the United States entered the war, they were not getting along. Walker rebuffed Almond's unsolicited advice on how to fight the Eighth Army by bluntly telling him to mind his own business. Almond no doubt portrayed Walker to MacArthur in the worst possible light, reinforcing the negative opinion MacArthur already had of him. Almond was sufficiently concerned with what he heard—or what he thought he heard—from his exchange with Walker to recommend to MacArthur that he fly to Korea as soon as possible to instill some backbone in his faltering ground forces commander. MacArthur and Almond did so the next day and met with Walker for ninety minutes. MacArthur said nothing about Walker's command post; instead, he emphasized that the Eighth Army must not withdraw to Pusan. Walker may or may not have understood the circumstances that prompted the conference, but as a soldier, he meant to obey his orders. After the meeting, Walker announced to his puzzled staff, "This army fights where it stands."[30] The incident was both unnecessary and counterproductive. It further soured the relationship between Almond and Walker, and it undermined MacArthur's confidence in Walker. As for Walker, it showed him that he lacked MacArthur's wholehearted support and that expressing opinions and undertaking actions contrary to those authorized by MacArthur's headquarters would get him into trouble.[31]

To make sure everyone understood his steadfastness, in the next few days, Walker expounded his message to as many Eighth Army personnel as possible, including his division commanders. On 29 July, he told an assembled group of Twenty-fifth Division staff and field officers at Sangju, "I am tired of hearing about lines being straightened. There will be no more retreating. Reinforcements are coming, but our soldiers have to be impressed that they must stand or die. If they fall back they will be responsible for the lives of hundreds of Americans. A Dunkerque in Korea would be a terrible blow from which it would be hard to recover."[32] In a schoolroom serving as the First Cavalry Division's headquarters, Walker elaborated to a group of journalists: "We have been trying our best to shore up the holes in our lines. As has been forecast, this is a fight for time. We will not give an inch of ground that's not already lost. . . . My army is not going to give up one more inch. We will stand."[33] The effectiveness of his message, of course, varied from individual to individual, but it certainly drove home to everyone Walker's intentions. Despite Walker's assertions, however, the Eighth Army retreat to the Naktong River continued throughout late July and early August. Indeed, even as he made his statement at Gay's headquarters, cynical reporters observed tanks heading southward and eastward. Walker was aware of the incongruity, but he figured that his "stand or die" order, even if not adhered to literally, bought him the time and support from MacArthur's headquarters he needed to implement his plan.[34]

As July ended and August began, thousands of weary Eighth Army troops crossed the Naktong River and took up new positions behind it. In the three and a half weeks since American ground forces had first entered combat, they had suffered more than 6,000 casualties, of whom 1,884 were killed, 2,695 wounded, and 1,400 missing or captured.[35] If the troops had not fought particularly well, they were learning fast. Infantrymen and artillerymen were becoming accustomed to sleeplessness, long hikes, tedious hours in trucks, and the incessant sound of rumbling vehicles, growling artillery, and sudden machine gun fire. They were now thinking in terms of fields of fire, ammunition allowances, defilades, and seizing the high ground. They were no longer repelled by the stifling heat, dusty villages, and fetid rice paddies or the stench of kimchi and night soil. Refugees—elderly men wearing black birdcage hats and smoking long-stemmed pipes, women in dresses and short jackets, and swarms of dirty children—became part of the war's backdrop. Rumors and evidence of North Korean atrocities against American prisoners hardened their hearts and steeled their resolve. Death ceased to be a rare phenomenon but was instead an omnipresent source of fear and repulsion. Soldiers adjusted to the constant turnover of personnel as men came and went with astonishing frequency. One general recalled the sad circumstances so many young officers experienced:

Many of them in less than forty-eight hours after departing division stations in Japan found themselves in command of front line units, where they were neither known nor did they know any member of their command. They assumed command during most confused situations and without orientation of any kind. In less than twenty-four hours after arriving in Korea many of these men were back in hospitals in Japan wounded or had been killed in action.[36]

At nightfall on 2 August, the last men of Hap Gay's First Cavalry Division crossed a bridge over the Naktong River at Waegwan and took up positions on the opposite bank. After the 8th Cav Regiment's First Battalion reached the other side, Gay prepared to give the command to blow the bridge up. Unfortunately, thousands of Korean refugees constituting the war's backwash surged across the span, seeking safety. Gay did not want the refugees on the other side because such throngs often contained North Korean infiltrators and spies. Several times he directed the 8th Cav to clear the bridge, but the troopers were unable to keep the refugees off long enough for Gay to carry out his plan. Finally, near dark, Gay ordered the explosives detonated anyway because he felt he had no choice but to make the "tough decision." The bridge blew up and killed and wounded hundreds of Korean men, women, and children. The Korean War may have been a limited conflict in broad geopolitical terms, but for those in its path, it was pitiless, awful, and indiscriminate.[37]

The Pusan Perimeter

In early August, the Eighth Army retreated into a rectangular-shaped area at the southeastern tip of the Korean peninsula that became known as the Pusan Perimeter, named after the all-important port it was designed to protect. Approximately a hundred miles long and fifty miles wide, the Pusan Perimeter was protected by the Sobaek Mountains to the north and the meandering, moatlike Naktong River to the west. Walker kept the slowly withdrawing ROK troops to the north and deployed his American forces to the west. Despite the heavy casualties they had sustained, the South Koreans were undertaking Herculean efforts to rebuild their army that included conscripting every military-age male they could find. As for the Americans, they were receiving reinforcements as well. The Hawaii-based 5th Regiment reached South Korea on 25 July, followed by the first elements of the stateside Second Division six days later and the 1st Marine Brigade between 2 and 4 August. Although Walker was not getting as many individual replacements as he wanted, more artillery and armor were flowing through Pusan, as well as equipment and supplies to make up for the Eighth Army's deficiencies at the war's start. As a result, by early August, there were approximately 92,000 American and South Korean combat troops on the peninsula facing 70,000 North Koreans. In addition to numerical superiority, the Eighth Army had uncontested control of the sea around and air over the peninsula, giving it access to enormous additional firepower. American intelligence officers were also providing Walker with astonishingly accurate information about North Korean intentions and movements through intercepted and decoded radio messages.

As for the North Koreans, they had suffered colossal casualties of their own, nearly 60,000 troops, in their march down the peninsula. Although they were rushing hastily trained replacements from the north and dragooned southerners into their ranks, these men lacked the prowess and commitment of the soldiers who had stormed across the 38th Parallel five weeks earlier. Moreover, the further south the North Koreans advanced, the more tenuous their supply and communication lines became. By August, the North Koreans at the front were desperately short of supplies, weapons, and equipment of all kinds. Worse yet, they faced a cruel operational dilemma. In order to break through the Eighth Army's lines, they needed to concentrate their forces, but doing so exposed them to American firepower that further depleted their finite and dwindling resources. Even if the geostrategic calculus was beginning to catch up with them, it was not readily apparent; the North Korean army still possessed a hard kernel of tenacious and fanatical troops perfectly capable of engaging the Eighth Army on almost any terms.

Considering the Eighth Army's numerous advantages, it was puzzling that the North Koreans maintained the initiative at the Pusan Perimeter as long as they did. One explanation to which some subscribed was poor American leadership, starting at the top of the Eighth Army with Walker. Walker had never been popular within the army, and this, combined with his apparent inability to stop the North Korean advance, led some to question his competence to command a field army. In early August, President Truman and the Joint Chiefs of Staff dispatched a high-level delegation to travel to East Asia to check up on the situation there. It included Truman adviser and troubleshooter Averell Harriman, air force deputy chief of staff Lieutenant General Lauris Norstad, and Norstad's army counterpart, Lieutenant General Matthew Ridgway. The team went first to Tokyo for talks with MacArthur. There MacArthur asked for four more divisions and complained that his replacements were not keeping up with his losses. He also raised the issue of the quality of his regimental and battalion commanders, noting that some of them were over fifty years old.

The delegation then flew to Taegu on 6 August to meet with Walker and take a short tour of the front. Harriman, Norstad, and Ridgway were all disappointed with what they found. They were especially dismayed with the poor quality of Walker's headquarters staff. Walker's chief of staff, Colonel Eugene Landrum, did not appear particularly forceful and energetic. He had a bad reputation to begin with because he had been relieved of his divisional command in Normandy during World War II. Many of Walker's key staffers were old artillerymen with pedestrian and provincial outlooks. An accompanying air force general called the staff presentation the delegation received one of the poorest he had ever witnessed. As for Walker, he did not even know the names of the principal ROK officers with whom he dealt. Finally, Ridgway's reports indicated that many of the Eighth Army's regimental commanders lacked both combat experience and aggressive instincts. Ridgway was a battle-hardened World War II division and corps commander, so he knew the importance of an efficient headquarters and strong leaders to winning victories. To Ridgway, Walker's failure to foster these fundamental qualities was evidence that he was not up to his job.

Comparing notes afterward, Harriman, Norstad, and Ridgway all agreed that Walker had to go. Certainly he had no business leading any breakout from the Pusan Perimeter. MacArthur appeared to feel the same way. He had never really liked Walker, and he told Norstad as much, adding that he would be pleased to have Ridgway as Walker's replacement. MacArthur, however, hated relieving people, so he balked at forcing the issue. When Norstad mentioned all this to Ridgway, Ridgway feared that people might think that he had traveled to East Asia to inveigle his way into Walker's job, which he insisted was not the case. Whatever Ridgway's discomfort, the basic problem remained: how to arrange Walker's relief. Soon after they returned to the States, Harriman and Norstad on 9 August met with Truman and recommended Walker's firing. Truman was unwilling to act unilaterally on an issue about which he was unfamiliar, so he referred them to Omar Bradley, the chairman of the Joint Chiefs of Staff. Bradley, for his part, chose not to bring the entire JCS into what was primarily an army affair. Instead, he consulted with Joe Collins, the army chief of staff. Meanwhile, Ridgway worked his end of the military establishment by talking with Secretary of the Army Frank Pace, Collins, and others in the Pentagon. He also undertook efforts to improve Walker's lackluster headquarters by sending him some new staffers to supplant those he deemed inefficient.

As for Walker, because Truman, MacArthur, and Bradley were unprepared to grasp the nettle, this left his fate in Collins's hands. Collins, though, hesitated to act. He had not known Walker well at the war's start, but he had been impressed with him during his whirlwind tour to East Asia in mid-July. On the other hand, Collins respected Ridgway and took seriously his assessment of the situation. Mulling things over, Collins figured he could replace Walker with either Ridgway or Lieutenant General James Van Fleet if it came to that. Of the two, Collins preferred to give the job to Van Fleet because he was grooming Ridgway as his successor as chief of staff. Collins finally opted to postpone any decision on Walker's future until he returned to Korea for a firsthand look at Walker and his headquarters.[38]

Walker may or may not have realized that his head was on the chopping block, but he was certainly aware that the latest North Korean offensive placed the Eighth Army in peril. Such knowledge, one journalist noted, made him "as grouchy as an old bear with bunions."[39] His chief concern in early August was the ongoing North Korean offensive toward Masan along the peninsula's southern coast. He had already dispatched John Church's Twenty-fourth Division there, but Church's exhausted soldiers proved unable to stop the enemy. Fortunately, the Eighth Army's retreat into the compact Pusan Perimeter freed up Kean's Twenty-fifth Division for other employment, so Walker sent it southward to reinforce Church. Moving an entire combat division, with all its weapons, equipment, supplies, and personnel, 150 miles by road and rail was difficult enough under the best of circumstances, but Korea's limited infrastructure exacerbated all the usual problems. Kean and his staff were up to the job, though, so the Twenty-fifth Division reached its destination in only two days.

Colonel Mike Michaelis's 27th Regiment was the first combat unit from Kean's division to reach the Masan area, arriving on 1 August. The thirty-seven-year-old Michaelis had been riding a desk at Eighth Army headquarters in Yokohama when the war began. Having seen his share of action as a regimental commander in the 101st Airborne Division during World War II, Michaelis was content to participate in this conflict from the comforts of occupied Japan. However, in his quest for younger and more energetic men to lead his regiments, Walker tapped Michaelis to take over the 27th Regiment just before the unit shipped out for Korea. Michaelis had only forty-five minutes to catch a plane to Taegu, from where he took a jeep to Pusan to meet the 27th Regiment at the docks three days later. There he was dismayed to discover that he did not know any of his chief subordinates, and also that many of the officers and men seemed distinctly unprepared for and unenthusiastic about the war. Undaunted, the hard-driving Michaelis ruthlessly weeded out and overhauled the regiment as rapidly as possible, and his draconian policy paid dividends when the outfit turned in a creditable performance in its first action at Hwanggan.

When he got his orders to take his regiment south, Michaelis was not optimistic, and in fact said to a journalist, "You may witness what well may be the last stand of the Americans in Korea."[40] Upon reaching Chung-ni, four miles northeast of Masan, Michaelis reported to Church for orders. To Michaelis, Church was a beaten man: lethargic, distant, and uninvolved. His headquarters seemed disorganized and unfocused. The Twenty-fourth Division as a whole was not in much better shape. It contained approximately 12,300 men, 2,000 of whom were conscripted South Koreans of dubious quality, and Church himself had grave doubts about the 34th Regiment's fighting qualities in particular. Michaelis wrote later, "I do not desire to be disparaging of the action of the Twenty-fourth Division at that time. However, it was a whipped Division with little initiative and my distinct impression was the inability of any of the Division staff or command to issue a concise and positive order."[41]

Michaelis was therefore more or less on his own, and on his own he and his regiment stopped the North Korean drive on Masan cold in a series of confused and bitter engagements west of the city on 2–3 August. Michaelis attributed his success to flexible tactics, seizing the high ground, luck, and defense in depth. His charisma, aggressiveness, and willingness to kick reluctant soldiers out from under trucks and jeeps and into the firing line helped as well. After a barrage of artillery fire so pulverized an enemy-held hill that one of his companies took it without losses, Michaelis explained to its commander over the phone, "You see, maybe that will show your men that they don't always have to get killed to get somewhere. Maybe that will show 'em we've got the finest artillery in the world."[42] His bright victory garnered considerable publicity and generated some jealousy within the Eighth Army. Walker, though, was thrilled to find an officer who could make American soldiers fight well, and thereafter he used the 27th as one of his fire brigades to plug the holes the North Koreans punched in American lines.[43]

Although the attitude among Walker's headquarters staff remained grim and downbeat, Walker himself was developing a more sanguine view of the military situation. He was rapidly getting a feel for the battlefield—an understanding not only of what his men could do but also of the enemy's capabilities. The North Koreans usually telegraphed their operational and tactical plans through their careless use of radio transmissions, and they repeatedly resorted to the same tactics. "[The North Koreans] operate Russian-style," Walker explained to one journalist. "When they are committed to a plan they stick to it."[44] In addition, Walker soon realized that the North Koreans lacked the logistical stamina to fight for more than a few days before they had to stop and bring up supplies. There was therefore a certain predictability to North Korean offensives that Walker could use to his advantage. He recognized that if he could deploy his reserves to threatened parts of his line quickly enough, the North Koreans would expend their limited resources fighting them at the edges of the Pusan Perimeter, so their attacks would peter out before they could exploit any breakthroughs.

Walker was a pugnacious general always looking for any opportunity to seize the initiative and hit back at the enemy. Now that Michaelis had stymied the North Korean drive on Masan, Walker saw an opening to counterattack in the area, retake Chinju, and perhaps roll up the North Korean right flank. Moreover, recently arrived American reinforcements made such an undertaking possible. Walker planned to deploy three army regiments—Horton White's 24th, Hank Fisher's 35th, and Colonel Godwin Ordway's 5th—and Brigadier General Edward Craig's 1st Marine Brigade for the operation. To lead it, Walker gave the job to Bill Kean and labeled his conglomeration "Task Force Kean." Kean was the logical choice because he and his headquarters were already in the area, and Kean had so far performed better than Walker's other American division commanders. Task Force Kean contained approximately 20,000 men, nearly twice as many as the opposing North Koreans, and had the usual advantages in logistics, air support, firepower, and mobility. The obvious problem, though, was that Kean was familiar with only half of his heterogeneous task force. His 35th Regiment was a comparatively solid outfit led by a capable if underrated officer, but White's 24th Regiment was already under a cloud. The independent 5th Regiment was new to Korea, and Ordway had limited combat experience. As for Craig's 1st Marine Brigade, it possessed great morale and élan as well as plenty of battle-hardened officers, tanks, army logistical help, and dedicated air support. On the other hand, it too was inexperienced, understrength, and bound to have problems cooperating with the army. Coordinating such a disparate collection obviously required close direction, but Kean usually did not ride herd over his subordinates.[45]

Unfortunately, Task Force Kean failed to live up to Walker's expectations. Kean's troops jumped off on 7 August and immediately ran into heavy opposition. For a week, the Americans and North Koreans slugged it out in a series of confused engagements in the mountains and passes west of Masan. The oppressive heat was bad enough, but enemy infiltration tactics were even worse. The 24th Regiment was chewed up early on in fighting around Battle Mountain, resulting in the relief of a clearly exhausted Horton White and more damage to the outfit's reputation. The 5th Regiment's baptism of fire was equally traumatic. Ordway seemed more interested in his personal safety than in his regiment's mission, so he did little to inspire his men. At first the rookie outfit made so little progress that a frustrated Kean placed it under marine command. When the 5th finally got moving, North Korean ambushes on 10–11 August at a place dubbed Bloody Gulch inflicted especially heavy losses on its artillery. Indeed, of the army regiments, only Fisher's 35th demonstrated much competence by overrunning a pass called the Notch and pushing toward the Nam River. The 1st Marine Brigade, on the other hand, performed so well that it found itself outdistancing and then rescuing the beleaguered 5th. In the end, Task Force Kean's offensive sputtered to an inconclusive halt, and Walker dissolved it on 16 August so he could use some of its units to confront a new North Korean attack to the north.[46]

Some participants later argued that Task Force Kean was a qualified success. It provided the untried 5th Regiment and 1st Marine Brigade with battle experience, raised morale in the Twenty-fifth Division, and led to the replacement of the inefficient White and Ordway with Colonel Art Champeny for the 24th Regiment and Colonel John Throckmorton for the 5th Regiment. It also mauled the North Koreans in the area, so that a defensive Kean wrote later, "If the action, resulting in the destruction of the combat effectiveness of a reinforced division, was not vital to the United Nations' mission, I have been laboring for many years under a misconception of the aims of warfare."[47] All this may have been true, but it was hardly what Walker intended. Chinju remained in North Korean hands, and there was no envelopment of the enemy's right flank. Instead, Kean failed to coordinate his troops effectively, two regiments got beat up, the marines made the army look bad by comparison, and the Eighth Army gained little ground. Moreover, Walker's decision to launch an offensive against the most remote part of the enemy's line was questionable. Such operations would not lead to American and South Korean victory any time soon.[48]

The main reason Walker disbanded Task Force Kean was because he urgently needed some of its units to confront a festering crisis to the north, where the Naktong River formed a bulge as it curved eastward toward Pusan. There Walker had placed John Church's three exhausted and understrength Twenty-fourth Division regiments. To guard the thirty-four winding miles of river for which he was responsible, Church had fewer than 10,000 men available. He deployed two of his regiments—Stephens's 21st and Beauchamp's 34th—north to south along the river, with the 19th Regiment, now under Colonel Edward Moore, behind them in reserve.

The North Koreans charged across the Naktong on 6 August toward the vital road junction of Miryang and quickly broke through Beauchamp's battered 34th. Unfortunately, Church misinterpreted the main axis of the North Korean offensive and initially focused his attention and resources in the wrong place. Even before counterattacks by the 34th and 19th regiments failed to stem the enemy advance, Church called on Walker for assistance. Walker, however, was reluctant to commit his scarce reserves, so he doled them out to Church in driblets. At the same time, though, he exerted considerable pressure on Church to push the North Koreans back across the Naktong as quickly as possible. Church therefore felt compelled to throw these reinforcements into action as soon as they showed up, and such a piecemeal commitment had predictably disappointing results. One after another, Church fed them into the Naktong Bulge maw: two battalions from Colonel John Hill's recently arrived 9th Regiment, Michaelis's 27th Regiment, and a battalion from Colonel Paul Freeman's fresh 23rd Regiment. Fighting was especially vicious around Cloverleaf Hill and Obong-ni Ridge. By the time Church managed to get all his men into action simultaneously, they were too drained to make much progress. Finally, on 14 August, Walker ordered Craig's 1st Marine Brigade in to help. The additional firepower and manpower tipped the scales, and after two days of bitter fighting on 17–18 August, the Americans practically destroyed what was left of an entire North Korean division still in the Naktong Bulge. Doing so was certainly an important victory, but Church's and Walker's performances left much to be desired. Church did not demonstrate sufficient control over his personnel or an understanding of the situation—at least not at first—and his decision to move his exposed command post in the middle of the battle further complicated matters. As for Walker, his hectoring and niggardly distribution of reinforcements was counterproductive and made Church's job more difficult.

In Walker's defense, he was chary about committing his reserves because the North Koreans were attacking across the Pusan Perimeter. Dispatching reinforcements to the wrong place at the wrong time might leave him with nothing with which to confront other, more serious, threats. While the fighting raged to the southwest of the Pusan Perimeter, Eighth Army intelligence uncovered evidence of an imminent North Korean offensive toward Taegu. Walker had deployed Gay's

First Cavalry Division and a couple of ROK divisions to defend the city. The First Cav Division soldiers had not fought well in their initial engagements around Yongdong, but since retreating across the Naktong they had had a few days to catch their breath and take stock. They used the time to clear fields of fire, register artillery, string barbed wire, absorb replacements, and receive supplies. In particular, they obtained their first tanks to counter the North Korean T-34s. Like his men, Gay was also learning from his earlier experiences. For example, he had created a reinforced battalion with lots of firepower to serve as a mobile reserve to respond to North Korean penetrations of his overextended lines. He explained, "There comes a time in every battle when both commanders think they are losing. Then the one who attacks, wins. I shall attack."[49] Operating from a horse barn at a Taegu racetrack, and dressed in shabby overalls, so he looked more like a Kansas farmer than a major general, he repeatedly toured the front to look over the situation and inspire his men. At one point, upon seeing a group of jittery replacements moving forward, he tried to reassure them by boldly exposing himself to enemy fire as he walked back from an inspection trip.[50]

When elements of five North Korean divisions charged across the Naktong in earnest on 9 August, the First Cavalry Division met them with heavy fire. Although most enemy units were decimated near the river, some still got through and behind the American lines, creating considerable mayhem in the process. Gay was not immune from the pandemonium. On 10 August, a North Korean mortar round landed amid a group of Americans and killed all of them except for Gay and his aide. With disarming modesty, Gay confessed to a journalist, "I hope the enemy is as confused about the situation as I am."[51] In the end, though, the First Cavalry Division held on and, helped by effective air support, cleared out the North Koreans and pushed them back across the Naktong. To the north, the South Koreans buckled under enemy pressure and retreated to within fifteen miles of Taegu. Walker pulled Michaelis's 27th Regiment and part of Freeman's 23rd from the Naktong Bulge and rushed them northward to bolster the ROK lines. From 18 to 24 August, Michaelis's veterans inflicted heavy casualties on the North Koreans in a long valley dubbed the Bowling Alley. With that, the North Korean offensive toward Taegu wound down. In maintaining the integrity of his lines, Gay had done much to redeem his poor showing around Yongdong several weeks earlier. As for Walker, his willingness to dispatch sufficient reinforcements in a timely manner demonstrated his growing ability to wage defensive warfare effectively.

The fighting west of Masan, in the Naktong Bulge, and outside of Taegu showed that American troops were capable of stopping the North Koreans. Of equal importance, the South Korean army, which defended the northern half of the Pusan Perimeter, continued its own dogged resistance. In a series of brutal battles from 5 to 18 August, the South Koreans lost and then retook the port of Pohang. If ROK troops were not yet able to defeat the North Koreans without American advisers, logistical support, and firepower, they were certainly improving. Moreover, the Eighth Army's American numbers continued to swell, despite losing another 6,000 battle casualties in August. By 1 September, Walker had approximately 83,000 American soldiers and marines at his disposal, as well as 91,700 South Koreans and a recently arrived British brigade of 1,600 men. Moreover, each of his regiments now contained three battalions apiece, making it easier for their commanders to maneuver and fight.

Walker was therefore in an optimistic mood when Collins arrived on 22 August to determine whether he should relieve his Eighth Army commander. Fortunately for Walker, Collins was satisfied with what he found. For one thing, the staffers whom Ridgway had dispatched had improved the tone and organization of Eighth Army headquarters. Collins and Walker toured the front, during which Michaelis made a particularly good impression on the chief of staff. Finally, and most importantly, the military situation had stabilized, and Walker seemed to have a firm grasp on tactical and operational matters. Collins was particularly struck by Walker's gung-ho attitude and his deft handling of his reserves to parry North Korean attacks. As Collins remembered later, "Tight as the situation was, I was gratified to find Walker fuming a bit, as usual, at having to give ground but fully confident that the Eighth Army and our ROK allies would hold the Pusan Perimeter."[52] Collins had a greater understanding of and sympathy for Walker than MacArthur, Ridgway, and other observers who had criticized Walker's actions. As a result of the visit, Collins decided not to replace Walker.[53]

Of all the reinforcements the Eighth Army received in August, the biggest was Major General Laurence "Dutch" Keiser's Second Division. The division had been stationed at Fort Lewis, Washington, when the conflict began, and was so seriously understrength that it required nearly 5,000 additional hastily assembled men to bring it up to par. Even then the army estimated that it needed four to six months of training before it was combat ready. The Eighth Army's desperate need for manpower, however, overrode such considerations, so it was shipped to Korea in stages in late July and early August. Its first regiment, John Hill's 9th, reached Pusan on 31 July, and Walker threw it into the Naktong Bulge battle nine days later. Paul Freeman's 23rd Regiment arrived on 5 August, followed by Colonel George Peploe's 38th Regiment two weeks later. As for the Philadelphia-born Dutch Keiser, he graduated from West Point in 1917 and went to Europe to fight in World War I. While in France, he won a Silver Star and rose to lead an infantry battalion—a remarkable accomplishment for a man in his early twenties. Keiser's interwar years were far more mundane and uneventful. He attended the Command and General Staff School from 1938 to 1939, but, like Church and Kean and

Gay, he did not go to the Army War College. During World War II, Keiser served as chief of staff of the Sixth Corps in Italy; he ended the conflict in the same capacity for the stateside Fourth Army. After Germany and Japan surrendered, Keiser worked in the United States Military Advisory Group in China before returning home to become the Second Division's assistant commander in February 1950. From there he ascended to the division's top spot in July.

Keiser had his admirers. Paul Freeman, for example, served under him both in Korea and in the interwar years and extolled his "fine military bearing, his clean appearance, his nice manner."[54] Another booster, Ned Almond, lauded Keiser's levelheadedness and experience. On the other hand, Michaelis later called Keiser a lousy division commander. Keiser never attended the Army War College, so he had to learn the finer arts of leadership on the job. Perhaps because he spent so much time as a chief of staff, Keiser tended to be a headquarters operator who communicated with his subordinates by phone. He relied on his assistant division commander, Brigadier General Joseph Sladen Bradley, to serve as his eyes and ears. His efforts to place his favorite officers in the division's important posts created an abnormal amount of dissension among its senior commanders, some of whom felt unappreciated and put upon. Although there was nothing wrong with Keiser's physical courage, some believed he was a little too old for his post. Finally, his willingness to defer to his staff on most issues underscored a diffidence and passivity people detected in his character. Whatever Keiser's positive qualities, he was an unlikely choice to take the Second Division to war in Korea.[55]

The Second Division's arrival gave Walker the opportunity to pull John Church's fatigued Twenty-fourth Division out of the line in late August for an overhaul. Not only did the Twenty-fourth Division receive replacements, weapons, and equipment to bring it up to strength, but also, of equal importance, Walker revamped its leadership and organization by relieving its assistant commander and a couple of battalion commanders. Most dramatically, he dissolved the 34th Regiment, sent Charles Beauchamp back to Japan to resume command of his Seventh Division regiment, and doled out the 34th's two battalions to the 19th and 21st regiments to bring them up to three battalions apiece. The 34th had acquired a poor reputation ever since it reached Korea, and Dean, Church, and others had commented negatively on it. Whatever Beauchamp's attributes, he was unable to turn the outfit around. In many respects the regiment was more sinned against than sinning. It was the least prepared of all the Eighth Army's regiments when the war began and the first committed to action; it had never recovered from its ordeal at Taejon. In fact, of the 2,000 men who disembarked at Pusan with it, only 184 were left by the end of August. To fill its slot in the Twenty-fourth Division, Walker eventually attached John Throckmorton's 5th Regiment. This divisional renovation, though, did not include John Church. The lackluster

Church had not performed especially well since he took over for Dean, but unlike many divisional officers, he was usually confident and upbeat. Moreover, assigning to the Twenty-fourth a third commander in two months might create more problems than it would solve. Perhaps for these reasons, Walker chose to keep Church in charge of the outfit.[56]

Walker's late August optimism, however well deserved, was about to be tested. The North Korean army had suffered colossal losses since the war began, but it remained a formidable foe. Despite relentless American air force interdiction bombing, the North Koreans continued to bring down enough weapons, supplies, and equipment to succor their soldiers trying to cut their way through the Pusan Perimeter. They had also built up their troop strength there to nearly 100,000, partly through the conscription of South Korean men. As American and South Korean power swelled, though, it was increasingly clear that time was running out for the North Koreans. Therefore, they gambled on one more big offensive to crush the Americans and South Koreans before the odds against them became insurmountable. This time, they planned to attack more or less simultaneously along all four avenues toward Pusan: though Masan, the Naktong Bulge, Taegu, and Pohang on the east coast. Success would require courage, tenacity, and ferocity, but the North Koreans certainly possessed those attributes. As one American air force general awkwardly acknowledged: "Yet, the North Koreans without any air support and in spite of tremendous casualties that they are receiving from our air, they are aggressive at all times. When one considers the tremendous havoc and casualties that we (air) are inflicting on personnel, armor, and on trucks, and they still keep coming one cannot but admire them as an enemy."[57]

The South Korean troops defending Pohang were the first to be subjected to the latest North Korean offensive. The ROK army had been fighting stubbornly for weeks in the mountains of eastern Korea without the support and resources its American ally enjoyed, so by late August it was near the end of its rope. On 27 August, a North Korean attack routed a ROK division and opened the door to Pohang. Walker recognized the danger immediately; Pohang was only sixty-five miles from Pusan. Walker also realized that he lacked sufficient information about the murky situation to make informed decisions. Fortunately, a solution presented itself in the person of Major General John Coulter. Coulter had recently flown to Korea to organize and lead the newly arrived First Corps headquarters, but Walker ordered him instead to travel to Kyongju, about fifteen miles southwest of Pohang, to take over all South Korean and American forces in the area as the Eighth Army's new deputy commander. Coulter had served in Korea in 1948 to 1949 and was presumably familiar with Korean culture, so he seemed like an ideal go-between. Walker also dispatched a regiment from the Twenty-fourth Division—Richard Stephens's 21st—to help out. He dubbed the 21st and the various American odds and ends around Pohang "Task Force Jackson" and put it under Coulter's control.

When Coulter and his staff reached Kyongju around noon on 27 August, they found considerable chaos and confusion. Some South Korean officers were clearly tired and losing heart, an attitude that soon infected a number of Coulter's staffers as well. In addition to substandard leadership, the ROK soldiers were poorly trained, ill-equipped, and badly supplied. They had fought better than anyone had a right to expect, but there were definite limits to their endurance. As they retreated southward, an anxious Walker sent the other Twenty-fourth Division regiment, Edward Moore's 19th, to bolster the South Koreans. Although the North Koreans seized Pohang for a second time on 5 September, South Korean and American opposition stiffened. Coulter used his American battalions as bases of resistance around which South Korean units coalesced. No matter how motivated the South Koreans were, they still required American advisers, air and naval support, and logistics to overcome the determined North Korean troops. An increasingly irritable Coulter relieved some South Korean commanders and threatened others. He also won a Silver Star for almost singlehandedly stopping a ROK division from retreating under fire. Despite these efforts, Walker did not believe that Coulter was sufficiently aggressive, and he was irked by his repeated calls for reinforcements, which were not available. Therefore, on 7 September, he dissolved Task Force Jackson, ordered Coulter to Pusan to continue planning for his corps, and put Church in charge. Church was clearly tired, but he had enough tactical acumen to conclude that Coulter had dispersed his American outfits too much, so he brought the 21st Regiment closer to Kyongju. In the following week, the North Korean tide ebbed, though there was nothing easy about it as American and South Korean soldiers fought their way from one hill to another. The South Koreans finally reoccupied Pohang for good on 12 September. To the west, the ROKs also held onto Yongchon, through which ran the railroad connecting Taegu with Pohang.[58]

The North Korean offensive in the Masan area began on the night of 31 August–1 September, when the North Koreans crossed the Naktong and assailed Bill Kean's Twenty-fifth Division. Two battalions in Art Champeny's 24th Regiment crumbled under enemy pressure, creating a hole in the center of Kean's line that the North Koreans quickly exploited. Kean committed Throckmorton's 5th Regiment and part of Michaelis's 27th Regiment to seal the breach. They did so after several days of hard fighting, during which Champeny was wounded and evacuated. To the north, the North Koreans surrounded Hank Fisher's 35th Regiment. Unlike Michaelis, there was nothing glamorous about the fifty-year-old Fisher. As one officer explained, "Col[onel] Fisher was not the best looking, not the most diplomatic, nor the best talker . . . but as far as a leader of a regiment in combat, I feel, he was by far the best. He was solely interested in the fighting ability of his unit."[59] Although Fisher had led a regiment in Europe in World War II, he was still willing and able to learn. Moreover, his men were by now tough veterans disinclined to panic under the adverse circumstances in which they found themselves. Fisher pulled his regiment into a tight perimeter and relied on air and artillery fire to decimate the encircling North Koreans. Kean quickly recognized the threat to Fisher and risked Walker's wrath by committing on his own authority the remainder of the 27th Regiment to rescue the 35th Regiment. After the 27th finally broke through, Fisher commented, "I never intended to withdraw. There was no place to go."[60] By the time the fighting petered out on 9 September, the North Koreans had been so badly gutted that they no longer possessed much combat power. Throckmorton, Michaelis, and Kean could all be proud of their performances. The three men showed considerable poise and professionalism in responding to the North Korean attack. On the other hand, poor leadership continued to plague the hard-luck 24th Regiment, and after the battle, Kean recommended that the Eighth Army inactivate it and distribute its men to other units.

To Kean's immediate north, at the Naktong Bulge, Dutch Keiser's Second Division was undergoing its own trial by fire. Keiser's outfit, though, operated under some disadvantages that made its battle dicier than Kean's outside of Masan. For one thing, Walker had deployed his outfit along the Naktong less than a week earlier, so the men were still unfamiliar with the ground they were defending. Veteran troops might have adjusted more quickly, but the Second Division was as yet untested. Although some of its battalions had been bloodied already, others had not. Moreover, Keiser and his headquarters had not yet fought the division as an integrated unit, so they were bound to make some mistakes in their first engagement. Two of the regiments—Hill's 9th and Freeman's 23rd—were understrength because they had only two battalions in line apiece. There also were some of the usual supply, equipment, and weapons shortages. Finally, American intelligence, which had worked well over the past month, missed the North Korean buildup in the area and failed to provide warning of the imminent North Korean offensive. It was therefore unsurprising that the enemy attack across the Naktong achieved considerable success at first. Along the northernmost part of the Second Division's front, George Peploe's 38th Regiment maintained its positional integrity, but the 23rd and 9th regiments, situated in the center and southern part of the division's line, respectively, had a much more difficult time. North Korean troops overran Freeman's command post and shattered Hill's 9th Regiment. In doing so, they split the Second Division in two and opened the door for an enemy advance on Miryang, through which ran the communications and supply lines between Taegu and Pusan.[61]

When Walker first learned about the North Korean attacks rippling up and down the Pusan Perimeter, he immediately zeroed in on the fighting in the Naktong Bulge as the most serious threat. He said, "I don't know where we should be-gin but there's one area where we cannot let them through, and that's the Bulge." He was so disturbed by the emotional reports he initially got from Keiser that he decided to fly to Second Division headquarters for a firsthand look at the situa-tion. As his small plane winged over the Naktong Bulge, Walker spotted 9th Regi-ment soldiers retreating so rapidly and disjointedly that they failed to take advantage of good ground available from which they could stop or delay the en-emy. Because there was no suitable place nearby to land, Walker ordered the pilot to cut the throttle and idle the engine so he could bellow at the troops through a bullhorn: "Get back there, you yellow sons of bitches! Get back there and fight!"

Walker's sour mood was not sweetened by the confusion he discovered at Keiser's headquarters. Indeed, Walker seemed to know as much about the situa-tion as Keiser. "Dutch, where's your division?" Walker asked. When Keiser tried to explain, Walker repeatedly interrupted him by demanding, "Where are your re-serves, and what are your reserves? What are you doing about positioning your re-serves?" Just to make sure Keiser understood the stakes involved, Walker explained to him, "We cannot lose Yongsan. If we lose that, we'll lose Miryang—we'll lose Pusan. Now, you're in the heart of this whole thing, and you don't know what the hell's going on." Warming to his subject, Walker resorted to his usual direct form of motivation by bellowing at Keiser, "If you can't run this Division, I'll run you out of the Goddamn army, but I'm not going to lose this battle!" After some dis-cussion, Walker returned to his plane, waving off Keiser's attempt to escort him. Before taking off, Walker examined a map for several minutes. Then tears rolled down his cheeks and he exclaimed to the pilot, "Here I'm an Army Commander and I can't—I can't do anything about what's happening to my command."[62]

Fortunately for the stressed Walker, a subsequent flyover of the entire Pusan Perimeter indicated that the overall military situation was not as bad as he thought, allowing him to concentrate on the Naktong Bulge crisis. Of Walker's three fire brigades, the 5th and 27th regiments were already committed to the ac-tion around Masan, and the 1st Marine Brigade was preparing to leave the Pusan Perimeter to join the Inchon invasion. Walker, however, asked MacArthur for per-mission to retain the marines, at least temporarily, to combat the North Korean threat in the Naktong Bulge. To emphasize his seriousness, Walker added that without the marine outfit, he could not guarantee the Eighth Army's safety. MacArthur too was concerned by the latest North Korean offensive, so he permit-ted Walker to hold onto the leathernecks for a few more days, even though this complicated preparations for the Inchon landing. Walker deployed the marines in the Naktong Bulge on 3 September. The leathernecks had fought there two weeks earlier, so they were thoroughly familiar with the terrain. Together with the 9th Regiment, the counterattacking marines rapidly ground down the North Koreans, who had expended most of their energy in their initial thrust across the Nak-tong. The Second Division continued its cleanup operations after the marines pulled out on 6 September, but by then the issue was no longer in doubt. Although Keiser's performance certainly left much to be desired, John Hill ended up the scapegoat because the enemy had broken through his regiment. Keiser relieved him as commander of the 9th Regiment and replaced him with Colonel Charles "Chin" Sloane.[63]

Unlike Keiser's Second Division, Hap Gay's First Cavalry Division around Taegu had warning of the upcoming North Korean offensive. Unfortunately, and ironically, Walker's patented aggressiveness nullified many of the advantages Gay should have derived from this intelligence. Walker ordered Gay to launch a spoiling attack to disrupt North Korean preparations. The operation, conducted by elements of Cecil Nist's 7th Cav Regiment on 2 September, not only failed but also threw the entire division off balance. As a result, the initial North Korean assaults met with more success than would have been the case had the First Cavalry Division stayed in position. Tabu-dong and Kasan fell on 3 September, providing the North Koreans with a vantage point from which they could shell Taegu. Predictably enough, Walker was displeased with this regrettable turn of events. He roared at Gay, "You will not withdraw your division beyond terrain from which it can cover Taegu. If the enemy gets into Taegu you will find me resisting him in the streets and I'll have some of my trusted people with me and you had better be prepared to do the same. Now get back to your division and fight it!"[64]

Despite Walker's admonitions, the First Cavalry Division's situation continued to deteriorate. Soon North Korean and American units were so intermingled north and west of Taegu that it was hard to tell who had isolated whom. Moreover, because all of Walker's reserves were committed elsewhere, Gay had to fight the battle with what he had. Walker grew increasingly jittery as he read his reports. Indeed, he considered withdrawing the Eighth Army south of Taegu to the recently surveyed Davidson Line. When Walker visited the First Cav Division's headquarters on 5 September, he pulled Gay aside and asked him if he could save his division by abandoning his artillery, armor, and transportation and directing his troops to walk overland to safety. Gay said that he did not know but would think about it. Next day he told Walker, "I have been a cavalryman all my life. I have never learned to walk. I am too old to learn now."[65] Such resolve apparently helped assuage Walker's momentary anxiety; he put his arm around Gay's shoulder and wished him luck. Walker had, however, already ordered Gay to withdraw a few miles to better positions outside of Taegu. The retreat was not well conducted, and it included abandoning Waegwan to the enemy. Even so, Gay remained stalwart. At one point he personally directed fire against a pesky North Korean roadblock and other targets of opportunity. After several hours serving as a line officer, Gay returned to his headquarters to face a stack of paperwork on his desk. With a dejected sigh, he said of his foray to the front, "I've been having myself a hell of a time, but I guess that's the sort of thing generals ought not be doing."[66]

At about the same time Gay was playing lieutenant, Walker ordered his cumbersome but irreplaceable signals equipment and much of his headquarters staff to evacuate to the Pusan area, leaving him and a small number of key personnel at his advanced command post in Taegu to oversee Eighth Army operations. In the end, the North Korean advance, here as elsewhere along the Pusan Perimeter, started to run out of steam as a result of insufficient supplies. Although the North Koreans seized Hill 314, only eight miles north of Taegu, on 11 September, the next day a battalion from the 7th Cav Regiment retook it. Of the 535 troopers who participated in the engagement, 229 were killed or wounded. The victory broke the back of the North Korean offensive against the First Cavalry Division. Subsequent mop-up operations were tedious and difficult, but by then the crisis had passed.

Gay was not surprised by the battle's outcome. Indeed, he fought it with increasing skill and professionalism. Gay never believed that Taegu was in serious danger of falling to the enemy, though he allowed that the situation was at times touch and go. Gay later explained that the problem was that his division simply had too much ground—thirty-five miles—to cover. Although beforehand he had received three new battalions to strengthen his three regiments, he was still short of the necessary manpower to hold his assigned front. Gay had, however, learned from August's engagements that because it was difficult to adequately outpost his line, the best solution was to keep each of his battalions as concentrated as possible so they could maneuver in a coordinated fashion. Doing so enabled them to systematically and methodically eliminate pockets of enemy resistance with the help of air and artillery support. The downside of this tactic was that it made North Korean infiltration behind American lines much easier and more likely, which accounted for their initial successes. It also made their offensive seem more dangerous than was actually the case.[67]

By mid-September, the North Koreans and Eighth Army were like two punch-drunk heavyweight boxers staggering in the center of the ring. The North Koreans had wagered on a short and violent conflict that would destroy South Korea before the United States could interfere. Although the North Koreans had demonstrated plenty of ferocity and determination in pursuit of that goal, South Korean resistance had bought enough time for the United States to intervene and stop the enemy advance down the peninsula. It had not been easy, though; the army had suffered 19,165 casualties, of whom 4,280 were killed, 12,277 wounded, 401 captured, and 2,107 missing.[68] As for the North Koreans, their casualties had been enormous, and with each passing day, the balance of power shifted inexorably against them. Whatever the successes they had achieved, the fact was that they had lost their gamble—and unless they received outside assistance, the war as well. Whether or not Kim Il Sung realized it, his fate was no longer in his hands but would instead be determined in Washington and Tokyo. For the Americans and South Koreans, victory may have become the proper application of their increasing power, but this did not mean it would be easy. There was no denying their growing resources and skill in defensive warfare, but they had not had much success offensively. Walker's only operational offensive, Task Force Kean, had fallen a good bit short of its objectives. Whether the Eighth Army could master this other type of warfare was still an open question. Although some American, North Korean, and South Korean soldiers may have recognized that the North Koreans had shot their bolt, almost no one in the Pusan Perimeter knew that MacArthur was about to forcefully and abruptly shift the focus of the war away from southeastern Korea to the port of Inchon.

Conclusions

The Eighth Army's retreat to and defense of the Pusan Perimeter provides an opportunity to evaluate the chief American ground forces commanders and their relationships with their superiors and subordinates during the first ten weeks of the conflict. Starting at the top, MacArthur usually took a hands-off approach toward the fighting on the peninsula. Indeed, he flew to Korea only twice that summer, first to Suwon in late June to size up the situation and then to Taegu a month later to keep Walker's nose to the grindstone. MacArthur ordinarily gave his lieutenants plenty of autonomy to do their jobs as they saw fit as long as they hewed to his strategic ideas, remained loyal to him, and stayed out of his limelight. Of equal importance, MacArthur concluded early on that the war would not be won by the Eighth Army in the Pusan Perimeter but at Inchon, so he focused his attention there. To MacArthur, the Pusan Perimeter was, in strategic terms, a sideshow to the main event—Inchon—that he concentrated on producing and directing. As a result, the one and only decision he made that directly affected the course of the campaign was to press for the deployment of American ground forces to the peninsula. To do so, he lobbied for and even anticipated Truman's verdict that protecting South Korea was vital to American national security. Had MacArthur spoken out against American intervention, it is unlikely that the Truman administration would have successfully committed the United States to South Korea's defense. MacArthur's advocacy, therefore, made the Pusan Perimeter possible. The subsequent nitty-gritty logistical, operational, tactical, diplomatic, and personnel details all flowed from this one decision. Even MacArthur's late July trip to Taegu merely confirmed what Walker already intended to do.

MacArthur's relationship with Walker was not the best. MacArthur had not asked for Walker as his Eighth Army commander, and once in Japan, Walker failed to ingratiate himself with his new boss. Simply put, MacArthur did not much care for the man and saw him as an outsider. After the Korean War began, MacArthur grew disenchanted with Walker's military performance. To make things worse, Almond's antipathy toward Walker helped stoke MacArthur's discontent. Almond filtered much of the information MacArthur received from Korea in such a way as to place Walker in a negative light, which reinforced MacArthur's preexisting opinion of him. Despite his distaste for Walker, though, MacArthur made no real effort to remove him from the Eighth Army during the Pusan Perimeter campaign. The biggest reason for this was that MacArthur found such actions unpleasant. Indeed, MacArthur was far more likely to manipulate his lieutenants and play them off each other for his own benefit than to fire them. During World War II, for instance, MacArthur did not remove any of his field army or corps commanders, even when some of them deserved it. He even retained the services of his chief of staff, Major General Richard Sutherland, after Sutherland had alienated almost everyone with whom he came into contact, had become too ill to do his job, and had brought his mistress to the Philippines with him in direct violation of MacArthur's orders. It is therefore not surprising that MacArthur refrained from relieving Walker even after Norstad suggested it. As long as MacArthur did not force the issue, no one in Washington was willing or able to do so. As a result, Walker was on safer ground than he perhaps realized.

However, by keeping a subordinate in whom he did not have complete confidence, MacArthur did a disservice to himself, Walker, and the war effort. Most obviously, MacArthur was never sure that Walker could carry out his orders. Their poor rapport inhibited open and frank communications between them, as evidenced by MacArthur's overblown fear in late July that Walker lacked sufficient wherewithal to stop the North Koreans. It also made Walker wary of speaking his mind and acting as he thought best for fear of providing MacArthur with an excuse to fire him. Walker consequently had to resort to subterfuge to fight the war his way by, for example, surreptitiously authorizing the withdrawal behind the Naktong River. Such miscues did not prove ruinous in the Pusan Perimeter, but they did a few months later during the advance to the Yalu River.

It was bad enough that Walker's immediate superior and his staffers did not have confidence in him, but he also lacked the support of much of the American military establishment. He had never been a popular man, so friends were few and far between. During the Pusan Perimeter fighting, one journalist quoted an anonymous Pentagon insider as saying, "The opinion is that while Walker is not a bad general, he is not a particularly good one."[69] This meant that Walker's colleagues did not give him the benefit of the doubt but instead highlighted whatever flaws in his generalship they identified. That many of these men were themselves skilled practitioners of their craft, with distinguished World War II records to prove it, did not help Walker. Nor did the fact that Walker did indeed make mistakes during the first ten weeks of the conflict. He was responsible for browbeating his subordinates, micromanaging his units, and establishing a mediocre staff, all of which hurt his cause. On the other hand, some of these errors were due to factors beyond his control. After all, he had to wage war with an army he had not had the time or resources to prepare for combat, one that was woefully understrength and underequipped. He also had to fight a defensive conflict for which he had neither training nor experience, and which many army officers found doctrinally suspect. Observers overlooked his fortitude, adaptability, and resolve. Walker compensated for the Eighth Army's growing pains with the skillful use of terrain, mobile reserves, interior lines of communications, intelligence, superior logistics, and air and artillery support. Fortunately for Walker, he found a friend in chief of staff J. Lawton Collins, who sometimes seemed to be the only high-ranking officer who understood and sympathized with Walker's problems.

Walker's tendency to badger his division commanders and meddle in their tactical dispositions indicates that he had as little faith in them as MacArthur had in him. Except for Dean, Walker at one time or another publicly yelled at and bullied all of them. He often denied them the autonomy to fight their own battles, and he interfered down to the battalion level. Indeed, he sometimes treated them as hindrances to his war effort and rarely sweetened his tart criticisms with much praise. The fact that he did not relieve some or all of them seems to show that he made the same mistake with them that MacArthur made with him. Walker never gave reasons for his sufferance, but there are some obvious explanations. For one thing, removing them might reflect poorly on him. Walker realized that MacArthur lacked confidence in him, so firing one or more of his division commanders might have provided MacArthur with sufficient evidence to relieve Walker by demonstrating that he was not running the Eighth Army effectively. It might also create a public relations problem by causing the American public to question the army's competence. In addition, removing a division commander in the middle of the touch-and-go Pusan Perimeter battles would have been unwise. Continuity under such circumstances mattered, and disrupting the divisional command structure for even a short time might have cost the Eighth Army dearly. Finally, Walker had cut his teeth as a corps commander in George Patton's Third Army in Northwestern Europe in 1944–1945. Walker greatly respected Patton and modeled himself after him. Patton discovered during the North African and Sicily campaigns that most new leaders made mistakes the first time they took their units into action. Relieving these men before they had the opportunity to settle down and learn from their experiences lowered morale and made other officers reluctant to take risks for fear of losing their jobs if they failed. Before the Normandy invasion, Patton assured Walker and his other corps commanders that he would not fire them for the occasional blunder, especially if it was due to aggressiveness. Patton continued to yell at his lieutenants as a form of rough encouragement, but he rarely replaced them. Walker likely internalized Patton's leadership philosophy and applied it to his own division commanders. Walker probably concluded that it was wiser to work with his current division commanders and hope that they grew into their positions than run the various risks trying to sack them entailed.

Indeed, Walker's division commanders—Church, Dean, Gay, Kean, and Keiser—all turned in substandard battlefield performances that summer. Dean's piecemeal commitment of his division, while arguably necessary, by his own later admission left much to be desired, and he abdicated his responsibilities during the fighting for Taejon. Neither Gay nor Kean succeeded in stopping the North Korean advance short of the Naktong River when they picked up where Dean left off. Dean's replacement, John Church, foundered in his first action at the head of the Twenty-fourth Division west of Masan. As for Keiser, his efforts in the Naktong Bulge were anything but the acme of military skill. These men undoubtedly labored under the same difficulties that afflicted all American army officers during the war's first weeks—poorly trained and ill-equipped soldiers—but they were hindered by other factors as well. Except for Dean, none of them had attended the Army War College or led large units in combat before, so they had neither experience nor training to guide them. As World War II staff officers, they were accustomed to the confusion of battle—the contradictory intelligence, untimely communications snafus, matériel shortages, overwork, stress, personnel problems, and so forth—but they were unfamiliar with the loneliness and isolation of the top spot. Until they arrived in Korea, they had never made the big, tough decisions that could cost the lives of hundreds of men. Having the weight of the world on their shoulders was bad enough, but they also had to cope with the demanding and abrasive Walker. He was apt to show up at the worst possible moment, impatiently ask hard-to-answer questions, and reject even legitimate explanations. However, these challenges, while formidable, were not insurmountable. At the regimental level, officers such as Michaelis and Fisher brought out the best in their units and got their soldiers to fight well. Although divisions were bigger and more impersonal organizations, their troops were not immune to good inspirational leadership. Unfortunately, the Eighth Army's division commanders were not dynamic and charismatic men but the kind of colorless professionals the army produced in such abundance throughout the twentieth century.

Happily, most of the division commanders proved themselves capable of learning and adapting as the war continued. In this Kean and Gay were the most impressive. The no-nonsense Kean may have failed to stop the North Korean advance around Sangju, but he conducted a tolerably efficient retreat to the Naktong. He got his division to Masan in a timely manner, though Michaelis deserves most of the credit for stopping the first North Korean push toward the city. Although Kean subsequently fumbled Walker's one and only operational counteroffensive during the Pusan Perimeter fighting, he redeemed himself by repelling the second North Korean attack on Masan. He did not panic when the 24th Regiment broke but instead used his reserves to seal the breach in his line. Perhaps most importantly, he demonstrated moral courage and initiative by committing part of the 27th Regiment to battle without Walker's consent. Hap Gay's learning curve was equally steep. He fought poorly in his first action at Yongdong, but he later succeeded in protecting Taegu from two ferocious North Korean assaults. He adjusted his tactics to compensate for the unforgiving terrain, enemy infiltration tactics, and the long frontages he had to defend. He did not panic when the military situation looked bad but maintained the poise that characterizes good generals. Dean was captured before he had a chance to fulfill his potential, and Keiser did not receive the opportunity to show his capabilities before the war entered a new phase. Finally, John Church was the most disappointing of the division chiefs. Although it is true that he led the weakest of the American divisions, he lacked the personality to shake it quickly into fighting form. He was particularly ineffective in stopping the enemy march to Masan and the Naktong Bulge, though he demonstrated a better grasp of tactics when he took over in the Pohang region. On the whole, then, Walker's implicit assumption that his division commanders would grow into their jobs was not without merit.

At the regimental level, the command situation in the first two and a half months of the conflict was more fluid and the turnover rate higher. In the late 1940s, the army had assigned many regiments to officers who had previously worked mostly as staffers in order to give them some command experience. When they were suddenly thrust into battle under terrible circumstances, it was hardly surprising that some of them did not measure up. Because regimental commanders were close to the action, they were more vulnerable to the vicissitudes of war. Several of them, such as Robert Martin and Stan Meloy, were replaced because they became casualties. Running a regiment was so physically demanding that other officers, such as Horton White, lost their jobs because they were simply too old or out of shape to perform their duties. Finally, it was easier to blame these men than their more remote divisional counterparts for battlefield setbacks. Regimental leaders were relatively low on the command food chain, so replacing them was unlikely to embarrass the army. Although a good many of the army's World War II–era division and corps commanders had retired, there were still plenty of officers around who had led regiments against the Germans and Japanese. The problem was getting these men where they were needed. Walker recognized this problem as soon as the war started and undertook efforts to weed out those he suspected were not up to snuff, which was how Michaelis got his job. Ridgway was equally prescient, and after he returned to the Pentagon from his visit to Korea in late July, he made it his business to identify and make available to Walker men he believed would make good regimental commanders. The shakeout did not occur all at once but was a gradual process that improved the Eighth Army's efficiency. Within a few months of the war's start, though, only three of the Eighth Army's original regimental commanders remained: Fisher, Michaelis, and Stephens.

On the whole, therefore, the army's leadership during the war's first two months was at best uneven. This was unsurprising considering the army's poor condition at the conflict's start, as well as the quality of some of the division and regimental commanders. Even a casual glance at the records of many of these men indicated that they were not the army's first team but rather second stringers who owed their positions to bureaucratic vagaries rather than combat prowess. Some of them fought well when they found themselves in Korea, but others did not. As the army flexed its muscles and dispatched more resources to the peninsula, these officers had more chances to demonstrate their value. Whether they could take advantage of these opportunities as the war entered a new phase was an open question.

3
MacArthur's Last Hurrah

Planning an Amphibious Landing

Amphibious assaults were among the most complex and difficult military operations in twentieth-century warfare. Conducting them entailed carefully loading and then transporting men and matériel across miles of ocean to hostile shores. Shepherding such convoys to their destination required innumerable warships, from aircraft carriers to minesweepers, to protect them and ensure naval supremacy. All this was complicated enough, but successfully placing the soldiers or marines on an enemy coast was an even more daunting task. After a preliminary bombardment that might last anywhere from a few hours to several weeks, troops boarded specially designed landing craft for the short voyage from ship to shore. Planners selected the appropriate beach on the basis of tides, currents, gradients, soil composition, and of course anticipated enemy opposition. Once the soldiers or marines reached dry land—assuming they overcame innumerable and often unexpected natural and man-made obstacles—they had to be protected, supported, succored, and reinforced faster than the enemy rushed troops to the area. Doing so necessitated a significant logistical investment and interservice cooperation. Not surprisingly, the century was full of instances of amphibious assaults gone awry—sometimes destroyed at the water's edge, but more often undone by an inability to muster sufficient strength to break out of the beachhead. In short, amphibious warfare was not the kind of thing undertaken lightly or on the fly.

Whatever its complexities and attendant risks, amphibious warfare served MacArthur well in the Southwest Pacific during World War II. There MacArthur used his limited resources to conduct scores of intricately coordinated amphibious assaults along New Guinea's northern coast and in the Philippines archipelago. By landing in lightly defended areas, Australian and American forces repeatedly and with minimal losses isolated and neutralized Japanese strongholds during MacArthur's advance toward Japan. Considering his success with amphibious operations, MacArthur's thoughts predictably turned in that direction as he watched ROK troops flee across the Han River during his late June visit to

Korea. As he saw it, a properly directed amphibious attack would take advantage of both American naval supremacy and Korea's long exposed peninsular coast to turn the war's tide. After consulting with his staff, MacArthur zeroed in on Inchon, a large port city only twenty-five miles west of Seoul. Seizing Inchon would open the door for an American push toward the South Korean capital, through which ran the North Korean army's logistical and communication lines southward. Once Seoul was in American hands, those North Korean troops battling along the Pusan Perimeter would be cut off from reinforcements and resupply. Walker's Eighth Army could then launch a counteroffensive to destroy the weakened enemy army and free South Korea. The concept, eventually dubbed Operation Chromite, was breathtaking in its elegance, simplicity, and directness.

Unfortunately for MacArthur, turning his notion into a workable design exposed its numerous weaknesses. Inchon was quite simply a horrible place to conduct an amphibious landing. Merely reaching the city required a fleet to steam through the constricting and windy Flying Fish Channel, where one well-placed mine or artillery round could disable a ship and bottle up the entire passage. Wolmi-do Island guarded Inchon's approaches, so its capture or neutralization was a prerequisite to the invasion's success. Worse yet, Inchon's thirty-foot tides were among the world's highest. Without careful timing, landing craft could end up stranded on mudflats far from the shore, vulnerable to enemy fire. There was no beach per se but rather a fourteen-feet-high seawall for troops to scale before engaging the enemy. Moreover, Inchon was a major city containing a quarter million people that could swallow up units in its sprawling urban environment. The numerous buildings and warehouses along the shoreline provided ready-made pillboxes for enemy soldiers to repel attackers. Small wonder one officer commented, "Make a list of amphibious don'ts and you have an exact description of the Inchon operation."[1] Finally, before MacArthur could even fight the North Koreans at Inchon, in a few weeks' time he had to formulate a plan, sell it to his superiors, and round up sufficient resources to implement it.

For all his serene self-assuredness, MacArthur was not a dictator, so he had to get support from President Truman and the Joint Chiefs of Staff to carry out Chromite. This would not be easy because of the palpable risks involved. Although everyone in the know recognized the advantages an amphibious assault offered, there was considerable doubt about the practicality of a landing at Inchon. Navy and marine officers were especially unhappy with the obvious difficulties in getting ashore there, the lack of knowledge about the city, and the compressed schedule. Some marines suggested assailing Posung-myon, an undefended beach thirty miles south of Inchon, instead. Army chief of staff Collins was equally dubious. He backed an attack on Kusan on South Korea's west coast because it was close enough to the Pusan Perimeter for mutual support.

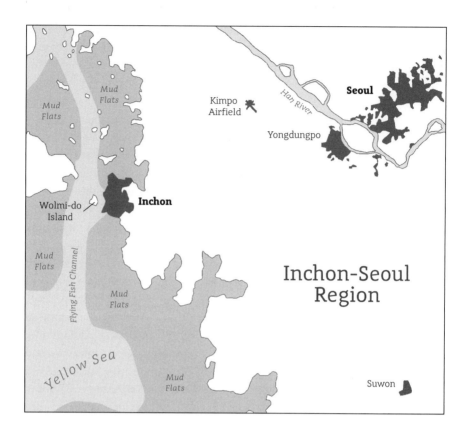

Inchon-Seoul
Region

MacArthur dismissed such counterproposals as too timid and remained focused on Inchon. He was a savvy bureaucratic operator who knew how to overcome opposition off the battlefield as well as on it. To sway those within his reach, he relied on his formidable powers of persuasion. For instance, when Harriman, Norstad, and Ridgway flew to East Asia in early August, they were inclined to oppose Chromite because of Inchon's high tides. MacArthur's magical rhetoric, however, brought them all on board, and when they returned to the States, they all reluctantly endorsed the plan. As MacArthur certainly intended, Harriman discussed Chromite with Truman. The president was loath to second-guess the man on the scene, and anyway he had recently pledged to support MacArthur's military efforts in any way possible, so he gave Chromite his blessing. All this was well and fine, but MacArthur still needed the Joint Chiefs' backing, or at least their acquiescence. MacArthur initially disclosed as few details as possible to the Joint Chiefs about Chromite. He pointed to operational security to justify his actions, but he no doubt realized that the further along the planning for Chromite had progressed, the harder it would be for the Joint Chiefs to cancel it.[2]

Ironically, it was MacArthur's stonewalling that finally galvanized the JCS into action. The Joint Chiefs were increasingly concerned that MacArthur was preparing to undertake a risky and important mission without their input or explicit approval. The JCS therefore dispatched two of its members, Collins and chief of naval operations Admiral Forrest Sherman, to Tokyo to learn Chromite's details. Late in the afternoon of 23 August, Collins and Sherman met with MacArthur, his staffers, and various naval officers in a Dai Ichi building conference room to discuss the operation. Although most of Chromite's important players were there, Almond excluded the high-ranking marine officers involved because, in all likelihood, he feared they would complicate matters by bringing up Posung-myon as a possible alternative landing site. At the meeting the naval officers ticked off a long list of problems with Chromite. As one officer later remembered, "We drew a list of every conceivable and natural handicap—and Inchon had 'em all." By doing so, however, they may have overplayed their hand because Sherman mistook their caution for defeatism and snorted, "I wouldn't hesitate to take a ship up there." Collins, for his part, again advocated an assault on Kusan as a safer alternative to Inchon. For an hour, Collins and the naval officers tore up Chromite, leaving no doubt that they believed the plan both prohibitively dangerous and unnecessary.

MacArthur listened impassively to the presentation while puffing his pipe, making few comments. When all the briefers had finished, he remained seated for a minute or two to collect his thoughts and build tension. His dad's advice that war councils bred timidity flashed through his mind. When he finally rose and began pacing, he spoke quietly at first, but gradually his voice built to a crescendo as he made his points. He had, he noted, more amphibious warfare experience than most of the naval officers in the room, so he was thoroughly aware of the dangers involved. However, Inchon was the quickest way to Seoul, and seizing the South Korean capital was the key to winning the conflict. Once Seoul was in American hands, the North Korean troops down around the Pusan Perimeter would be cut off from their homeland and vulnerable to destruction. Seoul was, he continued, the anvil to the Eighth Army's hammer. On the other hand, a landing at Kusan would do little to threaten the North Korean army's communication and supply lines. MacArthur emphasized his high regard for the navy and Marine Corps, and added that he apparently had more confidence in their abilities to implement Chromite than they did. Besides, he continued, the plan's very boldness was the best guarantee of its success. He compared it to British general James Wolfe's audacious scaling of the cliffs along the St. Lawrence River to reach the Plains of Abraham outside of Quebec during the Great War for Empire. And if North Korean resistance was too severe, he would be on hand to withdraw the invasion force before anything except his professional reputation suffered. "But Inchon will not fail," he intoned. "Inchon will succeed. And it will save 100,000 lives." Although most of the conferees had been exposed to MacArthur's rhetoric before, they were still spellbound by this virtuoso performance. One witness recalled, "It was an extraordinary moment. Even as it was happening, I realized I had witnessed something that would go down in history." The silence that filled the room when he finished his soliloquy indicated that he had won the argument. Collins and Sherman were persuaded, albeit against their better judgment and with continuing reservations.[3]

Everything thereafter was anticlimax. Although marine officers met with MacArthur the next day to pitch their plan for Posung-myon, MacArthur was in no mood for further discussion and dismissed their suggestion. The Joint Chiefs sanctioned Chromite on 28 August, but they qualified their approval by urging MacArthur to consider alternative landing sites if North Korean opposition at Inchon seemed too strong. To MacArthur, this wishy-washiness indicated that the Joint Chiefs might still change their minds, so he continued to keep them in the dark as much as possible. Indeed, he did not send a courier to Washington with Chromite's final plans until he knew it was too late for them to call off the operation.

At the same time he was lobbying for Chromite, MacArthur was also scrambling to secure the ground forces necessary to implement the operation. His original plan had been to use Hobart Gay's First Cavalry Division for the landing, but Walker's desperate need for troops compelled MacArthur to send the division to the Eighth Army instead. Once the First Cavalry, Twenty-fourth, and Twenty-fifth divisions had been deployed to Korea, Major General David Barr's Seventh Division was the only large outfit left in Japan. Unfortunately, the Seventh Division was completely unprepared for action because MacArthur's headquarters had gutted it for replacements for the hard-pressed Eighth Army in Korea. When Barr got the word on 26 July to ready his outfit for combat, it was short 9,117 officers and men. To bring it up to strength, MacArthur's headquarters temporarily diverted the Eighth Army's entire replacement flow from the States, nearly 5,800 officers and men, to the Seventh Division, despite Walker's urgent need for every soldier he could get. This placed some highly qualified people in the unit—for example, instructors and demonstration personnel from the infantry and artillery schools—but it was not enough. In desperation, MacArthur's headquarters also infused more than 8,600 poorly trained South Koreans into the division as part of the Korean Augmentation to the United States Army (KATUSA) program. Although this gave the Seventh Division sufficient manpower on paper, the quality of the KATUSAs was low for several reasons—particularly communications problems. As one officer put it, "The KATUSAs were hopeless because no one could talk to them."[4] Barr later elaborated:

Not by the mildest stretch of imagination should these personnel be referred to as "ROK" troops. They were civilians, in every sense of the word, picked up on the streets of Pusan without benefit of draft or prior notice of any kind. Many of them had only slipped from their doors or places of business for a moment's absence—but were never later permitted to communicate with relatives or business associates again. I believe within 48 hours after being picked up they arrived by ship in Yokohama. Their clothing consisted of what they had on ranging from a fairly presentable business suit for a few to the many in shirts and shorts only. The majority wore sandals or cloth shoes. They brought no other possessions. Upon arrival they were completely frustrated but amenable, they were stunned, confused and exhausted.[5]

Notwithstanding these Herculean efforts, it was clear to everyone that although the Seventh Division could serve in a supportive role, it was in no condition to spearhead an amphibious assault on Inchon.[6]

Happily for MacArthur, he acquired for Chromite the services of the country's foremost amphibious warfare experts: the Marine Corps. Despite persistent rumors to the contrary, MacArthur thought highly of the marines and had worked well with them in the Pacific during World War II. He recognized from the start that they had the know-how and equipment to make Chromite work, so he repeatedly pressured the JCS to dispatch a marine division to Korea as soon as possible. Although the Joint Chiefs acquiesced to committing the 1st Marine Brigade, they initially balked at sending an entire division. One reason for their reluctance was that doing so would further deplete the country's already bare strategic reserve at a time when global war with the Soviet Union seemed a possibility. However, personal prejudice also played a part. Many members of the American military establishment, including President Truman and JCS chairman Omar Bradley, disliked the Marine Corps and its penchant for publicity. As far as they were concerned, the Marine Corps was an anachronism in an era of atomic warfare that sucked up scarce resources better used by the army. The marines had, according to this line of thinking, simply outlived their usefulness. Whatever the reason, MacArthur's persistence gradually wore down the JCS, and in late July it authorized the deployment of two thirds of a division to East Asia, with the understanding that MacArthur could use the 1st Marine Brigade to round out a full division. The marines, always eager to justify their existence, hurried to meet MacArthur's timetable. They mobilized their reservists, scoured the world for personnel, and even sent an entire battalion from the Mediterranean Sea to East Asia through the Suez Canal. The Marine Corps had had the foresight to store enough leftover weapons and equipment from World War II at Camp Barstow,

California, to supply their units, so their shortages were not as acute as those of their army counterparts. There was nothing easy about the obstacles they had to overcome, but they met MacArthur's tight schedule. It was therefore the First Marine Division that conducted the amphibious assault on Inchon.[7]

As the American military's amphibious warfare specialists, the marines were the logical choice to lead Chromite. They had a headquarters designated for such amphibious operations, with an experienced general and personnel at its helm. MacArthur, however, wanted his own people planning and running Chromite, so he created "Force X" out of his headquarters staff and put Almond in charge of Inchon's preparations. Almond and Force X got to work in a motor pool far from prying eyes, but they had trouble requisitioning matériel and people because the army's bureaucracy did not recognize any Force X on its organizational tables. MacArthur and Almond put their heads together and decided to redesignate the team as the Tenth Corps. MacArthur was particularly pleased with the title because he had had a Tenth Corps with him during World War II. As for its commander, MacArthur surprised Almond by giving him the job. Although Almond was pleased with a combat assignment, he protested that he could not simultaneously take the Tenth Corps into Inchon and serve as MacArthur's chief of staff. MacArthur airily dismissed his concerns. The Inchon operation, MacArthur explained, would only last a few weeks, and after it ended in American victory, Almond could resume his chief of staff duties while Walker mopped up whatever North Korean resistance remained. Until then, Almond's deputy, Major General Doyle Hickey, could oversee MacArthur's headquarters.[8]

An American army corps like the Tenth was on paper little more than a headquarters to which divisions were attached for specific combat missions. The idea was to free up corps commanders from the mundane day-to-day paperwork that plagued their divisional counterparts so they could focus on planning and fighting their battles. As such, it was one of the purest combat posts the army could offer a general. It was also one of the most important, so usually the army chief of staff appointed corps commanders after consulting with their presumptive superiors. When Collins flew out to Tokyo in August, he was shocked to learn that MacArthur had chosen Almond to lead the Tenth Corps without discussing the matter with him first. Not only did this violate army protocol, but also there was bad blood between Collins and Almond dating back to their days as young officers. However, here, as elsewhere, Collins deferred to MacArthur's judgment and accepted the fait accompli. In the meantime, Almond set about with his usual energy in organizing a first-rate corps headquarters. He had already skimmed off some of the best personnel from MacArthur's staff and the Seventh Division for the Tenth Corps, and now he persuaded a reluctant Collins to send him a number of the army's finest and most promising young officers, even though this diluted the talent available for the worldwide military buildup the army was beginning. As for Almond's Tenth Corps chief of staff, MacArthur suggested Major General Clark "Nick" Ruffner. Although Almond knew Ruffner only by his good reputation, he accepted MacArthur's recommendation.[9]

Except for MacArthur, Edward "Ned" Almond was the army's most divisive Korean War general. The Virginia-born Almond received his commission after graduating from the Virginia Military Institute in 1915. He fought along the Marne River and in the Argonne during World War I, rising to command a machine gun battalion. He was also wounded in the scalp and received a Silver Star for gallantry. After Germany surrendered, he attended and later taught at the army's Infantry School at Fort Benning, Georgia. While there, he impressed assistant commandant and future army chief of staff George Marshall by suggesting more realistic night training. In the 1930s, Almond punched all the right tickets for an ambitious officer: Command and General Staff School, Army War College, Air Corps Tactical School, and even the Naval War College. He also saw troop duty by leading a battalion of Philippines Scouts. When the United States entered World War II in December 1941, Almond was a corps operations officer obviously going places.

Unfortunately for Almond, World War II failed to launch him into the army's stratosphere. In July 1942, Marshall appointed Almond commander of the all-black Ninety-second Division, which became one of the army's most controversial units. Deployed to Italy in late 1944, the Ninety-second Division did not fight particularly well. There were plenty of reasons for its poor performance, not the least of which was the army's institutionalized racism, but Almond did little to confront and overcome these obstacles. Indeed, he was part of the problem. He had scant respect for blacks as soldiers, so not surprisingly, he had difficulty relating to or respecting his men. Whatever the Ninety-second Division's woes, the army's leadership did not blame Almond for them. Almond himself certainly accepted no responsibility, but put the onus for the Ninety-second Division's failures on the troops themselves. Even so, he was aware that he had not exactly covered himself with glory during the conflict. Worse yet, personal tragedy accompanied his professional travails; both his son and son-in-law died during the war. Almond did not, however, give up but rather searched for the opportunity to refurbish his stagnant career. He turned down an offer to become military attaché to the Soviet Union and instead found himself transferred to MacArthur's Tokyo headquarters as head of personnel. Unlike Walker, he placed himself in MacArthur's orbit and worked hard to prove his value and ingratiate himself. MacArthur found Almond useful and promoted him successively to assistant chief of staff and then, in February 1949, to chief of staff. Almond was therefore well positioned to play a central role when the Korean War began.[10]

Years later, one officer tried to explain Almond's motivations: "General Almond desired one thing above all else in his life. Military glory. I do not say this in a negative sense. He sought fame as other men chase power, or money, or art. To gain it he was willing to subordinate his personal comfort, convenience or his life if that was what it would take."[11] For Almond, the Korean War offered him a rare second chance to achieve the glory that circumstances had denied him in World War II. His role, he well knew, was dependent on his relationship with MacArthur. Almond was therefore loyal to MacArthur to a fault. As MacArthur's chief of staff, Almond pushed himself by working the usual business hours as well as MacArthur's more evening-oriented schedule. He saw himself as MacArthur's gatekeeper and insisted that staffers run any ideas past him before pitching them to MacArthur. He was jealous and suspicious of those who gained access to MacArthur without his consent, especially MacArthur's alter ego, Courtney Whitney. MacArthur, for his part, valued Almond for his devotion and efficiency, which was why he put him in charge of the operation MacArthur was convinced would win the war.[12]

There was no doubt that Almond possessed an extraordinarily forceful personality. He was a man of medium height, with gray hair, frosty blue eyes, a weathered face, and a crisp voice. He was also one of the most aggressive leaders the American army had ever produced. Twentieth-century army commanders tended to be cautious professionals who focused on fulfilling their missions with minimum losses and the greatest margin for error possible. Almond, though, was one officer who never needed pushing and prodding but instead required careful oversight to keep him on the right side of recklessness. For Almond, taking the initiative was practically axiomatic. He coupled this ferociousness with phenomenal energy. He drove like a maniac and was always impatient with any delay or obstacle. He liked to be at the front, and he was so courageous that some officers speculated that he had some kind of death wish. He exposed himself to enemy fire so often and so irresponsibly that occasionally staffers had to physically remove him, and in one instance actually tackle him, to get him out of the line of fire. Almond combined this boldness with intelligence and organization. He ran a tight headquarters and made sure that his desk was always clean at the end of the day. He demanded that all directives be short and to the point, and had an aide take detailed notes of everything he observed during inspections. He even wrote up discussion points to refer to while talking on the phone long distance to his daughter. He was a first-rate tactician, capable of sizing up a battlefield at a glance and recognizing whatever opportunities were available. Although he prided himself as a combat general, he was not immune to the finer things his rank offered. His command post, for example, included fine china, silverware, and waiters wearing white coats and serving the best foods and wines. Not surprisingly, he was also mercurial, high strung, and excitable, so he sometimes let his emotions cloud his judgment. While he had a sense of humor and was capable of compassion—one regimental commander recalled that Almond yelled at him because the soldiers on sentry duty forgot to salute him whenever he arrived but laughed when the officer suggested that Almond try visiting another regiment instead—his more prominent traits overwhelmed and subsumed these humane qualities. Most officers acknowledged Almond's military abilities but also realized that he required firm supervision to bring out the best in him.

What made Almond such a polarizing figure, though, were his interpersonal skills—or lack thereof. He was, in fact, an overbearing and difficult man. Opinionated, officious, mean, and arrogant, Almond was always ready to point out the flaws of others and tell them what to do, whether they were Walton Walker, Syngman Rhee, or lowly company and battalion commanders. To bend others to his will and demonstrate his superiority, he resorted to intimidation and browbeating. For example, he sometimes held interviews with officers while under fire to cow those who lacked his reckless courage. He fired people without reflection and often in front of others, demonstrating an unbecoming cruel streak. His emotionalism interfered with his personal relations and contributed to an awkwardness that was often displayed in dealing with people. One officer recalled that Almond was once so angry with him that he feared Almond would assault him, but the next day Almond cried when he saw that the same officer had been wounded. Almond tried hard to relate to the rank and file by, for instance, freely handing out medals, but his clumsy efforts to ingratiate himself with enlisted men and noncoms got nowhere. On one occasion, he exclaimed to a bedraggled sergeant that it was so cold that the water in his basin froze in his trailer, to which the sergeant responded, "You're goddamned lucky to have a trailer and a basin of water."[13] Another time Almond yelled at a general in front of a bunch of enlisted men, "I don't care if your men get killed, you go and do this!"[14] To his credit, Almond had an eye for talent and selected capable men for his Tenth Corps staff, many of whom later became two-, three-, or even four-star generals. He could be reasoned with if the counterarguments were brief and to the point, and he respected those who stood up to him. Even so, Almond was not an easy man to work for or with. As one officer explained, "Ned Almond could precipitate a crisis on a desert island with nobody else around."[15]

Considering Almond's forceful personality, he not unexpectedly clashed with the Marine Corps officers tasked with Chromite's nitty-gritty tactical planning. Almond's ability to procure hard-to-get men and matériel for Chromite was counterbalanced by his obliviousness about amphibious warfare and his reluctance to listen to the experts. Most of the marines involved in Chromite possessed a wealth of amphibious experience from the Pacific War, so they understood the complexities such operations entailed. Chromite's short timetable and the limited intelligence about Inchon made the situation worse, as did the fact that the First Marine Division was arriving in driblets in vessels that were not always combat loaded. The marines realized that the antidote to these problems was to keep everything as simple as possible. Unfortunately, Almond and some of his Tenth Corps staffers did not see things in the same light, and they repeatedly interfered in ways that complicated planning and demonstrated their collective ignorance. For example, Almond wanted to use some marines for a commando-style assault on Kimpo airfield near Seoul on the day of the landing. The marines saw this as an unwise dispersion of their limited resources, but they could not dissuade Almond until the last minute. A more serious crisis, however, arose over the 1st Marine Brigade. Walker valued the outfit and wanted to hold onto it to help repulse the North Korean army's late August offensive. Almond figured he would simply substitute the Seventh Division's 32nd Regiment for it. Horrified marine and naval officers pointed out that the 32nd Regiment was in no way up to such a mission and protested vehemently. Eventually everyone involved agreed to a compromise in which the marines got their brigade for Chromite in return for deploying another Seventh Division regiment, the 17th, offshore from Pusan as a floating reserve should Walker need it. Such differences were regrettable enough, but Almond interpreted them as evidence of the Marine Corps' faintheartedness and inflexibility, an attitude that eventually metastasized once the campaign began in earnest.[16]

In fact, the differences of opinion between Almond and marine officers extended beyond Chromite's particulars; they were institutional as well. The army and Marine Corps were two separate branches of the American military. They had dissimilar organizational and doctrinal approaches that manifested themselves during and after Chromite. The Marine Corps was part of the navy and since before World War II had dedicated itself to amphibious warfare. Theoretically, amphibious assaults lasted only as long as it took for the marines to land on and secure a beachhead. As a result, the marines lacked the logistical infrastructure for prolonged operations that the army took for granted. Likewise, the Marine Corps did not have the army's artillery support but relied on naval and air power instead. Finally, the marines did not possess the army's mobility because its doctrine never envisioned wide-ranging campaigns inland. As for tactics, those of the Marine Corps were largely molded by its World War II experiences against the Japanese. The marines fought most of their battles on small Pacific islands whose geography often limited maneuverability. The Marine Corps' solution was to concentrate its forces and rely on its superior élan and training to overcome the enemy. Although this sometimes resulted in high casualties, it ended the battle quicker than more cautious tactics, thus limiting the amount of time the supporting fleet had to remain offshore, vulnerable to enemy attack. On the other hand, Almond believed in using motorized divisions to outmaneuver the enemy and keep casualties low, even though such tactics could be time consuming. There was something to be said for both army and Marine Corps doctrines, but the right one often depended on circumstances such as terrain, the enemy, and available resources. However, Almond, for whom subtlety and nuance were alien concepts, had a tough time understanding and accepting that his way might not be the only solution to military problems.[17]

Almond directed much of his antimarine antipathy toward Major General Oliver Smith, the First Marine Division's tall, white-haired, and rawboned commander. The two men were as different as night and day. Smith had the aura of a staffer and scholar, and he was easy to underestimate. He was a devout Christian Scientist who possessed such high moral standards that he practically oozed integrity, fairness, and kindness. A taciturn, aesthetic, thoughtful, and meticulous man, Smith rarely raised his voice or exhibited much anger or frustration. Indeed, he seemed so remote and reserved that few claimed to know him particularly well. Beneath his placid exterior, though, Smith had ample reservoirs of toughness, focus, moral courage, common sense, and military skill. Matthew Ridgway, who knew a thing or two about good generalship, later described Smith: "Oh, top flight. Very calm and extreme consideration for his troops; good tactical judgment and a gentleman. He was a splendid commander."[18] Almond, however, clashed with Smith from the get-go; he was not at all impressed with what he perceived as Smith's timorous attitude toward Chromite. He was disgusted with Smith's initial assertion that there was not enough time to mount the operation and by Smith's desire to solidify the beachhead before pressing inland. Almond said, "I got the impression initially (and it was fortified constantly later) that General Smith always had excuses for not performing at the required time the tasks he was requested to do. This is the real disagreement between General Smith and myself."[19] Smith, for his part, saw Almond as a loose cannon. Unlike so many army generals whom Almond browbeat, Smith had the poise, character, and institutional autonomy to resist what he believed to be Almond's imprudent directives. If Almond insisted on this or that, Smith intended to do so the Marine Corps way or not at all. The relationship between the two men, rocky from the start, got progressively worse as time went on, so that eventually, as one army officer remembered, "Smith and Almond were just like two dogs at each other's throats."[20]

If Smith seemed more scholarly than martial, he came about it honestly. Born in Texas in 1893, Smith graduated from the University of California at Berkeley in 1916. He worked for the Standard Oil Company until the United States entered World War I, upon which he secured a Marine Corps commission. Instead of fighting in the trenches of France, though, Smith spent the conflict on the other side of the world garrisoning the Pacific island of Guam. After Germany surrendered, he served successively in a marine detachment on the battleship USS *Texas*, in the Marine Corps' personnel office, and in Haiti. From that point, his career took on an increasingly educational hue. He attended the army's Infantry School during George Marshall's tenure there as assistant commandant, taught twice at the Marine Corps School in Quantico, Virginia, and took a two-year course at the École Supérieure de Guerre while working on the naval attaché's staff in Paris. In 1940 he got his own battalion and commanded it in the occupation of Iceland. He did not see action in World War II until 1944. He led a regiment in New Britain, was assistant commander of the First Marine Division at Peliliu, and finished the conflict as the Tenth Army's assistant chief of staff during the Okinawa campaign. After the war, he returned to the Marine Corps School as its commandant; then, in April 1948, he became assistant commandant of the entire Marine Corps. Although he and the commandant, General Clifton Cates, had very different personalities, Cates appreciated Smith's finer qualities and put him in charge of the First Marine Division when the JCS assigned it to Korea.

Despite the problems and snafus inherent in all amphibious operations, especially one thrown together as hastily as Chromite, the planners got the job done and met MacArthur's timetable. In late August and early September, Chromite's various task forces assembled in Japanese ports for their assigned roles. Ashore, soldiers and marines readied their gear and moved to their embarkation areas. As things turned out, the last big threat to Chromite came not from the JCS but from Mother Nature. On 3 September, a typhoon that swept through the region damaged some ships and delayed loading, but not enough to stop the operation. Eight days later, the troops began boarding their transport vessels for the voyage to Korea. It was impossible to hide such an enormous undertaking from prying eyes, and Chromite's planners did not try. Instead, they relied on a number of diversionary attacks on both sides of the peninsula to fool the North Koreans as to the target of all the men, ships, and matériel massing in Japan. After dodging yet another typhoon, the armada got under way starting on 11 September. The invasion fleet might have been unremarkable by the World War II standards to which so many of the participants were accustomed, but it was still impressive. It contained approximately 260 vessels of all kinds, from huge aircraft carriers and battleships to smaller minesweepers and rocket ships. The capital ships may have gotten most of the attention, but Chromite's workhorses were the lowly transport and supply vessels responsible for moving men and matériel. They included forty-seven invaluable Landing Ship, Tanks (LSTs), which could each carry over 2,000 tons of equipment and land them directly onto a beach. Thirty had been commandeered from the Japanese merchant marine and went to Korea still manned by Japanese crews. In all, the invasion fleet contained 53,000 troops, 6,629 vehicles, and 25,000 tons of supplies. As for the 20,000 marines spearheading the assault, they did their best to fill the downtime, settle their stomachs, and get some sleep.

Sleeplessness and anxiety were no respecters of rank but instead afflicted everyone from the lowliest leatherneck all the way up to Douglas MacArthur. MacArthur insisted on accompanying the invasion fleet just in case it ran into trouble. On 12 September, he and Courtney Whitney boarded the command ship USS *Mount McKinley* and set sail for Korea. Although initially voluble, MacArthur became progressively more nervous and seasick as time went on. He had staked his reputation on Chromite's success, and as D-day approached, doubts crept into his mind. A staffer found a nauseous MacArthur in the stateroom huddled in a West Point bathrobe. He and Whitney persuaded the general to relax with some scotch and water, and eventually MacArthur fell asleep. Late at night, though, he claimed he woke up and went on deck, listened to the rush of the sea, and thought, "I alone am responsible for tomorrow, and if I failed, the dreadful results would rest on judgment day against my soul."[21] MacArthur need not have worried; he was about to experience the highlight of his illustrious military career.[22]

Inchon to Seoul

Before dawn on 15 September, nineteen warships slipped into Flying Fish Channel to conduct the preliminary bombardment of Wolmi-do Island, which served as Inchon's geographical sentinel. For forty-five minutes, cruisers and destroyers pumped 2,845 shells into the island from 800 yards offshore, followed by a rocket barrage and naval airstrikes. By the time the navy was done, Wolmi-do looked, according to one correspondent, like a forest fire had swept over it. At 6:30 AM, a battalion from Colonel Raymond Murray's 5th Marine Regiment, tough veterans of the Pusan Perimeter, landed on the island and secured it within a few hours at the cost of only seventeen wounded. Back on *Mount McKinley*, MacArthur watched the battle intently. After he got word that the island was in marine hands, he stood up, looked around with a broad smile, and said, "Let's go below and get some coffee."[23]

There was then a pause in the action as the tide receded and left Wolmi-do's new owners surrounded by a sea of mud. When the tide returned in the late afternoon, so did the navy. This time the warships directed their fire at Inchon itself. The rocket ships alone threw 6,000 rockets at the city. Amid the evening haze and periodic rainsqualls, marines from the rest of the 5th Marine Regiment and Colonel Chesty Puller's 1st Marine Regiment boarded their landing craft and headed toward their two assigned beaches on either side of Inchon's wartlike peninsula. When the landing craft hit the seawall, the marines used aluminum scaling ladders to climb over it and descend into Inchon's urban sprawl. As at Wolmi-do, resistance was light. Indeed, there were only 2,500 North Korean troops in the area, and a good many of them had been killed or stunned by the navy's firepower even before the marines reached terra firma. The marines quickly pushed into Inchon and staked out positions on the high ground. As was often the case, there was considerable confusion back at the beaches as the follow-up waves struggled to sort themselves out, but by the time darkness arrived, more than 13,000 marines were ashore, all at the cost of less than 200 casualties.

Successfully establishing a beachhead at Inchon at such a bargain price was an impressive accomplishment, but everyone understood that doing so was preliminary to seizing the bigger and more important inland objective: Seoul. On the day after the landing, the marines quickly shook themselves out and pushed eastward toward the South Korean capital, with the 5th Marine Regiment on the left (north) and the 1st Marine Regiment on the right (south). The 5th Marine Regiment occupied Kimpo airfield on 17 September, and Yongdungpo, on the Han River, fell to the 1st Marine Regiment four days later. However, enemy resistance gradually stiffened as the North Koreans rushed men to Seoul to protect their supply and communications lines to the Pusan Perimeter. Unfortunately for the North Koreans, the Americans were pouring in reinforcements of their own through Inchon. The ROK Marine Corps regiment arrived on 16 September to mop up in the city before joining the First Marine Division, followed by the ROK 17th Regiment. Two of David Barr's Seventh Division regiments, Charles Beauchamp's 32nd and Colonel Richard Ovenshine's 31st, disembarked on 18–19 September. Finally, the First Marine Division's last regiment, Colonel Homer Litzenberg's 7th, came ashore on 22 September. At the same time, the generals were also setting up shop. Almond, for instance, activated his Tenth Corps headquarters on 19 September. As for MacArthur, on 16 September, he landed for a firsthand look at his handiwork. He insisted on visiting Chesty Puller, so Almond and Smith accompanied him to the 1st Marine Regiment's front. Almond drove MacArthur there in his usual monomaniacal manner, prompting one of his staffers to ask him if he possessed a driver's license. The marines had only recently cleared the area of North Korean troops, but MacArthur struck his usual nonchalant pose as he poked around. Almond and Smith, on the other hand, were not at all happy to see their boss exposed to land mines and snipers, and they did their best to wrap the inspection up as fast as possible. In the days that followed, this was one of the few things upon which the two men agreed.[24]

Smith's First Marine Division may have starred in Chromite, but David Barr's Seventh Division had an important supporting role of its own to play by protecting the marines' southern flank. Like most of the army's first batch of division commanders in Korea, Barr was an improbable choice for the job. Born in Alabama in 1895, Barr studied at Alabama Presbyterian College for three years until he received an army commission when the United States entered World War I. He fought with the First Division in France, then saw occupation duty after Germany surrendered. In the interwar years, he swam against the army's doctrinal current by specializing in armored warfare. He even attended the French tank school while posted with the American military attaché in Paris from 1926 to 1927. His record was impressive enough to earn him a spot at the Command and General Staff School from 1934 to 1936 and the Army War College from 1938 to 1939. During World War II, Barr was drawn into General Jacob Devers's convivial orbit. He worked as Devers's chief of staff when Devers was successively in charge of the American military buildup in England, American forces in the Mediterranean, and the Sixth Army Group in northwest Europe. In 1948, Barr became head of the Army Advisory Group in Chiang Kai-shek's China, during which time he recommended against arming Chiang's inefficient Guomindang forces. By now Barr wanted a command post, so after he was assigned to Japan, he lobbied hard for one until MacArthur and Walker gave him the Seventh Division in May 1949.

Most people liked Bob Barr. Officers noted his courteousness, integrity, and practicality. The rank and file, for their part, appreciated his obvious concern for their well-being and willingness to interact with them. Indeed, Barr sometimes eschewed his staff to eat with the enlisted men. Unfortunately, Barr also possessed some troubling traits that undermined his effectiveness. He had almost no leadership experience, having spent most of his career, including the all-important World War II years, as a staff officer. One officer later referred to him as more a "political soldier" than anything else. In addition, he was a chronic worrier who fretted constantly about enemy intentions, his men's welfare, and so forth. Accidents that killed or wounded his troops particularly upset him. There was something to be said for a general so deeply concerned about his soldiers, but Barr's obvious anxiety did not convey the kind of confidence that characterized good leaders. It also took a toll on his health, so he appeared increasingly fragile and tired as time went on. Barr simply lacked the forcefulness, enterprise, and poise necessary to inspire people and get things done. One of Barr's regimental commanders commented on his boss, "He just didn't seem to hold up under stress. . . . He just worried and worried. And he just didn't seem to have the drive and whatnot that he should have had."[25] Almond recognized Barr's meekness, questioned his ability to run his division properly, and ran roughshod over him. Finally, despite Barr's long experience as a staffer, he failed to organize an efficient headquarters. Observers described it as amateurish, disorganized, inflexible, and full of deadwood. The outfit contained some promising personnel, but it was also full of KATUSAs who required special care and were never properly assimilated. For all these reasons, some outsiders doubted the Seventh Division from the minute it landed at Inchon. During the war's first months, the Seventh Division often seemed disjointed and unresponsive, prompting one officer to inarticulately recall, "It was a disaster going somewhere to happen."[26]

By the time the marines reached the Han River, Smith's relationship with Almond had reached the breaking point. Smith planned to seize Seoul in the same methodical and systematic manner he had used getting there in the first place. He hoped to cross the Han somewhere downstream from Seoul and then swing north to cut the city off from North Korea and assail it with all his forces from that direction. He greatly resented Almond's efforts to hurry him. As Smith saw things, Almond's emphasis on skirting pockets of enemy resistance exposed rear echelon personnel to enemy attack. One marine officer later complained that Almond did not understand the North Koreans, adding, "An Oriental who is bypassed is not out of the ball game: he is not a German or an Italian, and he doesn't get out on the road and hold up his hands, he gets in a hole with a sack full of rice and a few rounds of ammunition and he'll kill anyone that he has a chance to kill."[27] Nor did Smith appreciate Almond's curtness toward him or his meddling in Marine Corps affairs by, he claimed, issuing orders to his regimental commanders without informing him. Smith was so displeased that he refused to accept Almond's directives unless they were in writing. To Smith, Almond seemed like an unappreciative and hyperactive glory hound. Smith remembered, "General Almond became so obsessed with the idea that Seoul had to be captured by September 25th, just three months after the North Koreans had invaded South Korea, he lost touch with reality. He also showed a surprising blindness to what the First Marine Division had accomplished for him and to the sacrifices its officers and men had made to accomplish these results."[28]

Almond, not surprisingly, saw things in a different light. MacArthur had forecast that Seoul would fall five days after the Inchon landing, but Almond argued that two weeks was a more realistic timetable, and one he was determined to meet. Almond worried that the North Koreans might turn Seoul into an urban fortress if given sufficient time, so he hoped to prevent that by getting there as quickly as possible. He was also cognizant of the laurels he would receive by facilitating the quick liberation of the South Korean capital. Therefore, he wanted the marines to sidestep pockets of enemy resistance and strike directly for Seoul, and he was frustrated by Smith's more meticulous tactics. Although he acknowledged marine courage, Almond concluded that Smith resented his presence, was insufficiently responsive to his wishes, and was chary in sharing information. In response, Almond often bypassed Smith by going directly to the field with his orders and questions. Scouring the front by helicopter and jeep, Almond seemed to be everywhere at once, prodding and pushing the marines forward. As the marines approached Seoul, Almond directed the 5th Marine Regiment to assail it from the west while the 1st Marine Regiment swung around to the southeast to hit the city from that direction. He was predictably outraged when Smith balked at the order because he wanted to keep his two regiments together on the north side of the Han. Under ordinary circumstances, Almond would have probably relieved Smith of his command, but Smith was a marine, and Almond knew that firing him would provoke an interservice brouhaha that would bring him nothing but trouble. If Almond expected to implement his plan, he had to find another way to do so.[29]

On 24 September, Almond met with his principal commanders and staffers, including Smith, Barr, and Beauchamp, at Yongdungpo to discuss the assault on Seoul. Because the marines were disinclined to do his bidding, Almond abruptly announced that he intended to use Beauchamp's 32nd and the ROK 17th regiments to cross the Han the following morning and attack Seoul from the southeast. Smith did not like this at all, in part because he did not think much of the Seventh Division and in part because he did not want anything to interfere with his current operations. When Almond added that he had cleared his plan with Smith's regimental commanders, Puller and Murray, Smith "just hit the ceiling" at this new evidence of Almond's meddling with his subordinates. Although Almond afterward assured Smith that he had not given direct orders to Puller and Murray, Smith was hardly appeased. Whatever the marines' sensitivities, though, Almond was determined to conduct the campaign his way, with or without the marines' cooperation.[30]

This new mission surprised Beauchamp. His 32nd Regiment had been protecting the marines' right flank and positioning itself to block the North Korean retreat from the Pusan Perimeter by seizing Suwon on 21 September. Doing so was more difficult than Beauchamp expected, requiring his inexperienced men to push the North Koreans from hill to hill as they advanced eastward and southward. Just about the only thing that Beauchamp knew about the marines' travails outside of Seoul was that Almond was unhappy with their progress. Now, out of the blue, Beauchamp learned that he had to immediately redeploy his regiment to the village of Sinsa on the Han River for an early morning crossing. Fortunately, Beauchamp was up to the job. He had seen plenty of desperate action in the war already as head of the 34th Regiment during the retreat to the Pusan Perimeter. Moving his regiment under these circumstances was nothing compared to the ordeals he had experienced in the Twenty-fourth Division a few weeks earlier. This prompted one officer to comment that Beauchamp was the only high-ranking Seventh Division commander who had a clue about military operations.[31]

On the morning of 25 September, Almond was at Beauchamp's command post on the Han River bank to make sure everything proceeded according to his plan. Although Almond growled at Barr for not being there too—Barr opted to stay at a nearby bluff to oversee the entire operation—the crossing went smoothly, as did the ROK 17th Regiment's a short time later. From there the 32nd and ROK 17th regiments drove northeastward to seize South Mountain and Hill 120, whose possession gave them control of the hills overlooking Seoul and cut the main roads east and south of the city. As far as Almond and a good many of his army colleagues were concerned, these events leveraged the North Koreans out of the South Korean capital. One of Almond's staffers explained, "As Almond had foreseen, the possession of South Mountain proved to be the key to the final capitulation of Seoul on September 26."[32] Almond could not help but compare the Seventh Division's responsiveness with the First Marine Division's obstinacy.[33]

The marines had a much different explanation for Seoul's fall. Murray's 5th Marine Regiment crossed the Han downstream from the city on 20 September, followed three days later by Puller's 1st Marine Regiment near Yongdungpo. After storming the hills blocking access to the capital, the two regiments assailed the city itself. Fighting raged until the end of the month. The two marine regiments, eventually joined by elements of the 7th Marine, 32nd, and ROK 17th regiments, battled house to house and street to street to cleanse Seoul of its die-hard North Korean defenders. The 1st Marine Regiment had a particularly difficult time clearing the center of the city. Almond incensed Smith by ordering a night attack on 25–26 September that not only disrupted marine plans but also ran headlong into a last gasp North Korean offensive. Nor were the marines amused by Almond's premature 25 September declaration that enemy opposition had ended when plenty of fighting remained to be done. By the time the last North Korean troops had been killed or driven out of Seoul, the Tenth Corps had lost 3,500 men (2,450 of whom were marines), inflicted 14,000 casualties, and captured another 7,000 prisoners. Because they bore the brunt of the combat and shed the most blood, the marines felt that they deserved the credit for liberating Seoul.[34]

Army and Marine Corps officers could argue all day long about who was most responsible for Seoul's capture, but MacArthur garnered the bulk of the praise for this dramatic turn of events. On the morning of 29 September, MacArthur landed at Kimpo airfield. From there he got into a Chevrolet sedan and led a motorcade of vehicles across the Han River and through Seoul's battered streets. Crowds of civilians who had survived the North Korean occupation and the recent fighting emerged to cheer him as he drove to the National Assembly for a restrained ceremony returning the capital to the Rhee government's control. The National Assembly was pockmarked by bullet holes and guarded by tired marines. Inside, an immaculately dressed military police platoon kept watch over the assembled journalists, South Korean government officials, and high-ranking American officers. MacArthur gave a short speech commemorating the occasion, saying, "On behalf of the United Nations Command I am happy to restore to you, Mr. President, the seat of your government that from it you may better fulfill your constitutional responsibilities." Ambassador Muccio added a few words on behalf of the American government, and then Rhee stepped forward to thank his allies for their help. Rhee's emotions got the better of him as he expressed his gratitude toward MacArthur in particular: "We admire you. We love you as the savior of our race." MacArthur closed the ceremonies by leading the audience in a recitation of the Lord's Prayer. As he did so, background artillery shook loose shards of glass from the roof, showering the floor below. Fortunately, no one was hurt. Although most of the military men prudently put on their helmets, MacArthur finished his oration without missing a beat. He flew back to Tokyo within the hour, confident that his masterstroke had won the war and that all that remained was the mopping up.[35]

Indeed, the Inchon landing and the subsequent capture of Seoul constituted one of the greatest victories in American military history. For this MacArthur deserved most of the credit. He envisioned the operation as a cost-effective way to dramatically alter the course of the war, and he insisted on its implementation over the opposition of almost the entire American military establishment. Once Seoul was in American and South Korean hands, North Korean forces around the Pusan Perimeter were doomed. Chromite's very success, however, paved the way for an equally devastating defeat only a couple of months later, for which MacArthur was also largely responsible. MacArthur was a dominating and intimidating figure even before the marines landed at Inchon, but Chromite gave him an unassailability no one was willing to challenge. Secretary of the Army Frank Pace later said, "As a result [of Inchon], if three weeks later, General MacArthur had said to me, black is white, I would have come very close to believing him."[36] J. Lawton Collins gave a more thoughtful response: "The success of Inchon was so great, and the subsequent prestige of General MacArthur was so overpowering, that the [Joint] Chiefs hesitated thereafter to question later plans and decisions of the general, which should have been challenged. In this we must share with General MacArthur some of the responsibility for actions that led to defeats in North Korea." Inchon further inflated MacArthur's already healthy ego and made him less willing to listen to the doubts, concerns, and criticisms of others. As Collins later put it, "From then on he seemed to march like a Greek hero of old to an unkind and inexorable fate."[37]

Pusan Perimeter Breakout

If Chromite was MacArthur's anvil, then the Eighth Army was his hammer. MacArthur wanted the Eighth Army to charge out of the Pusan Perimeter at about the same time the marines splashed ashore at Inchon. MacArthur figured that the North Korean army could scarcely survive as an organized combat force if squeezed between the Tenth Corps and Eighth Army. As an inherently aggressive commander, Walker had never been comfortable fighting defensively, so he also liked the idea of assuming the offensive. However, he worried that he lacked sufficient strength to undertake such a mission because the Tenth Corps was sucking up so many resources, but, considering his relationship with MacArthur, he was hardly in a position to argue the issue. Walker's division and regimental commanders were also ready to seize the initiative. When John Church heard the news, for example, he said, "Well, you know, we never had a chance to attack before. I think it's a good idea. We might get them moving out of this perimeter."[38]

Walker's plan was simplicity itself. He intended Gay's First Cavalry Division to punch through enemy lines in the Taegu area toward Taejon while the rest of the Eighth Army kept the North Koreans too busy to reinforce their comrades resisting Gay. Walker emphasized that he did not hope to simply push the enemy back a few miles but rather envisioned a breakthrough that would shatter the North Korean army. Although Gay had performed as well as or better than any of Walker's other division commanders, he got the starring role because his division was already deployed in the critical area. Gay approved of the basic concept, but he asked for and received an additional regiment—John Throckmorton's 5th, which had not yet been officially attached to the Twenty-fourth Division and was still serving as one of Walker's fire brigades—to carry out his part of the design. As for timing, Walker scheduled the offensive to begin on 16 September, the day after the Inchon landing. The news of the threat to their rear, they hoped, would demoralize those North Korean soldiers facing the Eighth Army.[39]

When the Eighth Army launched its counteroffensive, Walker had at his disposal four American and six ROK divisions. Ordinarily a field army commander such as Walker would have possessed one or more corps headquarters to manage so many divisions, but the previous March the army had inactivated the two Eighth Army corps as a cost-cutting measure. As a result, when the war began, Walker had to serve as his own corps commander. This became increasingly onerous when Walker gained authority over the ROK army and as more and more American units joined the Eighth Army during the summer. Collins and MacArthur understood the burden this imposed on Walker, so they provided him with two corps headquarters. The army organized the First Corps, formerly the Fifth, at Fort Bragg, North Carolina, on 2 August, and the bulk of its staff reached Korea on 6 September. To lead it, Collins appointed Major General John Coulter. Coulter got the assignment because he had combat experience, had served recently in East Asia, and was familiar to both MacArthur and Almond. The other corps, the Ninth, did not become operational until 23 September because Almond siphoned off much of the available communications equipment and personnel for his Tenth Corps. As for its commander, Collins selected Major General Frank Milburn, who had been slated to take over the Fifth Corps before it was re-flagged and shipped to Korea. Collins explained to MacArthur that Milburn "had a fine record in action in Europe and I know him to be the type of fighter you will need in Korea."[40]

Walker wanted to use one of his new corps to oversee Gay's First Cavalry Division and Throckmorton's 5th Regiment in the Pusan Perimeter breakout. The First Corps was the only one ready, but Walker had serious misgivings about Coulter. Although Walker acknowledged Coulter's great physical courage while leading ROK troops around Kyongju in late August and early September, he doubted that Coulter possessed the necessary forcefulness and drive to exploit his planned breakthrough. If not Coulter, then who? Walker wished Dean were available, but of course he was currently a prisoner of war. That being the case, Walker turned to the recently arrived Milburn. Walker knew something about Milburn from their service together as corps commanders in northwest Europe during the last months of World War II. Walker concluded that Milburn had the aggressiveness and temperament the mission called for, and after much thought he decided to turn the First Corps over to him and assign Coulter to the still-organizing Ninth Corps. Walker still felt that Coulter could be useful down the line, but Coulter no doubt recognized the implied lack of confidence. As for Milburn, he was embarrassed by the uncomfortable situation into which he was thrust when MacArthur informed him that he would lead the First Corps instead of the Ninth. Awkwardness notwithstanding, Walker was aware that his career was on thin ice; he was taking no chances on a battlefield setback that could give MacArthur an excuse to relieve him as Eighth Army commander.[41]

Although less well known than such famous Korean War personages as Almond and Walker, Frank "Shrimp" Milburn was one of the conflict's most important combat generals. The Indiana-born Milburn graduated from West Point in 1914, where he made his mark as an athlete despite his diminutive size. He spent World War I not in the trenches of France but garrisoning the Canal Zone in Panama. In the 1920s he had the usual mix of educational, line, and staff assignments, including a stint as University of Montana's football coach while he ran the school's Reserve Officer Training Corps detachment. He ranked eighteenth out of 125 in his 1932 Command and General Staff School class, but he did not go to the Army War College. Instead, he returned to the Command and General Staff School as an instructor for four years. After the United States entered World War II, Milburn steadily climbed the army's hierarchy from regimental to division to corps commander. However, his ascent took place stateside, so he accrued no combat experience in the process. Dwight Eisenhower wanted Milburn's Twenty-first Corps headquarters in northwest Europe, but not Milburn. Eisenhower had nothing against Milburn personally, but he was leery of giving such a responsible post to such an inexperienced man when he had several battle-hardened division commanders available who could do the job. Fortunately for Milburn, the army ground forces chief, Lieutenant General Benjamin Lear, persuaded Eisenhower to reconsider. When Milburn and his Twenty-first Corps headquarters reached Europe in autumn 1944, Eisenhower assigned them to Lieutenant General Alexander Patch's Seventh Army. Milburn's Twenty-first Corps participated in the bitter winter fighting in Alsace and in the drive across the Rhine River into Germany. Milburn performed so well that Patch referred to him as the most impressive of his three corps commanders. After the war Milburn took over the Twenty-third Corps, returned to the States to become head of the Fifth Corps, and then recrossed the Atlantic to run the First Division and serve as deputy commander of all army forces in Europe. From there Collins summoned him to lead the Ninth Corps in Korea.

Milburn and Ned Almond were polar opposites. The short and wiry Milburn was as nice and low-key as Almond was abrasive and arrogant. People invariably commented on Milburn's modesty, geniality, and taciturnity. Indeed, he said so little as to seem almost uncommunicative, but conversely he was a great listener and inherently friendly. He greeted everyone with a big smile and pleasant hello regardless of circumstances. Michaelis recalled a tired Milburn driving up to his command post in the middle of the Korean winter when American fortunes were at a low point and saying, "Hey, Mike, things are going great. How are you doing?"[42] He also possessed a quiet and self-deprecating sense of humor. One officer remembered witnessing Milburn intently studying a map in a First Corps headquarters tent with his hands behind his back and thought himself fortunate to see such a high-ranking military mind at work. After ten minutes or so, though, Milburn broke the silence and said, "You know, I have been watching people look at these maps for years, and I have never known what they get out of it."[43] Milburn's calm, stable, and serene personality provided a much-needed palliative to the chaotic conditions in which the Eighth Army frequently found itself during the war's first year. Beneath his withdrawn demeanor, though, lurked an aggressive and stout-hearted soldier with the poise, self-confidence, and decisiveness that good commanders require. At the same time, though, Milburn lacked that little extra centimeter of gray matter, that little extra spark, that separated competent generals from great ones, so he never rose to the top of the pantheon of American army leaders.

Milburn and Almond also had dissimilar leadership and relationship styles. Milburn scarcely knew MacArthur, and in fact had to wheedle his way past Almond just to meet with him when he first reached the theater. On the other hand, Milburn got along well with Walker. Walker respected Milburn so much that he never browbeat him like he did his division commanders. As for his headquarters, Milburn ran it, according to one officer, "with a light but firm touch of an accomplished horseman."[44] His chief of staff, Brigadier General Rinaldo Van Brunt, had worked for Milburn in the same capacity during World War II, so the two men were thoroughly familiar with each other's routines, habits, strengths, and weaknesses. Because he was shy and uncomfortable in groups, Milburn usually sent Van Brunt to represent him at Eighth Army meetings. Division and regimental commanders liked serving under Milburn because he was so friendly, sympathetic, and accommodating during even difficult circumstances. One person recalled, "He would listen to you, he'd also leave you alone. You know, he wouldn't be hounding you all day, where you are, why aren't you doing this."[45] Milburn never resorted to bullying or threats; he had other ways of getting his points across. When he did not think that Gay's First Cavalry Division was moving fast enough, for instance, he deliberately placed his First Corps command post ahead of Gay's as a subtle hint. Division commanders discovered that Milburn was an easy touch if they could get a few minutes alone with him to plead their case and make their requests. Van Brunt had to order a staffer to stay with Milburn at all times during his frequent inspection trips to learn what promises Milburn had made to whom. Unlike Almond, Milburn also managed to establish good rapport with the rank and file. He traveled everywhere with a shaggy dachshund named Ebbo that he had acquired in Europe. Soldiers enjoyed playing with Ebbo while Milburn conferred with their officers and were amused when Milburn invariably had to search for the dog before he left. It was a touch of humanity that Almond rarely showed.[46]

Walker kicked off his counteroffensive on 16 September, the day after the marines came ashore at Inchon. He had 140,000 troops with which to conduct the operation, of whom a bit less than half were American, organized into ten divisions, and a recently arrived British brigade. Opposing them were approximately 70,000 tired, hungry, and underequipped North Korean soldiers. Walker stressed to his subordinates that he wanted them to charge through the enemy and drive northward to link up with the Tenth Corps as quickly as possible. His determination was infectious; Dick Stephens, the 21st Regiment's commander, expounded to some of his men, "We're breaking out of the [Pusan] Perimeter and the 21st is going to spearhead it. I want you to be aggressive, bold, and to move fast! If anyone delays you, move around them. We have the numbers now to overflow 'em, so don't worry about leaving any enemy bypassed; there'll be lots of people behind you to mop up."[47]

Unhappily, things did not go as planned—at least not at first. Not only were the North Koreans dug in east of the Naktong in many areas but they were also still attacking along much of the perimeter. As a result, a lot of American and

South Korean soldiers had all they could handle just holding their own. The result was business as usual for many outfits. The First Cavalry Division and 5th Regiment were supposed to lead the breakout, but they did not make much progress. Indeed, Gay relieved one of his regimental commanders, the 7th Cav's Cecil Nist, for mishandling his men. Colonel George Peploe's 38th Regiment provided the only early bright spot for the Eighth Army by reaching the Naktong on the first day, which earned his division chief, Dutch Keiser, kudos from Walker. For the most part, though, a frustrated Walker did a lot of yelling and scowling. Throckmorton's 5th Regiment did not retake Waegwan until 19 September, the same day Edward Moore's 19th and Stephens's 21st regiments finally got across the Naktong downstream. Off Inchon on *Mount McKinley*, an impatient MacArthur watched the stalemate with increasing concern. During a 19 September dinner with Almond and some high-ranking naval officers, MacArthur opined that it might take another amphibious landing, perhaps at Kusan, to break the Pusan Perimeter logjam. He also noted darkly that he might need a new Eighth Army commander as well.[48]

Fortunately for Walker, the Eighth Army was just then finally breaking out of the Pusan Perimeter. It did so not because its officers demonstrated any particular tactical brilliance but rather through brute force. Although the North Koreans initially fought hard from prepared positions and mounted sharp counterattacks, American and South Korean firepower gradually ground them down until their brittle lines cracked. As the Eighth Army got over the Naktong River, Walker urged his division commanders to sidestep pockets of enemy resistance and drive northward as fast as possible. Division commanders responded by organizing battalion-sized task forces of tanks and infantry-laden trucks to barrel northward and westward along the dusty roads to link up with the Tenth Corps south of Seoul. This sudden new battlefield fluidity, however, caused almost as many problems as the defensive warfare to which the Eighth Army was accustomed. A lack of bridging materials made it difficult for vehicles and equipment to cross the Naktong. Michaelis's 27th Regiment, for example, had to build a bridge of sandbags to get over the river. The fast-moving columns ran short of food and lost touch with their headquarters. Commanders came under unexpected enemy fire while searching the countryside for their far-flung units. At one point, Gay used a shotgun to clear the way for his jeep. There were disputes over road usage between the First Cavalry and Twenty-fourth divisions, so Gay brandished his shotgun again, this time against his own countrymen, to make sure his men got priority. Milburn's efforts to pause and establish some order failed when Walker reemphasized his desire to keep moving northward regardless of enemy opposition, logistical constraints, or organizational cohesion.

Walker's hard-driving attitude produced results. George Peploe's 38th Regiment, for example, moved seventy-three miles in ten hours to reach Chonju. South Korean units made equally spectacular progress through the mountains to the east. American morale skyrocketed at evidence of the enemy's disarray. One officer said, "All along our route we saw the debris of war: burned out trucks and tanks, discarded ammo boxes, C-ration cans, empty shell casings. On the shoulders of the road, plodding south in a constant stream, were the pitiful refugees. . . . Further on, as we neared the scenes of more recent fighting, we began to see bodies of dead enemy soldiers sprawled grotesquely in the paddy fields."[49] Another recalled, "All along the way between Chonan and Osan we saw soldiers at bridges, on motorcycles, jeeps, trucks, bicycles, carrying supplies. These we shot up, not shooting the trucks and jeeps unless someone was in them."[50] One by one, American and South Korean troops recaptured those cities and towns the North Koreans had so painfully conquered weeks earlier: Sangju (23 September), Chinju (25 September), Yongdong and Chonan (26 September), and Taejon (28 September). The day before Taejon fell, elements of the 7th Cav Regiment rolled through Osan and linked up with Richard Ovenshine's 31st Regiment about ten miles north of the city. Except for the mopping up, the breakout from the Pusan Perimeter was complete.[51]

By most measures, the Pusan Perimeter breakout was something of which any general could be proud. In the space of two short weeks, the Eighth Army destroyed the opposing North Korean army as an effective and organized force and freed almost all of South Korea from North Korean control. In the process, the Eighth Army's American component suffered 790 men killed and 3,544 wounded. Like most good leaders, Walker knew what he wanted to do, and he went about achieving it with ruthless efficiency. He was greatly assisted by his corps and division commanders, all of whom understood his objectives and pushed their men hard to reach them. They may not have performed brilliantly, but none made any serious mistakes that upset the offensive either. On the other hand, Walker's plan itself is open to criticism. In their mad dash northward, the Americans and South Koreans bypassed lots of enemy soldiers who subsequently escaped to North Korea or melted into the countryside to resort to guerrilla warfare. Either way, the Eighth Army would have to deal with them at some future date. One officer recollected,

> We passed hundreds, I'd say thousands of North Koreans who . . . kept off the road, but then we could see them. They were unarmed, they had deposited their arms somewhere, not from any orders that we had given them, but I think they had stationed them somewhere, you know, and they were heading north. I thought we should have rounded them up and put them at least in some kind of temporary restraint . . . and not let them stream back.[52]

In short, a more methodical approach might have captured or killed more of the enemy and saved the Eighth Army considerable trouble later. Such a strategy, though, went against the grain of an old tanker like Walker, who had gained fame in World War II by dashing across France and Germany with his armored divisions. Nor would it have impressed MacArthur. As far as he was concerned, the Inchon landing and the conquest of Seoul had won the war, and all that remained was for Walker to mop up what was left of North Korean resistance. That being the case, MacArthur would probably not have approved a slower and most systematic advance northward. Moreover, there is little evidence that MacArthur was particularly impressed with the generalship Walker did display. Although he awarded Walker the Distinguished Service Cross, when Walker flew up to Kimpo airfield on 29 September to meet MacArthur and participate in the ceremony commemorating Seoul's liberation, MacArthur pointedly ignored him and showered attention on Almond instead.[53]

"On to the Yalu!"

South Korea's liberation created as many problems for the Truman administration as it solved. Among the most obvious was whether the Eighth Army should cross the 38th Parallel. When the conflict began, the Truman administration stressed that preserving South Korean independence was its main objective, but as the American commitment deepened and North Korea's military fortunes waned, Truman's advisers shifted gears. A consensus gradually emerged in the White House, the Pentagon, and the State Department in favor of forcibly reuniting the entire peninsula under Rhee's rule. American policy makers feared that leaving North Korea intact would merely give its communist rulers time to regroup, recover, and perhaps in a few years launch another attack that would necessitate another painful American intervention. Both MacArthur and Rhee certainly interpreted the facts in this light and advocated invading North Korea. After weighing the pros and cons, Truman reached a similar conclusion. On 27 September, the Joint Chiefs authorized MacArthur to overrun North Korea and destroy Kim Il Sung's regime once and for all. However, they also warned MacArthur to use only ROK troops near the Soviet and Chinese borders to avoid unnecessarily provoking those communist countries. Unhappily for everyone involved, the JCS chose not to make an issue of MacArthur's response that he considered all of Korea open to American forces because the new secretary of defense, George Marshall, had promised him a free rein to conquer North Korea. Either way, the door was now open for the Eighth Army to assail North Korea itself.

It was, as usual, MacArthur's job to implement the Truman administration's directives. To carry them out, he had by late September approximately 229,000 troops, including 103,000 American soldiers, 21,500 marines, 101,500 ROK personnel, and a few thousand men from various allied contributions. MacArthur's plan was twofold. The first part was simple enough—a direct assault across the 38th Parallel by Walker's Eighth Army toward Pyongyang, the North Korean capital. However, MacArthur also decided to withdraw Almond's Tenth Corps from the Inchon–Seoul area for use in another amphibious assault, this one on the other side of the peninsula against the North Korean port of Wonsan. This would establish a presence in northeastern North Korea and enable the Tenth Corps to push on toward either Pyongyang or to the Chinese border. Opening the port to supply the corps would also alleviate the Eighth Army's continuing logistical burdens.

Walker and his staffers opposed MacArthur's design for several reasons. For one thing, pulling the First Marine Division out through congested Inchon and transporting the Seventh Division down the equally crowded South Korean roads to Pusan for its embarkation would in the short run exacerbate the Eighth Army's already strained supply lines. Moreover, it looked increasingly likely that ROK troops advancing rapidly up the peninsula's east coast would seize Wonsan before the Tenth Corps got into position to attack the port, thus rendering any amphibious operation unnecessary. Finally, removing so many troops from the Inchon–Seoul region would make it easier for isolated North Korean soldiers in South Korea to escape northward. Walker and his staff were not alone in their objections. Although Almond was noncommittal, Dave Barr and Oliver Smith both doubted the wisdom of MacArthur's concept. As far as Walker and his staffers were concerned, the thing to do was to use the Tenth and First corps to charge across the 38th Parallel together and drive directly for Pyongyang. To these officers, it was unwise to remove an entire corps from the battlefield at such a critical time. However, when one of Walker's staffers asked him to forward their proposal to MacArthur's headquarters, Walker shook his head and explained that he had already expressed their views and received contrary instructions. Walker no doubt felt that he had already gone out on the limb far enough, and now he meant to obey his orders.[54]

MacArthur's command arrangements were equally perplexing. He originally intended for the Tenth Corps to revert to Eighth Army control after Chromite and for Almond to return to Tokyo to resume his duties as chief of staff. When MacArthur decided to send the Tenth Corps to Wonsan, though, he opted to keep Almond as its boss. Moreover, he also concluded that Almond should act independently of the Eighth Army and answer directly to him. On 11 October, MacArthur gave Almond authority over the ROK First Corps, which was also operating in the Wonsan area. This turned Almond into a de facto field army commander at the same level as Walker. Plenty of people questioned the wisdom of this decision, including Collins, Walker, and some of MacArthur's own staffers. Even Almond was "consternated" by MacArthur's thinking, at least at first. For the busy MacArthur to try to lead two independent entities from distant Tokyo seemed like a recipe for disaster. MacArthur was not much of a hands-on operator to begin with, so it was unlikely that he could provide the kind of day-to-day oversight Walker and Almond needed to prosecute the war in a coordinated manner. However, no one wanted to interfere with MacArthur's prerogative to organize his forces as he saw fit, especially when he had just proven the American military establishment spectacularly wrong by successfully conducting Chromite.[55]

MacArthur later claimed that no one expressed any reservations to him about his new command arrangements. He rationalized his decision by stating that the Taebaek Mountains, which extended down the middle of North Korea, made it impossible for Walker to effectively oversee Almond's tactical and logistical dispositions around Wonsan. Indeed, the only good lateral road over the mountains was well south of Tenth Corps operations. However, there was likely more to MacArthur's thinking than he let on. Although he later claimed that Walker and Almond got along well, he could not have been unaware of the enmity between the two men. Of the two, he clearly preferred the can-do Almond, who had so successfully implemented Chromite, to the abrasive Walker. Because he was unwilling to court drama and controversy by replacing Walker with Almond, he did the next best thing by giving Almond his own independent command. He also probably intended to play Almond and Walker off against each other to get the best out of both men. MacArthur had managed his personnel this way before. During World War II, for instance, he manipulated his Sixth Army and Eighth Army commanders, Walter Krueger and Robert Eichelberger, in a similar fashion during his campaign to liberate the Philippines. MacArthur wagered that the benefits of competition outweighed the weaknesses inherent in a divided command. That the North Koreans seemed beaten no doubt made this gamble even more attractive.[56]

As aggressive generals, both MacArthur and Walker wanted to assail North Korea as soon as the Truman administration gave its approval. ROK soldiers had already crossed the 38th Parallel on 30 September, and Walker was keen to follow suit with his Americans before the enemy had a chance to regroup and recover. Positioning the Eighth Army for such an operation, though, was not easy or simple. The troops were exhausted from their fighting in the Pusan Perimeter and the subsequent breakout. There were also some serious logistical difficulties. The air force had destroyed a good many of the railroads and bridges throughout South Korea, and Inchon's port was not yet operating at full capacity, so many units already faced matériel shortages. Withdrawing the Tenth Corps further clogged up the Eighth Army's supply pipeline. As a result, Walker was unable to deploy John Coulter's recently activated Ninth Corps, consisting of Dutch Keiser's Second and Bill Kean's Twenty-fifth divisions, for the invasion. Instead, Milburn's First Corps—Hap Gay's First Cav, John Church's Twenty-fourth, and Brigadier General Paik Sun Yup's ROK First divisions, as well as the British Commonwealth 27th Brigade—would have to continue to bear the brunt of the fighting. Because Gay's First Cav Division had spearheaded the Eighth Army's Pusan Perimeter breakthrough and reached the Tenth Corps first, Milburn felt that it was in the best position to lead the new offensive. Paik's division would advance on Gay's left while Church's men followed behind in support.

Elements of the First Cav Division crossed the 38th Parallel on 7 October and headed for Kumchon, about twenty miles north of the border. The 5th and 8th Cav regiments ran into heavy opposition and initially made little progress, but Colonel William Harris's 7th Cav Regiment, operating on the far left of the American line, unexpectedly broke open the enemy front with a successful crossing of the Yesong River. Kumchon fell on 14 October, opening the way for the First Corps to push northward toward Pyongyang. Gay, modest as ever, admitted to assembled journalists that his division had punched through the North Korean positions in spite of, not because of, his generalship. At that point North Korean opposition became sporadic and scattered. Crowds turned out in the dusty streets to welcome American and ROK forces. Even so, plenty of problems remained. Gay's and Paik's men, for example, bickered over road space allotment. The further north the Americans and South Koreans advanced, the worse the supply situation became. Although American self-confidence skyrocketed with each mile gained, this was not necessarily a good thing because many soldiers were now so sure of ultimate victory that they became gun-shy. After all, no one wanted to be the last man to die in a war practically won. Moreover, some officers concluded that the First Cav Division was not nearly as good as its members seemed to believe. One journalist watched a small North Korean rear guard hold up an entire First Cav Division battalion because the noncoms and low-ranking officers could not get their men moving. Despite these problems, Gay for one figured that it was merely a matter of when, not if, Pyongyang fell.[57]

Gay's confidence in Pyongyang's fate did not make his job any easier. Indeed, the closer his division got to the North Korean capital, the more stressed he became. Walker worried that Almond and his Tenth Corps might upstage the Eighth Army again by reaching Pyongyang first from Wonsan, so he exerted tremendous pressure on Gay to hurry up. Walker even threatened to relieve Gay from his command if he did not seize the city by 21 October. If that failed to spur Gay on, Walker and Milburn resorted to competition by giving Church and Paik the opportunity to vie for the Pyongyang prize. The result was an uncoordinated and haphazard dash toward the city by American and South Korean units eager for the distinction of getting there first. Troops jockeyed for the limited available road space, resulting in time-consuming traffic jams. Gay's anxiety reverberated up and down the chain of command. Gay removed a nervous and exhausted Billy Harris from the 7th Cav Regiment for his supposed lack of forcefulness but restored him to his post a short time later after his temper had cooled. Gay also suspected that Harris's temporary successor, Colonel James Wollnough, was not using all three of his battalions to clear enemy roadblocks because doing so might prompt Gay to put another regiment in the lead to maintain divisional momentum, thus depriving the 7th Cav of the honor of leading the way into Pyongyang. Gay punished the outfit by supplanting it with Colonel Marcel Crombez's 5th Cav Regiment. When the ordinarily placid Milburn criticized what he saw as the First Cav Division's sluggishness, Gay concluded that Milburn should exert his authority more and complain less.[58]

In the end, the unbridged Taebong River on Pyongyang's outskirts prevented the First Cav Division from reaching the city first. Instead, the honor went to Paik's ROK First Division, which came at the city from the northeast and took possession on 19 October. Despite this somewhat downbeat coda—for the Americans, anyway—the fact was that Pyongyang had fallen without the costly urban combat that characterized Seoul's liberation. Although there were pictures of Vladimir Lenin and Stalin everywhere, the locals still turned out to wave British, South Korean, American, and even Guomindang flags designed from hearsay. A happy and relieved Milburn stood in a field under intermittent sniper fire and commented to journalists, "I've fulfilled my orders. Here we are." Then, seemingly as an afterthought, he exclaimed with uncharacteristic and awkward flamboyance, "On to the Yalu [River]!" MacArthur was equally jubilant by this additional evidence of his superior generalship and flew to the city on 21 October for another victory lap. During an inspection of the first 5th Cav company to enter Pyongyang, MacArthur asked how many of the men had been with the unit since it arrived in Korea the previous July. Of the nearly 200 soldiers present, only five stepped forward, three of whom had been wounded and returned to duty. It was a poignant reminder of the price the Eighth Army had paid to secure the triumph that almost everyone thought was imminent.[59]

Pyongyang's fall seemed like good evidence that the war was all but over. Indeed, the Pentagon was already making plans to withdraw the bulk of American forces from the peninsula. As Milburn indicated, the last step was to push on to the Yalu River, which separated Korea from neighboring Manchuria, and snuff out what was left of Kim Il Sung's seemingly moribund communist regime. Although the Joint Chiefs reiterated to MacArthur their earlier directive prohibiting the use of non-Korean troops near the Chinese and Soviet borders, MacArthur blatantly disregarded their instructions by responding that military necessity required the presence of American troops. The JCS, however, was too intimidated by MacArthur's Chromite-enhanced reputation as a military genius to insist that he obey its orders. As it was, MacArthur did not have a lot of Eighth Army American ground units available to administer his coup de grâce because of continuing logistical problems. Coulter's Ninth Corps was still deployed in South Korea, so Milburn's First Corps was the only American arrow in his quiver. Unfortunately, Gay's understrength and exhausted First Cav Division was in no condition for renewed action, so Walker put it in reserve near Pyongyang. This left John Church's Twenty-fourth Division in the hopper. To it Walker added the British Commonwealth 27th Brigade and the ROK Second Corps. Walker decided that the Twenty-fourth Division and British Commonwealth 27th Brigade would advance along the western coastal roads toward the Yalu's estuary while the ROKs moved through the mountains to the east. It was a simple enough design based on the assumption of minimal enemy resistance.[60]

Church's division and his accompanying British Commonwealth brigade jumped off on 22 October and reached Sinanju on the Chongchon River two days later. To the east, the ROK Sixth Division seized Kohang, only eighteen miles from the Yalu, on 25 October, and the next day one of its battalions drove all the way to the Yalu and occupied Chosan. To Walker, everything seemed to be going according to plan. However, as the Twenty-fourth Division continued its northward advance in the last days of October, it ran into increasingly heavy, albeit sporadic, opposition. Even so, Dick Stephens's 21st Regiment got fewer than fifteen miles from the Yalu when he received orders to stop his advance. After one of these surprisingly bitter engagements, John Throckmorton's 5th Regiment found two Chinese soldiers among its eighty-nine prisoners. To Throckmorton, this was ominous and disconcerting news. He remembered, "I began to get the funniest feeling like the hair rising on the back of my neck."[61]

Conclusions

Chromite marked the highpoint of MacArthur's illustrious military career. His simply conceived and graceful plan took full advantage of Korea's geography, American air and naval power, and the enemy's limited resources to turn the war around in a matter of days. Once American and South Korean troops occupied Seoul, the now-isolated North Korean army along the Pusan Perimeter was finished as an organized force. As MacArthur explained to some correspondents on the *Mount McKinley* before the marine landing, "The history of war proves that nine times out of ten an army has been destroyed because its supply lines have been cut off. That's what we are trying to do."[62] Without its army, North Korea itself was doomed once the Truman administration made the decision to order MacArthur across the 38th Parallel—unless it received significant outside assistance. MacArthur was aware of Chromite's numerous logistical and topographical obstacles, but he consistently expressed confidence that they could be overcome. He preferred to focus on the enemy's problems rather than exaggerate his own.

MacArthur was certainly astute in recognizing the rewards a landing at Inchon offered, but he also demonstrated considerable skill in persuading the jittery American military establishment to go along with his risky idea. Indeed, his bureaucratic abilities proved as useful and impressive as his strategic ones. His single-minded determination and self-assuredness enabled him to surmount all the bureaucratic hurdles the JCS, the Marine Corps, and the navy put in his way. He used his moral authority as a senior and successful general to overawe the Joint Chiefs, and he used his control of information to keep them in the dark about important details they needed to make informed decisions. In addition, his formidable powers of persuasion made believers out of initially skeptical high-ranking officials such as Ridgway, Harrington, and Collins who visited him. By the time Chromite's final countdown began, the JCS could not have stopped the operation even if it wanted to. Such bureaucratic savvy was as important as anything else in guaranteeing Chromite's success.

Unfortunately for MacArthur, Inchon was a Pyrrhic victory. His success so inflated his already healthy ego and reputation that people thereafter hesitated to question his judgment. However, after Inchon MacArthur made a series of military mistakes that cost the United States dearly. Seoul's fall convinced MacArthur that the war was over except for the mopping up. In his urgency to wrap up operations, he encouraged Walker to push toward Seoul as quickly as possible instead of advocating a more methodical advance that might have killed or captured many of the enemy soldiers who escaped northward to fight another day. He also withdrew the Tenth Corps for an unnecessary assault on Wonsan. Doing so not only removed this powerful formation from the war for several crucial weeks but also forced Walker to invade North Korea with only two American divisions. Plenty of people up and down the chain of command recognized at least some of these errors, but no one had the audacity to tell him he was wrong, let alone the rank and moral courage to make him reconsider. Chances are that none of his missteps would have mattered if the North Koreans had remained the only enemy, but Chinese entry into the war exposed these miscalculations for the world to see and contributed to MacArthur's downfall.

It is also possible to question MacArthur's handling of his chief ground forces subordinates. He stuck with Walker as his Eighth Army commander even though he lacked confidence in him. He gave Almond the starring role in the Inchon landing as his Tenth Corps commander because he knew the man, valued his loyalty, and recognized that he possessed the forcefulness and single-mindedness to make Chromite a success. Indeed, Chromite turned Almond into MacArthur's favorite general. MacArthur's subsequent decision to divide the Korean command between Walker's Eighth Army and Almond's augmented Tenth Corps without providing an effective coordinating mechanism was simply asking for trouble, especially because there was bad blood between the two generals. If MacArthur did not trust Walker, he could have simply removed him from the Eighth Army and replaced him with Almond instead of resorting to such a convoluted stratagem. However, MacArthur hated relieving people; he much preferred working around such personnel problems with solutions that complicated the chain of command. Such expedients were manageable against a beaten and waning enemy such as North Korea, but they became crippling when the Chinese unexpectedly intervened.

MacArthur's top three ground forces commanders—Walker, Almond, and Milburn—all fought aggressively and doggedly in September and October. Although Almond sometimes displayed arrogance and ignorance in his Chromite planning, he met MacArthur's deadline despite a shockingly short timetable, uncertain resources, and coordination problems. No doubt the lack of enemy opposition at Inchon was a big factor in Chromite's success, but MacArthur and Almond still deserve credit for taking this into account. Almond never hesitated during his subsequent push toward Seoul; instead, he ruthlessly drove his soldiers and marines until the city was in his hands. He knew exactly what he wanted to do and went about accomplishing it with great energy and verve. Seoul's fall only two weeks after the marines came ashore at Inchon was a testament to his generalship. To the south, along the Pusan Perimeter, Walker and Milburn also overcame limited and uncertain resources to break through North Korean lines and reach the Tenth Corps near Seoul. Their plan was relatively simple, and like Almond, they followed through with great resolution and energy, so that the Eighth Army linked up with the Tenth Corps only eleven days after its offensive began. All three officers were combative by nature, but they also took their cues from an impatient MacArthur. Unfortunately, all three were also more focused on reaching their geographic objectives, be it Seoul or the Yalu River, than in demolishing enemy forces. Indeed, killing or capturing enemy troops became an incidental aspect of their operations. Here too their thinking reflected MacArthur's. Such tactics, though, diverted the Americans and South Koreans from the equally important task of destroying the North Korean army.

Walker, Almond, and Milburn interacted with their subordinates differently. Almond's rapport with his two division commanders, Dave Barr and Oliver

Smith, left much to be desired. Almond claimed to respect Barr's abilities and appreciated his cooperation, but during the fighting around Inchon–Seoul, he criticized both Barr's failure to reach Suwon in a timely manner and his division's combat worthiness.[63] Because Barr was a soldier with a diffident personality, Almond browbeat and dominated him. Smith, on the other hand, was a different animal. Beneath his taciturn exterior, he was every bit as tough as Almond. Moreover, as a marine leading a marine unit, Smith possessed a certain institutional autonomy that enabled him to resist Almond's habitual meddling. The two men clashed repeatedly during both Chromite's planning and execution over everything from logistics to tactics. Almond neither understood nor tried to understand Marine Corps doctrine. Had he done so, he might have been more sympathetic toward the marines' tactics against Seoul's North Korean defenders. To expect the marines to learn to fight the army's way in the middle of a campaign was unrealistic. As a result, his relationship with Smith degenerated into mutual antipathy that did not serve the Tenth Corps well then or later.

The introduction of Milburn's First Corps into the Eighth Army should have provided a cushion between Walker and his division commanders. Walker, however, often bypassed Milburn to deal directly with them in his usual direct and brusque manner. On the other hand, he treated Milburn with a certain deference he rarely showed his other subordinates. For his part, Milburn was still getting a feel for his new command during the Pusan Perimeter breakout and the invasion of North Korea. Although he respected both John Church and Hap Gay, the latter officer's tactics frustrated Milburn during the push to Pyongyang. As for Gay, he was ambivalent about Milburn's leadership style because he was more accustomed to Walker's heavy-handed approach than Milburn's lighter and more indirect touch. Considering his short time at the First Corps' helm in Korea, it was hardly surprising that Milburn's relationship with his subordinates was still a work in progress.

The American army and marine division commanders performed creditably that September and October. No doubt they had the advantage of combating a flagging enemy, but because most of them had contributed to the enemy's decline, this should hardly be counted against them. When Smith could operate as he wanted, he fought methodically and relentlessly in his drive from Inchon to Seoul. Barr played a secondary role in Chromite, but he did a good job despite Almond's reservations and his division's slapdash organization. In particular, he deserved credit for getting Beauchamp's regiment across the Han on such short notice. To the south, Keiser and Kean helped break out of the Pusan Perimeter, but logistics sidelined them from the invasion of North Korea. Instead, Gay got the starring roles because of his division's proximity to Seoul. Gay carried out his orders to punch through North Korean lines, link up with the Tenth Corps around Seoul, and then drive toward Pyongyang. Along the way, Gay overcame logistical obstacles, his men's growing weariness, occasional heavy enemy resistance, and conflict with subordinates and superiors. Church picked up where Gay left off and got within twenty miles of the Yalu before events elsewhere overtook his activities. These men had proven that they could defeat the North Koreans, but they were unaware that they were about to confront a far more formidable foe.

4
A Powerful New Enemy

Chinese Intervention

The Korean War did not take place in an international vacuum but was instead part of the Cold War struggle for world supremacy between the Soviet-dominated communist bloc and the democratic United States and its allies. Both the Soviets and Chinese were therefore acutely interested in the conflict. Indeed, Kim Il Sung could not have initiated the war without Stalin's and Mao's backing and approval. All three communist dictators gambled that Rhee's government would collapse before the United States could intervene effectively; they were surprised and distressed when events did not develop as they expected. Mao had as a precaution started redeploying his military from opposite Chiang Kai-shek's Guomindang stronghold of Taiwan to the North Korean border even before Inchon, and he grew increasingly alarmed as North Korean fortunes faded.

On 29 September, as American forces prepared to invade North Korea, a panicky Kim called for direct Soviet and Chinese military assistance to save him. Stalin had no intention of risking a full-scale conflict with the United States over North Korea, but he was not above manipulating his Chinese allies into doing his dirty work for him through vague promises of support. Orchestrating Chinese intervention would, he hoped, save North Korea, keep Mao dependent on Soviet largesse, and further bog down the United States in a confounding and peripheral war. For his part, Mao believed that American forces positioned on China's border in a reunited noncommunist Korea would endanger his nascent regime by reigniting the civil war with the Guomindang that he had so recently and painfully won. As he saw it, it was better to confront the United States in Korea than wait for the Americans to bring war into China. Although Mao and most of his advisers understood the price China was likely to pay by directly challenging American power in Korea, Mao was never one to worry much about human costs, appalling or not. After indirect warnings to the Truman administration not to violate the 38th Parallel failed to deter the Americans, Mao ordered Chinese forces into North Korea. On the night of 19–20 October, the first of 120,000 Chinese soldiers, under the command of Peng Dehuai, crossed the Yalu River and marched southward to engage the Americans and South Koreans.

The Chinese People's Liberation Army was nothing like its American counterpart. Most obviously, it lacked the American army's matériel abundance, heavy artillery, air and naval support, mechanized transportation, advanced communications equipment, armor, and state-of-the-art medical facilities. Its rank and file consisted largely of tough and stoic conscripted peasants accustomed to hardship and want. Its high-ranking officers, for their part, had learned to wage war mostly through years of on-the-job training against the Guomindang and Japanese. Indeed, the Chinese army's experiences had taught it to compensate for, and even make virtues of, its shortcomings by emphasizing maneuver and flexibility in achieving its objectives. Chinese units in Korea communicated through bugles and gongs, marched light and fast over even the roughest terrain, fought mostly at night, and employed superb camouflage techniques. Although the Americans often referenced "human wave" assaults, the Chinese usually used much more sophisticated and nuanced tactics. When on the offensive, Chinese soldiers sought out the weakest parts of the enemy lines to attack, enabling them to surround and isolate strongpoints. To keep out of the way of American artillery, the Chinese preferred an elastic defense that often avoided irrevocably committing to any particular geographic position. North Korea's forested mountains were tailor-made for these tactics and played no small role in the Chinese army's initial accomplishments. This same topography, though, overtaxed its always-tenuous supply lines, so that even when its troops managed to defeat the enemy, it lacked the logistical wherewithal to quickly exploit its good fortune. Even so, the Chinese army's ability to slip over 100,000 men into North Korea undetected was merely the first in a series of remarkable achievements that winter.

The various American intelligence agencies were well aware of the Chinese military buildup along the Yalu River in Manchuria but missed the introduction of Chinese troops into North Korea. No one denied that the Chinese had the ability to intervene in Korea; the question was whether they would. Unfortunately, a dearth of good reliable sources within China forced American policy makers to resort to guesswork that all too often reflected their preconceived notions rather than the facts on the ground. The Central Intelligence Agency and the State Department both doubted that the Chinese would enter the conflict and dismissed Chinese threats to do so as bluffs. Although the Armed Forces Security Agency picked up some electronic chatter indicating that there were Chinese units in Korea, the evidence was not sufficiently strong and persuasive to change minds. In Japan, MacArthur relied on his intelligence chief, Charles Willoughby, for his information. MacArthur and Willoughby's professional relationship dated back to World War II, and even then Willoughby tended to color his analyses with unsupported opinions, contradictions, and idle speculation. The basic thrust of his often wishy-washy reports, though, was that the Chinese would not get involved. MacArthur took his cue from that and acted accordingly. When MacArthur met with Truman on Wake Island on 15 October, he assured the president that there was little chance the Chinese would intercede on behalf of the North Koreans in a war that was practically over. And if Chinese troops did try to cross the Yalu, MacArthur declared that the air force would redden the water with their blood. MacArthur's certitude became self-reinforcing; once he committed to this line of thinking, he was loath to admit his error by reconsidering.

Throughout late October, the Eighth Army continued its uncoordinated lunge toward the Yalu River. Because North Korean resistance was almost nonexistent, there seemed little need to carefully synchronize the various motorized American and South Korean columns threading their way through the barren and unpopulated countryside. However, officers began picking up ominous evidence of Chinese troops in the vicinity. Mike Michaelis, for example, remembered that as his regiment moved northward to catch up with the First Corps, locals warned that the Chinese were not far away. Patrols spotted units that did not appear to be North Korean marching along the ridgelines. Most conclusively, the Eighth Army captured a number of Chinese soldiers. When one fell into South Korean hands on 25 October, Eighth Army headquarters personnel flew him to Pyongyang for an interrogation that easily revealed his nationality. Intelligence officers sent all this information up the chain of command but got no real response. Walker no doubt felt that questioning MacArthur's geostrategic assumptions and stopping the Eighth Army's drive on the verge of victory might give MacArthur an excuse to finally relieve him, so he authorized no changes and made no contingency plans. Milburn listened to reports of Chinese troops with Delphic silence. As for Church and Gay, they remained focused on fulfilling their missions by reaching the Yalu. Gay later noted that he never even considered the likelihood of Chinese intervention because no one mentioned it as a possibility. As late as 30 October, Church predicted that he would reach the Yalu within forty-eight hours, "barring any sudden and unexpected increase in enemy opposition."[1] Neither general realized that the war was about to change dramatically.[2]

While Church's Twenty-fourth Division approached the Yalu estuary and Gay's First Cavalry Division mopped up around Pyongyang, Milburn's last First Corps division, Paik Sun Yup's ROK First Division, was operating in the Unsan area. To Paik's north and east, Major General Yu Jae Hung's ROK Second Corps was pushing through the mountains toward the Yalu, and in fact a South Korean battalion even reached the river at Chosan and secured a bottle of its water for Rhee. On 25 October, however, the Chinese launched an all-out attack against the South Koreans. The outnumbered and poorly situated ROK units were caught completely by

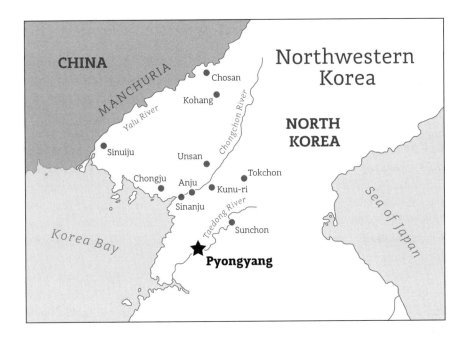

surprise, and one after another, they crumbled under the weight of the Chinese attack. Within a week, four ROK regiments had been destroyed, and the survivors fled forty miles to the Chongchon River. The Chinese also assailed Paik's ROK First Division around Unsan. Although Paik was not yet thirty, Americans considered him the ablest of the high-ranking South Korean generals, so Milburn had a lot of confidence in him. Even so, the ROK First Division gradually wilted under pressure. If the Chinese broke through here and seized Anju–Sinanju near the Chongchon's mouth, they would cut off and isolate Church's division.[3]

To bolster Paik and protect his suddenly exposed right flank, Walker on 28 October ordered Gay to bring his First Cavalry Division up from the Pyongyang area. Gay was surprised by the summons. Neither he nor his subordinates had heard anything about possible Chinese intervention. As far as they knew, the war was practically over. The division's rank and file was equally oblivious. Indeed, the rumor mill had it that the troops would soon return to Tokyo to participate in an Armistice Day parade there, and some units had even turned in their ammunition. As a result, few people clearly understood the seriousness of the situation and the enormity of the task before them. One officer noted that the soldiers in the first regiment to arrive, Ray Palmer's 8th Cav, seemed indifferent, unconcerned, and dismissive of their latest mission. Palmer disregarded warnings by stating that his outfit could take care of itself. His tone prompted one observer to note later, "I consider the catastrophe that overcame the 8th Cavalry Regiment the result of this attitude."[4]

As the 8th Cav took up positions around Unsan in the lasts days of October, though, some officers became increasingly alarmed. On 1 November, Gay and Palmer visited Paik and asked him if reports of Chinese soldiers were true, and Paik assured them there was no doubt about it. The whole region was covered in a spooky, smoky haze because the Chinese had set the surrounding forests on fire to obscure their movements from American air reconnaissance. Retreating ROK soldiers were everywhere, trying to escape the holocaust the Chinese had unleashed. One battalion commander saw through his binoculars waves of Chinese moving toward those ROK troops still holding their positions. As far as Gay was concerned, Paik's division was no longer combat effective, and Paik himself seemed mentally defeated. The 8th Cav was out on a limb on its own. He did not like the look of things at all.[5]

Having mauled Paik's ROK First Division, the Chinese focused their attention on the 8th Cav starting on 1 November. Gay and his artillery chief, Brigadier General Charles Palmer, listened to the radio chatter at the division command post that afternoon and overheard a forward observer in an L-5 plane exclaim, "This is the strangest sight I have ever seen. There are two large columns of enemy infantry moving southeast over the trails. . . . Our shells are landing right in their columns and they just keep coming."[6] Although the forward observer assured listeners that the slaughter was terrific, the Chinese flood of men continued to flow. As the day wore on, Gay became increasingly worried and frustrated. He wanted to pull the 8th Cav back and bring up the rest of his division to support it, but Milburn would not let him. To Gay, it was bad enough that Milburn was hamstringing his efforts to fight the battle, but Chinese numbers and strength seemed to grow exponentially by the hour. Referring to all the Chinese troops emerging from the woodwork, Gay exclaimed, "God, this is just like cutting paper dolls, cutting paper dolls here."[7]

At his First Corps headquarters at Anju, Milburn was that day equally frustrated and alarmed, which was no doubt one reason why he kept a tight leash on Gay. Early in the afternoon, he received a startling call from Walker. In his usual brusque manner, Walker got straight to the point: "You have no right flank. The [ROK] Second Corps on your right has ceased to be a fighting organization. They have lost all control of their units. Protect your flank."[8] Unfortunately, Milburn had no reserves immediately available with which to secure his vulnerable flank, but he ordered his chief of staff, Rinaldo Van Brunt, to scrounge up whatever service troops he could find and send them up the road toward Kunu-ri, about ten miles south of Unsan, to defend the bridges over the Chongchon. While Van Brunt got busy, Milburn took a jeep to Kunu-ri to confer with the ROK Second Corps commander, Yu Jae

Hung. Yu admitted that he had lost contact with and did not know the whereabouts of most of his men, and that he had only three combat-ready battalions with which to defend Kunu-ri. Milburn assured him that help was on the way—he did not, however, mention that that assistance consisted of whatever service troops Van Brunt could scrape together—and drove back to Anju. Once there, he summoned his three division commanders for an emergency meeting. By the time Church, Gay, and Paik had all arrived, it was getting dark. Everyone now understood the gravity of the situation; if the Chinese broke through at Unsan or Kunu-ri, they could descend on Anju–Sinanju and cut the Eighth Army in two. Paik, who had had more than his fill of Chinese by now, urgently recommended that the Eighth Army withdraw behind the Chongchon at once. After Paik finished making his point, Milburn abruptly reached for the phone and called Walker to explain the situation. Walker hated retreating, especially with victory so seemingly close, but it was hard to ignore the unpleasant facts Milburn presented. He authorized Milburn to go onto the defensive straightaway. Milburn thereupon recalled Church's Twenty-fourth Division from its march to the Yalu, ordered Paik to withdraw what was left of his division, and told Gay to pull back his exposed 8th Cav. These redeployments, they hoped, would place the First Corps in a better position from which to resist the Chinese onslaught.[9]

When Gay returned to his command post, he discovered that the 8th Cav was in deep trouble. He directed the regiment to fall back, but Chinese attacks throughout the night of 1–2 November pinned the men down and severed most of the roads out of Unsan. Even so, two of the battalions managed to get out, albeit with heavy losses. The regiment's Third Battalion, though, was trapped southwest of the village. Next morning Gay commanded elements of the 5th and 7th Cav regiments to try to reach it, but they were unable to break through. That afternoon Milburn drove over for a firsthand look at the situation. He and Gay concluded that they lacked the resources necessary to save the wayward battalion, so they abandoned their rescue efforts and ordered the battalion to escape as best it could. Milburn afterward referred to it only as a tough decision, but Gay was more emotionally invested and later said, "A soldier accumulates many sad memories over his lifetime, but I have never before or since made a decision that was more sad or more lonely."[10] He regretted that he had not ordered the regiment out earlier on his own authority, instead of asking Milburn's permission. Over the next few days, repeated Chinese assaults wore down and finally destroyed the isolated Third Battalion. Only a couple of hundred survivors made it through to American lines. Indeed, the 8th Cav suffered around 600 casualties in the Unsan fighting, though the initial losses appeared much heavier. After the regiment went to Sinanju to refit, for the next twelve days, the Eighth Army sent all its replacements to the First Cav Division to try to bring it up to strength.[11]

On a more positive note, Church's Twenty-fourth Division and its accompanying British Commonwealth 27th Brigade made a clean getaway. Operating on the far left of the Eighth Army line, Church was initially oblivious to the ROK Second Corps' late October debacle. In fact, he figured it was just a matter of days before he was at the Yalu. His men saw no reason to disagree, despite a series of sharp battles with the enemy at the end of the month. One spotter plane pilot gleefully radioed to his regimental command post, "Hey, you guys, I can see the Yalu!" Minutes later, however, the regimental operations officer entered the tent and announced, "Pack up, everybody. We're moving out—south."[12] Once Church got the word to bring his division back to the Chongchon, he moved with alacrity. Motorization gave the army the tremendous advantage in mobility that Church used to withdraw without serious losses. Within hours, bumper-to-bumper traffic filled the roads as hundreds of vehicles carrying thousands of men headed southeastward. The last units reached Anju on 2 November, providing Walker and Milburn with the resources they needed to bolster their fraying line. Milburn deployed the British Commonwealth 27th Brigade and Edward Moore's 19th Regiment north of the Chongchon to maintain a bridgehead there for future operations, and he sent John Throckmorton's 5th Regiment to the Kunu-ri area to help the ROK soldiers and Chin Sloane's newly arrived 9th Regiment protect the Eighth Army's exposed right flank. For the next five days, the Chinese attacked along the line, but the American, British, and South Korean troops held on. The Chinese surprised and scattered one 19th Regiment battalion at Hill 123, but Church brought Stephens's 21st Regiment across the river to restore the front. Then, on 6 November, as suddenly as they had appeared, the Chinese broke contact and vanished into the North Korean mountains.

The Chinese army's sudden disappearance gave the Eighth Army's leaders the opportunity to catch their collective breath and take a hard look at their poor performances. Indeed, there was plenty of blame to go around, starting at the top with MacArthur. In his haste to end the conflict on his terms, he downplayed and overlooked evidence that the Chinese were moving into Korea. He therefore ordered the Eighth Army to continue to charge headlong into the Chinese trap when a more methodical advance might have disclosed their presence. MacArthur, though, did not want to waste any time in finishing a war he believed was all but won. His mind-set had a chilling effect on Eighth Army personnel, who suspected the truth but were unwilling to speak up for fear of contradicting MacArthur's script. Even after it was clear that Chinese troops were involved, it took far too long to sound the alarm. As late as 1 November, almost a week after the Chinese first engaged the South Koreans, Hap Gay—a major general and division commander ordered forward to engage the enemy—remained unsure whether the Chinese were in the war.

Nor did Walker and Milburn have much of which to be proud. Both reacted sluggishly to Chinese intervention, and during late October and early November they were usually a step behind events. To this Milburn committed the additional sin of micromanaging Gay's fight at Unsan. Had Gay been able to maneuver all his battalions as he saw fit, it is possible that the 8th Cav might not have suffered so much damage. Humble as ever, Gay later acknowledged his role in the debacle, but at least he identified the danger sooner than a good many of his officers and men, who went into action believing that the conflict was just about over. This complacency played no small role in the 8th Cav's discomfiture. On the other hand, once Walker and Milburn recognized the Chinese threat, they redeployed their units in such a way as to establish a new line from which they could fight effectively. Church and his regimental commanders especially deserved credit for withdrawing quickly to the Chongchon and then holding their ground there. On the whole, however, the Eighth Army's debut against this new enemy was hardly auspicious.

Uneasy Interval

Chinese intervention sent shock waves through Washington. Unfortunately, the Truman administration was unable to agree on Chinese motivations and intentions, let alone formulate a coherent response. The Central Intelligence Agency, for instance, believed that the Chinese wanted to carve out a buffer zone along the Yalu River. The Joint Chiefs of Staff admitted that this was a possibility but added that the Chinese could be stalking horses for Soviet aggression elsewhere, or that they might aim to drive the Americans, South Koreans, and their allies off the peninsula altogether. The truth was that American policy makers did not know Chinese plans and objectives but were instead relying on guesswork and speculation for their analyses. In fact, the Chinese were determined to exterminate MacArthur's forces and reunite Korea under communist control. Although Chinese troops had suffered heavy casualties in their first battles, they had withdrawn deeper into North Korea not to lick their wounds but rather to tempt their enemies into an unwise offensive into the barren mountains. There the Chinese planned to attack and destroy the exposed American and South Korean columns far from their supply lines and artillery support. Mulling things over, the JCS concluded that the most reasonable and prudent strategy was for MacArthur to dig in along the Chongchon and wait for the situation to clarify itself, even if this meant surrendering the initiative. However, the Joint Chiefs were, like the rest of Truman's administration, disinclined to interfere with MacArthur's prerogatives as theater commander and intimidated by his Inchon-enhanced reputation as a military genius. They therefore reluctantly left matters in MacArthur's hands with the sole proviso that he could not expand the war into China without their approval.[13]

Unlike the Truman administration, MacArthur had no doubts about the proper response to Chinese intervention. Although he initially downplayed the number of Chinese troops in Korea, he soon realized that he could use a more flexible and ambivalent view of the situation to further browbeat the JCS into letting him fight the war his way. MacArthur argued that Chinese involvement limited his options to staying put along the Chongchon, withdrawing southward, or resuming the offensive toward the Yalu. He believed that retreating was contrary to his orders, was dishonorable, and would squander the last, best opportunity to end the conflict in victory. Digging in would not accomplish much either, especially because he lacked the resources to establish the kind of defense in depth necessary to repel Chinese attacks. By process of elimination, this left advancing toward the Yalu as the only realistic solution. Not coincidentally, it was also the alternative that most suited MacArthur's temperament. As MacArthur saw it, he was in a race against the clock. Every day he remained on the defensive brought the awful Korean winter closer and gave the Chinese time to import more reinforcements onto the peninsula. On the other hand, if the air force could destroy the Yalu River bridges and isolate those Chinese troops already in Korea from Manchuria, then the Eighth Army could quickly push northward and mop up the remainder. Because the Joint Chiefs' hints and suggestions that he stop and take stock of the situation were just that—hints and suggestions, not orders—he intended to implement his plan as soon as possible. To do so, he had approximately 425,000 personnel throughout his theater, of whom 224,000 were South Korean, 178,500 American, and the remaining 21,000 or so from other nations.[14]

Walker did not share MacArthur's certitude. In fact, he was extremely leery about sending his troops back into the Chinese maw from which they had so recently and fortuitously escaped. Unhappily, his poor relationship with MacArthur prevented him from freely expressing his reservations. Although Walker may not have known how close he had come to losing his job, he was well aware of MacArthur's antipathy. His soldierlike response had been to deny MacArthur any specific reason to relieve him by loyally and uncomplainingly obeying his orders. Now, however, Walker worried that following MacArthur's instructions might lead to a military catastrophe. He had plenty of reasons for his concerns. For one thing, the Eighth Army's logistical situation remained precarious, and Walker wished to wait until his troops were better supplied before he pointed them at the Yalu again. Simply getting to the Chongchon had stretched Eighth Army supply lines to the breaking point, and only now were Walker's logisticians getting a handle on it. He was also anxious about his lack of information about Tenth Corps operations across the Taebaek Mountains, and he wanted time to reorganize and reequip the recently battered ROK Second Corps. Most of all, though, he fretted about all those Chinese soldiers he strongly suspected were lying in wait beyond the Chongchon to assail the Eighth Army, but about whom he had precious little hard intelligence.

Walker's solution to this conundrum was to surreptitiously use his authority as Eighth Army commander to rein in and limit MacArthur's grandiose scheme for a major offensive. He referenced his continuing supply problems as an excuse to push back the date of the big attack by a week. He also designed the operation more like a careful reconnaissance-in-force to make contact with the Chinese than an all-out assault to destroy them. This included establishing fallback lines in case he had to retreat to the south. Such timidity was unlike Walker, who had a well-established reputation for aggressiveness dating back to World War I. As one of his staffers later noted, "General Walker by nature much preferred the offensive. However . . . he approached this one with caution unusual for him."[15] In fact, a visiting Tenth Corps officer was so appalled by what he saw as Walker's defeatist attitude that he later referred to him as a disgrace to the uniform. Nevertheless, Walker was taking no chances this time; if he had to assume the offensive, then he was going to do it his way.[16]

For this offensive, Walker planned to use all the resources at his disposal to cover his approximately seventy-five-mile-long front. To that end, he ordered up John Coulter's Ninth Corps, consisting of Dutch Keiser's Second and Bill Kean's Twenty-fifth divisions, and inserted it between Milburn's First Corps along the west coast and the regrouped ROK Second Corps in the mountains to the east. Both divisions had been engaged in mop up and counterinsurgency operations down south, but they were still better rested than the tired American, British, and South Korean soldiers recovering from their recent ordeals north of the Chongchon. Moreover, they were now veterans led by commanders who had seen plenty of action in the Pusan Perimeter and the subsequent breakout. Keiser's initial performance along the Naktong had left much to be desired, but since then, he had not made any major mistakes. As for Kean, although his record was hardly unblemished, he was probably the best division chief Walker had. Walker also gave Coulter the newly arrived Turkish Brigade as his corps reserve. Finally, Walker put Gay's First Cav Division, still recovering from its Unsan debacle, in army reserve just in case.

John Breitling Coulter's Ninth Corps had played a secondary role in the war since it became operational on 22 September. Coulter was born in San Antonio, Texas, in 1891, and secured a cavalry commission after graduating from West Texas Military Academy in 1911. He participated in John Pershing's Mexican expedition against Pancho Villa, went to France as an aide to the Forty-Second Division's commander when the United States entered World War I, and ultimately rose to lead a battalion in the St. Mihiel operation. After the conflict, he took full advantage of the military's educational system by attending the Cavalry School from 1921 to 1922, the Command and General Staff School from 1926 to 1927, the Army War College from 1932 to 1933, and the Naval War College from 1933 to 1934. He returned to the cavalry and had worked his way up to brigade command by the time the Japanese bombed Pearl Harbor. Chief of staff George Marshall eventually put Coulter in charge of the Eighty-fifth Division, which Coulter trained and took to Italy in 1944. The Eighty-fifth fought well along the Gustav and Gothic lines, for which Coulter naturally got the credit. After Germany and Japan surrendered, Coulter ran the Infantry Replacement Center, then in 1948 went to Korea as Seventh Division commander. He took over the First Corps in occupied Japan when the United States withdrew its last combat units from Korea, and, upon the First Corps' inactivation, was preparing to take over as deputy commander of the stateside Fifth Army when the Korean War brought him back to the peninsula as head of the resurrected First Corps.

Coulter no doubt owed his new job—or, more accurately, the return to his old job—to his prior relationships with MacArthur and Almond. Coulter and MacArthur had served together in the Forty-second Division in World War I, and he and Almond were old friends. Coulter saw his assignment as his best opportunity to gain a third star before he retired, so he was eager to play a prominent part in the war. Unfortunately, he failed to impress Walker when in late August Walker dispatched him to Kyongju to take over and stiffen ROK resolve there during the last North Korean offensive against the Pusan Perimeter. Although he won a Silver Star for rallying faltering ROK units, Walker concluded that Coulter was too jittery and uncertain. Walker had wanted Coulter's First Corps to spearhead the planned breakout from the Pusan Perimeter, but after watching Coulter in action, Walker opted to replace him with Milburn. Because he still valued Coulter, Walker refrained from relieving him outright; instead, he sent him to take over the nascent Ninth Corps. The Ninth Corps' participation in the Pusan Perimeter breakout was secondary and marginal, and thereafter Walker relegated it to mopping up and counterinsurgency duties because he could not supply the unit further north. Walker was, however, impressed with the speed with which Coulter relieved Milburn's men so the First Corps could quickly invade North Korea.

Chinese intervention gave Coulter the chance to show Walker of what he was capable. He possessed many of the ingredients of a good commander, such as military education, battle experience, ambition, and personal courage. Colleagues spoke well of his good judgment, loyalty, and alertness. He also demonstrated a sincere concern for and appreciation of the Korean people. On the other hand, he usually did not venture much beyond his command post, so he did not always have a good feel for battlefield conditions. He also neglected to establish positive relationships with his subordinates and the rank and file. Nor did he develop much rapport with Walker and his fellow corps commanders. Whatever his record in World War II, by the time he reached Korea, he did not seem particularly forceful, dynamic, or impressive.[17]

As his corps deployed north of the Chongchon, the Twenty-fifth Division on the left and the Second Division on the right, Coulter was optimistic about the upcoming offensive, believing that it would end the war in a matter of days. He no doubt wanted to appear positive and upbeat in his first big assignment at the head of a corps, and he also possessed the advantage of having not yet experienced the Chinese firsthand. As he saw things, his men were ready and raring to go, and his information indicated that there were few Chinese around. Indeed, Coulter was so gung-ho that Hank Fisher, Kean's able 35th Regiment commander, told him point-blank that he was underestimating the Chinese. The Chinese, Fisher claimed, were not like the Germans because they did not retreat or surrender when their tactical situation became untenable; instead, they had to be rooted out and killed. Coulter, however, refused to be swayed.[18]

Over at First Corps headquarters, Shrimp Milburn had a much different perspective and mind-set. Unlike Coulter, Milburn was well aware of Chinese capabilities, having recently been at the receiving end of their last military effort. He was unhappy with the continuing supply problems, and he worried about the Eighth Army's poor communications with the Tenth Corps. He was also bothered by the lack of concrete intelligence about Chinese whereabouts and intentions. He was not so much concerned about his immediate front as about his right flank. His patrols had been unable to penetrate the Unsan area, which indicated that the enemy was there in strength and would cause the Ninth Corps considerable trouble. Most distressing of all, though, was that he could not seem to get Eighth Army headquarters to acknowledge the gravity of the situation.[19]

Such reservations were by no means limited to the field army and corps levels; they were shared by division and regimental commanders as well. Fisher took his pessimistic cue from Walker. Soon after Fisher's 35th Regiment relieved Edward Moore's 21st north of the Chongchon, Walker came over for a look. Fisher was accustomed to Walker's aggressive attitude, so he was disconcerted with his boss's uncharacteristic cautiousness. Fisher, however, began to understand Walker's mind-set after his patrols were unable to penetrate much beyond American lines. It seemed to Fisher that many of the higher-ups did not appreciate the situation on the ground. Although Keiser feigned optimism in Coulter's presence, he too worried about all the Chinese he suspected were out there. The night before the Eighth Army kicked off its big assault, Keiser had dinner with his 23rd Regiment commander, Paul Freeman. Keiser confessed that he did not really understand what was going on or why the Eighth Army was attacking with so little good intelligence, but he concluded that MacArthur must have some secret high-level information that the Chinese would not fight hard. Freeman was not convinced. Like Fisher, his patrols were also encountering Chinese, but with unpredictable and odd results. One reconnoitering company commander who stumbled upon the Chinese was amazed that they waved at his men and let them withdraw without opening fire on them. Freeman talked things over with his friend Michaelis, who was still leading the 27th Regiment. Michaelis was, like Freeman, especially nervous about the reconstituted ROK Second Corps on the Eighth Army's right flank. The South Koreans had not fared particularly well against the Chinese in their first encounter, and neither officer saw any reason why things should be different this time. To Michaelis, the planned offensive had all the hallmarks of a disaster, and he later recalled, "I frankly had the gut feeling that this was the last damn thing we should be doing."[20]

Thursday, 23 November, was Thanksgiving. The army went out of its way to provide a good holiday meal for its troops, even though doing so further strained the Eighth Army's overstretched supply lines. Soldiers feasted on turkey, cranberry sauce, pumpkin pie, and mince tart. Division and regimental headquarters printed elaborate menus and set up tables covered with white cloth and decorated with candles and flowers. There were the inevitable wry and morbid jokes about fattening up the men for slaughter, but it was still an impressive display of the army's logistical prowess that it could deliver such sustenance to the rank and file so far from home. Although a good many officers were deeply concerned about all the Chinese they suspected were waiting in the mountains, morale was high among the men, especially those who had yet to encounter the new enemy. As far as they were concerned, the war was almost over.

As the men scarfed down their dinners, they could not help but notice the drop in the temperature as the brutal Korean winter took hold. The biting wind cut to the bone, obscured hearing, and blew away anything under a certain weight not tied down. The accompanying cold was hard on both machines and men. Vehicles failed to start quickly or easily, and rifles needed to be fired periodically to keep them in working order. Mortar baseplates broke during recoil, and illumination shells failed to light. Plasma and sedatives froze, as did emergency rations. Those soldiers who ate frozen food risked severe gastrointestinal problems. Most units did not get their winter clothing until the season was well under way. Prolonged exposure to the elements led to frostbite and turned soldiers into walking, benumbed zombies barely able to function, let alone fight or perform other duties. Troops learned to move often or else their sweat turned to ice in their uniforms, and to prevent trench foot by keeping their feet dry and changing socks frequently. Snow filtered into everything—sleeping bags, truck beds, radios—and turned slushy and icy under the weight of vehicles. Warming tents containing stoves offered refuge but also attracted enemy fire. For all the problems that waging war in Korea's stifling summer heat had caused, the Korean winter promised a whole new level of misery. As one journalist explained, "Winter, when you don't have a home and fireside, is an atrocity no matter how many clothes you wear."[21]

The Eighth Army's offensive began on 24 November, the day after the Thanksgiving feast. MacArthur and a gaggle of staffers flew in from Tokyo to mark the occasion, touching down at the bumpy Sinanju airfield around midmorning. Walker, Milburn, and their staffers were there to greet them. The sun was out, but it was bitterly cold, with temperatures hovering around fifteen degrees Fahrenheit. Walker was so bundled up that he reminded one journalist of the rotund Michelin man. Once everyone had deplaned and exchanged salutes, they all got into jeeps and drove to Milburn's First Corps headquarters for a briefing. Milburn expressed confidence that he could reach the Yalu without much difficulty—resistance had so far been light—but worried that the Ninth Corps might get into trouble around Unsan.

From there the generals motored to Coulter's headquarters for an update on his operations. Coulter gestured toward a big map full of blue and red arrows and circles as he explained his mission. He emphasized that his men were ready and eager to attack, and that so far everything was going as planned. Walker interjected that he wanted the Eighth Army to push as hard as possible for the Yalu, a notion with which both MacArthur and Coulter fully agreed. Indeed, MacArthur smiled and said to Coulter, "You tell the boys that when they get to the Yalu they are going home. I want to make good on my statement that they are going to eat Christmas dinner at home."[22] At Church's Twenty-fourth Division headquarters a short time later, MacArthur reiterated and expanded on his desire that this offensive end the war within the month: "I have already promised wives and mothers that the boys of the Twenty-fourth Division will be back by Christmas. Don't make me a liar. Get to the Yalu and I will relieve you."[23] From all the optimistic reports he had heard, MacArthur had no reason to think the goal was unrealistic or foolish, and in fact he issued a communiqué reflecting his sentiments. MacArthur skipped lunch and returned to the Sinanju airfield for the flight back to Japan. On the way, he ordered the pilot to take an impromptu and dangerous reconnaissance up to and along the Yalu. As he gazed down at the barren and seemingly empty mountains, MacArthur was unaware that more than 380,000 Chinese troops were just then getting into position to initiate the biggest ambush in American military history.[24]

Although MacArthur implied in his conversations with Walker that the presence of Chinese troops did not mean full-scale Chinese intervention in Korea, Walker remained skeptical. As usual, he refrained from expressing his honest opinions out of fear that doing so would give MacArthur a reason to remove him from his command. In MacArthur's presence, he echoed MacArthur's aggressiveness and optimism to show that he was a team player and obedient soldier, even though he did not agree with the strategy. As soon as MacArthur's plane disappeared into the sky, he returned to First Corps headquarters and told Milburn to ignore all the frothy and belligerent talk about driving straight to the Yalu. Instead, he reiterated his desire for a methodical march to contact to figure out what the Chinese were up to, and added, "The first time you smell Chinese chow, you turn around and start back."[25]

Eighth Army Debacle

Despite Walker's admonitions and forebodings, the first days of the offensive went smoothly for the First and Ninth corps. The weather was chilly but bearable, the skies were clear, and both corps made steady progress against minimal resistance. The biggest gains were along the flat west coast, where Church's Twenty-fourth Division seized Chongju without a fight on 25 November. Even so, there remained a certain ominousness in the air that reflected Walker's and Milburn's concerns. Dick Stephens, whose 21st Regiment had occupied Chongju, was not worried so much about the opposition in front of him but rather what was going on in the mountains on his right flank. As his regiment advanced, refugees trudged in the other direction. One correspondent remembered:

> Through it all by day and night the refugees trudged pitifully in the last grip
> of despair and exhaustion fording the frozen river with their naked feet, small
> boys and girls bearing their smaller brothers and sisters upon their backs,
> others, men, women and children, slumped by the river, the road, the rail
> track, perhaps not to rise again, their heads and hands hanging limply
> between their knees. I remember a boy with his small brother on his back
> picking his way bravely across a broken railway viaduct, leaping the breaks
> with a drop of fifty feet or more beneath him.[26]

Heartbreaking though the refugees were, their presence was also comforting because it usually meant that the enemy was not around. It was the absence of refugees that made the soldiers nervous.[27]

While MacArthur and the Truman administration pondered their options throughout much of November, Peng Dehuai waited impatiently for his enemies to walk into his trap. He focused his attention on the Eighth Army's weakest link, the ROK Second Corps. Not only were its three divisions operating in the rugged mountains on the Eighth Army's vulnerable right flank but they were also still recovering from their mangling three weeks earlier. All three divisions contained plenty of ill-trained and inexperienced men brought forward to fill their depleted ranks, and they lacked the firepower and matériel that helped their American counterparts compensate for their shortcomings. When the Eighth Army's offensive began, the ROK Second Corps ran into heavy resistance from the start and got nowhere, resulting in a gap between it and Keiser's advancing Second Division on its immediate left. This was troublesome enough, but on the night of 25–26 November, the Chinese hit the ROK Second Corps with sledgehammer-like force. While the South Koreans fought desperately to maintain their frontline positions, Chinese soldiers infiltrated behind them and set up roadblocks to prevent them from receiving supplies and reinforcements—or from retreating in any organized manner. By 28 November, the Chinese had driven off or destroyed all nine of the corps' regiments, rendering it combat ineffective. This exposed the remainder of the Eighth Army to Chinese troops maneuvering to get between it and Pyongyang.

Walker by now had plenty of experience dealing with sudden military crises, but he failed to immediately grasp the magnitude of this one. His initial reaction was to prop up Coulter's now-vulnerable Ninth Corps by reshuffling units and responsibilities. On 27 November, he ordered Coulter to take over the ROK Second Corps' zone. He also removed Gay's First Cav Division from army reserve, gave it to Coulter, and deployed it north and east of Sunchon to safeguard Pyongyang from that direction. Gay managed to do so in a series of confusing battles, but unfortunately his division's reach did not extend far enough to protect the Second Division's escape route to the south. Walker further augmented Coulter's resources by directing the British Commonwealth 27th Brigade to assemble near Kunu-ri in case Coulter needed it, and by authorizing Coulter to use the recently arrived Turkish Brigade to guard Keiser's exposed right flank. Finally, Walker placed Kean's Twenty-fifth Division in Milburn's First Corps so Coulter could focus on the emergency at hand. Although Walker informed MacArthur the same day he made these changes that the Chinese had attacked along part of his line, he claimed that he still hoped to resume the offensive and downplayed the seriousness of the ROK Second Corps' predicament.[28]

Walker's belated efforts to help the ROK Second Corps were hindered by all-out Chinese assaults along most of the Eighth Army's lines that began as early as the night of 24–25 November and persisted through daylight. "Calls were coming in for fighter support all over the front," recalled one air force general listening to the radio chatter.[29] Although Church's Twenty-fourth Division continued to encounter little opposition, the Chinese assailed Paik's neighboring ROK First Division with increasing ferocity and over the course of the next few days mauled it badly. By 27 November, it was backpedaling as rapidly as it was disintegrating. To

Paik's right, Kean's Twenty-fifth Division also came under heavy attack, but most of its units more or less maintained their integrity. Hank Fisher demonstrated considerable skill in withdrawing his 35th Regiment from its exposed position, and Michaelis fought his 27th Regiment with his usual competence. On the other hand, Colonel John Corley's 24th Regiment, on the division's far right, got turned around and fragmented and was lucky to escape. Despite his difficulties, Kean never lost his composure even when he lost some of the 24th Regiment's companies.

To the southeast, though, the Turkish Brigade had the most unfortunate experience of all. The Turks were new to Korea and had had little opportunity to acclimate to the strange new environment in which they found themselves. Most of the men were raw, and language barriers made communicating with the Americans and South Koreans problematic. When the ROK Second Corps collapsed, the Turks were Coulter's only available reserve, so on 26 November he dispatched them toward Tokchon to prop up his vulnerable right flank. In three days of chaotic fighting, the Chinese pummeled and vitiated the brigade, so that by 29 November it had lost most of its equipment and was no longer in any condition to fight as an organized unit.

To the right, or east, of Kean's Twenty-fifth Division, Dutch Keiser's Second Division straddled the Chongchon River. Morale among the rank and file was high for what the men assumed was the last big push of the war, and at first all went well. However, here too there were ominous portents. Chinese deserters indicated that there were lots of enemy troops nearby, as did air reconnaissance. When one such report revealed that large numbers of Chinese were repairing a road to the east, Keiser exclaimed, "Goddamn it, that's where they're going to hit. That will be the main effort—off our flank and against the ROK Second Corps."[30] Keiser actually underestimated the scale of the massive Chinese offensive, which soon engulfed almost every Eighth Army combat unit, including the Second Division. One of his regimental commanders, Chin Sloane of the 9th, briefly watched one of his companies struggle against Chinese dug in on a hill and concluded that this was far more than a run-of-the-mill engagement. "I think this is different; it may be the real thing," he radioed back to division headquarters. "We better watch it."[31]

Heavy Chinese attacks against the division began on the night of 25–26 November and soon became continuous. Although Keiser committed his reserve, Paul Freeman's 23rd Regiment, to try to stabilize his fraying line, it was not enough. The Chinese punched a hole in Sloane's regiment, splitting it in two. Sloane was a capable enough officer but inclined to be overly optimistic, so he failed to adequately communicate to Keiser the seriousness of his situation. In fact, Sloane's discomfiture meant that George Peploe's 38th Regiment on Sloane's right was suddenly separated from the rest of the division—and isolated from the remainder of the Eighth Army now that the ROK Second Corps was in the process of dissolving. Peploe redeployed his men to meet the threat, but he did not realize how dire Sloane's condition had become. Indeed, obliviousness of the division's danger extended up and down the chain of command. Keiser was a headquarters operator who relied on radio, telephone, and his assistant division commander, Joseph Sladen Bradley, to keep tabs on his units instead of traveling to the front to see things for himself. He therefore took Sloane's rosy word about his regiment's condition and did not respond adequately to the danger. Bradley might have set Keiser straight, but he was an impulsive man with questionable judgment who usually reported to Keiser alone, without the presence of staffers who could provide a more balanced assessment. As a result, he likely did not offer an accurate accounting of the 9th Regiment's plight either. The upshot was that the Second Division was in deeper trouble than anyone yet realized.[32]

MacArthur had left Korea believing that all was going according to plan, so the magnitude of the Chinese offensive shocked and surprised him. On 28 November, he summoned Walker and Almond to his Tokyo residence for a late-night conference with him and his key staffers. Despite the gravity of the situation, Walker sounded optimistic. Even so, he admitted that he needed to retreat in order to establish a solid line from which to fight. As it was, he had already earlier that day ordered the Eighth Army to fall back to the Chongchon River bridgehead, although in fact the Chinese were effecting such a withdrawal with or without his consent. After four hours of discussion, a consensus emerged that the Eighth Army and Tenth Corps should go over to the defensive. Shortly after the meeting ended, MacArthur in effect authorized Walker to fight the battle as he saw fit. He directed Walker to hold onto Pyongyang if possible, but he added that he also needed to protect his flank and rear. With these new marching orders, Walker returned to Korea the next day.

As soon as he reached his headquarters, Walker directed the Eighth Army to retreat from the Chongchon River line. For all its problems and losses, the Eighth Army possessed enough vehicles for most of it to escape the Chinese. Church's Twenty-fourth Division, still deployed along the coast, had seen almost no action, so it got across the river at Anju without much difficulty, and Throckmorton's 5th Regiment dug in there to act as rear guard for the remainder of the army. On 30 November, the ROK First and Kean's Twenty-fifth divisions crossed the river too and put the Chinese behind them for now. This left Keiser's Second Division as the last major unit near the Chongchon. By then it was in serious trouble. The collapse of the ROK Second Corps had exposed its right flank, and heavy Chinese attacks had depleted its strength and forced it back to Kunu-ri. Keiser blamed the division's woes as much on Coulter as the Chinese. Over the past few days, he had asked Coulter for permission to break contact with the Chinese and fall back five miles or so to reestablish his lines, but Coulter authorized only limited withdrawals that kept the tired soldiers engaged with the enemy. To Keiser, this defeated the purpose of such planned retrograde movements. In addition, because the Second Division's original mission was offensive, most of its artillery, command posts, supply depots, hospitals, and so forth were close to the front and vulnerable to enemy assault.[33]

By 29 November, the Second Division was deployed along a shallow valley just south of Kunu-ri. The Chinese recognized that it was vulnerable and assailed it mercilessly. Keiser believed that the Chinese would destroy his unit if it stayed there, so he was relieved to receive the order to pull out. Of the two roads to safety, one to the west to Anju and the other south to Sunchon, Keiser preferred the former, but he did not want to interfere with Kean's retreat. When he flew from Ninth Corps headquarters back to his command post, though, he observed what he believed were lots of Korean refugees to the south and east, which convinced him that the Chinese were not yet near the road to Sunchon in strength. Coulter had also flown over the area and reached a similar conclusion. Therefore, Coulter told Keiser to bring his division out to the south, and he promised to send the British Commonwealth 27th Brigade to attack northward up the road to help clear it of any enemy troops. Although the Second Division zone was full of the war's backwash—South Koreans, Turks, and Americans all blown loose from their commands—Keiser got his men more or less organized and sometime after noon on 30 November, the bulk of his division left Kunu-ri for Sunchon, leaving behind Paul Freeman's 23rd Regiment to serve as rear guard.[34]

Paul Freeman spent most of World War II as a staffer and planner. He did well in the role, but he did not get the opportunity to distinguish himself as a combat leader. As a result, he resigned himself to an unexceptional postwar career. He was therefore surprised and delighted when he received command of the 23rd Regiment just before the North Koreans invaded South Korea. Freeman's admirers lauded his intellect, low-key sense of humor, composure, and charisma. His critics, on the other hand, charged that he was actually a self-centered and pessimistic whiner. Before the Twenty-fifth Division fell back across the Chongchon, Freeman and Michaelis shared a command post for several hours. Michaelis did not like the look of things, so before he left—Freeman later complained that Michaelis absconded with his stove, a valuable commodity in the Korean winter—he recommended that Freeman follow him out via the road to Anju. Once the remainder of the Second Division pulled out of Kunu-ri, the Chinese nearby focused their attention on Freeman's beleaguered 23rd. As the afternoon wore on, Freeman wondered if his regiment would survive the battle. And even if it did, Freeman was increasingly convinced that it would perish on the road if it tried to retreat southward.

Mulling things over, Freeman concluded that the best option was to take Michaelis's advice and withdraw westward toward Anju. Getting permission from Keiser to do so, though, was difficult because Keiser was busy trying to prevent the Chinese from mangling the rest of the Second Division. Freeman finally got through to the division's assistant commander, Sladen Bradley. After a brief and garbled radio discussion, Bradley authorized Freeman to use his best judgment. He did not, however, realize that Freeman intended to exercise his new authority by taking his regiment off in a completely different direction. As the Chinese swarmed around his regiment, Freeman ordered his artillery and tanks to fire off all their ammunition reserves in a twenty-minute barrage, some 3,000 rounds. While the Chinese took cover, the 23rd made its escape to the west. It was not exactly a rout, but everyone got out as fast as possible. When the 23rd reached the safety of the 5th Regiment's lines after midnight on 1 December, Freeman reported to First Corps headquarters and explained, "Well, the rest of them [Second Division] went down this way so I pulled down this way. I didn't know what was over here but I knew what was there."[35] By doing so, Freeman probably saved his regiment, but he also abdicated his rearguard duties and exposed the balance of the Second Division to additional Chinese attacks.[36]

While Freeman fulfilled—or, from his detractors' more critical perspective, failed to fulfill—his rearguard responsibilities, most of the rest of the Second Division was undergoing its own ordeal on the road to Sunchon. It turned out that the Chinese were in the area in far greater strength than anyone initially suspected and had established innumerable fire blocks along the route, especially at a seven-mile stretch subsequently dubbed "the gauntlet." The 9th and ROK 3rd regiments from the north and the British Commonwealth 27th Brigade from the south had tried and failed to clear the way the previous day. Even so, Keiser had his orders to retreat in that direction, and he believed that if he stayed at Kunu-ri the Chinese would obliterate his division. In early afternoon on 30 November, while Chinese sniper fire peppered his command post, Keiser directed his division to head southward.

Once the long motorized columns got into motion and plunged into the gauntlet, though, Keiser lost all control over them and became just another unfortunate participant. Chinese soldiers dug in along the hills lashed at the trucks, jeeps, and tanks threading their way south with rifle, machine gun, and mortar fire. Soon disabled vehicles and artillery pieces cluttered the road and obstructed movement. Confused, injured, and stunned men were everywhere—in ditches, under broken-down and burning trucks, on the road itself. There were not enough officers around, and those who were present sometimes failed to exert their authority. Although some troops tried to find places for the wounded in their vehicles, many were left where they fell. Small groups of men opted to take their chances by moving cross-country rather than push through the Chinese shooting gallery. Keiser later recalled that the only man he saw fighting back was a sergeant firing a mortar from a truck bed. Both Keiser and Bradley demonstrated considerable physical courage by ranging along the gauntlet trying to rally the soldiers and help the wounded, but without much success. Bradley later recalled, "I take my hat off to Gen. Keiser. He was not well and he stood up and walked up and down the column showing himself to the men to build up their confidence. I think the man deserves a ribbon or medal."[37] Those who made it through did so by either barreling forward as fast as possible or by moving in short spurts when Chinese fire let up. The key to the latter strategy was the close air support the air force provided that periodically forced the Chinese to cease firing and take cover. Bradley remembered in a letter to an air force general, "It is my very definite opinion that had it not been for the closest cooperation and all-out help given us by your close air support we would not have gotten through that block in any order at all."[38] By the time the division's remnants reassembled at Sunchon the next day, it had lost around 5,000 casualties, sixty-four guns, and hundreds of vehicles, and had joined the list of other units the Chinese had rendered combat ineffective.[39]

No sooner had the Second Division reassembled than some surviving officers began assessing blame for the calamity. Freeman was an obvious candidate. Indeed, when the division's chief of staff, Colonel Gerald Epley, learned of Freeman's actions, he immediately sought out Keiser to ask if he had authorized Freeman to take the alternative road to Anju. Keiser said emphatically that he had not, but he later told Epley, who had no love for Freeman, to let the matter drop. Freeman and Keiser were friends, and Keiser concluded that no good would come of scapegoating. On the other hand, George Peploe, commander of the 38th Regiment, strongly believed that Freeman should be reprimanded for his actions, and there is evidence that Bradley felt Freeman deserved a court-martial. Bradley himself came under fire by some who argued that he should not have so impulsively given Freeman permission to use his best judgment to escape from Kunu-ri, though Bradley denied that he had in any way endorsed Freeman's decision. For all the finger-pointing within the division, however, others looked higher in the chain of command for culprits. Some observed that Coulter did precious little to support Keiser on 29–30 November. During the division's run through the gauntlet, Coulter was busy moving his corps headquarters to Pyongyang and did not seem to understand Keiser's plight. He failed to keep a close watch on the British Commonwealth 27th Brigade's activities, send reinforcements, and provide greater guidance to Keiser. Finally, Walker was oddly detached from the battle. By 30 November, the Second Division was the only major Eighth Army unit still heavily engaged with the enemy, yet Walker did not get involved, even though he was ordinarily ready to intervene at the regimental and even battalion levels if he thought it necessary.[40]

The most obvious scapegoat for the Second Division's debacle was not Freeman, Bradley, Coulter, or Walker but rather Dutch Keiser. After all, as commander of the division, he was ultimately responsible for its performance. Keiser had not been an especially successful or popular general before MacArthur's offensive went into reverse, so it was easy for some to blame him. Walker was among his chief detractors. Walker had questioned Keiser's leadership during the Pusan Perimeter fighting, and he had been appalled by the division's disorganization when he flew over it during its run through the gauntlet. A subsequent visit to Keiser's headquarters did nothing to restore Walker's confidence in him. On 6 December, Walker relieved Keiser of his command; Keiser eventually returned to the States to run the Infantry Replacement Center. By doing so, Walker no doubt hoped to put the unpleasant episode behind the army. Rather than fire him for cause, Walker seized on Keiser's health to explain his removal. Keiser had been battling a bad cold throughout late November, and after witnessing his division's ordeal, he was, as one surgeon put it, "more or less in a state of shock" that undoubtedly exacerbated his illness. The press attributed Keiser's relief to pneumonia, but a resentful Keiser believed that this was just a subterfuge created by Walker to get him out of the way. It was a sad ending for a man who had served his country honorably, but as one officer later noted, "That's the law out there— he got defeated so he got relieved."[41]

The same day that he and his staffers met with Walker and Almond, MacArthur informed the Joint Chiefs of the Chinese offensive and added that he now faced "an entirely new war" with implications beyond his immediate control. As the military situation deteriorated over the following days, MacArthur became increasingly pessimistic and erratic. He stated that the soldiers were physically and mentally exhausted, and that the South Korean army was now useless. Under current conditions, he said, he could not hold onto Pyongyang or even establish a defensive line across the peninsula's narrow waist. He also rejected the idea of incorporating the Tenth Corps into the Eighth Army as counterproductive and unnecessary. Finally, he wanted to bomb Chinese territory and negotiate with Chiang Kai-shek for the use of Guomindang troops on the peninsula. MacArthur emphasized that unless the JCS acceded to his requests for more resources and greater authority to wage the war as he saw fit, he was doomed to defeat.

At the same time MacArthur was seeking to make the Truman administration understand the stakes involved, he was also working frantically to elude responsibility for the rapidly unfolding disaster. He claimed that he had all along designed his offensive as a reconnaissance-in-force that had cleverly tripped the enemy snare, thus forcing the Chinese to commit their troops prematurely. Had he remained on the defensive, he argued, the Chinese would have had all winter to re-inforce their troops in Korea and would therefore have overwhelmed him in the spring. MacArthur explained in his memoirs, "I myself felt we had reached up, sprung the Red trap, and escaped it. To have saved so many thousands of lives entrusted to my care gave me a sense of comfort that, in comparison, made all the honors I had ever received pale in comparison."[42] Even so, MacArthur was depressed by this sudden turn of events, which translated seemingly inevitable victory into crushing defeat and cast doubt on the image of military infallibility that he had so carefully cultivated over the years.[43]

The Truman administration was equally concerned. The deteriorating military situation greatly alarmed State Department and Defense Department officials charged with recommending policy to Truman. Fashioning a proper response to the crisis, though, led to nothing but additional questions and problems. They rejected MacArthur's recommendation to expand the conflict to China because they believed that this would likely lead to Soviet involvement and World War III. As far as many Pentagon officials were concerned, the solution was to abandon South Korea to its fate and focus on protecting Japan, whose value everyone acknowledged. After all, Korea had never been strategically important to the United States. Because MacArthur had concluded that it was impossible to win the war on the peninsula under current circumstances, it seemed best to just get out under the best conditions possible. The question, though, was how to arrange such a withdrawal. Doing so without complete humiliation required negotiating a deal with the Chinese, whose cooperation could hardly be expected as long as they held the military upper hand. State Department officials, on the other hand, pointed out that forsaking South Korea, while perhaps logical from a cold-hearted realpolitik perspective, would do great harm to American prestige and credibility at home and abroad. For the Truman administration, the Korean War was turning into a hopeless puzzle that had no good resolution.

Some Truman administration officials also believed that MacArthur's mercurial, panicky, and contradictory statements prevented them from getting a clear picture of the conflict and making informed recommendations to the president. To them, this was symptomatic of his poor judgment. For example, his refusal to incorporate the Tenth Corps into the Eighth Army struck some as militarily unsound, if not downright foolish. As usual, though, the Joint Chiefs refrained from giving MacArthur direct orders out of respect for his long service and enormous prestige. Such deference was perhaps understandable when MacArthur was winning the war, but now there seemed a direct connection between MacArthur's decisions and the unfolding military disaster on the peninsula. After one early December JCS meeting, Matthew Ridgway, still serving as deputy chief of staff for administration, asked air force chief of staff General Hoyt Vandenberg why the

Joint Chiefs did not simply tell MacArthur what to do. "What good would that do?" Vandenberg responded. "He wouldn't obey the orders. What can we do?" An exasperated Ridgway exclaimed, "You can relieve any commander who won't obey orders, can't you?"[44] Ridgway would have been right had MacArthur been an ordinary general. Vandenberg, however, recognized that MacArthur's status as an American military icon provided him with a certain autonomy that the JCS had to tolerate. The reality was that removing MacArthur from his command was a political decision that could only be made at the presidential level. Unless the Joint Chiefs were willing to initiate a disruptive political and military brouhaha by asking Truman to replace MacArthur, they had to tolerate his intractability.

To get a clearer understanding of the military situation, Secretary of Defense George Marshall dispatched Collins to East Asia for a firsthand look. Collins arrived in Tokyo on 4 December and met with MacArthur and his staff for several hours. MacArthur reiterated the point he had made since the Chinese launched their second offensive: he could not win the war without additional resources and authority. Collins replied that there were no stateside reinforcements available and that the administration would not grant him the greater powers he sought. That being the case, MacArthur recommended that the United States get out of Korea under the best terms possible.

Collins then flew to Seoul to confer with Walker. Although Walker was ordinarily a team player eager to please MacArthur, he was probably unaware of MacArthur's current pessimistic attitude toward the war. Walker admitted that the Eighth Army had taken a pounding, but he also sounded surprisingly upbeat. To be sure, he doubted that he could hang onto Pyongyang or even Seoul because he lacked the strength to protect his exposed right flank. On the other hand, he stated that he could, if necessary, fall back to the old Pusan Perimeter and, if reinforced by the Tenth Corps, hold out there indefinitely. From Seoul Collins traveled to Tenth Corps headquarters at Hungnam on North Korea's east coast to talk with Almond. Gung-ho as always, Almond was confident that his corps could dig in there if required or evacuate without difficulty.

Collins found such positive testimonies enlightening for a couple of reasons. For one thing, they indicated that the military situation was by no means as dire as MacArthur believed, and that the Eighth Army and Tenth Corps could in fact maintain themselves in Korea. They also showed that MacArthur did not understand military conditions in his own theater. Collins stopped off in Tokyo on 6 December for another conference with MacArthur before returning to the States. MacArthur repeated his previous arguments, but he was now amenable to placing the Tenth Corps under Walker's orders and made it official the next day. When Collins reached Washington, his optimistic reports helped reinforce an emerging consensus within the Truman administration that the United States should remain in Korea and await developments. Lost in the shuffle, and implicitly abandoned, was any desire to reunite the peninsula under Syngman Rhee's rule.[45]

While MacArthur and the Truman administration debated policy, the Eighth Army undertook the longest retreat in twentieth-century American military history. Walker decided to evacuate Pyongyang right after he returned from his late-night meeting with MacArthur and Almond in Tokyo, and thereafter he made no attempt to stop and face the enemy until his army reached the Imjin River near the 38th Parallel. Doing so meant foregoing a stand along Korea's constricted waist, but Walker had his reasons. He had almost no knowledge of enemy intentions and whereabouts, and he had received little guidance from MacArthur. Moreover, North Korean guerrillas were active north of the 38th Parallel setting up roadblocks, ambushing convoys, and attacking isolated troop detachments. As far as Walker was concerned, his top priority was to save his army, and he was not sure he could do that anywhere north of Seoul. In fact, he doubted he could even hold onto the city as long as ROK troops were unable to protect his exposed right flank. When a worried Rhee asked for reassurances that Walker would fight for the South Korean capital, Walker could only respond vaguely that he was focused on destroying the enemy.[46]

Considering the unfortunate circumstances in which he found himself, it was unsurprising that Walker was a depressed man as the year came to an end, even if he tried hard to remain upbeat when, for example, talking with Collins. He was always conscious that he was on thin ice with MacArthur, and he knew that the defeat along the Chongchon did nothing to endear him to his boss. Furthermore, as he explained to Collins, he was leading a weakened and hurt army. The Second Division and Turkish Brigade were combat ineffective, as were all but one of the divisions in the ROK Second Corps. Despite his problems, Walker tried to accentuate the positive. Although he did not know much about Tenth Corps operations, he was pleased that the outfit would finally come under his command. He figured that once he got to the old Pusan Perimeter, he could eventually launch a counteroffensive. He searched for any evidence that his men were not beaten and took heart when some of them waved at him when his plane flew over them. "My Army isn't whipped," he explained to a journalist somewhat wistfully. "I'm proud of the way it came out of the offensive. And they will fight again."[47]

Walker may have been indomitable, but the same could not be said for a good many of his Eighth Army's American personnel, whose morale plummeted with each backward step. Although there was little fighting once they broke contact with the Chinese near the Chongchon, many Americans behaved as if hordes of Chinese soldiers were rapidly closing in on them to finish the job they had so promisingly begun. The scale and suddenness of the Eighth Army's defeat led some Americans to attribute to the Chinese army greater military prowess than it deserved. In fact, the Chinese lacked the motorized transport and logistical wherewithal to aggressively pursue the Eighth Army, and their losses had been enormous. Even so, many Americans had had their fill of the war for now, and they hoped that rumors that the Truman administration intended to abandon Korea were true. Some officers contributed to this defeatist attitude by questioning everything from the tactics used along the Chongchon to the original decision to commit American forces to defend South Korea.

On 5 December, the last Americans and South Koreans evacuated Pyongyang. By then looting and wanton destruction had gotten out of hand. One officer returned from Eighth Army headquarters with Walker's armchair in tow; he explained that he would have secured his fine rug as well had Walker not been standing on it at the time. A couple of nights earlier, a burning truck set fire to a huge ammunition dump on the outskirts of the city. The resulting explosions consumed an enormous amount of ordnance. Troops demolished large stockpiles of supplies, equipment, and ammunition because there was not enough time or transport to move them. Massive traffic jams clogged the roads south as the soldiers drove through the cold and isolated countryside. One man remembered, "At the end of seven days we had retreated well over a hundred miles. When we stopped I fell asleep immediately, in a cornfield next to the road, and when I woke up I saw thousands of infantrymen walking along the road, long long columns of them, retreating from the north."[48] Hungry and cold refugees hovered near the convoys, prompting another soldier to recall, "There were hundreds of thousands of refugees streaming south. It was the most pitiful thing I've ever seen. If they got within a hundred yards of the road they were shot. There was only one road to move Eighth Army on, and the road had to be kept open."[49] The road ended along the Imjin River, where the Eighth Army, shaky and demoralized, finally turned to confront the Chinese, who came up to reestablish contact around 20 December.[50]

For all of Walker's woes, he remained as pugnacious as ever. He was already thinking about launching a counteroffensive once the Tenth Corps arrived to reinforce his Eighth Army. On the morning of 23 December, Walker drove north from his new Seoul headquarters to Uijongbu to present a Republic of Korea Presidential Citation to Church's Twenty-fourth Division and the British Commonwealth 27th Brigade for their actions along the Naktong River the previous summer. Walker was an impatient passenger who did not like to wait for anything. Therefore, when his jeep suddenly came upon a traffic jam, he ordered his driver to detour around it. Unfortunately, the South Korean truck ahead of him had the same idea and pulled out in front of Walker's jeep. Walker's jeep hit the truck's bumper, skidded to the side of the road, and turned over down an embankment. Walker suffered massive head injuries in the crash and was pronounced dead at a field hospital a short time later. His body was sent to Eighth

Army headquarters at the University of Seoul campus and placed in the auditorium. Milburn gently draped the casket with an American flag and consoled Walker's son, an officer in the Twenty-fourth Division. Next morning Walker's remains were put in a truck and taken to Kimpo airfield for a flight to Japan. On 30 December, MacArthur, Walker's son and widow, and the diplomatic corps attended a ceremony for the general before his body was loaded on a plane for interment in the States. Walker's death came as a shock and surprise to almost everyone. Even Almond, hardly the most sympathetic or introspective observer, noted that the tragedy made their differences in personality and strategy appear insignificant. Walker was not the best-liked commander, but most of his colleagues respected him for his determination and toughness. Many commented on the incongruity of his dying in a mundane traffic accident when he regularly exposed himself to danger on the battlefield. One diplomat remembered that his death seemed to epitomize the irony and frustration of the conflict. Joe Collins, though, probably best summed up the feelings about Walker's demise when he called it "a sad and inglorious ending for a fine battlefield commander."[51]

Defeat and change were in the air that Christmas. Although the fighting had tapered off dramatically once the Eighth Army began its retreat from the Chongchon, the day-to-day wear and tear of war still took its toll, as Walker's death and Keiser's departure demonstrated. The day before Walker was killed, the Twenty-fifth Division's assistant commander, Brigadier General Vennard Wilson, broke his back in a plane accident that put him in a cast for several months. Both the 9th Regiment's Chin Sloane and the 35th Regiment's Hank Fisher were evacuated because of illness and exhaustion. Fisher had been a reliable Eighth Army mainstay since the conflict's early dark days, but more than five months of continuous grinding combat wore him out until he was "completely whipped." Before he left, he commented that he was simply too old to fight this kind of war. Sladen Bradley, the Second Division's assistant commander, also left, albeit not permanently, to recover from the shock and sickness brought about by his division's recent travails and did not return until after the new year. Milburn took over the Eighth Army temporarily while the Pentagon decided on Walker's replacement. He had throughout the long retreat tried to stay positive and upbeat. When the ROK's First Division commander, Paik Sun Yup, asked him if the Americans planned to abandon South Korea, Milburn responded, "We are soldiers. We will fight to the last even if it means surrendering our lives."[52]

As Christmas approached, it appeared increasingly likely that the Chinese would test this assertion sooner rather than later. Intelligence officers predicted another Chinese attack on Christmas Day, so the Eighth Army fed its soldiers their holiday meal on 24 December and braced for the expected onslaught. When it failed to materialize, everyone breathed a sigh of relief and tried to appreciate the holiday. A group of Twenty-fifth Division artillery officers went from tent to tent at division headquarters caroling to ease the homesickness that Christmas instills in people away from their families. They even called the no-nonsense Bill Kean, sitting in for Milburn at First Corps while Milburn oversaw the Eighth Army, and sang "Silent Night" to him over the phone.[53]

The Tenth Corps' Misadventure

On 26 October 1950, right after Pyongyang fell and the war's end seemed just around the corner, a plane carrying Bob Hope and his United Service Organizations entertainment troupe touched down at Wonsan's airfield to put on a show for the servicemen in the area. No one was around to greet them, so they walked over to an abandoned hangar and waited for twenty minutes until an embarrassed Ned Almond and assorted bigwigs and staffers drove up from the beach to explain that they had not expected them to land there. As an experienced performer, Hope immediately recognized comedic opportunity when someone updated him on the bizarre local military situation. MacArthur had ordered the First Marine Division to attack Wonsan with an amphibious assault, but the South Koreans had seized the city first on 11 October. Unfortunately, the North Koreans had laced Wonsan's harbor with over 3,000 mines, so it took the unprepared navy two weeks to clear a passage for the marines to land. While logistical personnel arrived overland to help transform Wonsan into a military base, the marines remained stranded offshore, killing time, until the navy gave the all clear. Catcalls greeted the marines when they finally hit the beach shortly after Hope and his entertainers deplaned. The situation had everything an astute comedian such as Hope needed for a surefire performance: absurdity, relevancy, immediacy, and a high-profile subject to ridicule. That afternoon, in a hastily cleaned burned-out hangar, Hope peppered his monologue to the crowd with references about the tardy leathernecks, starting with his opening line: "It's wonderful seeing you. We'll invite you to all our landings." Most of the audience roared with laughter. Some marines, though, did not see the humor and remarked unfavorably on the way they had been mishandled.[54]

Almond was inclined to agree with this sullen assessment. Of course, he did not believe he was in any way responsible for this fiasco, which kept an entire American army corps out of action for several vital weeks and consumed much of the theater's logistical support. Instead, he blamed the navy—or, more specifically, the Japanese crews manning some of the minesweepers operating under navy command—for holding up the campaign. Almond himself had embarked from Inchon on the *Mount McKinley* on 17 October, but he did not set up his headquarters on

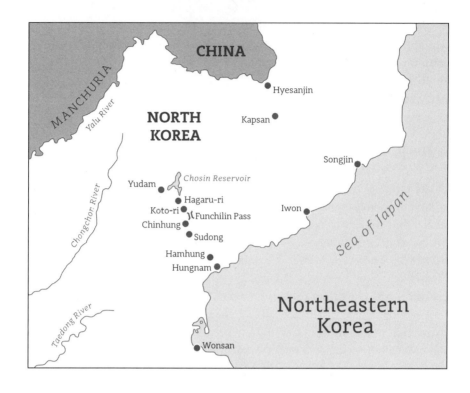

CHINA

MANCHURIA

Hyesanjin

NORTH
KOREA

Yalu River

Kapsan

Songjin

Chongchor River

Yudam

Chosin Reservoir

Hagaru-ri

Koto-ri

Iwon

)(Funchilin Pass

Chinhung

Sudong

Sea of Japan

Hamhung

Hungnam

Northeastern
Korea

Taedong River

Wonsan

Wonsan until a week later. Although many officers questioned the wisdom of sending the Tenth Corps around the Korean peninsula on a mission independent of the Eighth Army, Almond had overcome his initial doubts and embraced the idea. He concluded that Walker could not adequately direct the Tenth Corps across the mountains, so it made military sense for MacArthur to order him to act on his own. Besides, Almond liked the autonomy of independent command. Almond also persuaded MacArthur to assign Major General Kim Pac Il's ROK First Corps to him, giving him his own little field army of around 85,000 men. Almond believed that since the Inchon operation and the Eighth Army's Pusan Perimeter breakout had broken the North Korean army's back, all that remained of the conflict was the mopping up. MacArthur wanted Almond to push north and northeastward from Wonsan and Hungnam to the Yalu River in one last offensive to finish the war. Almond anticipated little organized North Korean resistance, but he figured increased guerrilla activity was likely as he approached the hydroelectric plants along the Yalu. Occupying northeastern Korea would require him to disperse his units over a wide area, but considering the disorganized and spasmodic state of North Korean opposition, this seemed like an acceptable risk.[55]

Almond had more confidence in his mission than in his Tenth Corps division commanders. Although he had nothing but praise for the leathernecks in the First Marine Division, he had serious problems with their leader, the taciturn Oliver Smith. Almond and Smith had clashed repeatedly during the planning for Operation Chromite, and the subsequent fighting for Seoul had destroyed whatever remaining trust and confidence the two men had in each other. As far as Almond was concerned, Smith was slow, obstinate, cautious, and borderline insubordinate. Indeed, Almond would probably have relieved Smith earlier if Smith had been an army general. Unfortunately for Almond, Smith's Marine Corps moniker provided him with an institutional autonomy that Almond dared not challenge.

To fulfill MacArthur's strategic plan, Almond wanted the First Marine Division to march from the Hamhung–Hungnam area to the Chosin Reservoir region preparatory to a final advance northwestward to the Yalu. Smith, however, was not so sure. The Inchon–Seoul campaign had convinced him that Almond was a loose cannon who did not understand the marines' capabilities and limitations. He had doubted the wisdom of deploying his division to Wonsan by sea from the start and was equally dubious of the newest scheme MacArthur and Almond had concocted. Smith believed it was foolish to disperse his battalions in winter over such a wide area in such unforgiving terrain, especially when enemy whereabouts and intentions were unclear. Doing so would also expose his left flank. Moreover, the marines were designed for amphibious assaults, so they lacked the vehicles to move inland very far or very fast. Almond had little patience for Smith's Cassandra-like concerns. He thought that the best way to learn what was happening to the northwest was for the marines to go there and find out. As for Smith's left flank, the Third Division's 65th Regiment would protect it after it disembarked at Wonsan on 3 November. Despite Almond's assurances, Smith remained unconvinced that the war was as close to over as Almond and MacArthur seemed to think. Still, it was hard to argue with MacArthur's strategic acumen after Inchon; as Smith put it, "Well, he got away with it there at Inchon, so he'll probably get away with it here."[56]

Three days after the first marine combat units splashed ashore at Wonsan, elements of Dave Barr's Seventh Division—specifically Colonel Herbert Powell's 17th Regiment—landed at Iwon, about 150 miles up the coast. Almond picked the spot himself after reconnoitering the area from his helicopter. When naval officers worried about mines, an exasperated Almond retorted that the North Koreans could scarcely have sown them along the entire coastline. Although Almond's concerns about the marines were limited mostly to Oliver Smith, he had serious doubts about both the Seventh Division and its leadership. The Seventh Division had been fleshed out with hastily conscripted South Koreans before the Inchon landing, and these men had not been successfully integrated into the outfit.

Charles Beauchamp's 32nd Regiment had played an important role in sealing off Seoul, but the division's other two regiments, the 17th and 31st, had seen little action so far. After Seoul fell, Almond concluded that the 31st's original commander, Robert Ovenshine, had not moved rapidly enough to secure the Suwon area, so he successfully pressured Barr to replace him. Almond was also displeased with the Seventh Division's conduct in subsequent training exercises, as well as with the excessive straggling he saw when the division moved overland to Pusan for its shipment to northeast Korea. Almond assured MacArthur on 7 October that the division was improving, but he continued to view it as a work in progress. As for Almond and Barr, their longtime friendship was wilting under the pressures of war. Almond criticized Barr for his division's poor performance in a formal letter of reprimand and continued to browbeat him afterward. On the other hand, he also laced his criticism with praise by, for instance, congratulating Barr for getting the division ready for future operations in a timely fashion. Almond seemed to think that if he was sufficiently forceful and energetic around Barr, some of these characteristics might rub off on his retiring subordinate.[57]

Barr for his part had a jaded view of both Almond and his new mission. He had opposed the seaborne assault on Wonsan, arguing that an overland drive from Seoul made more military sense. Once he reached Iwon, Barr, like Smith, worried that Almond was dispersing his division too widely. Unlike Smith, though, Barr possessed neither the force of personality nor the institutional autonomy to resist Almond's will. In fact, Barr was unhappy serving under Almond and recognized that Almond lacked confidence in him. Some observers felt that deep down, Barr shared Almond's reservations and that the strains of the war were eroding whatever reserves of self-assurance he had. Nothing exemplified the growing chasm between the two officers like their reactions to a training accident before the Seventh Division departed for Iwon, during which an errant mortar shell killed two of Barr's men. Barr was so upset that he was almost in tears, but Almond nonchalantly accepted the incident as part and parcel of war and ordered no investigation.[58]

In early November, the lead elements of Major General Robert "Shorty" Soule's Third Division began disembarking at Wonsan for service with the Tenth Corps. The Third Division was the last American combat division to reach Korea during the conflict's first turbulent year. The army had at the war's start gutted the stateside Third to provide replacements for other units either on the peninsula or on their way there but had since then gradually brought it back up to strength. Doing so included incorporating Colonel William Harris's Puerto Rican 65th Regiment and adding 8,500 South Korean conscripts, making the Third the army's most polyglot division. Although the 65th saw some action mopping up in South Korea after the Pusan Perimeter breakout, the division's other two regiments, the 7th and 15th, were still green. As for Soule, he was born in 1900 and commissioned in 1918 after spending two years at the University of Wyoming. Instead of fighting in France in World War I, Soule found himself stationed in Siberia as part of President Woodrow Wilson's quixotic Russian adventure against the Bolsheviks. He stayed in the army and spent a good part of the 1930s in China. There he learned to appreciate Chinese culture and speak the language fluently. He attended the Command and General Staff School at the end of the decade but not the Army War College. He spent the first part of World War II working on the General Staff and in the Transportation Corps. From there he led a regiment in the Eleventh Airborne Division in Leyte and Luzon in the Philippines. After becoming assistant commander of first the Eleventh Airborne Division and then the Thirty-eighth Division, he served as military attaché to Guomindang China from 1947 to 1950. His background in East Asia no doubt played a role in his appointment to lead the Third Division in Korea.

As his nickname indicated, Soule was a short, squat man who, according to one officer, seemed tailor-made for airborne operations. Although something of a character, he was respected for his sound judgment, determination, energy, and professionalism. Tough but fair, he set the highest standards for his troops and could be strict in attaining them. Soule thoroughly understood leadership, so he knew that, for instance, the best way to learn what was really happening in his outfit was by talking with the noncommissioned officers. His pugnaciousness meant that he was unlikely to back away from a confrontation or flinch in the face of adversity. Unfortunately, some alleged that he drank too much. One officer recalled, "He was wont to have a few too many martinis in the evening and his judgment at those times was erratic."[59] There was, however, no evidence that this interfered with his generalship. Almond was pleased to get the Third Division, and he intended to use the outfit to guard his left flank and clean out guerrillas in the southern part of his corps zone. He was unfamiliar with Soule but during the difficult winter grew to appreciate his abilities.[60]

As the Tenth Corps' various units landed, assembled, and deployed in late October and early November, they began picking up evidence of a Chinese presence in the region. Here, as on the other side of the peninsula, the South Koreans were the first to recognize the danger. The ROK Third Division ran into heavy Chinese opposition in the Koto-ri area in late October and made little progress. Almond pulled the division out and sent in the marines. As the marines moved in to relieve the ROKs, they confirmed what was already obvious to the South Koreans. One ROK battalion commander produced a half dozen Chinese prisoners for a marine officer and said bluntly, "This area is full of these people. We're convinced that they're here in organized units."[61] The marines, though, had a hard time believing that such bedraggled troops were part of a formidable coherent force. So did Almond. When he learned at the end of October that the ROKs had sixteen Chinese prisoners at Hamhung, he flew over for a look. With an interpreter, he interviewed each one privately, then put the group through close-order drill. The Chinese were obviously hungry, and some of them wore gunnysacks around their feet instead of shoes. They did not seem particularly impressive, and Almond dismissed them as a bunch of laundrymen. Although he reported the news to MacArthur, he did not think that these men represented full-blown Chinese entry into the war. Instead, he figured that they were volunteers the Chinese surreptitiously and informally sent to Korea to help their faltering communist ally. Besides, the air force would certainly identify and destroy any large-scale Chinese units attempting to cross the Yalu. In this Almond took his cue from Willoughby, who had reached a similar conclusion. Almond still felt that most organized enemy resistance in Korea was over and that his Tenth Corps would from now on deal mostly with pesky guerrilla bands.[62]

At that very moment, however, Homer Litzenberg's 7th Marine Regiment was engaged in heavy fighting with the Chinese around Sudong. The battle raged for four days until the bloodied Chinese suddenly broke contact and faded into the hills on 7 November. This, as well as the inclement weather and difficult terrain, gave Almond pause. Although he did not suspend his offensive, he agreed to Smith's request to concentrate his division along the road to the Chosin Reservoir. As November wore on without any more significant encounters with the Chinese, Almond's confidence gradually returned. On 18 November, he admitted that there were indeed Chinese units in his zone, but he still could not bring himself to recognize the implications. Instead, he concluded that they had learned their lesson: "I do not take too dim a view of the situation because I believe the Chinese Communists are fighting, for the first time in their history, a first class opponent and the punishment that we have dealt out to them has been terrific. This, I hope, will sober some of their aggressive aspirations."[63] As things turned out, it was Almond's expectations that were about to face the cold light of a Chinese dawn.[64]

While the ROK Third Division and the 7th Marines fought around Koto-ri and Sudong, Herbert Powell's 17th Regiment landed and assembled at Iwon. Powell's mission was to push to the Yalu while the division's other two regiments came ashore and moved inland to protect his left flank. Barr still worried about scattering his division too much, and he feared the kind of casualties it might sustain in the process. Powell was aware of the dangers too. He flew over the region Almond wanted his regiment to traverse and was appalled by the awful topography: "It is the wildest and most desolate country I have ever seen."[65] Powell noted the freezing cold, the bitter and cutting Siberian wind, the high altitude, and the snow. Moreover, the road Almond expected Powell to use was so torn up that supplying his regiment was bound to be difficult. Powell understood that he would be pretty much on his own, but considering the disorganization he increasingly believed existed at Seventh Division headquarters, did not think this was necessarily a bad thing.[66]

Sure enough, all the problems Powell identified manifested themselves as his regiment started northward in early November. The regimental column stretched twenty miles along the narrow road and was surrounded by snowdrifts ten to twelve feet deep. The tanks had a particularly hard time maneuvering. Powell complained that the air force had destroyed all the buildings, making it impossible for his troops to find adequate shelter. Fortunately, opposition was sporadic and light, though still dangerous. Powell was wounded in the leg in one skirmish, but he wrapped it with an elastic bandage and used a cane to hobble around. When Barr drove up to see how the regiment was doing, a North Korean boy threw a grenade at his jeep that luckily bounced off the windshield before exploding. The 17th crossed the Ungi River on 14 November, seized Kapsan after a fight five days later, and reached Hyesanjin on the Yalu on 21 November.[67]

No one knew it at the time, but Hyesanjin was the only point along the Yalu that a major American combat unit reached during the war. There was not much to the town. Air force bombing had destroyed almost all the buildings, and the population had fled. American troops dug in among old Russo-Japanese War fortifications and looked across the Yalu toward the bluish Manchurian mountains in the distance. The iced-over river was less than a hundred yards wide, so the Chinese soldiers on the opposite bank were clearly visible. No matter how mundane Hyesanjin was, its symbolic value still attracted the brass and press. Almond and Barr both showed up to be photographed, to congratulate the men, and to urinate in the river. Although Almond was pleased with this evidence that everything was going according to plan, Barr was more relieved than anything else. As for Powell, he was justifiably proud of his achievement. In less than three weeks, his regiment had advanced two hundred miles over a primitive road under difficult conditions, and at a cost of only forty-seven killed and 169 wounded. Back in Tokyo, MacArthur was thrilled with the news and radioed Almond, "Heartiest congratulations, Ned, and tell Dave Barr the Seventh Div[ision] hit the jackpot."[68]

While Powell's regiment slogged its way through the snow toward the Yalu, Smith's First Marine Division was also on the move. Even after the Chinese engaged the marines around Sudong, Almond still wanted Smith to march to the Chosin Reservoir to ascertain enemy strength and intentions there and see if they constituted a threat to the Eighth Army. Smith, though, was more leery than ever about dispatching his marines into the unknown now that he had experienced the Chinese army firsthand. Doing so entailed operating in incredibly rugged terrain, the Korean winter, and along one poor and vulnerable road. Almond assured Smith that the Third and Seventh divisions would protect the marines' flanks, but

Smith was more concerned that the Tenth Corps was not establishing a continuous front from which to operate. Almond was his superior, though, so Smith had to obey orders. Even so, he intended to go about it his way and, to the extent possible, on his own timetable. He used the apprehension generated by the first Chinese offensive to persuade a temporarily cautious Almond to let him concentrate his division along the road to the Chosin Reservoir. He sent two of his regiments to the reservoir against intermittent opposition but kept the third, Chesty Puller's 1st Marines, deployed along the road. He also made sure that the marines operated within the range of their artillery at all times. Finally, Smith ordered, over Almond's objections, an airfield constructed at Hagaru-ri and fortified several positions along the road—the soon to be fabled Main Supply Route, or MSR— from which Puller's regiment could operate, even though this consumed time and resources. Almond complained repeatedly about the slowness of the marine advance, but Smith refused to be hurried and continued to worry about what was up ahead. Defending his dilatory actions later, he said, "I believe that a fair consideration of some of the factors influencing the situation would indicate that the Division had considerable justification for its caution."[69] As November came to an end, two of Smith's regiments, Ray Murray's 5th and Homer Litzenberg's 7th, were at Yudam, about eighty miles inland and fourteen miles from Hagaru-ri and its airfield.[70]

Like their Eighth Army comrades on the other side of the peninsula, Tenth Corps personnel celebrated Thanksgiving with a big holiday meal. Almond invited most of his division and regimental commanders to dine with him at his Hamhung headquarters. Almond laid out a fine spread, which some appreciated and others thought was somewhat excessive under the circumstances. Despite the good cheer, though, Smith for one remained apprehensive about what might be waiting for his leathernecks west of the Chosin Reservoir. The next day, 24 November, Almond issued orders for the First Marine Division to attack out of Yudam with Murray's and Litzenberg's regiments to make contact with the Eighth Army somewhere to the west. When they did so three days later, they ran into heavy resistance almost immediately. That night the Chinese went onto the offensive. Marines and Chinese fought bitterly for the barren high hills around Yudam. Chinese whistles, bugles, and gongs echoed across the hills and valley floor as they repeatedly assailed the marine positions. Rifle and machine gun fire punctured the cold night air while flares illuminated the skies.

Smith set up his command post at Hagaru-ri on 28 November and listened to the battle's progress over the squawky radio net while rocking in a chair. However, the Chinese brought the war to him by unsuccessfully assailing the base that same night. Smith became increasingly concerned as Chinese fire gradually depleted his hard-pressed companies. Moreover, he heard reports that the Eighth Army was retreating, rendering his mission moot. After informing Almond of the situation, Smith on his own authority ordered Murray and Litzenberg to go over on the defensive, though the Chinese had in fact already put the marines in that position.[71]

The ferocious Chinese offensive caught Almond flat-footed. As some marine officers had observed, the Tenth Corps had no continuous front but was instead scattered across northeast Korea. As Collins later put it, Almond "was dispersed from hell to breakfast."[72] Fortunately for Almond, the enemy's reach did not extend much beyond the Chosin Reservoir region. Therefore, only the marines and elements of Barr's Seventh Division felt its initial sting. Almond's frenetic inspections kept him in close touch with his units, so he quickly recognized the scale and violence of the Chinese attacks and reported the news back to MacArthur. When he returned to his Hamhung headquarters on 28 November after pushing through a four-and-a-half-hour-long marine traffic jam on the road from Hagaru-ri south—he blamed it on poor marine convoy discipline—he received orders to fly to Japan for an emergency meeting with MacArthur and Walker.

Almond left immediately and reached Tokyo later that evening. The consensus among the participants was that the Eighth Army and Tenth Corps should abandon the offensive until a clearer picture emerged of enemy intentions. For Almond, this meant that the Tenth Corps had to pull back toward the coast. Almond was confident that he could do so without much difficulty, and upon returning to Hamhung, he wasted no time in implementing MacArthur's directive. He did so with a skill and decisiveness his critics sometimes overlooked, despite a headquarters atmosphere tinged with anxiety, doubt, and alarm. As one staffer remembered, "Emotions were running very high, casualties were high, people were cut off all over the place and heroic measures and wild schemes and so forth were floating around."[73] On 30 November, Almond summoned Barr and Soule to his headquarters to work out the details of his plan, then flew to Hagaru-ri to bring Smith up to speed. His basic idea was to use Soule's Third Division to cover the marine withdrawal southward. At the same time, Almond ordered the Seventh Division concentrated and brought the ROK First Corps, which had been advancing practically unopposed up the North Korean east coast toward the Manchurian and Soviet borders, back toward Hungnam. There were plenty of moving parts involved, but it was the only way to quickly redeploy the Tenth and ROK First corps into a position from which they could resist the Chinese onslaught in an organized fashion.[74]

Extricating Smith's First Marine Division from the Chinese trap around the Chosin Reservoir was clearly the trickiest part of Almond's design. To do so, Smith intended to withdraw to the coast down the MSR in stages, using the various fortified positions he had established earlier as temporary refuges for his leathernecks to catch their breath, resupply, and evacuate the wounded. The first step, bringing Murray's 5th Marines and Litzenberg's 7th Marines from Yudam back to Hagaru-ri, promised to be the most difficult one. Not only were the Chinese pressing hard on Yudam but they had also severed the road back to Hagaru-ri in several places, meaning that the marines would have to fight their way to safety. When an officer at a Hagaru-ri conference referred to the planned marine movement as a "retreat," Smith mused, "Well, really, in the tactical position in which we find ourselves, having to fight forward—in other words having to attack to seize our own MSR—but going 180 degrees from where we are now, this is really not a retreat, because in every case we must attack." Later Smith explained the situation to a reporter in a pithier and more headline-grabbing manner: "Retreat, hell, we are simply attacking in another direction."[75]

Whatever Smith labeled the operation, he could not mitigate the misery the leathernecks in the two marine regiments endured in carrying it out. In fact, when Murray described it to a journalist a short time later, he admitted that he never thought they would make it, then broke down and wept. The marines left Yudam on 1 December for the fourteen-mile trek back to Hagaru-ri. They ran into heavy opposition almost immediately. They relied on their discipline and courage, firm leadership up and down the chain of command, and superb air and artillery support to repeatedly clear the Chinese from their positions overlooking the road. It was so cold that blood froze into a pinkish hue before it could coagulate, saving the lives of wounded marines who would have died of exsanguination under warmer conditions. Riflemen seized one hill and ridge after another, and fended off fierce Chinese attacks. Engineers rebuilt destroyed bridges, often under enemy fire. Vehicles broke down, bringing the winding column to unwelcome halts. Finally, Mother Nature dumped six additional inches of snow on the moving battlefield. The marines could take some comfort in the fact that the outgunned, lightly clothed, and poorly supplied Chinese suffered even more, which did much to even the odds. The first leathernecks reached Hagaru-ri late on 3 December, and by the end of the following day, the entire column was secure. When one group of cold and exhausted marines arrived, a lieutenant called them to attention and yelled, "All right, you guys, square yourselves away. We're gonna go in like marines."[76] And so they did.[77]

On the other hand, those Seventh Division soldiers deployed along the Chosin Reservoir's eastern shore did not share the marines' good fortune. Before the Chinese launched their big late November offensive, Almond had ordered Barr to send some of his troops there to help protect the marines' supply and communications line from Hagaru-ri to Hamhung. The bulk of Barr's division was deployed to the north, so he hurriedly dispatched whatever outfits he could find to comply with Almond's orders and timetable. Most were part of Colonel Allan MacLean's 31st Regiment, but a battalion from Charles Beauchamp's 32nd Regiment went along as well. MacLean had been leading the 31st for only a couple months, and most of his men had minimal combat experience. However, Barr and others lauded MacLean's courage, aggressiveness, and energy. If anyone could quickly turn this version of the 31st Regiment into an effective fighting force, it was MacLean. MacLean's troops relieved the marines on 26 November and prepared to push northward. They did not get far before the Chinese assailed them in strength on the night of 27–28 November. Almond took a helicopter in for a look the next day and undertook his usual awkward efforts to raise morale, including the indiscriminate distribution of medals. He found MacLean cheerful and self-assured, so he left confident that the 31st could fulfill its mission.[78]

In the following days, though, the Chinese attacks grew in number and intensity. Barr flew in on 30 November but apparently offered MacLean little guidance. The problem was that by now Almond had placed everyone in the Chosin Reservoir region under Smith's command, and Smith focused more on rescuing his two regiments retreating from Yudam than on MacLean's deteriorating situation. Moreover, the marines at Hagaru-ri had their hands full protecting their base from Chinese assaults and had little to spare to help the 31st. With the road from Hagaru-ri to Hamhung cut, there was no way to rush reinforcements quickly to rescue MacLean. Almond found the situation first frustrating, then maddening. For the sensitive Barr, though, it was much worse. His inability to assist MacLean affected him so deeply that one officer claimed he came close to a nervous breakdown. Another remembered, "General Barr was in a near state of catatonic shock at the way events were running."[79] In the end, the Chinese overran and destroyed the regiment. MacLean was captured and died in captivity. What was left of the force tried unsuccessfully to break through to marine lines around Hagaru-ri on 1 December. Of the approximately 3,200 soldiers deployed to the Chosin Reservoir's eastern shore, only 385 escaped to Hagaru-ri, most by crossing the ice to safety.[80]

For Smith's marines, Hagaru-ri offered only temporary sanctuary. It was still more than fifty-five miles to Hamhung, and Smith wanted to go about getting there in his usual thorough and methodical manner. He spent several days evacuating his wounded via the airfield he had fortuitously insisted on building, accumulating ammunition and supplies, reorganizing his forces, and letting his tired leathernecks, as well as Seventh Division refugees, catch their breath. Doing so gave the Chinese time to deploy their forces southward along the MSR to impede the marine withdrawal, but Smith figured that the benefits of a short delay outweighed the risks. He was heartened by the marines' stalwart morale after their recent ordeals and increasingly confident that his men could successfully escape the Chinese trap. Almond felt the same way. Although he labeled the situation serious, he concluded that it was by no means dire and that the marines and soldiers should get through without substantial losses. Moreover, he set about evening the odds for them by bringing as many resources to bear along the MSR as possible to help the marines. Most obviously, he positioned Soule's Third Division in the Hamhung region to provide support. With his usual intrusiveness, he suggested to Smith that he abandon some of his equipment to facilitate his getaway, but Smith responded that he needed every asset he had to fulfill his mission.[81]

Smith conducted his retreat in stages, with short halts at the fortified bases previously established along the MSR. The marine–army column, 10,000 men and 1,000 vehicles strong, abandoned Hagaru-ri on 6–7 December and, after an eleven-mile journey that included a good bit of combat, reached Koto-ri thirty-eight hours later. From there it pushed through Funchilin Pass to Chinhung, picking up elements of Chesty Puller's 1st Marine Regiment as it progressed southward. Along the way, the tired leathernecks and soldiers slogged through the heavy snow, fought off repeated Chinese attacks, and blasted the enemy from one ridge and hill after another. Overhead, marine, navy, and air force planes machine-gunned, bombed, and napalmed Chinese positions along the MSR. The vehicular convoy's jerky, stop-and-go procession frustrated everyone and offered the Chinese a tempting target, but it also provided refuge for the wounded and frostbitten, although almost no one else; Smith insisted that everyone walk to keep warm except for drivers, radiomen, and medics. Engineers repaired the road and rebuilt bridges, including one three and a half miles south of Koto-ri that required air-dropped treadway sections and two days of work to span a twenty-nine-foot-long chasm. Refugees shadowed the column despite the cold and danger. With each mile, marine confidence in their ultimate success increased. Smith remembered sitting in a hospital tent at Koto-ri, listening to a group of singing leathernecks: "The very air had a lift to it. The column was dog-tired, but the men knew they were going to get through. We all had the feeling that we 'were in.' I remember that night at Koto-ri hearing singing in the tent next to mine. . . . They were singing the Marine Hymn and they were doing it in a spirit of exultation."[82] The marines reached Chinhung on the morning of 10 December, then pushed through Sudong to the Third Division's lines. One leatherneck recalled the incongruity of the scene:

> We raced down the road. It's amazing how all hell can break loose in one place and somewhere else nearby it's as calm as a summer's day. The armored personnel carrier I rode in pulled into an Army outpost about a mile below where we'd hit a roadblock. There was a lone soldier out in front of a little Korean house. The rest of his outfit was up in the hills.[83]

By the end of the next day, all the marines and accompanying soldiers were safely ensconced in the Hamhung–Hungnam beachhead. When Smith counted noses, he learned that the marines had suffered 7,300 casualties during their two-month sojourn to and from the Chosin Reservoir, though a good many of those were due to frostbite rather than combat. By way of compensation, the leathernecks gained little from their exertions and hurts except for their inclusion in a new chapter in Marine Corps lore. Smith was the last man to gainsay marine courage, but he admitted that their success in reaching the coast was partly the result of Chinese mistakes. "I can't understand their tactics," he said later. "Instead of hitting us with everything in one place, they kept on hitting us at different places."[84]

The First Marine Division was not the only retreating Tenth Corps outfit during those dark December days, just the most endangered one. Indeed, the bulk of Almond's forces were falling back to the coast as fast as possible. The ROK First Corps' two divisions had encountered almost no enemy resistance as they pushed along the North Korean east coast toward the border and were far removed from the Chinese army's outstretched tentacles. They therefore had comparatively little trouble turning around and marching to the port of Songjin, from where they were transported by sea to Hungnam on 9–11 December. Of the Seventh Division units not chewed up along the Chosin Reservoir, Herb Powell's 17th Regiment was the most exposed. The Chinese offensive overshadowed his march to the Yalu, transforming him almost overnight from military centerpiece to afterthought. Powell learned of the Chinese attack not through official channels but by listening to radio chatter from his divisional colleagues along the Chosin Reservoir. When Barr finally ordered the 17th Regiment to pull back to the Hamhung–Hungnam beachhead, Powell moved with celerity. Although he faced no enemy opposition, snow and ice on the poor road southward caused considerable trouble. There was no way to quickly repair many broken-down vehicles, so the soldiers pushed them out of the way and abandoned them on the road. This included a majority of the seventeen tanks assigned to Powell, as well as half-tracks, trucks, and jeeps. Powell was ashamed of the resulting clutter and later wrote, "It looked like the trail of a defeated army and it was most embarrassing to professional soldiers to see this in back of an American army."[85] On the other hand, Powell was proud that he got his bedraggled and unshaven troops out of their cul-de-sac with minimal casualties, and with their discipline and morale intact.[86]

Throughout December, more than 105,000 American and South Korean troops flowed lavalike into Hamhung–Hungnam and began fortifying the beachhead in the bitter cold. MacArthur flew in on 11 December for a meeting with Almond and his staff. Almond was his usual forceful and confident self; he stated that he could hold out there as long as necessary. After all, the ROK First Corps and Soule's Third Division were pretty much intact. With the notable exception of its 31st Regiment, so was Barr's Seventh Division. Finally, despite its recent ordeal, the First Marine Division remained a cohesive entity. All these troops, as well as the awesome amount of air and naval support available, made the beachhead practically impenetrable. Almond's subordinates were inclined to agree. Barr, for instance, told a reporter, "They may come in on us in force but we have a terrible lot of firepower concentrated in this small area now and we can just mow 'em down."[87] After Almond finished his briefing, MacArthur took him aside and informed him that he was incorporating the Tenth Corps into the Eighth Army. That being the case, Almond could not officially continue as both the Tenth Corps' commander and MacArthur's chief of staff, so MacArthur asked him to pick one or the other. Despite his poor relationship with Walker, Almond opted to remain with the Tenth Corps. He proudly explained later, "I chose command in the field instead of the easier staff job back in Tokyo, and I never regretted the decision."[88] Although Almond mourned Walker's death less than two weeks later, he also no doubt recognized that it made his integration into the Eighth Army's command structure easier than would have otherwise been the case.[89]

Despite Almond's confidence that the Tenth Corps could remain in Hamhung–Hungnam indefinitely, MacArthur opted to bring it back to South Korea to help the retreating Eighth Army make its stand along the 38th Parallel. Doing so necessitated the largest seaborne evacuation in American military history. The Chinese chose not to assail the beachhead, enabling Almond to focus on the innumerable logistical challenges that removing his corps entailed. Almond was determined to depart on his own terms: in a systematic manner, with all his weapons and equipment, and leaving nothing of value behind for the enemy. When naval officers complained that this would require too much time and shipping, he replied, "I came in like a soldier, I'm going out like a soldier."[90] To his credit, he also insisted on taking out as many of the thousands of refugees who had crowded their way into the beachhead as possible.

Hungnam gradually turned into a vast smoky swamp of slush and mud as thousands of soldiers and marines drove vehicles down to the docks and engineers set fire to empty warehouses. Troops boarded landing craft that took them to transports bobbing in the harbor's choppy winter waters. Because it had undergone the worst ordeal, Almond sent Smith's First Marine Division off first, on 15 December. The ROK First Corps left next, on the 18th, followed by Barr's Seventh Division several days later. Finally, Soule's Third Division, which had done yeoman's service guarding the beachhead, departed on Christmas Eve. Everything went smoothly, though there were some hiccups and close calls. For instance, while his 65th Regiment was marching onto landing craft, Colonel William Harris noticed a long string of boxcars on a nearby railroad spur. Peeking inside one of them, he saw thousands of artillery shells with wires protruding from many. Curious, Harris followed the wires to an unattended hand-generated detonator sitting on the dock. Had someone activated it, there would have been one less regiment for Almond to evacuate. Fortunately, no such catastrophes occurred. Instead, the navy brought out 105,000 soldiers and marines, 98,000 refugees, 17,500 vehicles, and 350,000 tons of cargo. As for the air force, it flew out another 3,600 troops, 196 vehicles, and 1,300 tons of cargo. It was an impressive display of the American military's logistical and organizational prowess.[91]

Almond was proud of his skillful withdrawal, but there was no disguising that it was in fact the denouement of an unsuccessful campaign. Almond's two-month misadventure to northeast Korea cost his forces 10,495 battle casualties. Of them, the First Marine Division lost 4,345 men, the Seventh Division 4,362, the Third Division 590, and the ROK First Corps 930. The Americans and South Koreans had very little to show for their efforts beyond the infliction of enormous casualties on the enemy. Considering the low return on their investment, it was unsurprising that many Americans were demoralized as they sailed southward and disembarked at Pusan. Herb Powell, for example, wrote, "I don't know what this war's 'all about' anymore, but the soldier's job is to do his part of the picture as ordered. I can't help but feel that our army should be out of Korea sometime soon."[92] Almond was inclined to share Powell's discouragement. He believed that the Tenth Corps could have served as a thorn in the side of the Chinese and North Koreans if it had remained at Hamhung–Hungnam, and he disagreed with the decision to evacuate. Doing so highlighted and confirmed a defeat attributable to his military record. Almond, though, was nothing if not resolute and looked forward to returning to the fray. Even so, the campaign had been as stressful for him as everyone else. After he boarded the *Mount McKinley* on 24 December for the journey to Pusan, he attended dinner, went directly to bed, and slept until the middle of next morning. His exhaustion did not prevent him from dispatching to his men a holiday message to remind them of the stakes involved:

This Christmas Day finds us locked in a desperate struggle with those who seek to destroy the principles and concepts without which life itself would have little meaning or purpose. The bitterness of conflict, however, will neither dim the luster nor lessen the spiritual significance of Christmas Day. Although separated from our families and loved ones, I am confident that our desire to defend and preserve our way of life will continue to give strength and courage to all so that we may pursue with unfailing resolution the ultimate accomplishment of that end for which Angelic Heralds announced, "Peace on Earth."[93]

Conclusions

Considering the changed environment in which he was practicing his chosen profession, Herb Powell's confusion and demoralization that Christmas was hardly unexpected. In two short months, MacArthur's forces had gone from the verge of victory to incontrovertible defeat. By late October, the Americans, South Koreans, and their allies had destroyed the North Korean army, seized their capital, and were charging hard toward the Yalu to end the war. Korean unification seemed just around the corner, and with it conclusive evidence that the United States could protect its friends and allies from communist aggression. Chinese intervention changed all that. The Chinese surprised and beat MacArthur's forces not once but twice, then drove the befuddled Eighth Army and Tenth Corps out of North Korea and back to the 38th Parallel. It was the American army's biggest twentieth-century defeat. To be sure, the army had failed on the battlefield before, but never with success so seemingly close and certain. Worse yet, the Chinese showed every indication that they planned to finish the job Kim Il Sung had started by throwing the American army out of Korea, destroying Syngman Rhee's government, and establishing a communist regime throughout the peninsula. Perhaps worst of all, in these new altered circumstances, American policy makers were unsure how to define victory, let alone go about achieving it.

The Truman administration was ultimately accountable for the American failure to detect and respond adequately to Chinese intervention. After all, it was Truman who ordered the invasion of North Korea and who disregarded Chinese warnings against doing so. This does not, however, absolve MacArthur for his counterproductive actions. He recommended crossing the 38th Parallel and discounted the possibility of large-scale Chinese participation in the conflict. In fact, his belligerent implementation of Truman administration directives by, for example, ordering the Eighth Army and Tenth Corps to drive to the Yalu River actually made Chinese interference more likely and potent. MacArthur later claimed that figuring out Chinese intentions was not his responsibility, but this ignores the intelligence assets at his disposal and the certitude he displayed in his faulty analysis of the information they acquired. MacArthur's inability to foresee Chinese involvement was due to a number of factors. For one thing, he trusted his intelligence chief, Charles Willoughby, who failed to sound the alarm in time. Moreover, MacArthur could not believe that Chinese troops could cross the Yalu in strength without the air force spotting and destroying them. Finally, there was a psychological angle. Recognizing and acknowledging the Chinese threat required a prudence that was not part of MacArthur's makeup. Aggressiveness had marked MacArthur's military actions throughout his career, regardless of his opponent or circumstances. Sometimes this boldness paid enormous military dividends, such as at Inchon against the weakening North Koreans. At other times, though, this forcefulness turned into a foolhardiness of which the Chinese took full advantage.

The inability of the Truman administration and MacArthur to foresee and detect Chinese intervention in October 1950 cost the Eighth Army dearly along the Chongchon. Even after these events, however, the American government and military still failed to appreciate the extent and implications of Chinese participation. Although the damage the Chinese inflicted on the Eighth Army should have served as a wake-up call for MacArthur, he continued to downplay and discount their involvement for the same reasons he used before. His willful blindness paralyzed the chain of command. From above, the Joint Chiefs of Staff remained disinclined to order MacArthur to stop his advance and take stock of the new situation. The Joint Chiefs were leery to second-guess the man who had almost single-handedly turned the war around with his Inchon landing. That victory in particular, as well as his long track record of military success, gave him a certain military credibility that was hard to gainsay. Moreover, MacArthur's stature as a military legend with long-standing political ties made the JCS wary of precipitating a political crisis by issuing him orders he might question or disobey. Finally, the Joint Chiefs respected the American military tradition of giving local commanders such as MacArthur considerable autonomy to fulfill their missions. From below, MacArthur's subordinates were unwilling or unable to raise questions about Chinese intervention or make overt contingency plans for it. Many of them strongly suspected that there were lots of Chinese troops in front of them, but they did not know what to do with their suspicions. Although MacArthur usually gave his lieutenants leeway to implement his directives as they saw fit, he was much less forgiving of those who questioned those directives. The result was MacArthur's disastrous end-of-war offensive.

MacArthur's response to the second Chinese offensive in November–December was, at the strategic and operational levels, sound enough. Once he understood the seriousness of the Chinese attacks, he summoned Walker and Almond to Tokyo for a conference. Had he been militarily obtuse, he might have ordered Walker and Almond to continue their offensives, which might have resulted in even greater losses than they actually sustained. Instead, he directed them to go over to the defensive and fight their battles as they saw fit. This no doubt saved the lives of many American, South Korean, and allied personnel who the Chinese would have otherwise cut off and destroyed. Both the Eighth Army and Tenth Corps therefore escaped more or less intact and were able to fight again. On the other hand, MacArthur's reactions at the policy level were much more counterproductive and controversial. He tried to rewrite history and escape blame for the debacle by relabeling his final offensive a reconnaissance-in-force designed to expose Chinese intentions and spring their trap ahead of schedule. He also overstated the damage his forces suffered to make the situation appear grimmer than was actually the case. This enabled him to use Chinese intervention as a club with which he tried to bludgeon the Truman administration into giving him the resources and expanded authority he wanted to fight the war on his terms. He claimed that if the Truman administration did not provide him with what he wanted, he could not win the war. By doing so, he placed his personal agenda ahead of his government's and called into question his military competence.

MacArthur's dysfunctional relationship with Walker also played a role in the Eighth Army's discomfiture. Walker may have been surprised by the initial Chinese intervention in October 1950, but he strongly suspected the presence of large numbers of Chinese troops before he launched MacArthur's end-of-war offensive the following month. He went along with it anyway because he recognized that MacArthur lacked confidence in him and might relieve him of his command if he expressed his doubts fully and freely. Instead, Walker used his authority to surreptitiously turn the full-fledged offensive MacArthur wanted into the glorified reconnaissance-in-force MacArthur later claimed he ordered. Walker's big operational mistake was not the attack itself but rather his placing the weakened ROK Second Corps in the most vulnerable part of the Eighth Army's line. The Chinese destruction of the ROK Second Corps threw Walker so off balance that he never regained the initiative. Once he got MacArthur's permission to fight as he saw fit, he broke contact with the enemy and retreated back to South Korea as rapidly as possible. He did not try to hold onto Pyongyang or dig in along Korea's narrow waist because he worried that he lacked sufficient strength to protect his exposed right flank. In the process, he failed to exercise the tight control over his units that had characterized his actions in the Pusan Perimeter. Back then he had directly supervised his divisions, but along the Chongchon he worked through corps commanders whom he trusted to oversee the evacuation of their units. This inattention to detail probably contributed to the Second Division's woes around Kunu-ri. Although Walker's actions throughout December appeared defeatist, he intended to initiate his own counteroffensive as soon as the Chinese overextended their supply lines and the Tenth Corps came under his control. His death, however, rendered his plans academic.

During the second Chinese offensive, Walker had at his disposal a complete field army. He went into battle with three corps (two American, one ROK), eight divisions (four American, four ROK), and several unattached brigades. Of the two American corps commanders, the more experienced Shrimp Milburn saw the least action and managed to extricate his First Corps without suffering crippling losses. On the other hand, Breitling Coulter had a much more difficult time. Although Coulter had run a division in Italy during World War II, he had never led a corps in a major engagement until the fighting along the Chongchon in late November and early December 1950. Walker had until then kept the Ninth Corps on the back burner because he lacked the resources to support it and because he did not believe that Coulter was as skillful a general as Milburn. Many officers later criticized Coulter's response to the Chinese attack. Coulter had naively accepted MacArthur's rosy narrative that his drive to the Yalu would end the war, even though some of his lieutenants warned him that there were plenty of Chinese in front of them. Once MacArthur's offensive went into reverse, Coulter failed to co-ordinate his headquarters with those of the First and ROK Second corps. Nor did he keep close tabs on his divisions. Critics claimed that this was because he did not get into the field enough to develop a good appreciation of the battle. He therefore neglected to use all the resources at his disposal to fight more effectively. In short, Coulter never demonstrated the kind of operational awareness and sure-footedness that enabled good generals to control events. Instead he was swept along by the Chinese tide. Had he possessed a better grasp of the situation, the Second Division might not have suffered as much as it did during its retreat to and from Kunu-ri.[94]

The performances of the Eighth Army's division commanders during the second Chinese offensive varied. John Church and his Twenty-fourth Division, on the far left of the Eighth Army's line, saw comparatively little combat and withdrew southward without difficulty. Hap Gay's First Cavalry Division was in reserve until Walker deployed it to safeguard Pyongyang and protect the Eighth Army's exposed right flank. Gay fulfilled his orders, but he could not do much to facilitate the Second Division's disastrous withdrawal from Kunu-ri. Of the Eighth Army's American divisions, Keiser's Second and Kean's Twenty-fifth divisions did the bulk of the fighting along the Chongchon. Although Kean labored under serious handicaps—one of his regiments failed to effectively engage the enemy and both his flanks became exposed—he still managed to extract his division more or less intact. As for Keiser, he bore the blame for the destruction of two of his regiments, so Walker relieved him of his command. No doubt Keiser was dealt a bad hand, but in a situation that called for more than basic competence, he did not rise to the occasion.

On the other side of the Korean peninsula, the Chinese also defeated Ned Almond's Tenth and ROK First corps. Whereas Walker suspected and, to the degree his authority and personality allowed, prepared for the second Chinese offensive, Almond failed to understand and appreciate Chinese potential. Throughout most of November, he accepted MacArthur's and Willoughby's argument that Chinese involvement was small in scale and limited, despite evidence to the contrary. Doing so reflected his loyalty to MacArthur and his chauvinism toward the Chinese.

Because he believed that the war was practically over, Almond spread his corps all over northeastern Korea. When the Chinese attacked in late November, Almond's corps was scattered in regiment-sized packets, without a continuous front. Fortunately for Almond, as well as the thousands of American, South Korean, and allied troops under his command, the Chinese focused most of their attention and assets on Walker's Eighth Army. As a result, the Chinese only had sufficient resources east of the Taeback Mountains to assail those Tenth Corps units—mostly the marines and MacLean's 31st Regiment, as well as some Third Division outfits subsequently committed to the area—around the Chosin Reservoir. Had the Chinese hit Almond's soldiers with the kind of strength they used against the Eighth Army, the Tenth and ROK First corps might not have survived. Once Almond realized the seriousness of the threat, he moved with skill and speed to consolidate his corps along the coast. With the exception of MacLean's 31st Regiment, the Tenth and ROK First corps reached and were evacuated from the Hamhung–Hungnam area more or less intact and ready to fight again. On the other hand, the Chinese armies in the region were so decimated by American firepower, disease, and hardship that it took them months to recover.

Almond owed his incongruous independent command at least to an extent to his rapport with MacArthur. MacArthur trusted Almond and preferred working with him to Walker. Almond, for his part, had nothing but respect and confidence in MacArthur. When the Chinese launched their second offensive in late November, MacArthur directed Almond first to go over to the defensive and then to evacuate Hamhung–Hungnam. Other than that, though, MacArthur was content to leave operations in Almond's hands. Almond's relationship with his division commanders, on the other hand, was not as smooth. He got along best with Shorty Soule. Although Soule played a limited, albeit important, role in securing the Hamhung–Hungnam beachhead and protecting the marines' left flank, Almond then and later lavished a disproportionate amount of praise on him.[95] As far as Almond was concerned, Soule obeyed his orders promptly and without fuss. Almond's respect for Soule did not extend to Barr and Smith. Almond had had his doubts about Barr even before the Seventh Division came ashore at Iwon, and his efforts to infuse some forcefulness into Barr through example seemed to backfire. The retiring Barr simply could not live up to Almond's high standards. Almond's problems with Barr, however, paled compared to his difficulties with Smith. Almond had repeatedly complained about what he interpreted as Smith's truculent and timorous behavior before and during the Inchon–Seoul campaign, and the fighting in northeast Korea did nothing to change Almond's opinion. After the marines were safe in Hamhung–Hungnam, Almond downplayed Smith's accomplishment in orchestrating their escape from the Chosin Reservoir. Almond had nothing but praise for the average leatherneck but claimed that the First Marine Division was never in mortal danger once the Tenth Corps focused its attention on the problem of extracting it from the Chosin Reservoir. The division's injuries, Almond later stated, were more psychological than physical. Whatever his other achievements, Almond failed to forge a harmonious corps command structure.

Of the Tenth Corps' three American division commanders, Smith garnered the most laurels during the campaign. Smith recognized the risks involved in pushing toward the Chosin Reservoir and planned accordingly. He possessed the character and institutional autonomy to do so despite Almond's objections. Once the Chinese launched their offensive, Smith led his outnumbered and trapped marines to safety in one of the epic events in American military history. All the things about Smith that irked Almond—his meticulousness, stubbornness, cautiousness, and independence—were the very traits that helped save the First Marine Division from destruction. Although Almond downplayed Smith's achievement, the rest of the American officer corps recognized and appreciated it. Matthew Ridgway, for example, later noted, "If it hadn't been for his courageous moral courage and doing some of the things he did, which were not in full accord with the instructions he received, why he'd have lost a great part of that division."[96] As for Soule, Almond was right to point out his credible performance at the Hamhung–Hungnam beachhead, but his contribution was comparatively limited. Finally, Almond's concerns about Barr were justified. Barr disliked the way Almond scattered his division, but unlike Smith, he could do little about it. He became increasingly anxious and emotionally frail under the stress of operations, and his disorganized headquarters failed to take up the resulting slack. The fact that he never had the kind of control over the Seventh Division that Smith had over his First Marine Division contributed to Barr's feelings of helplessness. Indeed, Barr never had the opportunity to fight his division as an integrated whole, which interfered with his ability to provide it with the leadership it needed.

Chinese intervention marked one of the greatest foreign policy and military setbacks in twentieth-century American history. American field army, corps, and division commanders cannot be held accountable for Chinese entry into the conflict, but they were the ones defeated on the battlefield. Although an increasing number of officers strongly suspected the presence of large numbers of enemy soldiers, they were unable to respond in a way that significantly changed the military outcome. They were trapped between MacArthur's insistence that Chinese involvement was marginal and that their obligation was to obey orders. Some of them did what they could within the limits of their authority to anticipate the Chinese attacks, but it was not enough to stave off defeat. Some of them made serious military mistakes—Walker's decision to deploy the less powerful South Korean divisions in the mountains opposite the main Chinese armies, for example, or Coulter's poor handling of his corps—but most of them fought competently enough under trying and confusing circumstances. Once the Chinese went over onto the offensive, American and South Korean forces made no attempt to regain the initiative but instead broke contact and retreated as fast as they could. By the time they reached the 38th Parallel or evacuated from Hungnam, they were a beaten and demoralized group of men.

5
Ridgway to the Rescue

A New Broom

On Friday evening, 22 December 1950, Lieutenant General Matthew Ridgway and his wife attended a get-together at the home of an old army friend at Fort Myer, Virginia. As the party was breaking up, the host summoned Ridgway to take a call from Joe Collins. "Matt," said Collins, "I'm sorry to tell you that Johnny Walker has been killed in a jeep accident in Korea. I want you to get your things together and get out there just as soon as you can." The news caught Ridgway by surprise, even though he had had a premonition a few weeks earlier that he might get sent to Korea and had gone into his attic and readied his combat gear just in case. Despite his wife's raised eyebrows, Ridgway kept the big news to himself until breakfast next morning so she could get a good night's sleep. He then drove over to the Pentagon to take care of some housecleaning duties before he left. He sent a condolence note to Walker's widow, picked up some papers, checked his will, arranged a salary allotment for his wife, and talked with Collins and a few others. Ridgway had kept close tabs on the war since it began, so he was thoroughly familiar with the current bleak conditions he would face as the new Eighth Army commander. Although he had hoped to spend Christmas with his family, Collins insisted that he leave as soon as possible. By the time Ridgway returned home, journalists and photographers were there in search of news. Ridgway eventually shooed them away so he and his family could celebrate an abbreviated and early Christmas dinner in peace before his flight departed. His last memory as he left home was of his baby son playing with a silver cigarette holder. Many of his friends interrupted their holiday schedules to meet him at the airport terminal to say good-bye. As his plane got off the ground, Ridgway took comfort in the confidence everyone expressed in him and looked forward to the challenge he was about to meet with "warmth and brightness" in his heart. Matt Ridgway was going to war.[1]

Ridgway embodied everything that the twentieth-century army strove to achieve in its generals. The son of an artillery officer, Ridgway was born in 1895 in

Fortress Monroe, Virginia, and graduated from West Point in the middle of his 1917 class. Although he hoped to fight in France in World War I, he ended up patrolling the Mexican border and teaching languages back at his alma mater. He was still at West Point when MacArthur became superintendent there. MacArthur took a shine to Ridgway and appointed him athletic director. Ridgway gained another powerful mentor a few years later when he served under future army chief of staff George Marshall first in China and then at the Infantry School. Because he was one of the army's few officers who spoke Spanish, Ridgway participated in an American delegation overseeing elections in Nicaragua from 1927 to 1930. After working as military adviser to the governor general of the Philippines from 1931 to 1933, Ridgway attended the Command and General Staff School (1933–1935) and the Army War College (1936–1937). He was part of the War Plans Division when Marshall became chief of staff and World War II broke out. Marshall remembered Ridgway and recognized his potential, so he renewed his relationship with him by taking him on a diplomatic trip to Brazil.

For ambitious midlevel army officers such as Ridgway, World War II offered a once-in-a-lifetime opportunity to make their mark and prove their worth. Fairly itching for a combat command, Ridgway parked himself in Marshall's office suite so often that Marshall finally barked at his staff secretary, "Tell Ridgway I'm tired of seeing him hanging around out there every time my door opens. When I have something for him, I'll send for him."[2] Marshall was as good as his word, and eventually he selected Ridgway as assistant commander, then commander, of the Eighty-second Division. The Eighty-second's conversion into an airborne outfit gave Ridgway the inside track to a prominent role in the conflict by making him a leading expert on airborne operations. He directed his division in the confused fighting in Sicily, then demonstrated considerable moral courage by strongly and successfully recommending against a foolhardy plan to drop the Eighty-second on Rome when the Allies invaded the Italian mainland. Instead, the Allies used his paratroopers to reinforce the threatened Salerno beachhead in September 1943. Ridgway and the Eighty-second fought so well in Normandy the following summer that the Allied supreme commander, General Dwight Eisenhower, put him in charge of the new Eighteenth Airborne Corps. Although two of his divisions participated in Operation Market-Garden, the unsuccessful British effort to secure a bridgehead across the Rhine River in the Netherlands, Ridgway had little authority over them and was mostly a frustrated bystander. On the other hand, he played a prominent and effective role in the Battle of the Bulge. Acting with a ruthless energy that increasingly characterized his actions, he helped secure the First Army's northern flank and spark the counterattack that drove the Wehrmacht back into Germany. He subsequently led his corps across the Rhine and into Germany in the war's final weeks. After Japan surrendered, Ridgway chaired the Inter-

Allied Defense Board from 1946 to 1948, became head of the Caribbean command from 1948 to 1949, and finally took over as deputy chief of staff. Collins was grooming him for the army's top spot when the Korean War broke out.

Ridgway was an impressive officer for numerous reasons. Strapping, hawkish, austere, and ramrod straight, he looked like a soldier's soldier. His intellect matched his appearance. He was highly intelligent, articulate on paper and in person, knowledgeable, and equally astute in the classroom and on the battlefield. He read Marcel Proust and Rudyard Kipling, and he kept in shape by chopping wood and ice-skating. He augmented his brainpower and physicality with a formidable personality. Observers noted his forcefulness, aggressiveness, and energy. Indeed, he seized the initiative as if it was his birthright. His frankness, alertness, and superficial affability all bespoke a man brimming with self-confidence and optimism. He possessed a thick religious streak that he combined with his abundant patriotism to create a nationalistic spirituality in which God and the United States worked hand in hand for humanity's benefit. It also served as the wellspring of his enormous physical and moral courage. Conversely, by the time the Korean War began, he was on his third wife, having divorced the first two. He expected the best from both himself and those around him. One staffer noted that Ridgway had a knack for giving people assignments that were almost, but not quite, impossible. Put together, he was the epitome of the alpha male. One admirer noted:

> General Ridgway, from the moment I first set eyes on him, had extraordinary daring, magnetism, and strength of character, and looked like my idea of a leader and an officer. When he walked into the officers' mess you could feel his presence. He had this look of eagles in his eyes. There was a certain vibrancy that exuded from him. He was broad chested and square shouldered. He walked with a bounce, and had a wonderful jaw and aquiline nose. He just looked like a fantastic officer. He spoke in lofty terms and said the right things. He was physically fit. He exercised, and he had a demeanor and a bearing that was very inspiring.[3]

Another person upped the ante by attributing to Ridgway almost superhuman powers: "The force that emanated from him was awesome. It reminded me of Superman. You had the impression he could knock over a building with a single blow, or stare a hole through a wall, if he wanted to. It was a powerful *presence*."[4] In short, if anyone was able to turn the Eighth Army's fortunes around, it was Ridgway.[5]

Of course, Ridgway had his share of foibles, blind spots, and weaknesses. There was a bull-in-the-china-shop quality to his behavior that sometimes made him appear overbearing and egotistical. He often treated people brusquely, could be overly demanding, and was intolerant of even honest mistakes. He sometimes judged people by their combat experiences instead of their actual capabilities, and he made snap judgments that were based on hunches and preconceived notions rather than an objective analysis of available information. He skirted the line between self-confidence and arrogance. For example, he once crossed out the phrase "with due humility" from a speech written for him, remarking, "I am not humble in this job or any other. I am only humble before God, but no one else."[6] Although capable of bonhomie and good cheer when it suited his purposes, he was frequently standoffish, self-centered, and moody. Critics pointed out that self-promotion and showmanship played no small role in his career advancement. Ridgway was likely to get the job done, but in the process he occasionally left behind a lot of hurt feelings and bruised egos in people whose help he might need in the future.[7]

Although his selection as Eighth Army commander caught Ridgway by surprise, Collins and MacArthur had designated him as Walker's successor during Collins's visit to East Asia the previous August. Collins later claimed that they did so because of Walker's habit of exposing himself to danger, but in all likelihood they were also making contingency plans in case MacArthur ever chose to remove Walker from his command. MacArthur had Ridgway in mind even before Collins discussed the subject with him, and Collins was happy to go along with MacArthur's thinking. Indeed, Collins greatly respected Ridgway's generalship. As Collins saw it, Ridgway's brilliant record, his familiarity with the war, his sterling character, and, not least, the confidence MacArthur had in him made him the perfect choice to lead the Eighth Army. When MacArthur got the news of Walker's death, he immediately phoned Collins and asked him to send Ridgway out as soon as possible. Collins issued the necessary orders after consulting with Secretary of Defense George Marshall and Secretary of the Army Frank Pace, then securing the president's approval. Collins regretted losing Ridgway's invaluable services in the Pentagon, but, upon reflection, he figured that it had always been a matter of time before Ridgway found himself at the point of greatest immediate military need. In a letter to Ridgway, Collins wrote, "As you know, I hated to ask you to take on these new responsibilities in Korea at this critical time. Unfortunately, one of the penalties of great ability is that it inexorably draws to itself great responsibilities. It was almost inevitable that General MacArthur would turn to you to assume command of the Eighth Army after Johnny Walker's tragic death."[8]

During his long flight from Washington to Japan, Ridgway mulled over the difficult situation into which he had been thrust, scribbling notes of questions to ask and issues to raise. The situation reminded him of the training exercises he had faced as a younger officer working his way through the army's educational system. The first hurdle to overcome, he knew, was located not on a Korean battlefield but rather in Tokyo. Ridgway was under no illusions about MacArthur. He admired MacArthur's forceful personality, but he also recognized his many weaknesses: his obsession with the limelight, his inability to admit error, his sycophantic coterie, and his enormous ego. Ridgway realized that unless the two men established a good working relationship with mutually agreed-on boundaries, he would be as hobbled in exercising his authority as Walker had been before him.

Ridgway reached Haneda airport shortly before midnight on Christmas and next morning met with MacArthur at the Dai Ichi building for a full and frank discussion. To Ridgway's surprise and relief, MacArthur was all sweetness and light. He was not optimistic about the deteriorating military situation on the peninsula, complaining that he was operating in a "military vacuum" without clear instructions—meaning instructions to his liking—from the Truman administration and the JCS. MacArthur asked Ridgway to try to hold onto as much of Korea as possible, including Seoul, and added that the way to do so was through inflicting massive casualties on the Chinese. Without a trace of irony, he also warned Ridgway not to underestimate the Chinese. Most important of all, from Ridgway's perspective, was MacArthur's pledge of full support and autonomy. No doubt MacArthur gave it because of the confidence he had in Ridgway, but he probably also wanted to minimize his involvement as much as possible in what he saw as a losing cause. When Ridgway, pugnacious as ever, asked if MacArthur had any objections to him assuming the offensive, MacArthur responded by giving him carte blanche: "The Eighth Army is yours, Matt. Do what you think is best." A grateful Ridgway noted years later, "That is the sort of orders that puts heart into a soldier."[9] Ridgway left Tokyo knowing that unlike his unfortunate predecessor, he did not have to worry about MacArthur looking over his shoulder and questioning his competence.[10]

With that flank secured, at least for now, Ridgway flew to Taegu to see his new army, arriving in the chilly late afternoon. An old friend, Eighth Army chief of staff Lev Allen, greeted him and drove him north to army headquarters. Along the way Ridgway reacclimated himself to the combat environment: ever-present dirt and mud, constant noise, crude living conditions, tents, trucks, refugees, and exhaust fumes. Never much of a headquarters operator, Ridgway, in his first few in-country days, went into the field to see for himself the attitude of the rank and file. He later explained, "I held to the old-fashioned idea that it helped the spirits of the men to see the Old Man up there, in the snow and sleet and the mud, sharing the same cold, miserable existence they had to endure."[11] By walking among them, driving through them, listening to them, watching them, and talking to them, he quickly ascertained that their morale was low and that a good many of them were ready to quit the war and go home. As one officer noted years later, "The skies were far from sunny. The Eighth Army had lost a very fine leader in General Walker; it had been beat up, punched around, disorganized; its morale was nearly nonexistent; its rations were bad. . . . Weather terrible, Chinese ferocious, morale stinko."[12] Ridgway rapidly reached a similar conclusion, recalling later:

> For my own part I had discovered that our forces were simply not mentally and spiritually ready for the sort of action I had been planning. Their courage was still high and they were ready to take on any mission I might have assigned. But there was too much of a looking-over-your-shoulder attitude, a lack of that special verve, that extra alertness and vigor that seems to exude from an army that is sure of itself and bent on winning.[13]

Ridgway undertook immediate and determined efforts to raise morale. He started with Rhee, whose day Ridgway made by telling him, "I'm glad to be here, Mr. President, and I intend to stay."[14] He drove among the troops in an open jeep so everyone could see him, striking a pose with his trademark grenade and first aid kit taped to the webbing of his combat vest. He listened to the men's gripes and moved quickly to address them. He procured more stationery, gloves, and rations, and he ordered kitchens closer to the front to provide hot meals. He assembled the soldiers into large groups and made it clear to them that he cared about their safety and well-being, and that he would not abandon surrounded and overrun units. Through it all, he emphasized that he intended to assume the offensive and that doing so required an aggressive mind-set. He reminded them that their superior firepower and matériel could compensate for enemy numbers. Nor did Ridgway ignore the staffers who did the planning and ran the Eighth Army's machinery. Although he respected Lev Allen, the Eighth Army chief of staff, he did not think much of the staff as a whole; he eventually marginalized much of it from his consultations and planning. At one army conference, he listened patiently to a briefing, then commented, "That's fine, gentlemen. Now, I'd like to hear your plans for attack."[15] In the ensuing awkward silence, Ridgway's intentions became clear to everyone. To another group of staffers, Ridgway explained, "All right. Throw away all your defense plans, I'm not interested in listening to them, I'm not going to listen to them. We're through going backwards, and we're going to kill them right here."[16] Changing attitudes did not occur overnight— some persisted in calling him "Wrong Way Ridgway," whereas others claimed that Walker had already started repairing morale before he died. However, in a remarkably short time, spirits began to improve. For this Ridgway could claim a good bit of the credit.[17]

Ridgway did not neglect his commanders. Indeed, he had the highest expectations of them. Ridgway thought that soldiers did not fight well unless they had confidence in their combat generals, so an army's potency was directly proportional to its leadership. Ridgway desired his fighting generals to be energetic, self-confident, optimistic, and physically and mentally tough. He did not want them operating out of their headquarters but rather in the field at the scene of the hottest action. As he explained later:

> Well to me, a basic element of troop leadership is the responsibility of the commander to be where the crisis of action is going to happen. He does not belong back at his command post, and I would say that goes right down the line, maybe not quite as far as the company commanders, platoon commander of an infantry unit, and certainly you don't want to be the lead scout. From the battalion on up, I think the commander should be where the crisis of action is, where the going is the toughest. He is not there to trespass on the sphere of his subordinates. He is there to drink in, by his senses and all his experience, the actual situation, the human element above all else. What is the state of feeling in that unit?[18]

Nor was he sympathetic to those who used their rank to luxuriate. For Ridgway, waging war was almost a monastic experience. He set a personal example by placing his advanced army command post with First Corps headquarters to save resources and manpower. It consisted of little more than two tents put together with a cot, sleeping bag, and gasoline heater in one and a small table, a couple of chairs, and a plywood panel with a relief map of Korea in the other.

Ridgway had been hard-nosed in relieving those commanders who did not live up to his exacting standards during World War II, and he was determined to act the same way now, telling Collins, "Let's be ruthless with our general officers if they fail to measure up."[19] Although he was not friends with most of his American division and corps chiefs, he figured he was familiar enough with them to size them up with reasonable accuracy. Within days of his arrival, he visited all but one of the American and ROK division and corps commanders. By looking the generals in the eyes, watching their postures, asking them tough questions, observing their gestures and mannerisms, and measuring the tone of their voices, he sought to determine if they possessed sufficient wherewithal to serve under him. Ridgway did not believe in removing an officer from his post until he had observed him firsthand over a period of time, knew the impact that his relief would have on his unit, and had a replacement handy. Because he recognized he could not fairly evaluate his combat commanders until he had seen them in action, he instead initially sought to build them up by extravagantly praising them in front of their staffs, even if he did not actually feel that way about some of them.[20]

As things turned out, Ridgway soon got the opportunity to observe and evaluate his corps and division commanders under the kind of difficult combat circumstances that separate the wheat from the chaff. On New Year's Eve, the Chinese launched their anticipated offensive. Unfortunately, the Eighth Army was not ready for it. Ridgway had been on the job for only a few short days, and the Eighth Army's redeployment from North Korea was not yet complete. Church's Twenty-fourth and Kean's Twenty-fifth divisions were situated north of Seoul, with Gay's First Cavalry Division in reserve behind them. The Second Division was still recovering from its Kunu-ri ordeal and was only now moving northward into position. In addition to over 5,000 replacements, it had also received the newly arrived French and Dutch detachments. Even so, it remained below authorized strength, especially in its combat units. Smith's First Marine Division was reorganizing around Masan, and Soule's Third and Barr's Seventh divisions had just finished disembarking at Pusan. As for the ROK army, its units had by no means recovered from their recent bloodletting up north, and were short of almost everything except apprehension.

The Chinese focused their attack on the seam between two ROK army divisions and quickly broke through. Ridgway raced to the threatened point, but he could do nothing to stop the truckloads of fleeing South Korean soldiers heading toward the rear. The sudden ROK collapse, as well as his continuing doubts about the fighting abilities of the remainder of the army, convinced Ridgway that he had to fall back, and he issued the necessary orders on 3 January. Both Milburn and Coulter agreed. Of the division chiefs involved, only the tough Bill Kean felt that the Eighth Army should continue to fight north of the Han River. Although Ridgway authorized a retreat, he made it clear that he wanted it done in an organized manner that used advantageous geography to inflict maximum casualties on the Chinese. The stickiest part of the withdrawal was getting everyone across the Han River. Ridgway gave the First Cav Division's artillery commander, Brigadier General Charles Palmer, authority over everyone in the area and told him to keep the bridges clear and the military columns moving. Palmer did his job so well that the army got across without serious incident. Michaelis's 27th Regiment served as rear guard. Michaelis set up his command post in a Seoul dining room and talked with Church. Both men had seen their share of desperate fighting over the past six months and were not inclined to panic. After scanning the maps, Church grinned at Michaelis and said, "We've been in tighter spots than this before. We'll get out all right."[21] As for Ridgway, he was ordinarily the last person to find any humor in defeat, especially one charged to his record. However, before he left the city, he tacked on his office wall a pair of striped flannel pajamas split at the seat and wrote above it: "To the commanding general, Chinese Communist forces—with compliments of the Commanding General Eighth Army."[22] The capital fell to the Chinese on 4 January, followed by Inchon the following day. In the process, more than 1.6 million gallons of petroleum and 9,300 tons of engineering matériel were destroyed. Having outrun their supply lines, the Chinese called a halt to their latest offensive on 7 January. By then Ridgway had established a new position about sixty miles south of the 38th Parallel along a line running from Pyongtáek in the east to Chumunjin on the west coast.[23]

Ridgway was disappointed with the performances of most of his senior combat leaders in the Chinese New Year's offensive, and he said as much to them. To Ridgway, they lacked the aggressiveness characteristic of good generals. He had expected them to conduct a dogged and stubborn retreat, but some of them seemed more intent on escaping the Chinese than fighting them. Their unwillingness to seize and hold the high ground, use all available firepower, and coordinate effectively with neighboring units was symptomatic of the defeatism Ridgway saw all around him. As a result of these half-hearted efforts, the Eighth Army failed to inflict the kind of casualties on the Chinese he expected. He attributed this faintheartedness to demoralization and the wear and tear of months of continuous action. Some of these men, Ridgway believed, were just plain tired. Although Ridgway planned to assume the offensive as soon as possible, he did not think this was likely with so many used-up officers running his divisions and corps. Ridgway wanted to supplant them with tough, dynamic, and energetic men whom he could trust, but was aware that doing so would humiliate those relieved and roil the officer corps. Fortunately, before Ridgway took over the Eighth Army, Collins had decided to start rotating senior commanders back to the States after six months in Korea. Collins figured that there would be no stigma attached to bringing these battle-experienced men home to train stateside units mobilized in the Truman administration's military buildup. Ridgway could therefore replace those he wanted to be rid of without controversy and fuss. MacArthur was amendable to the idea as well. However, Collins advised Ridgway to go about the removals gradually so the public and Congress would not question and lose confidence in the army's leadership.[24]

At the corps level, Ridgway targeted Breitling Coulter for replacement. Coulter had not impressed Ridgway much during the Chinese New Year's offensive. In particular, Ridgway criticized Coulter's inability to launch timely and effective counterattacks, as well as his willingness to countenance retreat. There was not much in Coulter's recent record to contradict Ridgway's conclusion that he was an ineffective general. Rather than simply rotate Coulter back home, Ridgway opted to kick him upstairs by appointing him the Eighth Army's deputy commander. He also got Collins to recommend Coulter's promotion to lieutenant general to soften the blow to his ego. Ridgway explained to Coulter that his primary responsibility would be to represent the Eighth Army to the South Korean government, which would require him to maintain an office near Rhee and his ministers. Coulter officially left the Ninth Corps on 31 January and assumed his new duties a couple of weeks later. His tenure as Ninth Corps commander had been undistinguished at best, and at worst a good deal less than that. Although he deserved credit for helping the South Koreans hold onto Pohang, he played a marginal role in the Pusan Perimeter breakout. Walker had claimed that he respected Coulter's generalship but did not give him any important assignments as a corps commander until MacArthur's end-of-the-war offensive. Along the Chongchon River, Coulter never demonstrated the kind of operational awareness a good combat leader needs, and as a result the Second Division in particular suffered heavy losses.[25]

Ridgway's autonomy from MacArthur and friendship with Collins enabled him to choose his own man to replace Coulter. He sent a list of candidates to Collins, at the top of which was Major General Bryant Moore. Born in Maine in 1894, the ruddy and red-mustached Moore was educated in France before graduating from West Point in 1917. He served in Hawaii and China after World War I and later taught military science at the City College of New York and the University of Illinois. Although he attended the Command and General Staff College from 1938 to 1939, he did not go to the Army War College. Instead, he learned how to manage large units on the job during World War II. He led a regiment on Guadalcanal, moved to Europe as assistant commander of the 104th Division, and finished the conflict at the head of the Eighth Division. His division was part of Ridgway's Eighteenth Corps during the advance into Germany, and Moore's successful transformation of the temperamental Eighth into a first-rate outfit impressed Ridgway. Moore became superintendent of West Point in 1949. During his tenure, Ridgway visited him and asked him if he would be willing to serve under him as a corps commander should circumstances warrant it. Moore responded, "I'd thoroughly enjoy it." Indeed, Ridgway thought the world of Moore, even though he recognized that they had very different leadership styles. Moore was as mild-mannered and taciturn as Ridgway was abrasive and forceful. Although devoted to the army, Moore spent as much of his free time as possible on board his big sailing yacht, enjoying the sea breeze and open air. Ridgway believed that the dignified, imperturbable, and thoughtful Moore could run the Ninth Corps with more skill and deftness than Coulter had demonstrated.[26]

Ridgway was as disappointed with Shrimp Milburn's performance during the Chinese New Year's offensive as he was with Coulter's, and for most of the same reasons. In addition, he admonished Milburn for directing the Twenty-fifth Division and British Commonwealth 29th Brigade to maintain their bridgehead north of the Han River at all costs. Ridgway believed that issuing such drastic orders was a field army commander's prerogative, not a corps commander's. Ridgway simply did not think that Milburn possessed sufficient aggressiveness, forcefulness, and presence for his job. Milburn was a quiet and low-key person not much given to tooting his own horn, so it was easy for Ridgway to underrate him. Despite his reservations, though, on Collins's recommendation, Ridgway opted to keep Milburn at his post. For one thing, Milburn was an old friend. Moreover, he had a track record as a capable corps commander dating back to World War II that belied his seeming diffidence. He was also popular throughout his corps, so relieving him might damage morale at a time when spirits were already low. Finally, there were currently no stateside positions available for someone of Milburn's rank. Years later, Ridgway summed up his reasoning: "Now I had one commander there—everybody loved him. He was brave, he was conscientious, he was loyal, but he was mediocre. . . . But I wouldn't have relieved that fellow for anything. He was a lovable fellow, and it would have hurt the whole unit."[27] Although Ridgway claimed that he placed his advanced command post with Milburn's First Corps headquarters to save resources, it is also likely that he did so to keep an eye on and light a fire under Milburn.[28]

On Christmas Day, the *Mount McKinley* docked at Ulsan, and two days later, Ned Almond flew up to Seoul to report to Ridgway. Almond's recent close call in northeast Korea had not taught him the value of prudence or dampened his spirits. Instead, he remained as bellicose and aggressive as ever, and he was ready and willing to reengage the enemy on whatever terms necessary. As far as Almond was concerned, the key to defeating the Chinese was to figure out some way to overcome their numerical superiority. He did not yet have an answer, but he was confident that Ridgway would. Indeed, Almond believed that Ridgway was just the man to lead the Eighth Army, writing his wife, "I think Ridgway's selection was a good one and I am sure he is a brilliant leader. I prefer him to anyone else who might have been selected. I hope that with us combined all in the Eighth Army we can do something effective, and more effective than in the recent past, to destroy the avalanche of yellow fiends."[29]

Ridgway had known Almond for years and was well aware of his strengths and weaknesses. Ridgway considered Almond a fine combat leader and had no desire to relieve him, but he recognized that his rashness made him a loose cannon on the battlefield. Therefore, Ridgway concluded that he needed to carefully supervise Almond to check his recklessness. Unlike Coulter and Milburn, Almond fully agreed with and enthusiastically supported Ridgway's desire to resume the offensive as soon as possible. For Ridgway, Almond's can-do attitude was like a breath of fresh air after the discouragement and pessimism he encountered throughout much of the Eighth Army.

Ridgway's big problem with Almond, however, was not his personality or generalship but rather his special status with MacArthur. Despite MacArthur's pledge of support, Ridgway understood that he could not run the Eighth Army effectively if Almond's relationship with MacArthur was different from that of any other corps or division commander's. During their first meeting, Ridgway apparently made it clear to Almond that he would tolerate no end runs or back channels to MacArthur. Whatever his less admirable attributes, Almond knew how to obey orders, and from that point on, he loyally supported his new boss. After their conference, Almond flew to Eighth Army headquarters and spent the night there. He discovered that most of the staffers were gloomy and demoralized about the army's prospects. Gung-ho as ever, Almond responded, "I have just joined the Eighth Army and I do not know the potentialities of its troops, but I expect to see that the Tenth Corps units fight the enemy wherever met and to retire only when forced to do so."[30] For Almond, flinching in the face of the enemy was never an option.[31]

Ridgway was more ruthless in replacing his division chiefs. In doing so, he had the support not only of Collins and MacArthur but also of the corps commanders, all of whom concurred with Ridgway that the army needed younger men for these positions. Although Ridgway wanted to make these changes as soon as possible so he could conduct operations as he saw fit, he heeded Collins's advice to go about the process gradually and under the guise of routine rotations home. When Collins and Ridgway met in mid-January, they originally agreed that Gay and then Kean should come out first because they had fought the longest. However, Ridgway ultimately opted to move Church's and Barr's names to the top of the list. Ridgway had been unimpressed with Church's recommendation that the Eighth Army retreat behind the Han River, and he was even more unimpressed with Church's obvious poor health. Church's arthritic back prevented him from getting out into the field much, and as a result his division was looking increasingly slovenly. At MacArthur's suggestion, when Ridgway relieved Church on 25 January he emphasized Church's accomplishments in Korea. In a letter to Church, Ridgway congratulated him on his "superior leadership" and his "brilliant employment" of his division under difficult circumstances. In fact, Church's record had been unexceptional. He deserved credit for resurrecting the division after the drubbing the North Koreans inflicted on it during its withdrawal behind the Naktong River, though his performance along the Pusan Perimeter was uneven. He subsequently played a supporting role in the Pusan Perimeter breakout and invasion of North Korea. The Twenty-fourth was deployed along the west coast during the two Chinese offensives and saw comparatively little action. Church's main contribution on each occasion was getting his outfit out safely and then keeping the escape hatch open for other units to do the same. Church returned to the States to take over the Infantry School, thus ending his direct role in the conflict.[32]

On the same day that Church was replaced, Dave Barr ended his tenure with the Seventh Division. Ridgway and others had noticed that Barr was clearly worn out and emotionally frail, and Barr himself admitted that he was frustrated with the conflict's indecisive nature. Despite their prewar friendship, Almond had never been completely happy with Barr's personality or performance, and he likely urged Ridgway to ease him out. Indeed, Barr's tenure with the Seventh Division had been thoroughly lackluster. Although he played an important role in the conquest of Seoul by getting his 32nd Regiment across the Han River in a timely manner, Almond had subsequently marginalized him because he lacked confidence in him. In northeast Korea, Barr sat on the sidelines while Almond parceled his division out in penny packets over which Barr had minimal control. Indeed, Barr rarely had the opportunity to lead his entire division in action. Because of this, Barr stood by helplessly while the Chinese destroyed his 31st Regiment along the Chosin Reservoir. The defeat took such a mental toll on him that some observers worried that he might become completely unglued. Barr also failed to establish a well-run headquarters, which contributed to his division's inefficiency. Barr might have proven more useful under a more accommodating commander with a lighter touch. Almond, however, tended to dominate everything and everyone within his reach in a coarse and rough manner that merely exacerbated Barr's resentful diffidence. At a farewell ceremony Almond awarded Barr the Distinguished Service Award and lauded his "exceptionally meritorious conduct," leadership, courage, aggressiveness, and devotion to duty, but he was no doubt happy to be rid of his troublesome subordinate. Barr returned to the States to run the Armored School at Fort Knox and, like Church, played no further part in the war.[33]

Ten days later, Hap Gay left his First Cavalry Division. Before he decided to relieve Gay, Ridgway first consulted with Milburn and some of Gay's subordinates. They all agreed that Gay was worn out and needed a rest. Gay apparently realized this too because he was amenable to a change that included a transfer back to the States and promotion to deputy commander of the Fourth Army. Gracious as ever, before he left for home, Gay stopped to see Lieutenant General George Stratemeyer, the head of the Far East Air Force, to thank him for what Gay stated was the fine air support his outfit had provided the First Cav Division. Despite his modesty, Gay could not help but claim that his division was as good as any on the peninsula. In fact, Gay performed credibly in his five months in Korea. Like almost everyone else at his level, he made mistakes during the retreat to the Naktong River, but he fought with increasing skill along the Pusan Perimeter in some of the war's most desperate actions. His division spearheaded the Pusan Perimeter breakout, then led the advance to Pyongyang. The biggest black mark on Gay's combat record was the destruction of part of his 8th Cav Regiment around Unsan during the first Chinese offensive. However, Milburn's interference prevented Gay from fighting the battle the way he wanted, and it is likely that he would have extracted the regiment had Milburn given him more operational freedom. In the second Chinese offensive, Gay thwarted Chinese efforts to sweep around the Eighth Army to Pyongyang, though he might have done more to support Keiser's Second Division. Leading men in combat requires making tough decisions, but Gay seemed to confront a disproportionate number of these situations during his tenure in Korea. These included blowing up a bridge over the Naktong full of refugees and abandoning efforts to save one of his battalions around Unsan. As one officer noted, Gay was certainly no George Patton, but he saw his division through some of the most desperate campaigns in modern American military history with a rare humility and devotion.[34]

Finally, on 24 February, the Twenty-fifth Division commander, Bill Kean, left the peninsula. His departure was the only one Ridgway seemed to regret, no doubt because of the combativeness Kean demonstrated during the Chinese New Year's offensive by arguing that the Eighth Army should fight north of the Han River. Kean was probably the best of the original Korean War division chiefs. There was nothing brilliant about him, but he was solid and dependable during a time when those traits were often in short supply. He fought as well as any of his colleagues during the retreat to the Naktong River. Although he fumbled the abortive offensive toward Chinju, he succeeded in protecting the Pusan Perimeter's back door by blocking two North Korean attacks on Masan. He played a secondary role in the Pusan Perimeter breakout, the invasion of North Korea, and the first Chinese offensive because of logistical constraints and the division's geographic location. His finest moment occurred during the second Chinese offensive, when his division maintained its integrity and retreated in good order in the face of heavy Chinese assaults. It is true that Kean was blessed with two good regimental commanders in Michaelis and Fisher, but throughout his tenure, he was also handicapped by the problematic 24th Regiment. After five months in the field, though, Kean was pleased to learn that Collins had assigned him to lead the stateside Third Corps.[35]

While the Eighth Army withdrew south of the Han River, Shorty Soule's Third Division finished unloading at Pusan after its evacuation from the Hamhung–Hungnam beachhead. Although Ridgway condemned most of his combat commanders, he made no attempt to remove Soule from his post. For one thing, Soule had not been in Korea for long and had not seen nearly as much action as Barr, Church, Gay, and Kean—and therefore had less of a record to defend. He was also fresher than the others. Perhaps not coincidentally, he still possessed that gung-ho attitude that impressed Ridgway, especially in comparison to the gloom and doom that so pervaded the Eighth Army. At about this time, Soule said to a journalist, "We can stop the Chinese on this line or any other line they tell us to hold. And if they order us, we will go back and take Seoul."[36] Ridgway did not know

Soule well, but he noted his competence and concluded that his previous experience in China would prove useful. Finally, Almond had approved of Soule's handling of the Third Division during the desperate fighting in northeastern Korea and likely vouched for him to Ridgway.[37]

The leathernecks in Oliver Smith's First Marine Division watched the Eighth Army's woes unfold from their assembly area near Masan. The rumor mill among the officers was that the marines would act as rear guard when the Eighth Army evacuated the peninsula through Pusan. Indeed, there seemed to be plenty of evidence nearby that the Eighth Army planned to withdraw soon: Korean laborers building fortifications, army officers searching for bivouacs, tanks held back, and so forth. On 30 December, though, Ridgway flew in for a visit. His stalwartness and can-do attitude made a good impression on the marines who saw him, including Oliver Smith. When Smith and Ridgway met at Almond's headquarters at Kyongju, Smith stressed that his division had done most of the fighting and suffered a disproportionate number of casualties in northeast Korea, so it was not yet ready for action. He also emphasized that he did not want to serve under Almond's command again and explained his reasons why. Under ordinary circumstances, Ridgway would not have sympathized with such concerns. However, he understood that the marines were a separate branch of the American military that necessitated more delicate handling. The last thing Ridgway wanted to do was jeopardize interservice harmony at this crucial time. Moreover, he recognized that some good officers did not respond well to Almond's abrasiveness. Finally, and perhaps most importantly, Ridgway respected Smith from the start. If someone of Smith's obvious caliber had complaints, then Ridgway needed to take them seriously. As a result, Ridgway promised Smith that he would not put the marines in the line immediately, and that when he did, they would not be subject to Almond's authority.[38]

Relieving the various division commanders was merely the first, and in some ways the easiest, part of Ridgway's combat leadership transformation. The more difficult problem was finding effective replacements. With carte blanche from MacArthur and Collins, Ridgway had pretty much the entire officer corps at his disposal. He resisted the temptation to appoint only battle-experienced officers of whom he had personal knowledge; instead, he also looked for men with good reputations within the army. To head the Twenty-fourth Division, Ridgway turned to Brigadier General Blackshear "Babe" Bryan. Born in Louisiana in 1900, Bryan graduated from West Point in 1922. While at West Point, he earned a reputation as a fine football player, and he later worked as an assistant coach there while Ridgway was athletic director. He attended the Command and General Staff School from 1934 to 1936 and the Army War College from 1939 to 1940. During World War II, he was a policy planner in Washington in the Prisoner of War Division, and at the end of the conflict, he was appointed provost marshal general. He got his big break by serving as Ridgway's chief of staff during Ridgway's stint running the Caribbean command. Ridgway was impressed with Bryan's performance and summoned him to Korea soon after Collins sent him there to replace Walker. Although Bryan had no combat experience, Ridgway concluded that he was the officer for the job. Bryan was a big, friendly man who enjoyed pheasant hunting. John Throckmorton later referred to him as "wonderful." Others praised his sterling intellect and outstanding character. Unlike the departed Church, Bryan got out into the field often, which not only set an example for his subordinates but also brought about observable changes in the rank and file. One officer remembered that after Bryan took over the Twenty-fourth Division on 26 January, the men consistently appeared clean shaven, kept their helmets on at all times, and wore neat uniforms.[39]

For the Seventh Division, Ridgway appointed as its new leader Brigadier General Claude "Buddy" Ferenbaugh. The New York–born Ferenbaugh graduated from West Point in 1918, was stationed in Hawaii and the Philippines, and attended the Command and General Staff School from 1936 to 1937 and Army War College from 1939 to 1940. During World War II, he worked as the Second Corps' operations officer in North Africa, as a Pentagon planner, and finally as assistant division commander for the Eighty-third Division. After the conflict, he served as chief of staff for atomic testing, ran Schofield Barracks in Hawaii, and led the Fifth Armored Division. Along the way, he impressed all three postwar army chiefs of staff: Dwight Eisenhower, Omar Bradley, and J. Lawton Collins. Although Ridgway approved of him, Collins apparently took the initiative to send him to Korea. Ferenbaugh was well liked and respected in the army for his informality and cheer. One officer described him as a "big rough, tough old fellow."[40] Another noted, "He was a tremendous man physically, with a great heart to match. He was a sincere, warm, and friendly guy. He was the kind of man for whom I would have fought and died if it were necessary for victory."[41] On the inside, though, Ferenbaugh was similar to the departed Barr in that they were both anxious men. Ferenbaugh worried incessantly about all aspects of his division, even to the point of losing sleep. Indeed, his new chief of staff, former 17th Regiment commander Herb Powell, learned that the best way to deal with Ferenbaugh was to keep as many nitty-gritty details from him as possible. Unlike Barr, though, Ferenbaugh did not let his fretfulness inhibit his effectiveness.

Although Almond had warned him beforehand, Ferenbaugh was appalled by the Seventh Division's disorganization and slipshod standards when he took over the outfit on 26 January. He immediately concluded that Barr had not run a sufficiently tight ship. Ferenbaugh and Powell quickly determined that the division lacked zip and responsiveness, and that its headquarters was amateurish, disordered, inflexible, poorly administered, and full of deadwood. There seemed little coordination not only among headquarters personnel but also with other units. With Ferenbaugh's approval, Powell undertook a thorough housecleaning that included relieving a good number of staffers. In addition, Ferenbaugh initiated efforts to improve morale among the rank and file. He circulated more movies, organized mobile PXs, ensured the prompt distribution of *Stars and Stripes,* and emphasized proper military appearance. He also organized several division bands—a regular one, a thirteen-piece dance orchestra, a four-piece hillbilly quartet, an eight-piece Dixieland jazz ensemble, and a novelty band to play European folk music and classics—and sent them to the front to entertain the troops there. As for the officers, Ferenbaugh consulted regularly with his regimental commanders and gave them plenty of autonomy to fulfill their missions. The soldiers nicknamed Ferenbaugh "Fireball" for his whirlwind reforms, and later an officer wondered, "What a difference between Barrs [*sic*] Division and Ferenbaughs [*sic*] Division."[42]

Whereas Ridgway imported Bryan and Ferenbaugh into the theater, he found Hap Gay's replacement within the First Cavalry Division's family when he elevated the unit's artillery chief, Brigadier General Charles "Charlie Dog" Palmer, to fill the role. The Illinois-born Palmer—his older brother Williston also rose to the four-star level—graduated from West Point in 1924. He attended the Command and General Staff School from 1937 to 1938, but not the Army War College. He was deployed in the British West Indies when the United States entered World War II, but he made his mark as General Edward Brooks's chief of staff when Brooks served in Europe first as Second Armored Division commander and then as head of the Sixth Corps. When the Korean War began, Palmer was leading the First Cav Division's artillery, and in this role, he saw considerable action up and down the peninsula. Ridgway knew Palmer by his good reputation, which prompted him to put Palmer in charge of keeping the bridges over the Han River open and the military traffic moving across them during the Chinese New Year's offensive. As Ridgway explained later, "I had not served with him before, but I knew he would carry out my instructions."[43] Ridgway originally slated Palmer to take over the Twenty-fourth Division, but he shifted him to the First Cav Division instead. Palmer was well regarded throughout the army for his even temper, strict discipline, and ability to get things done without drama or fuss. As one put it, "Charlie Palmer was a top-notch man. He's absolutely marvelous."[44] The First Cav Division had always had a reputation as a spit-and-polish outfit, so Palmer had little difficulty keeping it up to snuff.[45]

Finally, Ridgway selected Brigadier General Joseph Sladen Bradley to replace Bill Kean as head of the Twenty-fifth Division. Born in Washington State in 1900, Bradley graduated from West Point in 1918 and was subsequently stationed in the

Philippines and China. He attended the Command and General Staff School from 1936 to 1937 and was an instructor at the Infantry School when World War II began. He compiled an enviable combat record during the conflict as a chief of staff and regimental commander in the Thirty-second Division in the Southwest Pacific. After Japan surrendered, Bradley served in the Mariana Islands and back at the Infantry School, then went to Korea as the Second Division's assistant commander. Although he survived the division's horrific retreat from Kunu-ri, he was hospitalized for illness and shock. Ridgway appointed him assistant commander of the Twenty-fifth Division after Vennard Wilson injured his back in a plane accident, and from there he ascended to the division's top spot.

Opinions about Bradley varied. Some extolled him as a courageous leader who knew a lot about combat in practice and theory, never shirked his responsibilities, met issues squarely and resolutely, and ran a by-the-book outfit. Dogged, feisty, and determined, Bradley stayed close to the scene of hottest action to make the tough decisions; at one point during the fighting in the Pusan Perimeter, he even entered battle wearing a T-shirt. At the same time, though, he knew how to delegate authority. On the other hand, some observers focused on Bradley's less admirable character traits. He was an intensely ambitious man who practically ached to run his own division, and he exhibited an off-putting pretentiousness to secure one. For instance, when he discovered that Keiser had been relieved of his Second Division command, he said to a group of assembled officers at morning mess, "Gentlemen, I have just learned that General Keiser is being relieved as commander of the division. I want that command. I deserve it. Now each of you must know something to do that will help me. What do you suggest?"[46] He tended to shoot from the hip, so his decisiveness sometimes might be more accurately described as impulsiveness. Indeed, he often reacted so emotionally under stress that he seemed erratic and borderline irrational. Small wonder that some questioned his intelligence. Finally, Bradley suffered from hepatitis and occasionally became violently ill before battles. He tried to hide his bouts of sickness by holing up in his trailer until he felt better, which prevented him from closely overseeing his division. Ridgway either did not know of or chose to overlook these flaws. As he saw things, Bradley was just the kind of hardworking and combat-experienced officer the Twenty-fifth Division needed at its helm for the battles yet to come.[47]

Ridgway not only replaced half of his division and corps commanders but he did so without provoking the backlash from the public, Congress, or the officer corps that Collins and others feared. He succeeded by making the changes gradually over a period of four weeks, and by portraying them as routine assignments, not demotions. Indeed, *Time* magazine reported in early March 1951: "Nearly all of the old command teams are back in the US for jobs of first importance: applying battle experience gained in Korea to the training of the expanding army at home."[48] The new commanders were a homogeneous group in some ways but disparate in others. All were West Pointers whose graduation from the Command and General Staff School in the 1930s indicated that the army had marked them as future leaders. World War II, however, prevented three of them—Bryan, Ferenbaugh, and Moore—from attending the Army War College. They were somewhat younger than their predecessors, averaging around fifty years of age. Four of the five had combat experience in World War II or Korea, but Bryan and Ferenbaugh had not previously led large units under fire. Bradley and Palmer were already in Korea; Ridgway transferred in the rest. Although Ridgway was familiar with some of them before he took over the Eighth Army, others he knew only by reputation. Most important of all, Ridgway believed that all these men met his requirements for combat leaders. He felt that they all possessed the positive attitude, competence, aggressiveness, and sturdiness he needed to carry out his plans.

The quality of Ridgway's division and corps commanders was irrelevant unless he developed an effective strategy with which to wage the war. As MacArthur noted during his first meeting with Ridgway, the problem was that the Eighth Army was operating in a mission vacuum. Chinese intervention had thrown the Truman administration's Korea policy into a disarray that policy makers were only now starting to sort out. By the time Ridgway reached Korea, though, a consensus was starting to emerge that whatever else the United States did in the region, it should at a minimum try to preserve South Korea's independence. This was something with which MacArthur could agree. Mulling things over, Ridgway concluded that the key to protecting South Korea was to defeat the Chinese and North Korean armies on the battlefield by killing as many of their soldiers as possible. As he saw it, seizing territory was irrelevant except to the extent that it facilitated the destruction of enemy forces. One British officer pithily stated, "Ridgway's interests are homicidal and not geographical."[49] Doing so would give the United States the upper hand in the negotiations that would be necessary to end the conflict short of total victory.[50]

Ridgway believed that the first step to accomplish this was for the Eighth Army to establish a solid and cohesive line from which to fight and maneuver. Once it did this, it could use its massive firepower to decimate the enemy's ranks. If the Chinese and North Koreans assailed the Eighth Army in their nighttime attacks, Ridgway planned to button down his men in prepared positions until the sun came up. Then the Eighth Army could employ its artillery, air support, and armor to rescue surrounded units and obliterate enemy troops who had penetrated its lines. After the Chinese and North Koreans had shot their bolt, Ridgway intended to assume the offensive in a methodical, deliberate, and systematic manner that took full advantage of the Eighth Army's mobility, firepower, and logistics. He did not plan on bypassing any enemy troops but rather to sweep them up as his army advanced. To do so, he expected his men to get off the roads and up in the hills: "You must dominate the heights before you can operate in the valleys. We have neglected that principle at times and have paid through the nose."[51] The more territory the enemy tried to hold, the easier it would be for the Eighth Army to locate and crush its soldiers in the kind of numbers Ridgway wanted. In essence, Ridgway aimed to apply the twentieth-century army doctrine of annihilation to the peninsula, albeit in the seemingly unusual context of a limited war. This would force the Chinese and North Koreans to fight on his terms. Ridgway summed it up by stating, "Find them! Fix them! Fight them! Finish them!" His men, though, dubbed it the meat-grinder strategy.[52]

After stopping in Tokyo to see MacArthur, on 15 January, Collins and air force chief of staff General Hoyt Vandenberg flew into Taegu to check up on Ridgway. For three days, Collins and Ridgway toured the rear areas and reviewed the military situation. They also finalized plans for rotating the division commanders out of the theater and discussed their replacements. Collins was pleased and reassured with what he saw. With the notable exception of the South Korean army, Ridgway seemed to have infused into the Eighth Army some of his can-do attitude. Ridgway believed that, barring something drastic such as Soviet intervention, he could hold out in Korea for at least three months. Collins breathed a sigh of relief because this offered the Truman administration a reasonable third option between evacuating the peninsula and expanding the war into China. At a press conference, Collins summed up his feeling by stating, "There is no shadow of a doubt in my mind that the Eighth Army can take care of itself."[53] However, for all the optimism that the meetings generated, the fact was that the Eighth Army had yet to prove that it could defeat the Chinese in battle.[54]

Fight for the Central Corridor

While the Chinese overran Seoul, revitalized North Korean units filtered into South Korea through the Taebaek Mountains and started cooperating with the local guerrillas. In doing so, they threatened to unravel Ridgway's new line before the Eighth Army had even settled in. Ridgway recognized that the three weak, poorly equipped, and demoralized ROK divisions in the vicinity lacked the strength to resist North Korean pressure for long, so he moved quickly to remedy the problem by dispatching the Second Division there. It was not an easy assignment. The region possessed few of the roads on which the mechanized Americans relied, and heavy snows made fighting in the mountains a miserable experience. Moreover, the Second Division was still recovering from its horrific experience at Kunu-ri, and its new commander, Major General Robert B. McClure, had been at his job for less than a month. Ridgway, though, felt that he had little choice if he wanted to keep the central part of South Korea out of enemy hands. He assigned the Second Division and the various ROK outfits in the area to Almond's Tenth Corps, and he directed Almond to make his stand at Wonju, a village at the center of the local road network.

Born in Georgia in 1896, McClure entered the army after washing out of the naval academy in 1916. He secured a commission, fought bravely in France in World War I, and decided to make the army his career. He became fluent in Chinese during two tours of duty in Tientsin from 1927 to 1933, and he later attended both the Command and General Staff School (1934–1936) and the Army War College (1938–1939). While at the Army War College, he met and impressed Collins, who was one of his instructors. When Collins was appointed head of the Twenty-fifth Division in 1942, he discovered McClure there working as a staffer. Collins took McClure under his wing and elevated him first to regimental command and then to assistant division commander. In these roles, McClure saw action on Guadalcanal and New Georgia in the Solomon Islands. Later he was put in charge of the Americal Division and led it through the fighting on Bougainville. At one point, he remarked that the "smell of a dead Jap is perfume to my nostrils."[55] When the war ended, he was back in China serving as chief of staff to Lieutenant General Albert Wedemeyer, chief of the American military mission there. McClure later trained Guomindang forces during their losing struggle with the communists, then was stationed in the Mariana Islands. McClure's familiarity with China, extensive combat experience, and personal relationship with Collins no doubt accounted for Collins's decision to dispatch him to Korea to succeed Keiser.

McClure had the unenviable task of putting together a division maimed in both body and spirit. The physical damage could be remedied by resupplying, reequipping, and reinforcing the outfit, but the psychological injuries were more intractable. The division's officer corps had seen an unusual amount of dissension even before it arrived in Korea, and the controversy surrounding the Kunu-ri battle had done nothing to dampen it. Nevertheless, McClure did what he could. Nicknamed "Uncle Bob," he was an outspoken, ruddy, stocky, and homespun man who enjoyed golf. He came into the division with a good reputation, and Paul Freeman later claimed he was a fine tactician. Some were less impressed. The division's chief of staff, Gerald Epley, concluded that McClure lacked the necessary intelligence for his new job. Others disapproved of his order for all division personnel to grow beards so they could easily differentiate themselves from the Chinese during their nighttime attacks. Worst of all, though, was evidence that McClure drank too much in an effort to steady his nerves. Army historian S. L. A. Marshall recalled talking with a slightly inebriated McClure shortly after he as-

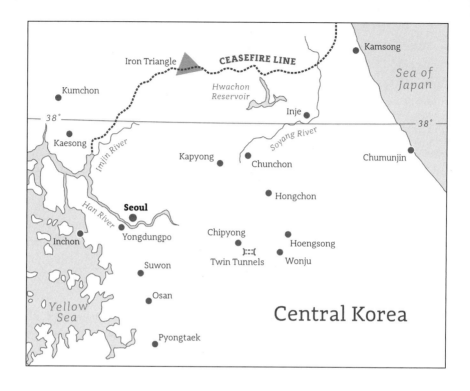

Central Korea

sumed command of the Second Division. McClure stated that he had been shocked to receive orders for Korea and admitted that he was not fit for his new post: "I can only brace myself by hitting the bottle. I'll be doing a lot of drinking."[56] That Collins would appoint such a man to such a critically important position is not as shocking as the fact that he evidently suspected these problems yet assigned McClure to lead the Second Division anyway.[57]

Almond and McClure clashed from the start. Almond was a hard-driving officer to begin with, but his intensity was no doubt heightened by his desire to impress his new boss and the seriousness of the current military situation. In early January, at the same time as the Chinese army was pushing toward Seoul, North Korean forces shattered ROK units north of Wonju. Although the Third and Seventh divisions were moving up to the Second Division's left and right, respectively, they were not yet in position. The Second Division was therefore exposed in its Wonju salient. In their first meeting, Almond was disturbed by McClure's unshaven and slovenly appearance and by the whiskey on his breath. Moreover, the two men argued heatedly over the disposition of American and ROK troops in the area. McClure wanted to intersperse them, but Almond insisted on keeping them separate because he believed that the South Koreans would probably fold under pressure. Even after Almond issued a direct order to McClure to segregate the two nationalities, McClure continued to kvetch. Almond was so unhappy with McClure that he left his operations officer behind at Second Division headquarters to keep an eye on him.[58]

Almond's already shaky relationship with McClure quickly deteriorated. The two men bickered over the best way to conduct operations around Wonju. McClure believed that holding onto the town was militarily unsound. He thought that the local topography was unsuited for defensive warfare and that remaining there would expose his division to enemy assaults on both flanks. Moreover, persistent guerrilla activity and heavy snowfall made resupply efforts difficult. The bad weather also inhibited the air support on which the infantry so heavily depended. Finally, there was a defile south of Wonju, and McClure worried that retreating through it, if and when it came to that, would invite the kind of enemy attacks that brought the division so much grief at the gauntlet south of Kunu-ri. Although Almond was willing to permit a limited redeployment to positions a few miles south of Wonju that kept the village within artillery range, he emphasized that the Second Division must maintain an aggressive posture. McClure used this leeway to pull out of Wonju on 7 January, and on his own authority, he established a new line about a dozen miles to the south. The withdrawal was poorly conducted through a blinding snowstorm that did little credit to any of the participants. Almond was, not surprisingly, furious with McClure's unauthorized actions, and he ordered an immediate counterattack to regain the lost ground. Efforts by Freeman's 23rd Regiment to do so made little progress, however, bringing the fighting in the area to a confused and uncoordinated impasse.[59]

Although Almond likely determined to relieve McClure of his command as soon as he learned the details of the Second Division's unauthorized retreat, he refrained from doing so immediately. Instead, he waited several days to accumulate more evidence of McClure's wrongdoings just in case Ridgway, MacArthur, or Collins questioned his decision. He had already complained to McClure about some of the deficiencies he believed existed in the division, so it was simply a matter of making them part of the record. Almond inspected the division several times over the course of the next few days, and he found plenty of problems to buttress his case against McClure: improperly placed foxholes, badly sited weapons, incorrect fields of fire, insufficient winter clothing, slipshod staff work, uncoordinated headquarters operations, a lack of timely hot meals for the rank and file, inadequate troop supervision to prevent frostbite, and slow artillery support. As far as Almond was concerned, McClure was running a slipshod organization. On 13 January, Almond finally pulled the trigger and removed McClure from his post because of his "poor leadership." Ridgway was ambivalent about Almond's action. His first impression of McClure had been good, but he also believed that commanders should have men of their own choosing. He therefore went along with Almond's decision and rather blandly informed MacArthur that he trusted Almond's judgment on this particular issue. When Collins visited Tenth Corps headquarters during his mid-January tour of Korea, he questioned Almond about McClure's relief. Almond claimed that Collins said little after he explained his rationale. One of Almond's staffers, however, later stated that Almond told him that Collins asked if McClure had been drinking. Almond said yes, but added that that was not why he fired him.[60]

To replace McClure, Ridgway, on Almond's strong recommendation, turned to Major General Clark "Nick" Ruffner, the Tenth Corps' chief of staff. Born in Buffalo, New York, in 1903, Ruffner graduated from the Virginia Military Institute in 1924. He started out in the cavalry, taught at Norwich Military Academy, and attended the Command and General Staff College from 1940 to 1941. During World War II, he made his mark as a staffer and logistician. He served as deputy chief of staff for the Seventh Corps from 1942 to 1943, then transferred to the central Pacific theater and rose to be chief of staff for all army forces in that vast region. When MacArthur formed the Tenth Corps and put Almond in charge of it, he suggested Ruffner as chief of staff because he recognized Ruffner's intelligence and resourcefulness. Almond did not know Ruffner well, so he only reluctantly agreed. Fortunately, Ruffner more than lived up to Almond's always demanding expectations; Almond later lauded Ruffner's leadership, judgment, and foresight. While Ruffner performed his chief of staff duties skillfully, his biggest contribution was acting as a buffer between Almond and everyone else by smoothing out some of Almond's countless rough edges. Almond deeply regretted losing Ruffner's invaluable services as his chief of staff, but he recognized that it was only a matter of time before he moved on to greater responsibilities. Like Almond before him, Ridgway only knew Ruffner by his good reputation; he might not have followed Almond's advice to give him a division had not MacArthur again intervened on Ruffner's behalf by persuasively pointing out his many attributes. Ridgway had initially planned to assign Ruffner to the Seventh Division after Barr left, but McClure's displacement opened up the slot in the Second Division first.[61]

Ruffner had been waiting for a division of his own for some time. Assuming a new command is never an easy job, but in Ruffner's case, it was more difficult than usual. Not only was he the third Second Division boss in a little more than a month, but he was also taking over an outfit full of dissension, still recovering from its recent defeats, and in the middle of complicated operations. Happily, Ruffner had the character and personality to pull the division together and make it fight. For one thing, months of experience had taught him how to handle Almond, in whose Tenth Corps the Second Division was attached. Unlike some others, Ruffner understood that Almond usually respected those who stood up to him. Moreover, he was tactful enough to do so without angering him. As a result, Almond was pleased with Ruffner's performance at the head of the Second Division. He later wrote of his decision to recommend Ruffner's appointment, "I never made a stronger move and a more appropriate one."[62]

Although some of Ruffner's new subordinates initially had doubts about him because he had so little combat leadership experience, Ruffner won them over as well. He presented that aura of authority that good commanders possess and took full advantage of his subordinates' collective experience. He quickly made his presence known by, for instance, rescinding McClure's dictate that everyone in the division grow a beard. He ran his staff well. He usually received a morning briefing, spent the day in the field, and returned to his command post in the evening to review the day's events and to discuss future plans. He impressed almost everyone with his calm demeanor, clear thinking, and wit. Indeed, Ruffner was something of a character with a fine sense of humor. One of his staffers, Edward Rowney, recalled that at meetings Ruffner invariably gave him full credit whenever something went right, even when he had done nothing to deserve it. On the other hand, Ruffner always chewed out another staffer named Forney whenever anything went wrong, even if Forney was completely innocent. Embarrassed with this unmerited praise, Rowney finally went to Ruffner privately and asked him to stop. Ruffner responded, "Forney, you're doing a good job.[63] Ruffner also won the respect of such Second Division mainstays as Gerald Epley and Paul Freeman, two men who rarely agreed on anything. Ruffner's ascension to the top of the Second Division certainly did not end all of its woes, and in fact under his supervision the outfit experienced both highs and lows, but he gave it some of the steady leadership that it had been missing and sorely needed.[64]

So far, the Eighth Army operations in South Korea's mountainous central corridor had left much to be desired, and in fact seemed to be sputtering to an unsuccessful halt. Not only were the North Koreans pushing down toward Wonju but they were also infiltrating southward to conduct attacks against the Eighth Army's supply and communication lines. Almond, however, was determined to turn things around; he wrote to Ridgway on 15 January, "You may rest assured that the troops under Tenth Corps will fight aggressively under any condition."[65] To deal with the threat to the Eighth Army's rear, Ridgway and Almond deployed part of the Seventh Division, the 5th Cav Regiment, the 187th Airborne Regiment, and the First Marine Division. Their operations were more akin to a counterinsurgency war than a conventional conflict, but they gradually wore the enemy down through constant and aggressive patrolling.

While these units secured the Eighth Army's rear, Almond focused on the Wonju region. He sent Colonel Ed Messinger's 9th Regiment into the village on

19 January, then followed up by dispatching Freeman's 23rd Regiment to the Twin Tunnels, about a dozen miles to the northwest. As its name indicates, the Twin Tunnels was a pair of railroad tunnels southeast of Chipyong. On the night of 31 January–1 February, the Chinese launched a ferocious attack on the 23rd Regiment and its attached French battalion. Because overcast skies grounded American air support, the Chinese continued their assaults into the next day before they finally broke off the engagement. Freeman had seen considerable combat in the Pusan Perimeter and at Kunu-ri, but nothing he had experienced compared to the unmitigated ferocity of the Twin Tunnels. He later wrote, "That was probably the most desperate fight that I participated in during my time in Korea and we were lucky that we weren't overrun because we were truly making our last stand."[66] When Ridgway arrived two days later to survey the scene, he was amazed by the number of Chinese dead around the 23rd Regiment's perimeter. Indeed, the Chinese probably lost over 4,000 men in the engagement, compared to about 250 American and French casualties. From there, the 23rd Regiment marched three miles to Chipyong and dug in. Thus, in the space of a few weeks, Almond managed to prop up the Eighth Army's sagging line and bring some stability to the central corridor. It was small wonder that Ridgway was full of praise for his Tenth Corps commander.[67]

Unhappily for Almond, no sooner had he stabilized his line than it unraveled again. The Chinese launched a full-scale offensive in the area starting on the night of 11–12 February. They focused their attention on three understrength ROK divisions deployed north of Wonju toward Hoengsong. Chinese attacks rapidly destroyed one of the divisions and drove the other two southward toward Wonju in disarray. In an effort to increase their combat effectiveness, Almond had recently attached American artillery units—dubbed support teams—to these divisions and placed them under ROK command. The Chinese overran and decimated some of the support teams during the retreat in an area near Hoengsong subsequently termed Massacre Valley. It reminded some of the gauntlet south of Kunuri. When elements of the First Marine Division came though a few weeks later, they discovered hundreds of bodies frozen in place where they had fallen, as well as dozens of burned-up vehicles, busted typewriters, a Catholic chaplain's mass kit, discarded letters, and even a Raggedy Ann doll. Almond later estimated that the Eighth Army lost 12,000 men, forty-seven artillery pieces, and huge amounts of equipment in the debacle.

Although Almond was quick to blame the South Koreans for the disaster, Ridgway held him responsible. He had had his doubts about Almond's command arrangements earlier and warned Almond to be careful, and now saw his concerns come true in the worst possible fashion. One staffer remembered, "General Ridgway showed up at the Tenth Corps headquarters and I never heard anybody get chewed out worse than he chewed out General Almond for his reckless misuse of artillery and a few other things, and he said this will never happen again."[68] To make matters worse, Almond could not respond to the crisis as quickly as he wanted because so many of his units were tied down with counterinsurgency operations to the south. For example, guerrillas sabotaged an entire trainload of ammunition for Buddy Ferenbaugh's Seventh Division the night the Chinese initiated their offensive. Thoroughly alarmed, Ridgway ordered Wonju held at all costs. He rushed in the British Commonwealth 27th Brigade and the ROK Sixth Division to help the Second Division's 38th Regiment and the 187th Airborne Regiment defend Wonju. These reinforcements, as well as plenty of air and especially artillery support, gradually brought the Chinese advance to a halt by 16 February.[69]

The sudden Chinese offensive isolated Paul Freeman's 23rd Regiment at Chipyong, where it had set up shop after its fight at the Twin Tunnels. Neither Freeman nor Ruffner liked the look of things, and both officers recommended withdrawing the exposed regiment to a less vulnerable position as soon as possible. Even the combative Almond agreed with their assessment. Ridgway, though, insisted that the 23rd stay put because Chipyong was the hinge that connected the Tenth Corps with the Ninth Corps to the west. If Chipyong fell, the Chinese could sweep down the Han River valley. Almond accepted the order, of course, but noted that he did not have a rescue force available because all his units were committed to Wonju's defense. Ridgway therefore agreed to send Colonel Marcel Crombez's 5th Cav Regiment to open up the road to Chipyong. Meanwhile, Freeman and his 5,000 troops—three battalions, the attached French battalion, and various odds and ends—prepared for battle. As Freeman explained, "There is no place to go. We are cut off and surrounded. This is a key point of the Eighth Army effort, so we will stay here and kill Chinese."[70] Fortunately, they had been at Chipyong since 3 February, so they had had plenty of time to dig in. Indeed, Freeman had accumulated so much ammunition that he worried he would be accused of hoarding if the expected Chinese attack failed to materialize. Freeman lacked the manpower to cover all the hills surrounding Chipyong, so he instead deployed a light screening force on them by day and pulled all his troops into a tight perimeter at night. It was a shrewd tactical decision that played no small role in his defeating the Chinese.[71]

The Chinese assailed Freeman's position around Chipyong on the night of 13–14 February. The attacks were not well coordinated, so Freeman's French and American soldiers repelled them without much difficulty. Shortly after dawn, an exploding mortar round wounded Freeman in the calf. The injury was not serious—Freeman could still hobble around—but when Almond heard the news, he seized the opportunity to make a change in command. Almond considered Freeman too pessimistic and defeatist, and he had criticized Freeman's management of his regiment. After consulting with a reluctant Ruffner, Almond dispatched his operations officer, Colonel John Chiles, to Chipyong by air to relieve Freeman. When Chiles arrived, though, Freeman refused to be evacuated and persuaded Chiles to stand down and let him finish the battle. One journalist quoted Freeman as saying, "I brought them in here. I'll take them out."[72] That night, thousands of Chinese troops bravely charged the regiment's perimeter. Tracers and flares illuminated the darkness, and the sounds of machine gun and rifle fire, gongs and bells and whistles, explosions, and hollering men reverberated across the hills. The Chinese usually broke off their operations at daylight rather than expose their soldiers to American air support, but this time the combat continued long after the sun came up. The situation became so desperate that Freeman had to commit his last reserves to restore his line. It was effective American air power, however, that turned the tide and saved the 23rd Regiment. By the time Crombez's relief column reached Chipyong in the late afternoon, the Chinese had started melting into the hills. The engagement cost the French and Americans 408 casualties. Chinese losses, on the other hand, ran into the thousands. For Ridgway, Chipyong was important for reasons other than the disproportionate amount of Chinese blood spilled. He had monitored the action closely, listening to reports on the radio in his tent while sipping tea. The Battle of Chipyong was the first time an Eighth Army unit had stopped an all-out Chinese offensive cold. Ridgway hoped it was a harbinger of things to come.[73]

The assaults on Chipyong and Wonju marked the climax of the Chinese and North Korean offensive down South Korea's central corridor. Had they succeeded in overrunning both places, the Eighth Army would probably have retreated to the lower third of the peninsula, or even into the old Pusan Perimeter. Instead, the Eighth Army repulsed the enemy attacks and put itself in position to drive northward to the 38th Parallel. There was plenty of credit to go around for this accomplishment. Ridgway, for one, was willing to make a stand in the mountains despite geographic and climatic factors that nullified many of the army's usual advantages. He also recognized the threat quickly enough to rush the Second Division northward to confront it. In addition, American and ROK division and regimental commanders—including Freeman, most obviously—deserved credit for successfully combating both conventional and guerrilla forces under confusing and challenging circumstances. And of course the rank and file who did the actual fighting cannot be overlooked. However, it was Ned Almond who was the spark plug behind Eighth Army operations there. Almond was certainly an overbearing, arbitrary, and insensitive man who made mistakes, but his innate aggressiveness and single-minded determination to win paid big dividends for the Eighth Army in the central corridor. Small wonder Ridgway endorsed Almond's promotion to lieutenant general.[74]

Ridgway's Offensive

While the Chinese and North Koreans focused their attention and resources on the central corridor, there was little contact between the opposing forces on the western part of the peninsula, south of Seoul, where the Eighth Army had positioned itself just above Pyongtaek after the Chinese New Year's offensive. From a military perspective, the Chinese army's local quiescence was not surprising. The area's flatter topography was more conducive to the use of American mechanization and firepower, the bulk of the Eighth Army's American troops were concentrated there, and the Chinese had to fight with the Han River directly behind them. It did not take Ridgway long to notice this inactivity, wonder about the reasons behind it, and formulate ways to take advantage of it.

Ridgway decided that the best way to ascertain enemy strength and intentions south of the Han was through an aggressive reconnaissance-in-force. To do so, he had at his disposal on the peninsula nearly 180,000 American soldiers and marines, as well as around 224,000 ROK and assorted allied troops. If successful, his reconnaissance-in-force would not only collect valuable intelligence on Chinese activities but might also raise Eighth Army morale and tempt the Chinese into a foolhardy and costly counterattack. Ridgway walked into Mike Michaelis's 27th Regiment headquarters one day and asked, "Mike, what are tanks for?" Michaelis was familiar enough with Ridgway's modus operandi to respond, "To kill." Nodding his approval, Ridgway said, "Well, I want you to take your tanks and your regiment and go forward to Suwon."[75] Ridgway's reconnaissance-in-force actually encompassed a good deal more than just Michaelis's outfit; it also included some ROK troops, artillery and armor units, and a couple of Third Division battalions. The probe, dubbed Operation Wolfhound, began on 15 January and met little resistance until the Eighth Army columns approached Suwon the next day, upon which they fell back unmolested south of Osan and dug in. A similar mission, mounted a week later by some ROK outfits and elements of the First Cav, Third, and Twenty-fifth divisions, also failed to provoke a violent response. To Ridgway, this enemy docility provided an opportunity he wanted to exploit.

The success of these reconnaissances-in-force convinced Ridgway to undertake a limited offensive in the area. His goal was not to seize territory but rather to inflict casualties. To that end, he decided to attack in a systematic, methodical, and mutually supporting manner, rather than engage in the haphazard and uncoordinated lunges that characterized Walker's and Almond's operations the previous year. Ridgway was determined to avoid tactics that created bypassed pockets of enemy resistance that could cause trouble later. He therefore set clear unit boundaries, established phase lines for units to advance to, and insisted that commanders tie in their flanks and button up at night so they could ride out any enemy assaults. Doing so forced infantrymen off the roads and onto high ground, making them less vulnerable to the kinds of ambushes that brought the Second Division to grief south of Kunu-ri at the gauntlet. He also wanted to synchronize air, armor, and artillery support to generate the tremendous firepower necessary to overcome enemy defenses without suffering unacceptable losses in return. If Ridgway seemed cautious, he had his reasons. For one thing, Eighth Army morale and resolve remained tenuous after its recent defeats. Moreover, because the air force had lost some of its airfields closest to the front and had withdrawn many of its aircraft back to Japan, he could not take air supremacy for granted. Finally, Ridgway's turnover of senior combat commanders was just beginning, so he had to entrust his corps and divisions to some men in whom he had little confidence. Despite these problems, Ridgway figured that doing something was better than surrendering the initiative and doing nothing.

Ridgway's limited offensive in the west, dubbed Thunderbolt, began on 25 January. His plan called for the gradual accumulation of pressure on the enemy. From left to right, Milburn's First Corps (the Twenty-fifth and Third divisions, as well as the Turkish Brigade) and Coulter's/Moore's Ninth Corps (First Cav and Twenty-fourth divisions), pushed forward, backed with as much firepower as Ridgway could provide. Chinese resistance ran the gamut from nonexistent to fierce, but the Eighth Army made slow, steady progress northward. The Chinese army's heavy commitment to operations in the central corridor, as well as an unexpected thaw that inhibited its resupply efforts by melting ice on the Han River, undermined its efforts to effectively oppose the Eighth Army. Suwon fell on 26 January, and on 10 February the Third Division's 65th Regiment was the first outfit to reach the Han. That same day, elements of Kean's Twenty-fifth Division occupied Yongdungpo, seized Kimpo airfield, and entered Inchon. With this, Ridgway terminated Thunderbolt.

Encouraged by Thunderbolt's success, and loath to surrender the initiative, Ridgway initiated a series of broad-front offensives that lasted through April: Killer (21 February–6 March), Ripper (7–31 March), Courageous (22–28 March), Rugged (1–6 April), and Dauntless (6–22 April). Each one followed the Thunderbolt model: careful, mutually supporting, and methodical advances that relied on massive firepower to overcome enemy defenses. The primary goal remained the destruction of North Korean and Chinese forces, not the seizure of territory, though the reclamation of ground was a welcome by-product. Heavy rains from the continuing thaw initially hindered operations by washing out bridges, rendering roads unusable, and complicating resupply efforts. Despite such problems, well-coordinated air, artillery, and armor support repeatedly helped the infantry surmount Chinese and North Korean resistance.

The Ninth and Tenth corps slowly cleared out the area east of Seoul, forcing the Chinese to relinquish the South Korean capital without a fight on 14 March rather than risk encirclement there. Having exchanged hands four times, the city was a shattered husk containing only a small percentage of its prewar population. One army officer recalled, "I'll never forget the picture of that, seeing Seoul for the first time in my life—just total devastation. . . . It was just a whole bunch of cardboard shelters, little wooden plywood shacks that they had been able to put together after the Chinese withdrew, and that was it."[76] From there the Eighth Army pushed gradually and relentlessly northward to the 38th Parallel across the peninsula. After the Truman administration decided that the 38th Parallel should not interfere with or influence military objectives, the Eighth Army crossed into North Korea and established itself at and beyond a line Ridgway designated "Kansas." It ran along the Imjin River north of Seoul, through the Hwachon Reservoir in the central mountains, and on to the east coast. Although these offensives garnered Ridgway plenty of acclaim, they did not kill the enemy in the kind of numbers necessary to compel the Chinese to negotiate a cease-fire favorable to the United States, South Korea, and their allies.

MacArthur shunned Korea during Ridgway's first weeks as Eighth Army commander. No doubt he wanted to give Ridgway some time and space to establish his authority over the Eighth Army, but he also probably wanted to avoid association with what at the time seemed like a losing cause. As the Eighth Army's fortunes rebounded, though, MacArthur showed renewed public interest in events on the peninsula. He flew to Korea eight times between 20 January and 3 April, putting in an appearance about every other week. His visits were brief, usually lasting a few hours, and consisted of cursory inspections, press conferences, and discussions with Ridgway. He was extremely complimentary of Ridgway, inundating him with high praise for his success in reversing the military tide. Unlike with Walker, MacArthur had a certain proprietary interest in Ridgway that contributed to his positive feelings for him. In addition, MacArthur could not help but be impressed with Ridgway's accomplishments. At an operational level, MacArthur largely agreed with Ridgway's ideas, though he placed more value on seizing territory, especially Seoul, than did Ridgway.

However, there is also evidence that MacArthur grew to resent Ridgway's achievements. MacArthur was, after all, a vain and egotistical man who disliked sharing the limelight with anyone, especially someone who was equally adept at public relations and self-promotion. In early April, MacArthur summoned his acting chief of staff and operations officer, Major General Doyle Hickey and Brigadier General Edwin Wright, respectively, into his office and complained that Ridgway had disobeyed orders by advancing further north with more troops than MacArthur thought appropriate. "I want you to write a letter to General Ridgway," said MacArthur, "and in effect tell him that this won't happen again." Taken aback, Hickey and Wright explained that this was obviously not a deliberate affront to MacArthur's authority but rather one of those simple miscommunications common in wartime. MacArthur was unmoved. The two men thereupon drew up a mildly worded reprimand and presented it to MacArthur for his signature. MacArthur angrily rejected it and insisted on a stronger rebuke. When Hickey and Doyle balked, he wrote it out himself and had Wright fly to Korea to hand-deliver it to a stunned Ridgway.[77]

The unmerited censure was one of several grievances Ridgway developed against MacArthur that spring. Ridgway was grateful that MacArthur initially kept his distance from Korea so he could focus on the Eighth Army and the immediate military situation without distractions from Tokyo. When the military situation improved, though, MacArthur resumed his periodic trips to the peninsula. As far as Ridgway was concerned, the costs of these visits outweighed any resulting benefits. Minding MacArthur and his entourage, including journalists hungry for news, required lots of Ridgway's time when he could least afford it: at the beginning of important operations. Moreover, Ridgway worried that MacArthur's expansive pronouncements tipped off the enemy about Eighth Army intentions. For example, during his 20 February visit, on the eve of Operation Killer, MacArthur announced, "I have just ordered a resumption of the offensive."[78] Ridgway finally wrote MacArthur a tactful letter asking him to refrain from flying to Korea until after the battle was already under way, which, to his credit, MacArthur gracefully accepted. The thing that really irked Ridgway, however, was MacArthur's public insinuation that he was responsible for the Eighth Army's recent successes. Ridgway remembered, "I knew he had no part in any way of suggesting or even influencing that operational plan, none whatsoever."[79] Ridgway had known MacArthur for thirty years, so he could hardly have been surprised by MacArthur's efforts to horn in on the limelight. In the larger scheme of things, though, these aggravations were relatively minor and could have been much worse.[80]

Ridgway's relationships with his corps commanders that winter and spring were relatively good, and he was largely satisfied with their performances. He was least concerned about Bryant Moore, who was, after all, a hand-picked and known entity. Almond, of course, presented his own set of challenges for Ridgway. However, the thing that worried Ridgway the most about his senior combat leaders—insufficient aggressiveness—was not one of them. To be sure, Ridgway hauled Almond on the carpet on several occasions that winter, most notably for his misuse of artillery units north of Wonju, but on the whole, Ridgway considered him an asset and was grateful to have him. Ridgway was willing to tolerate Almond's faults because he brought such unbounded initiative and energy to the battlefield. Indeed, Ridgway later rated Almond as a superior, though not top-level, corps commander. As for Almond, he maintained his belligerent and can-do attitude throughout the Eighth Army's counteroffensive. At one high-level meeting, Milburn wondered why the Eighth Army was not taking more prisoners, to which Almond responded that it was because whenever an enemy soldier stuck his head out of his hole, he was shot at. It was Milburn whom Ridgway fretted about the most. Ridgway doubted that someone he considered so mediocre should hold this important position. Because removing such a popular officer would cause too much trouble, Ridgway resorted to encouragement and close oversight to get the best out of him by, for example, placing his advanced command post with Milburn's headquarters. It is hard to say whether Ridgway's motivational strategy had much of an impact on Milburn, though it certainly stressed out his staffers, who had to respond immediately to Ridgway's tough questions and high demands. Milburn was not a brilliant general, but Ridgway mistook his humility, shyness, and self-effacement for a timidity that his overall record did not support.[81]

On 24 February, only a bit more than three weeks after assuming command of the Ninth Corps, Ridgway lost Bryant Moore. That morning, Moore's helicopter crashed into the Han River after its rotor blade hit an unseen cable. Although the helicopter flipped over in the shallow water, troops fished Moore out before he drowned. Moore was shaken up but seemed unhurt except for a twisted knee. He took a hot bath in the trailer of the Twenty-fourth Division's artillery commander, drank some coffee, and pulled a blanket around him. Shortly after phoning his headquarters, though, Moore suffered a fatal heart attack. Ridgway mourned Moore's passing. He had specifically asked for Moore and had expected great things from him.[82]

With what must have been a feeling of déjà vu, Ridgway sent Collins the names of three officers whom he believed were most qualified to succeed Moore. His first choice was Major General Joseph Swing, the commandant of the Army War College, but Collins nixed the idea because he wanted Swing where he was. Instead, he dispatched to Korea another name on the list: Major General William Hoge. The Missouri-born Hoge graduated from West Point in 1916. Although commissioned as an engineer, he commanded a battalion at St. Mihiel and in the Argonne during World War I. In the 1920s, he honed his engineering skills at the Massachusetts Institute of Technology, served with the Philippine Scouts, and attended the Command and General Staff School. He spent most of his time, however, working on various civil engineering projects. After the United States entered World War II, Hoge oversaw the construction of the Alcan Highway, a thousand-mile-long road connecting Alaska with the lower forty-eight states, until he was relieved because his boss felt he was not making sufficiently fast progress. From there, Hoge went to Northwest Europe to lead a combat command in the Ninth

Armored Division. He was in the thick of the fighting in the Battle of the Bulge, gained fame for seizing the Ludendorff Bridge across the Rhine River at Remagen, Germany, and ended the war at the head of the Fourth Armored Division. He ran the Engineering Center at Fort Belvoir, Virginia, after Germany surrendered and was in charge of American troops in Trieste, Italy, when the Korean War began.

Hoge's skillful handling of his men at the Battle of the Bulge and during the invasion of Germany greatly impressed Ridgway, who made a mental note to keep tabs on him. When Ridgway drew up his list of possible corps commanders, he concluded that Hoge's methodical approach to military problems would suit his strategy of attrition and make Hoge a valuable addition to his leadership team. After a grueling flight from Italy across the Atlantic, the continental United States, and the Pacific, Hoge assumed command of the Ninth Corps on 5 March. He appreciated his appointment to the Ninth Corps, later referring to it as the best assignment of his career because he had more autonomy there than in any other army job he had held. He was a self-effacing, dedicated, thoughtful, and blunt officer who read voraciously and kept physically fit through horseback riding and tennis. Although he understood the importance of delegating authority, he sometimes had trouble identifying and recruiting good staffers to implement his directives. His subordinates liked him, including the capable Oliver Smith. Hoge greatly admired Ridgway as "one of the best commanders I ever saw," but he was willing to argue with him when he received orders he felt were impractical. He had a more baleful view of Almond and criticized his headquarters as a "regular traveling circus." Within a month after arriving in Korea, Ridgway recommended Hoge's promotion and lauded him as an "aggressive, determined and experienced" officer who fulfilled his responsibilities in a "superior manner."[83]

As for the new slate of division commanders, they reacted to the military situation according to their different personalities. Over in the Tenth Corps, Nick Ruffner worked hard to bring the Second Division up to par. He took over a unit plagued by matériel and manpower shortages, disorganization, low morale, and inadequate leadership. He had to address these difficulties at the same time he was fighting the Chinese in the central corridor at Wonju and Chipyong. He was initially appalled by the horrible conditions in which the Second Division operated: poor or nonexistent roads, washed-out bridges, supply shortages, land mines, and so forth. Fortunately for Ruffner, Almond had great confidence in him and gave him some leeway that he did not usually accord to his subordinates. Ruffner's familiarity with Almond's intimidating methods from his time as Tenth Corps chief of staff provided him an additional advantage in running his division. Finally, Ruffner's serenity and sense of humor proved beneficial in his new post. As the Eighth Army gradually gained the upper hand over the Chinese and North Koreans, Ruffner's confidence in his outfit increased accordingly. He even claimed that students in military academies would someday study Second Division tactics. He was equally proud of the administrative reforms his regimental commanders instituted, some of which impressed even Almond.[84]

On the other hand, Buddy Ferenbaugh had a more difficult time adjusting to division command. Like Ruffner, Ferenbaugh worked hard to improve the lackluster outfit he inherited from Barr, with equally impressive results. Unlike Ruffner, though, Ferenbaugh was a worrywart, especially when his men were in contact with the enemy. He fussed about everything from the scattered condition of his division to the quality of the intelligence at his disposal. He and Almond also disagreed over the use of the approximately 2,500 black troops in the division. Ferenbaugh wanted to integrate them immediately, but Almond insisted on segregating them in the rear, where they remained underutilized until Almond finally rotated home. Despite his tiff with Almond, Ferenbaugh fretted more about alienating Ridgway; at one point he feared dismissal because bad weather prevented him from attending a meeting Ridgway had called.[85]

At the corps level, Moore was not around long enough that spring to register any hard opinions about his division commanders. As for the easygoing and taciturn Milburn, he approved of both Bradley and Soule. Bradley impressed Milburn by skillfully handling his Twenty-fifth Division during the approach to Seoul. When the Third Division reached Pusan the previous December, Soule had asked for ten days to reform and refit his men, but Ridgway ordered them to the front immediately. Even so, Soule remained upbeat and belligerent, and was confident that his troops were now sufficiently seasoned to defeat the enemy. "All they have is hordes," he exclaimed to one journalist. "And how many hordes are there in a battalion?"[86] His drinking continued to raise eyebrows among some of his staffers, but when one officer voiced his concerns to Milburn, Milburn dismissed the complaint: "Well, Christ, the Third Division is doing as well with that guy as any others are."[87]

During their first meeting, Ridgway had promised Oliver Smith that he would not place the First Marine Division under Almond's command and that the marines would get some time to refit after their Chosin Reservoir odyssey. After giving the division a short rest around Masan, Ridgway deployed it first to the Andong for counterinsurgency operations, then to backstop the 187th Airborne Regiment and Second Division's stand at Wonju. Ridgway initially kept the First Marine Division under his direct command, but he eventually sent it to serve in the Ninth Corps. Smith had no problem working under Moore and Hoge, but he disliked abandoning the marines' long-standing amphibious role. Ridgway, however, explained to Smith, "I agree with you on the principle of what you said. The First Marine Division is the most powerful division we have in Korea. But we have to use you where the principal threat is, and that is in the Seoul corridor."[88] With that, the marines mothballed their amphibious vehicles and equipment and became just another infantry division, albeit a powerful and proficient one. The division participated in the fighting around Hoengsong and Hongchon, and recovered the remains of the South Korean and Second Division artillerymen killed at Massacre Valley. Through it all, Smith performed in his usual low-key, skillful, and professional manner. He certainly impressed Ridgway, who later referred to Smith as the best of all his division chiefs in Korea. When Moore died, Ridgway appointed Smith temporary Ninth Corps commander out of respect for his seniority and ability. Although some floated the idea of making the assignment permanent, it did not happen. Collins and Ridgway certainly valued Smith and wanted to foster cooperation between the army and marines, but they had no intention of putting a leatherneck in charge of entire army divisions. Smith accepted the temporary promotion and subsequent demotion with his usual grace.[89]

On 10 April, Secretary of the Army Frank Pace flew to Korea on an inspection trip. Escorting visiting dignitaries was one of Ridgway's more distracting jobs as Eighth Army commander. Ridgway was friends with Pace, but shepherding him around the peninsula kept him from other equally important tasks that competed for his attention. On 11 April, Pace and Ridgway landed at the Twenty-fourth Division's airstrip to review some of its units. While at the 5th Regiment's command post, Major General Lev Allen, the Eighth Army's chief of staff, phoned looking for Pace. The switchboard operator initially claimed that there was no one in the regiment by that name, but someone sorted out the misunderstanding and summoned a napping Pace to take the call. Allen read to Pace a message from Secretary of Defense George Marshall instructing him to inform Ridgway that President Truman had fired MacArthur and appointed Ridgway to replace him as supreme commander in the theater. A shocked Pace said, "Read that to me once more, Lev. I don't want to relieve General MacArthur upon one reading."[90] Neither Pace nor Ridgway realized that the big story had already leaked out. Indeed, that afternoon a journalist had shouted congratulations to a puzzled Ridgway. Pace hustled over to a tent and asked Ridgway to join him outside in a hailstorm for a private conversation. After joking with Ridgway that a hailstone might detonate his ever-present grenade and kill them both, Pace delivered the news. Ridgway exclaimed, "I can't believe it, Mr. Secretary." The two men cut their visit to the Twenty-fourth Division short and headed back to the airstrip as soon as they could to return to Ridgway's advanced command post at Yaju. Although responsibility came easily to Ridgway, even he was stunned by his sudden elevation. One observer recalled that Ridgway looked as if the weight of the world had descended onto his shoulders.[91]

Ridgway's tenure as Eighth Army commander lasted less than four months. By the force of his character and personality, Ridgway transformed his demoralized army into an aggressive force that reclaimed the initiative and pushed the enemy northward. Ridgway's achievements, though, were limited and still incomplete when he left the peninsula to assume MacArthur's job. Although the Eighth Army had driven the Chinese and North Koreans back across the 38th Parallel, it had not inflicted on them the kind of losses necessary to force them to negotiate from a position of weakness. The North Koreans and Chinese had given up ground, but they maintained the integrity of their lines. As for Ridgway's new division and corps commanders, they may have performed well under the comparatively controlled combat conditions that Ridgway had orchestrated that spring, but most of them had not been tested under the kind of stressful and chaotic circumstances that undid some of their predecessors. Despite nine months of seesaw fighting that had brought each side to the brink of victory and defeat at least once, the war's military climax had not yet arrived.

A New Eighth Army Commander

The Korean War's circumscribed nature appeared anomalous to an American public accustomed to the totality of World Wars I and II, but historically, most of the conflicts in which the United States had fought required less than the maximum mobilization of American resources. Indeed, the American military had waged so many low-intensity wars against groups as disparate as American Indians, Barbary pirates, and Filipino *insurrectos* that it was actually the world wars that were incongruous. What made the Korean War so different was its scale and profile. Although the conflict may have been limited, it still required a significant commitment by the American military and public to conduct it, and it exacted thousands of casualties in the process. It was also part of the Cold War competition with the communist Soviet Union for global domination. Not only did the Soviets provide the North Koreans and Chinese with matériel assistance but also some American policy makers worried that the Soviets might enter the conflict themselves. As a result, the United States had to simultaneously engage in a real war with the North Koreans and Chinese in Korea and contend with a Soviet challenge that had the potential to turn into armed conflict. Therefore, for the Truman administration, Korea was merely one piece in an enormously complicated Cold War geopolitical puzzle in which policy makers had to balance American interests on the peninsula with larger ones throughout the globe.

MacArthur understandably viewed the conflict through his parochial lens as supreme American commander in East Asia. Chinese intervention convinced MacArthur that American options were limited to expanding the war to the Chinese mainland or abandoning South Korea to its fate. Although Ridgway's unexpected success provided a third alternative—preserving South Korea—MacArthur continued to advocate taking the war directly to China. As he saw it, negotiating a cease-fire based on the antebellum status quo meant accepting an outcome short of the kind of victory the large American investment of blood and treasure on the peninsula demanded. Moreover, Americans were temperamentally unsuited for the halfway measures Truman wanted. As MacArthur explained to one official, "The American people will never understand this war. War is to be won or lost; it is never to be temporized."[92] MacArthur defined victory as removing communist China as a threat to the United States and its East Asian allies. To achieve this goal, he wanted to bomb Chinese transportation and industrial targets, blockade the Chinese coast, utilize Guomindang troops in both Korea and on the Chinese mainland, and commit more American resources to the region. He also sought greater freedom to use the tools at his disposal. MacArthur understood that the United States had worldwide obligations, but he believed that defeat in Korea—which he interpreted as the continued existence of a militarily potent communist China and North Korea—would undermine American efforts to wage the Cold War everywhere.

Truman administration officials, on the other hand, saw the Korean War in a more global context. They believed that in the larger scheme of things, it was a bloody and aggravating sideshow, not the main event. To them, the Soviet Union was the United States' chief Cold War adversary and the wellspring of international communist aggression throughout the world. Therefore, the United States needed to focus its efforts on confronting and thwarting Soviet geopolitical ambitions in vital areas such as Western Europe and Japan, not wasting finite resources on a remote peninsula with little direct economic, political, and military significance. Expanding the war into China and mounting a full-scale invasion of North Korea, as MacArthur recommended, would further suck the United States down a rat hole in which victory was hard to define and harder to achieve—and which might even lead to World War III with the Soviets. Ridgway's military victories had given the Truman administration a viable middle option between MacArthur's vision of a Sino-American conflagration or a humiliating withdrawal from Korea. Truman administration policy makers intended to use the Eighth Army's success to strong-arm the North Koreans and Chinese into negotiating a cease-fire based on preserving South Korea's independence. Protecting South Korea had, after all, been the objective when Truman made his initial decision to intervene, and unification came into the picture only in the euphoric afterglow of Inchon. Cutting such a deal would maintain South Korea's independence and American credibility while freeing up American resources for use elsewhere.

The fundamental differences in Korean War strategy between MacArthur and the Truman administration were problematic enough, but there were other factors involved that ultimately led to MacArthur's dismissal. One was MacArthur's tendency to twist directives in such ways that advanced his agenda. Although he never explicitly disobeyed orders, he certainly violated the spirit in which some of them were issued by treating them more as suggestions and topics for discussion than as instructions. Most notably, he used semantics to justify deploying American forces near the Chinese border even though the JCS disapproved. A second factor was MacArthur's willingness to go public with his disagreements with the Truman administration in the hope that public opinion would compel policy changes more in line with his thinking. At the beginning of the war, for example, he strongly hinted that he opposed the Truman administration's decision to separate its Korean and Formosan policies. Later, he openly claimed that he could not effectively respond to Chinese intervention because the Truman administration forbade American forces from pursuing the enemy beyond the Yalu. In response, on 6 December 1950, Truman prohibited all overseas officials from making public statements on foreign policy unless they cleared them with the State Department first. MacArthur, however, continued to interfere and speak out. On 24 March 1951, he undercut Truman administration attempts to open talks with the Chinese by issuing his own ultimatum threatening the Chinese with annihilation in Korea unless they negotiated. Finally, on 5 April, the House of Representatives' minority leader, Republican Joseph Martin, read a statement from MacArthur dissenting from the Truman administration's policies. In it, MacArthur argued that a more aggressive approach in Asia would actually promote, not hinder, American national security:

> It seems strangely difficult for some to realize that here in Asia is where the Communist conspirators have elected to make their play for global conquest, and that we have joined the issue thus raised on the battlefield; that here we fight Europe's war with arms while the diplomats there still fight it with words; that if we lose this war to Communism in Asia the fall of Europe is inevitable, win it and Europe most probably will avoid war and yet preserve freedom. As you point out, we must win. There is no substitute for victory.[93]

For Truman, MacArthur's letter to Martin was the final straw. After reading a copy of the speech, he angrily concluded that the time had come for him to remove MacArthur from his command. He had, he felt, tolerated MacArthur's penchant for flouting presidential authority long enough. His closest civilian advisers, Secretary of State Dean Acheson and troubleshooter Averell Harriman, firmly agreed. However, they suggested that Truman secure the support of the American military establishment to avoid the appearance that he had fired the

Republican-leaning MacArthur for political reasons. When consulted, Secretary of Defense George Marshall hesitated to counsel such a drastic course of action, but after reading the cable traffic to and from MacArthur for the previous two years, he came around to Truman's point of view.

Truman also asked Omar Bradley, the chairman of the JCS, to meet with the Joint Chiefs and solicit their views. Neither Bradley nor the Joint Chiefs was aware of Truman's growing displeasure with MacArthur, but they had plenty of grievances of their own against him. Their main charge was that the president—and by extension the JCS—should have someone in charge of the theater who supported administration policy. By his own admission, MacArthur did not, and as far as the Joint Chiefs were concerned, his vocal recalcitrance constituted a threat to civilian control of the military. In addition, the Joint Chiefs believed that MacArthur had violated the presidential directive to clear policy statements before making them public. As Collins later put it, "[MacArthur] had exceeded his authority in his public statements, which were contrary to the President's directives, and frankly he'd gotten too big for his britches."[94] Finally, some JCS members questioned MacArthur's military judgment, especially his decision to divide his command between the Eighth Army and Tenth Corps. After two hours of discussion on 8 April, the Joint Chiefs walked down to Marshall's office and recommended MacArthur's relief, carefully noting that they did so on purely military grounds. Over the course of the weekend, various people suggested a number of less drastic options—summoning MacArthur home for consultations, leaving him in charge of Japan, or writing a carefully worded letter explaining the president's concerns—but none seemed wise or practical. On 10 April, Truman signed orders dismissing MacArthur, but he made it clear that he wanted him informed in a way befitting his rank and long service to the country.[95]

As it was, MacArthur had an inkling that his professional head was on the chopping block. In early April, Almond went on leave to Japan to see his family, but before he returned to Korea, he stopped by the Dai Ichi building to visit MacArthur. In the course of conversation, MacArthur said, "Ned, this may be the last time you see me over here," and went on to explain that Truman might remove him from command because he had injected politics into the policy dispute by sending his letter to Martin. Almond dismissed the possibility, but MacArthur was more prescient. Although Truman wanted MacArthur informed of his relief in a dignified and proper manner, a press leak upset the arrangement. One of MacArthur's aides heard the news on the radio and got word to MacArthur, so he knew what to expect when the official orders arrived a short time later. He perused them briefly, hugged his wife, and said, "Jeannie, we're going home at last." His equanimity, though, had its limits. He exclaimed to one official, "Publicly humiliated after fifty-two years of service in the army." He would, he continued, have retired quietly and without fuss had Truman intimated that he was dissatisfied with him. He returned to the States on 16 April to a hero's welcome, and three days later, he gave an emotional speech to Congress in which he defended his positions. He expanded on them in subsequent congressional hearings, but the bulk of the American military establishment lined up behind the Truman administration, and his popularity faded. Whether he realized it or not, his most remembered line from his congressional address, "Old soldiers never die; they just fade away," turned out to be a fit epitaph for his geostrategic ideas.[96]

Determining on Ridgway as MacArthur's successor generated neither debate nor hesitation within the Truman administration. Marshall, Bradley, and Collins had been his admirers even before he took over the Eighth Army, and his magnificent performance in Korea had only enhanced his standing. Indeed, his presence in the region made removing MacArthur easier than would have been the case had someone less successful been leading the Eighth Army. Upon the recommendation of Marshall and the JCS, Truman designated Ridgway as supreme commander in East Asia at the same time he pulled the trigger on MacArthur. Ridgway flew to Japan on 12 April, but he kept a low profile until MacArthur departed. That afternoon, the two men met privately in the American embassy's library. Ridgway's worries that MacArthur would react badly proved groundless. Indeed, MacArthur was the epitome of grace and solicitousness, exhibiting little rancor or resentment. He expressed his appreciation of Ridgway's work with the Eighth Army and added, "I hope when you leave Tokyo you will be chief of staff. If I had been permitted to choose my own successor, I'd have selected you."[97] As Ridgway settled into his new job, he impressed people with his energy, good looks, frankness, and decisiveness. Some, though, noted that the position lost some of the grandeur and allure that had characterized MacArthur's tenure.[98]

Walker's sudden and unexpected death the previous December had confirmed Collins's belief in the importance of planning for smooth command transitions. Because Ridgway exposed himself to as much danger as Walker had, Collins concluded that it made sense to designate his successor beforehand just in case he met a similar fate. Collins therefore nominated Lieutenant General James Van Fleet for the job soon after Ridgway took over the Eighth Army and secured Pace's and Marshall's approval. Van Fleet had served under Collins and Bradley in World War II in northwest Europe, during which he skyrocketed from regimental to corps commander in nine months. Collins, Bradley, and Eisenhower lauded Van Fleet's combativeness, tenacity, and upbeat attitude, and all three did what they could to nurture his career. After the war, Van Fleet further enriched his reputation by running the American military mission to Greece. When he arrived there in 1948, the Greek noncommunist government was slowly losing its war with communist rebels. Van Fleet helped turn the conflict around by rebuilding the

Greek army from the ground up and leading it in an aggressive series of counterinsurgency campaigns that gradually destroyed the rebels. Collins hoped that Van Fleet could work similar wonders on the beleaguered South Korean army. Although Van Fleet had never been stationed in Asia, Collins also figured that because Korea and Greece were both located on peninsulas, Van Fleet would find the situation geographically familiar. Collins informed Van Fleet of his decision in early February. He also directed Van Fleet to keep the news to himself and be ready to fly to Korea at a moment's notice. When the time came to relieve MacArthur and promote Ridgway, all Collins had to do was secure Truman's approval for Van Fleet's appointment.[99]

Van Fleet's rise through the army's hierarchy was surprising for a number of reasons. New Jersey born and Florida raised, Van Fleet graduated from West Point in 1915 in the same class as Eisenhower and Bradley. Unlike them, though, he went overseas to France in World War I and led a machine gun battalion in the Argonne campaign. After the conflict, he spent many years teaching in various Reserve Officer Training Corps programs and coaching football. He also commanded an infantry battalion in Panama and served as an instructor at the Infantry School at Fort Benning, Georgia. However, he attended neither the Command and General Staff School nor the Army War College, making him the only active World War II corps commander who did not darken the door of either place. When the United States entered World War II, many of Van Fleet's colleagues were quickly promoted to general and given increasingly responsible posts. Van Fleet, though, remained a colonel of a Fourth Division regiment. People noted and commented on this odd situation, but Van Fleet tried to be philosophical and focused on the job at hand. Later Collins and Bradley attributed his career stagnation to Marshall's confusing Van Fleet with an alcoholic officer with a similar name. Van Fleet doubted this because, he said, Marshall knew full well he was a teetotaler from their time together at the Infantry School at Fort Benning, but Van Fleet may have underestimated Marshall's tendency to confuse and forget names.

Whatever the truth, Van Fleet began to attract attention after his regiment shipped to England in preparation for the landing in northwest Europe. Collins noticed Van Fleet's qualities even before D-day, and with Bradley's encouragement, he made a mental note to keep an eye on him. Van Fleet fought so well in Normandy that Collins recommended his promotion to brigadier general, and Bradley later compared him to Ridgway and noted that he earned about three medals a day. At one point Van Fleet was wounded in the stomach, but after getting bandaged up at a field hospital, he opted to return to the front. Bradley found him there and said, "I came here to decorate you, but I ought to court martial you. You are AWOL; you left that hospital without being discharged." Considering his record and new patrons, it was unsurprising that Eisenhower and Bradley elevated Van Fleet first to assistant commander of the Second Division, then to lead the Ninetieth Division. He impressed George Patton during the grueling fighting in Lorraine in the fall of 1944, and he took over the Third Corps in the spring of 1945 and marched it through the Ruhr and into Germany. After his adventure in Greece, Van Fleet returned to the States to run the Second Army, from whence Collins summoned him to replace Ridgway in Korea.

Van Fleet was nicknamed "Big Jim" for the husky frame and physical strength that had made him a football star at West Point. At first glance he did not seem particularly complicated, sophisticated, or even clever. Shortly after he reached the peninsula, a reporter asked him what American goals were in Korea. Van Fleet responded, "I don't know. The answer must come from higher authority." There was, however, plenty of substance behind his simplistic facade. He lacked Ridgway's scary intensity, but he was just as much of a straight shooter. Fortunately, his open-mindedness, even temper, modesty, and innate friendliness helped mitigate his bluntness and kept him from making enemies and ruffling feathers. He possessed a low-key sense of humor that enhanced his appeal. When journalists dismissed his complaints that they were divulging too much information about the Eighth Army by stating that it was silly for a modern military to even try to keep secrets, Van Fleet asked, "Well, then, why don't you play it fair for both sides and furnish me with the enemy's order of battle?" As a result, he got along well with almost everyone: the rank and file, officer corps, politicians, South Koreans, and other American allies. Before visiting Korean orphanages, he stuffed his pockets full of candy to guarantee a good reception. Aggressiveness had marked his entire career, so no one doubted his combativeness. His self-assuredness, slowness in pulling rank, and unmistakable competence inspired confidence in others. Like all good leaders, he knew what he was doing and made it seem easy. He did not drink or smoke, and he possessed a thick, albeit quiet, religious streak. For all his amiability, though, he was a hard man to know because he kept his feelings to himself. This detachment contributed to the suspicion some had that he lacked sufficient gray matter for such an important job. Indeed, he had spent relatively little time in staff positions, so he was not as familiar with the housekeeping aspects of command as most high-ranking officers. No one ever claimed that Van Fleet was any kind of military intellectual, but he was certainly a fighter who got results. As it was, Van Fleet needed every advantage he had because he took over the Eighth Army just as the war reached its military climax.[100]

Van Fleet was on vacation at his Florida home, overseeing the planting of an orange grove, when Collins phoned him in the middle of the night and ordered him to Washington at once. Collins was anxious for Van Fleet to get to Korea to assume his new duties, so their Pentagon meeting was brief. Collins pledged Van

Fleet maximum autonomy, saying, "Now, Van, you have complete say in Korea. That is your job and we'll interfere as little as possible." Van Fleet was glad to hear this and delighted to get another big assignment. However, upon meeting with Ridgway in Taegu on 14 April, he learned that although Collins might give him freedom of action, Ridgway would not. Although Ridgway promised Van Fleet, "I won't get into your hair," he did not mean it. Instead, Ridgway planned to keep close watch over Eighth Army operations from Tokyo. Ridgway later claimed, "I had no desire to try to hold all the reins in my own hand, as MacArthur had done prior to my assuming command of the Eighth Army. Nor had I ever thought it proper for a distant commander to try to keep tactical control when he had able and trusted commanders on the spot." However, in the next sentences, he contradicted himself, writing:

> I would accord the Army Commander, General Van Fleet, the latitude his reputation and my high respect for his ability merited, while still retaining the right of approval or disapproval of his principal tactical plans. And in appraising these plans I intended on each occasion to consult personally and separately not only with the Army Commander himself, but with the Corps and Division Commanders of the Eighth Army, all of whom I knew intimately. I wanted in each instance to get for myself the feel of the situation as these officers responsible for execution of the plans might sense it. With this firsthand knowledge of their views added to all other relevant information, I would be in position to make sound decisions—for which I as Theater Commander would accept full and sole responsibility.[101]

Indeed, Ridgway meddled in Eighth Army operations in ways MacArthur never would have contemplated and that Ridgway himself would not have tolerated.[102]

Ridgway had his reasons for keeping such a tight grip on the Eighth Army. For one thing, he was a controlling officer who found it difficult not to interfere in military operations. In addition, he did not have complete confidence in Van Fleet. Collins had not consulted with Ridgway on his successor, so Van Fleet's appointment caught Ridgway by surprise. When Ridgway learned he would supersede MacArthur, he made a mental list of officers to recommend to Collins as his replacement. Van Fleet was not on it. Ridgway later admitted that Van Fleet had not crossed his mind, but he added that, considering his record in World War II and Greece, he could, in retrospect, understand Collins's thinking. Instead, Ridgway hoped that Joe Swing would take over the Eighth Army. Swing had led the Eleventh Airborne Division in the Philippines during the Pacific War, and Ridgway had tried unsuccessfully to secure him as a corps commander after Bryant Moore's death. He had much less combat leadership experience than Van Fleet, though, and probably lacked the temperament for such a high position. When Ridgway learned of Van Fleet's elevation, he accepted the order like the good soldier he was and praised Van Fleet to his subordinates. Later he claimed he was satisfied with Van Fleet's performance as Eighth Army chief, stating, "Van was a fine commander and I thought very highly of him. I still do."[103] At the time, though, Ridgway and Van Fleet were not very close, and one of Ridgway's aides later argued that Ridgway initially doubted Van Fleet's ability and intelligence. Whatever the truth, and whatever Ridgway's inclinations to micromanage the war from Tokyo, the fact was that he had to work with and rely on Van Fleet in the important fighting to come.[104]

Fortunately for Van Fleet, his other relationships began on a more solid footing. He got along well with the American ambassador, John Muccio, and South Korean officials. Unlike Ridgway, he respected and liked the Eighth Army staff. The rank and file appreciated Van Fleet's bluff, easygoing, and unpretentious manner. As for his chief combat commanders, he was savvy enough to know that he needed to treat them as individuals. One officer remembered, "He understood commanders, and he was very foxy and very clever in the way he handled commanders."[105] He had worked with Almond a few years earlier during the postwar demobilization. Like Ridgway before him, he grew to appreciate Almond's battlefield talents; he later referred to him as a "brilliant tactician" who could grab an idea and run with it. "He was an aggressive soldier," Van Fleet observed, "a type I like very much."[106] Almond, for his part, wrote of Van Fleet, "He is an honest fellow and a fine combat leader—much better than Walker."[107] Van Fleet knew Milburn from West Point and the Infantry School, and as a fellow corps commander in northwest Europe during World War II. He thought highly of him, believed he could rely on him, and appreciated his attitude. Van Fleet initially worried that Milburn would resent his elevation to Eighth Army command because Milburn was his senior, but Milburn instead gave him a warm welcome, saying, "Van, I am sure glad you are the commander. I would rather have you than anybody I know to work for."[108] Of course, it is also possible that Milburn was just grateful to get some breathing space between himself and the overbearing Ridgway. Finally, Van Fleet was familiar with Hoge from West Point and subsequent postings. Hoge thought the world of Van Fleet and later referred to him as a "crackerjack soldier."[109]

Chinese Spring Offensive

Throughout mid-April, the Eighth Army continued its methodical and cautious advance northward against varying resistance. Ridgway and Van Fleet were not interested in the ground gained but instead hoped to provoke a massive enemy offensive that would give the Eighth Army the opportunity to inflict so many casualties on the Chinese and North Koreans that they would agree to negotiate from a position of weakness. If and when the Chinese and North Koreans attacked, Ridgway and Van Fleet planned to retreat slowly to prepared defensive lines just south of the 38th Parallel while simultaneously using the Eighth Army's abundant firepower to make the enemy pay dearly for every mile won. Once the Chinese and North Korean wave had broken against the Eighth Army's defensive rocks, Ridgway and Van Fleet intended to use Charlie Dog Palmer's First Cavalry and Nick Ruffner's Second divisions to strike against each side of the enemy salient, thus, they hoped, cutting off and destroying even more Chinese and North Korean troops. Ridgway had great confidence in Palmer and his men; he had placed them in reserve to deliver his knockout blow.

Indeed, Ridgway and Van Fleet were both optimistic about the outcome of the battle they foresaw, and they communicated as much to their subordinates. As Ridgway put it, "If our experienced and veteran trained troops are carefully positioned in defense in depth, any penetration by the enemy should be defeated without difficulty."[110] They were not alone in believing that the Eighth Army could meet any challenge. Over at the Seventh Division, chief of staff Herb Powell noted, "Our division is at its peak, with experienced confident officers and men with high morale."[111] As April wore on and the Eighth Army pushed deeper into North Korea, evidence mounted of an imminent enemy offensive. Billows of smoke from fires set by the enemy to obscure troop movements filled the air. On 22 April, the Twenty-fourth Division captured a talkative Chinese soldier whose story convinced Babe Bryan that the balloon was about to go up. He called Milburn and said, "I think this is what we have been waiting for."[112]

As Bryan predicted, the enemy offensive began that night. Approximately a quarter of a million Chinese and North Korean soldiers assailed the Eighth Army along a forty-mile front on the western side of the peninsula. Milburn's First Corps was deployed along the far left of the Eighth Army line. It consisted of the ROK First Division, Soule's Third Division, the British 27th Brigade, the Turkish Brigade, Bradley's Twenty-fifth Division, and Bryan's Twenty-fourth Division. Unfortunately, the Turkish Brigade broke, forcing Milburn to pull his corps back. His efforts to do so, however, were complicated by the British Brigade's plight. It got boxed in along the Imjin River while serving as the corps' rear guard. Milburn ordered Soule to rescue it, but neither Milburn nor Soule initially recognized the seriousness of the situation because of the British habit of understatement. To the First Corps' right, Hoge's Ninth Corps—the ROK Sixth Division, Smith's First Marine Division, and the British Commonwealth 29th Brigade—was in even worse shape. The poorly positioned ROK Sixth Division, west of the Hwachon

Reservoir, disintegrated under the weight of the Chinese assault, creating a big hole in Hoge's line. This exposed Bryan's Twenty-fourth Division to the west and Smith's First Marine Division to the east, so both units had to fall back and refuse their uncovered flanks. The key to the Twenty-fourth Division's flank was the town of Kapyong, through which ran a vital lateral road. Hoge dispatched the Commonwealth Brigade there, and it fought off the Chinese in a ferocious battle. On the other side of the gap, an army artillery battalion and the marines managed to hold onto the Chunchon area long enough to permit the marines to retreat in an orderly fashion.

For all the confidence in Van Fleet that he later expressed, Ridgway was not about to give him carte blanche to conduct what was fast shaping up to be the war's climactic battle. Upon hearing the first discouraging reports from the peninsula, Ridgway on 24 April flew to Korea to assess the situation firsthand. He was distressed that Van Fleet wanted to deploy the First Cavalry Division to plug the holes in his lines because this deprived the Eighth Army of the Sunday punch he had planned to use to spearhead his counterattack. Considering the seriousness of the situation, though, Ridgway acquiesced. He also directed Van Fleet to rescue the British 27th Brigade and then fall back, but he emphasized that the Eighth Army should continue to employ all its firepower to wreak as much destruction as possible on the enemy. Ridgway's initial inclination was to withdraw behind the Han River and fight from there, even though this meant abandoning Seoul yet again. Van Fleet, however, argued persuasively that surrendering the capital, even one that was little more than a glorified ghost town, would demoralize the South Koreans. Besides, he doubted the military necessity of doing so. He explained to Ridgway, "Matt, this enemy doesn't know how to fight. They have no firepower behind them, they have no airpower. We have all of that. We can just finish them off right here, and you'll never find a better battlefield on which to do the job. I am confident we'll hold."[113] He made the same point to his subordinates. For example, when Milburn informed him that Sladen Bradley wanted to retreat fifteen or twenty miles to reorganize his division, Van Fleet responded, "Well, that is not in my book. I know all about withdrawing, too, but that doesn't apply in this war."[114] Van Fleet intended to duke it out where he was, and although he was willing to make readjustments to his lines to save surrounded units, he made it clear that he would do so only as a last resort.[115]

The Eighth Army began a fighting retreat southward on 25 April, falling back to a defensive position just north of Seoul dubbed Line Lincoln. Doing so involved some of the most intense combat of the entire war, during which Eighth Army artillery inflicted gruesome and terrible destruction on the charging Chinese and North Koreans. Extracting the British 27th Brigade proved especially difficult, and it lost a quarter of its personnel and much of a battalion in the process. Although there was plenty of blame to go around for the brigade's plight, Ridgway was inclined to assign a good bit of it to Soule and Milburn because neither officer actually visited the threatened sector for a firsthand look at the situation. Van Fleet, on the other hand, was more sympathetic toward his subordinates and concluded that they had acted reasonably. Heavy rains starting on 28 April further complicated operations by turning the roads to mud, reducing air support, and swelling the Han River. That day, the first Eighth Army combat units reached Line Lincoln and settled in. Despite the difficulties of the past few days, Van Fleet remained optimistic and hoped that the Chinese and North Koreans would assail his new line. Indeed, Line Lincoln fairly bristled with miles of interconnected trenches, layers of barbed wire, sandbagged bunkers, and plenty of mines and booby traps. Behind the Han, battalions of artillery with tons of ammunition emplaced awaited fire plans. Van Fleet hoped to bury the enemy under a mountain of artillery shells—so much so that Hoge later recalled, "He was a great person for firepower. You couldn't shoot enough for him. It didn't make any difference what kind of a cannon or gun it was, but he wanted just an avalanche of artillery poured on everything."[116]

As far as Van Fleet was concerned, Line Lincoln was practically impenetrable. At a 30 April meeting with his chief combat commanders, he noted that the Eighth Army had so far engaged only half of the available Chinese and North Korean troops, of whom he estimated half had become casualties. He wanted to finish off the remainder here and now:

> May is the month in which to defeat him. We can do it better in this area than in any other. If he is not given a bad set-back here, he can infiltrate forever. To stop him then in that type of operation we would have to meet the enemy man for man which we can't do. If we don't beat him now we will have more and more unfavorable weather for some months—less air—less mobility; the enemy will have better concealment. *Now is the time to destroy him. I would like to make this our maximum effort and do it north of the Han.*[117]

As it was, the Chinese and North Koreans had already suffered enormous losses, perhaps as many as 70,000, to gain a few hundred square miles of blasted and torn real estate. One officer observed, "They're spending people the way we spend ammunition."[118] Eighth Army casualties, on the other hand, amounted to only 7,000.[119]

Ridgway and Van Fleet concluded that the Eighth Army's southward displacement required some reorganizing of units. During their 24 April meeting, they opted to transfer Oliver Smith's First Marine Division from the Ninth Corps to the neighboring Tenth Corps so Hoge could focus on his most beleaguered outfits. However, the previous December, Ridgway had promised Smith that he would never again serve under Almond. Fortunately, a solution presented itself. In January, the Marine Corps commandant, General Clifton Cates, decided to rotate Smith home in April. His replacement, Major General Gerald Thomas, was already in Korea waiting to take over the division when Ridgway and Van Fleet made their decision. Ridgway and Van Fleet figured that the thing to do was to move up the turnover by a few days. Smith was reluctant to surrender his command in the middle of a battle, but Thomas bluntly informed him that there was only room in the division for one major general, and he intended to be it. Smith backed down and gave up the division earlier than planned, but it was shabby treatment of one of the war's most honorable and proficient generals. As things turned out, Thomas and Almond got along very well, and before he left Korea, Almond wrote Thomas to express his gratitude for Thomas's leadership and cooperativeness. This convinced some that perhaps Smith was responsible for the marines' difficulties with Almond. Others, though, pointed out that by the time the First Marine Division returned to the Tenth Corps, some of the more difficult corps staffers had left for other duties, and that Almond himself demonstrated greater tact and respect for the marines than when they originally served in his corps.[120]

Once the First and Ninth corps had settled in front of Seoul, Van Fleet remained convinced and hopeful that the Chinese would launch an all-out attack on the capital. To strengthen the Ninth Corps for the anticipated enemy assault, he decided to move Buddy Ferenbaugh's Seventh Division from the east central side of the peninsula to the Ninth Corps' right flank and put it under Hoge's command. The Seventh Division had been part of the Tenth Corps ever since the Inchon landing, so the transfer proved discombobulating for staffers accustomed to Almond's temperamental and hard-driving ways. Oddly enough, Ferenbaugh had a more difficult time working with Hoge than Almond. The two men did not see eye to eye on tactics, leading to arguments that did not seem to solve anything. Although Hoge actually had considerably more combat leadership experience than Ferenbaugh, Ferenbaugh failed to look past Hoge's engineering background. After one such dispute, Ferenbaugh fumed to an aide, "When I let a goddamn engineer tell *me* how to fight an infantry battle, it'll be a sad day for the [doughboys] of this fine division."[121] Almond, for his part, was sorry to lose the outfit because Ferenbaugh had done such a good job bringing it up to par.[122]

Because Van Fleet expected the Chinese and North Koreans to renew their offensive against the First and Ninth corps defending Seoul, he concentrated his resources and attention there. Unfortunately, the communists instead opted to launch a massive assault in the mountainous eastern half of the peninsula. They hoped to break through the Eighth Army's weak front there and sweep toward

Wonju, which would position them to assail the First and Ninth corps' exposed right flank and seize the South Korean capital. The Tenth Corps had recently fallen back to a line Almond dubbed No Name to remain abreast of the retreating First and Ninth corps. Van Fleet may have anticipated a push on Seoul, but Almond concluded that his corps was the enemy's next target. With his usual frenetic energy, Almond toured his divisions—from west to east, Thomas's First Marine, Ruffner's Second, the ROK Fifth, and the ROK Seventh—to make sure they were ready to resist the attack he believed was in the offing. His frequent reprimands and admonitions helped gird his American outfits, but they did little good for the South Koreans. When approximately 175,000 Chinese and North Korean soldiers charged forward starting on the night of 16–17 May, Almond's two ROK divisions, as well as the entire ROK Third Corps to their right, immediately crumbled under pressure. This created a huge hole in the Eighth Army's line through which the enemy rushed.[123]

Nick Ruffner's Second Division, dug in behind the Soyang River, found itself in a situation strikingly similar to the one it had faced around Kunu-ri the previous November and December. The collapse of ROK units to the east had again exposed the division's right flank to ferocious Chinese attacks. Happily, there were some important differences that enabled the Second Division to turn in a more creditable performance this time. For one thing, the weather was warm and supply lines more secure. In addition, the division's personnel had taken Almond's instructions to dig in seriously, so they had strung plenty of barbed wire and set thousands of mines and booby traps to cushion their front. There was abundant artillery support available; on the first day of the Chinese offensive, batteries cratered the area with 30,149 rounds. The Second Division was also now a veteran division led by a competent general and overseen by a corps commander who paid great attention to detail. Finally, Van Fleet made it clear that he expected the division to stay put, fight it out, and inflict as many casualties as possible on the enemy. Almond and Ruffner understood Van Fleet's thinking, but they were savvy enough to permit limited withdrawals if tactically necessary. Despite these advantages, the Second Division still made its share of mistakes in the ensuing week of brutal combat. Jack Chiles's 23rd Regiment lost many of its vehicles in a poorly conducted retreat, and two of Colonel John Coughlin's 38th Regiment battalions were cut up. At one point the division's attached Dutch battalion refused to assail an enemy-held knoll. Ruffner was fortunate to escape serious injury when his helicopter crashed into a hillside, forcing him to hike to the nearest battalion command post. Notwithstanding such errors and mishaps, the division hung on with grim determination. By 22 May, the Chinese had clearly shot their bolt and faded from contact. Ruffner rejoiced at his division's success. He claimed that the Second Division had just won one of the world's most decisive battles and singled out his artillery for particular praise. Almond was inclined to agree, claiming that the Second Division's victory confirmed his contention that Ruffner was a wonderful combat commander.[124]

Although the Second Division's brave stand along the Soyang stopped the Eighth Army's line from crumbling further, Chinese and North Korean soldiers continued to pour through the gap to the east. Van Fleet not only wanted to plug this gaping hole quickly but was also determined to use the opportunity to kill as many enemy soldiers as possible in the process. He flew to the east coast to visit Paik Sun Yup, now doggedly leading the ROK First Corps there, and ordered him to counterattack to "clean up this mess." Not surprisingly, the crisis brought Ridgway back to the peninsula from Japan to check up on the situation. On 20 May, he and Van Fleet flew to Almond's headquarters at Wonju to formulate a coordinated response to the Chinese and North Korean offensive. Almond did not downplay the stakes involved. He claimed that Pusan might fall in a week unless they took drastic action. Van Fleet had already dispatched part of his army's reserve, the Third Division's 15th Regiment, to the area to bolster the beleaguered Second Division, but Almond now wanted to deploy the entire division in regimental-sized islands to obstruct the flow of enemy troops southward. At the same time, he asked to use Colonel Frank Bowen's 187th Airborne Regiment to spearhead an assault out of Hongchon toward Inje to slice across the base of the enemy's salient. Ridgway's desire to entrap and destroy large numbers of Chinese and North Korean troops outweighed his distaste for employing elite paratroopers as ordinary infantry, so he and Van Fleet approved the scheme. Van Fleet also ordered the First and Ninth corps to attack out of Line Lincoln to give the enemy something else to worry about.[125]

Despite Almond's theatrics, there was never much chance of the Chinese and North Koreans reaching Pusan. Their armies lacked the logistical wherewithal to support active operations for more than a few days before their frontline troops exhausted their supplies and ammunition. As a result, their offensive began to run out of steam even before Almond implemented his plan. The Tenth Corps' attack, though, certainly exacerbated the enemy's discomfiture. Soule's Third Division reached the front between 19 and 21 May, followed by Bowen's 187th Airborne a day later. Almond ordered these units, as well as Ruffner's remarkably resilient Second Division, to attack on 23 May. As Almond saw things, this was his big opportunity to place his name in the pantheon of American military heroes, provided he moved fast. He explained to one journalist:

The enemy has committed the unpardonable sin of elongating himself. . . . I am trying to split the enemy in two. Two days from now may be too late. One day may be too late. Today is the day. . . . This is the psychological time to get in the best licks. The enemy is like a boxer reeling to the edge of the ring, and we want to clip him again before he bounces off the ropes.[126]

The Tenth Corps made some progress in the face of forbidding terrain, uncertain supply lines, and heavy opposition, but not enough to suit the demanding Almond. He was particularly disappointed with the sluggish 187th Airborne. His knowledge that the enemy was getting away increased his frustration, leading one officer to note that he seemed "emotionally upset." Flying overhead in a small plane, Almond observed thousands of Chinese and North Korean troops streaming northward to safety. They were clearly demoralized and beaten, and had abandoned all march discipline in an effort to escape. Many of them fell victim to hunger, exhaustion, disease, air and artillery strikes, and accidents. For the first time since they intervened the previous October, large numbers of Chinese soldiers surrendered. Paik remembered, "We took Chinese prisoners like plucking apples from a tree."[127] Although a good many enemy troops eluded the Tenth Corps' trap, Van Fleet was still impressed with Almond's celerity and energy. It is impossible to accurately gauge Chinese and North Korean casualties, but they undoubtedly numbered in the tens of thousands.[128]

Aggressive as ever, Ridgway and Van Fleet decided to assume the offensive even before Chinese and North Korean operations in the east had fizzled. As usual, they were more interested in inflicting casualties than in seizing territory. On 20 May, Milburn's First and Hoge's Ninth corps jumped off from Line Lincoln, north of Seoul. Hoge's divisions—Ferenbaugh's Seventh, Bryan's Twenty-fourth, and two South Korean ones—pushed toward Hwachon while Milburn headed for the Imjin River. Three days later, Almond's Tenth Corps joined the attack as well. Washed-out bridges and trails, rugged and remote terrain, limited air and artillery support, resupply problems, and occasionally tough enemy opposition all retarded progress. It was often impossible to commit more than a company at a time to action.

Van Fleet was especially frustrated with the slow pace of Hoge's operations; he chastised him for his dilatoriness and failure to use his artillery efficiently. Hoge defended himself by noting that his men had to hand carry artillery ammunition over the mountains because there were not enough roads available. He also responded by leaning on Ferenbaugh and Bryan. Ferenbaugh had a more difficult time than Bryan in accepting and complying with Hoge's orders. For one thing, he and Hoge continued to bicker over tactics, especially the proper employment of armor. Moreover, on the afternoon of 24 May the Chinese ambushed Ferenbaugh's jeep as he drove to a 32nd Regiment observation post. Enemy fire killed Ferenbaugh's guards and forced Ferenbaugh and his aide to take cover in some nearby heavy brush for the rest of the day. Toward evening a tank approached and cut its engine; an officer popped his head out of the turret and hollered Feren-baugh's name. Ferenbaugh and his aide could not reach the tank until dark, and by the time they arrived at Seventh Division headquarters, they were the worse for wear. Searching for Ferenbaugh brought Seventh Division operations to a virtual standstill for the day. On the other hand, Ridgway and Van Fleet remained pleased with Almond's energetic performance. Despite these problems, the Eighth Army steadily advanced. By the end of the month, it had regained almost all the real es-tate lost to the two big Chinese offensives and had killed and captured plenty of enemy soldiers in the process. On 3 June, Van Fleet ordered the Eighth Army for-ward again into North Korea in Operation Piledriver, which in two weeks brought it to Line Kansas/Wyoming, which extended from the Imjin River through the base of the so-called Iron Triangle to the Hwongchon Reservoir to Kamsong on the east coast.[129]

At this point, though, Ridgway suspended large-scale offensive operations. He concluded that he had achieved his goal of inflicting sufficient casualties to enable the Truman administration to approach the Chinese for negotiations from a posi-tion of strength. These negotiations, it was hoped, would lead to a timely cease-fire agreement that preserved South Korea. Ridgway believed that the Eighth Army could have continued its advance all the way to the Yalu River if necessary, but he doubted that it would be worth the cost. As he explained later:

> If we had been ordered to fight our way to the Yalu, we could have done it—if
> our government had been willing to pay the price in dead and wounded that
> action would have cost. From the purely military standpoint the effort, to my
> mind, would have not been worth the cost. A drive to the line of the Yalu and
> the Tumen [rivers] would have cleared Korea of the Chinese enemy. But he
> would have still been facing us in great strength beyond those rivers. The
> seizure of the land between the truce line and the Yalu would have merely
> meant the seizure of more real estate. It would have greatly shortened the
> enemy's supply lines by pushing him right up against his main supply bases in
> Manchuria. It would have greatly lengthened our own supply routes, and
> widened our battlefront from 110 miles to 420. Would the American people
> have been willing to support the great army that would have been required to
> hold that line? Would they have approved our attacking on into Manchuria?
> Or into the heart of the great mainland of Asia, a bottomless pit into which all
> the armies of the whole free world could be drawn and be ground to bits and
> destroyed? I doubt it.[130]

There were other factors to which Ridgway alluded but did not specifically men-tion. The Eighth Army was about to begin a rotation policy that would reduce its effectiveness by stripping it of some of its most battle-hardened officers, non-coms, and enlisted men. Moreover, many of the United States' allies were already leery about the war expanding into a global conflict and would not look sympathetically on actions that might enlarge the Korean sinkhole. Finally, enemy resistance had increased as the Eighth Army pushed northward, especially around the strategically vital Iron Triangle, which indicated that the North Koreans and Chinese were not as whipped as Ridgway implied. Whether the Eighth Army could really have reached the Yalu as easily as Ridgway claimed is therefore debatable.[131]

There were high-ranking Eighth Army combat commanders who disagreed with Ridgway's recommendation to the Truman administration and wanted to continue the push northward. Although Van Fleet recognized the logic in Ridgway's thinking and initially went along with it, he increasingly questioned the wisdom of suspending offensive operations and eventually became an outspoken critic of the policy. Almond was even more adamant in his disapproval. When Van Fleet told Almond about Ridgway's decision, Almond exclaimed, "Stop the attack! It has just begun to be successful for us. We have a chance to destroy those people down here, and that would end it."[132] As Almond and others saw things, halting the Eighth Army's northward march deprived the United States of its best weapon with which to bend the enemy to its will. They doubted that decreasing pressure on the Chinese and North Koreans would make them more pliable at the negotiating table but would instead give them time and opportunity to refit their battered armies, thus nullifying the military advantage that the Eighth Army had so painfully won.[133]

The catastrophic failure of their spring offensive and the Eighth Army's subsequent drive north of the 38th Parallel convinced the Chinese and North Korean leadership that they could not forcefully reunite the peninsula under communist rule. They were therefore open to a negotiated settlement of the conflict. After a delicate and complicated exchange of diplomatic signals and feelers, the Chinese and North Koreans agreed to meet at Kaesong on 10 July to discuss a resolution to the war. Truman administration hopes for a speedy resolution, however, proved illusory. Instead, negotiations dragged on for two years as the two sides bickered over the cease-fire line and prisoner repatriation. During that time, an additional 63,200 Americans were killed, wounded, or captured in the static fighting along Line Kansas/Wyoming. Moreover, the Eighth Army discovered that the North Koreans and Chinese had indeed used the respite provided by Ridgway's decision to suspend offensive operations to refurbish their forces and strengthen their lines. Overcoming these defenses would have required enormous resources. As Almond had predicted, stopping the Eighth Army's northward push cost the United States its most effective means of pressuring the enemy to bargain seriously. In the meantime, Eighth Army morale and public support for the conflict ebbed in the face of continuing communist intransigence at the peace talks. Not until July 1953, after Joseph Stalin had died and Truman had left office, did the Chinese and North Koreans prove willing to sign an agreement acceptable to the United States, South Korea, and their allies, one that preserved South Korean independence and established a demilitarized zone across the peninsula where the fighting ended.

Conclusions

It is impossible to overstate Ridgway's impact on the Korean War in early 1951. Collins's decision to appoint him as Walker's replacement, though predictable and logical, was an inspired choice. Ridgway took over a defeated and demoralized army, turned it around, and led it to victory. To be sure, he possessed some advantages that Walker lacked. He got along well with and had the support of both MacArthur and Collins, so he did not have to constantly look over his shoulder. In addition, the military situation in Korea was sufficiently desperate that MacArthur willingly gave Ridgway the kind of autonomy Walker never possessed. On the other hand, Ridgway faced his share of obstacles. He initially got little guidance from Tokyo and Washington, received few reinforcements, and assumed command of a thoroughly whipped army ready to go home. That he succeeded was in large part due to his forceful personality and powerful intellect. Despite the often contradictory policy proposals swirling around the Pentagon and State Department, Ridgway came to Korea knowing exactly what he wanted to do. As things turned out, his decision to hold there was something American policy makers from Truman to MacArthur could agree on. He also made his views known to everyone from his senior commanders to the lowliest private, thus providing a certitude that improved the Eighth Army's effectiveness. Not only did Ridgway have a goal but he also developed a plan to achieve it. He decided early on that seizing real estate was secondary to inflicting casualties on the Chinese and North Koreans. In doing so, Ridgway married the army's traditional strategy of attrition to military operations on the peninsula. It worked in that it compelled the enemy to enter into negotiations that ultimately led to a cease-fire that maintained South Korean independence, though it took longer than anyone anticipated.

Ridgway's plans would have mattered little had he not possessed senior combat leaders capable of implementing them. When he reached Korea, he was disappointed in the quality of most of his division and corps commanders. He believed that as a group they were tired and lacked the aggressiveness necessary to execute his strategy. Unlike Walker, Ridgway's relationships with Collins and MacArthur enabled him to remove most of them. He did so by rotating them out of the theater or kicking them upstairs to new posts. By portraying these personnel changes as routine, he spared the careers and reputations of those replaced and avoided embarrassing questions from Congress and the press. Moreover, he undertook this delicate task in the middle of active operations. Had Ridgway acted with his usual tactlessness, he might have roiled the officer corps and undermined the Eighth Army's effectiveness. Instead, he worked subtly to create a more skilled leadership team that could wreak the kind of damage on the enemy necessary to achieve his objectives. However, doing so terminated the ruthless personnel policies George Marshall instituted as chief of staff during World War II and established the precedent for the army of easing out unsuccessful combat commanders that characterized subsequent conflicts in Vietnam, Iraq, and Afghanistan.

These personnel changes were most obvious at the division level. Ridgway inherited seven American division commanders when he took over the Eighth Army, four of whom he replaced. Two of the four—Barr and Church—were clearly not up to their jobs physically or emotionally. The other two, Gay and Kean, had fought well enough, but Ridgway concluded that they were simply too tired after months of continuous action to continue as effective combat leaders. Of the three spared Ridgway's velvet-covered ax, McClure had just taken over the Second Division and had no record to defend. However, Ridgway raised no objection when Almond fired McClure a few weeks later, indicating that he might not have been too enamored with him to begin with and had only kept him because he was a Collins protégé. Oliver Smith's case was unique because the marines were responsible for his presence on the peninsula as First Marine Division commander. Ridgway therefore could not remove him without the consent of the Marine Corps commandant. As it was, Smith impressed Ridgway from the start, so there was no chance of Ridgway relieving him even if he could. Finally, Shorty Soule had been leading the Third Division in Korea for only a couple of months when Ridgway arrived and had done a good job in his relatively minor assignments. Moreover, Almond vouched for him, so Ridgway opted to leave him alone.

Things were more complicated at the corps level. Replacing corps commanders without jeopardizing their careers, reputations, and pride was difficult because there were so few jobs of commensurate prestige in the army, and most of those were held by men who were fulfilling their duties perfectly well. Ironically, of Ridgway's three corps commanders, Ned Almond presented the fewest problems. Despite his difficult personality, he possessed the kind of energy, aggressiveness, and determination that Ridgway looked for in his combat leaders. Besides, Ridgway knew full well that relieving Almond would alienate MacArthur. As it was, Almond proved his worth in the bitter fighting in the central corridor and during the second part of the Chinese spring offensive. At the other end of the competency spectrum, Ridgway quickly supplanted Breitling Coulter. Coulter's performance at the head of the Ninth Corps failed to impress him, so he kicked him up-stairs to become the Eighth Army's deputy commander, a position with responsibilities more diplomatic than military. Ridgway's biggest personnel conundrum, though, was Shrimp Milburn. Ridgway concluded that Milburn was a mediocre commander in an army that deserved better. However, he also recognized that removing him would cause more problems than it solved. Because there were no postings of equal or greater value available, there was no way to present a transfer as anything other than a demotion. Moreover, Milburn was loved and respected within his corps, so firing him could lead to dissension and hard feelings when Ridgway wanted everyone focused on killing the enemy. Besides, Milburn had not done anything wrong—or nothing meriting dismissal. Ridgway's solution was to keep Milburn with the First Corps but to ride herd over him in an effort to improve his military skills. During the fighting that winter and spring, Milburn functioned with his usual competence, but rarely in the stellar manner Ridgway wanted.

The seven officers Ridgway selected as his corps and division commanders seemed to have little in common with each other beyond their profession and Ridgway's confidence in their abilities. Except for Ruffner, who graduated from the Virginia Military Institute, they were all West Pointers. Each of them had attended the Command and General Staff School, but just two—Bryan and Ferenbaugh—went to the Army War College; the rest relied on World War II to complete their military educations. Only four of them had led units larger than a battalion when Ridgway chose them: Bradley, Hoge, Moore, and Palmer. Bryan, Ferenbaugh, and Ruffner had each had important and respectable World War II posts, but until they took over divisions in Korea, they had never made the life-and-death decisions that were part of a high-ranking combat commander's job description. Although it seemed to some that Ridgway brought his new team with him, three of them—Bradley, Palmer, and Ruffner—were already in Korea when they assumed their new duties. Ridgway had worked with Bryan, Ferenbaugh, Hoge, and Moore but knew the rest mostly by reputation. Indeed, Ruffner in particular was more MacArthur and Almond's pick than Ridgway's. Their personalities were equally varied. Ruffner was as affable and serene as Bradley was erratic and brittle. They all fought well, if not brilliantly, that winter and spring, and Ridgway was generally pleased with their performances. However, Ridgway's cautious, methodical, and systematic strategy played to their collective strengths. They each faced sticky situations during the Chinese winter and spring offensives, but they never experienced the extraordinarily chaotic circumstances—poorly trained men, uncertain supply lines, exposed flanks, inadequate equipment and weaponry, insufficient coordination—that had plagued their predecessors during the first six months of the war. For all their differences in background and temperament, they were all typical products of the early twentieth-century army—men trained to get the job done by applying American matériel superiority in a cost-effective and conventional manner.

Ridgway had an incongruous relationship with James Van Fleet, his successor as Eighth Army commander. Collins selected Van Fleet without consulting Ridgway, who later admitted that he would have recommended someone else for the post if asked. Despite Ridgway's reservations, Van Fleet was probably the best man for the position. Although he had not attended the Command and General Staff School and Army War College, he had had plenty of on-the-job training as a regimental, division, and corps commander in World War II and later as the head of the American mission to Greece. He was therefore thoroughly familiar with the heavy responsibilities leading a field army in battle entailed. Ridgway, however, had a difficult time letting his old position go, and he often treated Van Fleet like his deputy. During the Chinese spring offensives, Ridgway on several occasions flew to the peninsula to help Van Fleet make operational decisions. He did so partly because he was a hands-on leader who could not resist being at the scene of the action and partly because he was unsure of Van Fleet's abilities. Ridgway had complained about MacArthur's meddling, but MacArthur never interfered the way Ridgway did. Fortunately, Van Fleet agreed with Ridgway's strategy and put up with his impositions with good grace. Both Ridgway and Van Fleet were strong-willed men, and it is questionable whether they could have maintained their rapport if active campaigning had continued.

Conclusion

Transforming the Eighth Army

On 27 July 1953, stone-faced negotiators at Panmunjom silently signed a cease-fire agreement that ended the Korean War. It was not a peace treaty but rather a truce that terminated the fighting, established a demilitarized zone along the existing battle front just north of the 38th Parallel, and called for the repatriation of prisoners. The settlement therefore confirmed the peninsula's division between noncommunist South Korea and communist North Korea. Though its denouement was inconclusive, the conflict's human costs were substantial. In a bit more than three years of combat, the United States suffered about 140,000 battle casualties, including 36,500 dead. ROK losses totaled 621,500. South Korea's non-American United Nations allies added an additional 17,000 killed and wounded to the butcher's bill. It is difficult to accurately determine North Korean and Chinese casualties, but they probably numbered around 1.5 million. Finally, approximately a million Korean civilians died of various causes, including hunger, starvation, disease, and injuries.

The Korean War was a conflict that no American policy maker wanted in a place of little direct strategic importance to the United States. Frustration and confusion seemed to characterize American policy and its implementation from start to finish. To an American public accustomed to the totality and finality of the world wars, the Truman administration's actions in Korea seemed opaque and bewildering. However, although the players and context changed, the basic American objective remained remarkably consistent. Except after Inchon, when the unification of the peninsula appeared attainable, the fundamental American aim was always, first and foremost, the preservation of South Korean independence. The United States therefore achieved its goal and from this perspective "won" the war even though North Korea and communist China remained extant.

The conflict also had some far-reaching and unintended consequences for the United States. Truman's original pledge to protect South Korea stretched out into decades and cost the United States much more than the conflict's original $30 billion price tag. The belief that the Soviet Union was behind North Korean aggression convinced American policy makers to undertake a massive military buildup that, for better or worse, deepened American involvement in Western Europe, Japan, and Indochina. The conflict also poisoned Sino-American relations for a generation and contributed to Truman's declining popularity. Indeed, he did not run for reelection in 1952, so it was his successor, Republican Dwight Eisenhower, who was in office when the cease-fire was signed. Most important of all, though, the Korean War proved that the United States was serious enough about waging the Cold War to put its blood and treasure on the line, a commitment that lasted more than forty years until the Soviet Union's collapse.

Fewer than thirteen months separated the North Korean invasion of South Korea from the solidification of the battle lines just north of the 38th Parallel. It was, however, a traumatic roller coaster of a year for the United States Army. The army had not expected war, so it initially suffered a series of severe and humiliating reverses at the hands of the North Koreans. No sooner had it overpowered the North Koreans at Inchon and along the Pusan Perimeter than the Chinese entered the conflict and routed it. By the time the army overcame that challenge by trouncing the Chinese spring offensive, the Truman administration suspended the Eighth Army's northward advance and sought a negotiated settlement. Although these negotiations ultimately proved successful, they took much longer than anyone expected. During this time, the fighting degenerated into a squalid stalemate that created the impression that the army had been unable to defeat the enemy on the battlefield. This was a bitter pill to swallow for army officers who believed that they had had the North Koreans and Chinese on the run by June 1951 and could have pushed all the way to the Yalu. It contributed to the frustration and distaste many of them associated with the war.

It is impossible to accurately evaluate the army's performance during the Korean War's first decisive year without examining its combat leadership at the field army, corps, and division levels. After all, an army's potency is usually directly proportional to the skill of its generals who run its machinery and execute directives. The decisions these men made helped determine the outcome of battles such as along the Pusan Perimeter, on the Chongchon River, and at Wonju. The quality of the army's commanders on the peninsula initially left something to be desired, but as time went on, they became increasingly proficient and gradually achieved battlefield dominance over the Chinese and North Koreans. There was nothing inevitable or accidental about this leadership transformation. The army's top generals in Washington, Tokyo, and Korea recognized the problem, identified solutions, and implemented them. By doing so, they helped secure South Korea's independence.

The army was completely unprepared in almost every respect to fight the Korean War. This was especially true of its senior combat leadership. Before the conflict, army policy gave priority to staff officers for combat posts. The idea was to develop a more flexible officer corps by providing everyone eligible with experience leading combat units, and to make sure that the careers of World War II staffers were not penalized simply because they had not had combat leadership opportunities. However, the process sometimes degenerated into securing prestigious sinecures for men near retirement so they could inflate their records before they left the army. In the Eighth Army, three of the four divisions and ten of the twelve regiments were commanded by men with little combat leadership experience when the war began. To be sure, Dave Barr, Hap Gay, and Bill Kean were capable men who had held important staff positions during World War II, but they rose through the army's senior hierarchy because they had hitched their wagons to the stars of other, more accomplished officers. Barr and Gay both procured their divisions as much through wheedling and back-scratching as through any rational selection process designed to put these outfits in the hands of the most capable individuals. Neither of them had expected to take their divisions into action but instead looked forward to cushy and prominent assignments to cap their careers. These men were certainly not bad soldiers, but no one expected them to become chief of staff. Although Gay and Kean turned in adequate, if not spectacular, performances in Korea, Barr did not. For all three men, their learning curves were steeper and longer than those of more experienced officers deployed to the peninsula. No doubt they faced serious deficiencies for which they were not responsible—poorly trained and equipped troops, most obviously—but officers such as Michaelis managed to overcome these problems in a short time and fight well. The fact is that there were more battle-hardened and proficient officers available to run these divisions who might have given the Eighth Army that extra edge that made the difference between victory and defeat.[1]

Partly because of poor combat leadership, the Eighth Army did not fight well in its initial encounters with the North Koreans in the summer of 1950 and with the Chinese a few months later. The army's high command—Collins, Ridgway, MacArthur, and Walker—recognized this difficulty early on. During his August battlefield inspection, Ridgway pointed out that the quality of regimental commanders was especially poor. Later, after he took over the Eighth Army, Ridgway reached a similar conclusion about many of his division and corps commanders. Although such assessments seem commonsensical and obvious in retrospect, there was nothing inevitable about them. Large organizations such as the army often have trouble identifying the roots of problems and those responsible for them, especially if those in charge are out of touch and unfamiliar with the situation on the ground. Fortunately, Collins, Ridgway, and Walker were tough, skilled, and experienced officers who had led divisions and corps during World War II. They were therefore thoroughly familiar with the challenges of taking men into battle and could quickly sniff out deficient leadership. They also understood the seriousness of the matter because they knew full well that a unit's performance was almost always tied to the quality of its commander.

Not only did the army's top commanders recognize the Eighth Army's leadership problem but they were also willing to do something about it. Here, too, there was nothing inevitable about their actions. The army's general officers composed a small and tightly knit family where everyone knew everyone else personally or by reputation. They often worked and socialized together, so there were a lot of personal relationships at stake. Removing commanders perceived as failures was awkward and unpleasant for everyone involved. Those relieved faced humiliation and career stagnation. They could also cause dissension and undermine morale within the officer corps by griping and kvetching about what they perceived as unfair treatment. This could not only decrease the army's efficiency but might also provoke embarrassing questions from the press and Congress. A purge of regimental, division, and corps chiefs could, in sum, reflect badly on the army and those who led it. Collins, MacArthur, and Ridgway might have simply ignored the issue and hoped that the army's advantages in matériel, weaponry, and equipment would compensate for poor leadership. Fortunately, they opted to bite the bullet and try to fix the flaws they had identified in this area. It was relatively easy to remove regimental commanders because they were colonels with little institutional power. At the division and corps levels, though, Collins, MacArthur, and Ridgway used more finesse because the men involved were often well-respected and well-connected friends. They portrayed reliefs as routine reassignments, and they gave the transferees promotions in rank and responsibility. This preserved reputations, avoided disgrace, and generated no controversy. On the other hand, it set a bad precedent that came back to haunt the army in subsequent wars in Vietnam, Iraq, and Afghanistan.

Happily for the army, there were plenty of capable and veteran officers available to replace those commanders deemed unsatisfactory. Indeed, the army's personnel bench was deeper than at any time in its history. During World War II, hundreds of officers led its regiments, divisions, and corps. These men proved their worth by defeating the Germans and Japanese in some of the most complex and difficult operations in world military history. Most of those who had failed had already been weeded out one way or another. These tested leaders were therefore thoroughly familiar with the awesome responsibilities of command and the confusion of battle. Although some of them had retired or left the service, large numbers remained to serve in Korea. Of the army's 125 major generals, for example, more than fifty of them had headed divisions in World War II. The pool for brigadier generals and colonels was equally rich. Experience did not always equal proficiency—McClure's case proved this—but it was usually an important ingredient for combat prowess. This overabundance of skillful personnel was some-what mitigated by the need to oversee the massive military buildup the Truman administration had simultaneously undertaken in case of global conflict with the Soviet Union, but there were still enough qualified people for Korea. Collins made some of these officers accessible to Walker at the regimental level soon after the war began. After Ridgway took over the Eighth Army, he tapped into this reservoir of talent for many of his division and corps commanders. Moreover, the war generated its own proven leaders—men such as Charlie Palmer who rose to command regiments and divisions. As a result, by the time Ridgway suspended offensive operations, the Eighth Army was perhaps the best-led field army in American history up to that point.

Improved leadership was the most important component in the Eighth Army's transformation into an effective fighting force. Better-trained personnel, up-graded weapons and equipment, and greater coordination and communications also played important roles. Moreover, by the spring of 1951, it had a leader in whom everyone had confidence and who had developed a clear military objective and a plan to achieve it. Ridgway's strategy did not require brilliant generals to perform battlefield miracles. Rather, it required competent men capable of using the tools placed at their disposal. Fortunately, the army possessed such officers and succeeded in placing them in command of the Eighth Army's corps and divisions.

Command Relationships

With his powerful personality, extensive authority, and high public profile, MacArthur dominated the Korean War's first year more than any other American. However, he played a surprisingly inert role in personnel matters. Although he went out of his way to procure the Tenth Corps for Almond and wholeheartedly agreed with Collins that Ridgway should succeed Walker at the head of the Eighth Army, he rarely interfered in the selection and relief of the army's major combat commanders in his theater. For instance, he quietly acquiesced without protest to Collins's and Ridgway's decision to overhaul the Eighth Army's corps and division leadership after Ridgway took over the Eighth Army. This passivity was not new but was instead part of MacArthur's modus operandi. Even during World War II he had given his lieutenants wide latitude in choosing their own people as long as they completed their missions successfully and did not horn in on his limelight. This hands-off attitude worked when MacArthur had a capable field army commander sure of his role, such as Ridgway. On the whole, though, this forbearance in Korea probably did greater damage to the war effort than a more intrusive leadership style would have. MacArthur clearly lacked confidence in Walker and wanted someone else to run the Eighth Army, but he refused to take the initiative to secure a replacement. Instead, he sought to dilute and undercut Walker's authority by setting up Almond as a second de facto field army commander on the eastern part of the peninsula. He also failed to communicate freely and openly with Walker, thus undermining the mutual trust on which good relationships are based. Had MacArthur taken a more active interest in ensuring that the Eighth Army had a proficient combat commander on whom he felt he could rely, the Chinese might not have intervened so effectively in the conflict.

Conversely, MacArthur interfered too much in policy matters determined by the Truman administration and the Joint Chiefs of Staff. The problem was that MacArthur was no ordinary general. He had been chief of staff when Collins and his JCS colleagues were midlevel officers, giving him psychological seniority over the Joint Chiefs and making it difficult for them to exert their authority over him. MacArthur was also a public figure with a large following ready and willing to voice their support for him. Finally, he possessed an impressive and intimidating military record dating back to World War I. The successful Inchon operation, undertaken against the JCS's better judgment, served as a potent reminder of his military genius and made it even more difficult for the Joint Chiefs to question his judgment. For these reasons, he possessed a certain immunity from the usual command constraints that the JCS felt compelled to tolerate.

MacArthur's unique stature was not an insoluble problem early in the war when he and the Truman administration more or less shared the same goals on the peninsula, but it became one once Chinese intervention beckoned. MacArthur disagreed with the Truman administration's efforts to limit the conflict and did not respect the men who formulated it. His arrogance made it impossible for him to see matters from their perspective or to recognize that his views might not square with the realities on the ground in Korea. He was instead prepared to twist and circumvent Truman administration and JCS directives, such as the one prohibiting the deployment of American forces near the Yalu, when it suited his purposes. Truman and the JCS, for their part, were willing to abide his intransigence rather than undertake the extraordinary efforts necessary to remove him from his post—at least at first. After Chinese intervention proved MacArthur devastatingly fallible and created insurmountable policy differences with the Truman administration, Truman and the JCS decided that they could not accept his public dissent from their stated objectives. Had MacArthur simply obeyed his orders and kept his reservations to himself—or at least kept them in house—he would not have lost his command. But he would not have been Douglas MacArthur either.

Walton Walker was an experienced and capable combat leader with a sterling World War II record to prove it. In the first weeks of the Korean War, he overcame tremendous difficulties to stop the North Korean juggernaut along the Pusan Perimeter. His biggest challenge, however, was not the enemy but rather his poor relationship with MacArthur. Walker realized early in the war that MacArthur lacked confidence in him and saw him as an outsider, and he worried that MacArthur might relieve him if given a reason. Moreover, he had few friends in the Pentagon to look to for support. Walker responded to this awkward situation by promptly and unquestioningly carrying out MacArthur's directives—or anyhow seeming to. Obedience is of course the hallmark of a good soldier, but Walker also refrained from giving MacArthur his candid and frank views of the military situation so he would not appear contrary or disloyal. For instance, he never forcefully expressed to MacArthur his serious reservations about resuming the offensive after the initial Chinese intervention. Instead, Walker resorted to subterfuge when his military judgment conflicted with MacArthur's wishes. Sometimes it worked, such as his decision to surreptitiously retreat behind the Naktong River despite MacArthur's insistence that the Eighth Army stand in place and fight. On the other hand, it failed miserably when Walker attempted to convert MacArthur's end-of-war offensive to the Yalu into a reconnaissance-in-force. Whatever the result, it was a poor way for a field army commander to deal with his superior. Walker was no doubt in a difficult position, but honestly voicing his opinions to MacArthur behind closed doors would have benefited the war effort more than the Kabuki tactics Walker embraced. In failing to do so, Walker put his career above the welfare of the army in his charge, with tragic results.

There was nothing subtle about Walker's relationships with his corps and division commanders. With the exception of the amiable Milburn, Walker treated them all roughly, directly, and bluntly. He often yelled at them and threatened to replace them when they failed to achieve their objectives according to Walker's timetable. For all his browbeating, though, Walker demonstrated considerable forbearance toward them. Although they all made mistakes, he did not fire any of them for incompetence. Instead, he transferred Breitling Coulter to the Ninth Corps rather than send him home, and he used illness as a pretext to remove Dutch Keiser from the Second Division after the Kunu-ri debacle. Walker's restraint was probably due to his belief that new combat leaders needed time to settle down and learn their trade, an unwillingness to relieve such high-ranking combat leaders in the middle of crucial operations, and a concern that doing so might reflect poorly on him. There is certainly a logic to his thinking, but considering the quality of some of his corps and division commanders and the talent pool available, he tolerated more mediocrity than he should have.

One of the reasons Matthew Ridgway proved a more successful general in Korea than Walker was his ability to establish and manage beneficial relationships with his superiors. Whereas Walker had little contact with or backing from the army's top leadership, Ridgway was the quintessential Pentagon insider who knew everyone worth knowing. Ridgway kept in close touch with Collins during his tenure as Eighth Army commander. Working together, the two men not only purged the Eighth Army of most of its corps and division chiefs without generating much controversy but also procured more effective replacements in whom Ridgway had confidence. Of equal importance, Ridgway had MacArthur's respect. MacArthur agreed to Ridgway and Collins's plan to overhaul the Eighth Army's combat leadership and let them select their own men. In addition, MacArthur's support made it easier for Ridgway to put Almond in his place. Finally, by the time Ridgway reached Korea, MacArthur had more or less washed his hands of the dismal military situation there that he had helped create, giving Ridgway the time and space he needed to settle in and stamp his own imprint on the Eighth Army. Even after MacArthur showed renewed interest in the peninsula, Ridgway's victories there and his own forceful personality prevented MacArthur from overshadowing him. MacArthur and the army's leaders may have treated Walker like a neglected stepchild, but Ridgway went into battle knowing that the American military establishment was behind him.

Ridgway was every bit as tough and direct with his corps and division commanders as Walker had been. He was also more ruthless and guileful. Walker tolerated a certain mediocrity from his top combat chiefs, but Ridgway had higher standards and moved quickly to replace many of those generals he deemed ineffective with men of his own choosing. As far as Ridgway was concerned, there was no need to accept second-rate generals when there were so many well-qualified up-and-comers available capable of running corps and divisions more proficiently. Within two months of arriving in Korea, Ridgway removed six of the Eighth Army's nine army corps and division commanders. Moreover, unlike Walker, he had the connections to do so in a way that preserved the careers of those relieved. Ridgway was equally hard on his new team but was sufficiently satisfied with their performances to keep them all in place. Of course, he was largely responsible for creating a relatively familiar and predictable strategic environment in which they operated, enabling them to fight with greater skill than some of their predecessors had displayed in the war's chaotic first months. He also had a proprietary interest in them that probably colored his opinions.

Van Fleet's attempts to run the Eighth Army were complicated by his relationship with Ridgway. Despite his subsequent claims to the contrary, Ridgway was determined to closely oversee the Eighth Army from his new Tokyo headquarters. He was a hands-on general to begin with, and he was not familiar enough with Van Fleet to give him carte blanche. As a result, Ridgway interfered with Eighth Army operations in ways that never would have occurred to MacArthur. Fortunately, Van Fleet tolerated this meddling. As a good soldier, he understood that subordinates must accommodate themselves to their superior's methods, not vice versa. Besides, he was initially too busy responding to the big Chinese spring offensive to make an issue out of it. Finally, that spring he and Ridgway saw eye to eye on the best way to fight the war. If anything, Van Fleet was more adamant than Ridgway about using firepower to kill the enemy. As for his corps and division commanders, Van Fleet shared Ridgway's belief that some of them were too slow, but he was largely content with them. Because he had a warmer and more understanding personality than the flinty Ridgway, he established a greater rapport with his lieutenants.

Ned Almond was easily the most controversial and divisive of the five American corps commanders the Eighth Army employed in the war's first year. He got along reasonably well with his superiors by giving them exactly what they wanted. At the beginning of the conflict, he served as MacArthur's efficient chief of staff and planner for the Inchon landing. Almond did such a good job running MacArthur's headquarters and organizing Operation Chromite that MacArthur appointed him head of the Tenth Corps and later gave him an autonomous command in northeast Korea. Almond did not seek either of these roles, but he certainly made the most of them to gain the glory he sought. Whatever operational errors Almond committed in his independent command, MacArthur did not recognize them or hold them against him. After the Tenth Corps became part of the Eighth Army, Almond won over first Ridgway and then Van Fleet with his loyalty, aggressiveness, and combativeness. Almond's relationships with his divisional chiefs, on the other hand, were much more checkered and strained. He liked tough and can-do subordinates who were not afraid to stand up to him but who still faithfully carried out his orders. Ferenbaugh, Ruffner, Soule, and Thomas met these criteria, so Almond worked well with them. However, he did not click with Barr, McClure, and Smith, all of whom often disagreed with Almond's operational ideas, lacked the kind of personality Almond respected, or both. Almond could and did fire McClure, but he had to endure Smith because Smith was a marine who, as things turned out, was more often right than wrong in his battlefield instincts. Perhaps because they had been prewar friends, Almond tried to buck up Barr through force of will, but he later agreed with Ridgway that Barr should be sent home.

Almond and Shrimp Milburn were as different as black and white. The abrasive Almond was hard to work for and harder to like, but everyone appreciated Milburn's affability. However, his friendly taciturnity was a two-edged sword. He was so withdrawn that Ridgway in particular underestimated his abilities, but his geniality also prevented Ridgway from acting on his assessment by replacing or chastising him. Walker liked and respected him so much that he desisted from his usual browbeating. Milburn in turn served as Walker's mainstay during the Pusan

Perimeter breakout, during the invasion of North Korea, and in the fighting along the Chongchon. Ridgway had a dimmer view of Milburn's talents, but he refrained from removing him because doing so would have hurt Eighth Army morale at a time when the army's collective spirits were already low enough. He dealt with Milburn by riding herd on him and prodding him to be more aggressive. Van Fleet came to the same conclusions as Ridgway but was more sensitive to Milburn's feelings. On the other hand, division commanders enjoyed serving under Milburn. Milburn visited them often, acknowledged their problems and concerns, and tried hard to secure the resources they needed. Through it all, Milburn maintained an almost Zenlike equanimity and serenity toward his superiors and subordinates.

Of the remaining three corps commanders, Bryant Moore led the Ninth Corps for less than a month before dying of a heart attack, so he had little opportunity to form and express any firm assessments of his superiors and subordinates. Hoge thought the world of Ridgway and Van Fleet, and loyally served both men. They in turn appreciated Hoge's doggedness, but they believed that he should have advanced faster after the Chinese spring offensive failed. Hoge leveled the same charge against some of his division commanders, especially Ferenbaugh, but he understood that the horribly difficult terrain contributed to their sluggishness. As for Coulter, he was the least successful in fitting into the Eighth Army. Although Walker never questioned his physical courage, he doubted that Coulter was sufficiently forceful to lead the Pusan Perimeter breakout. Walker therefore transferred Coulter from the First Corps to the embryonic Ninth Corps and gave the starring role to Milburn. Three months later, Coulter did little along the Chongchon to prove himself to Walker. However, Walker was more inclined to blame Keiser for the debacle there. Unfortunately for Coulter, he failed to impress Ridgway either during the Chinese New Year's offensive. Ridgway quickly concluded that Coulter was not up to running a corps and kicked him upstairs to a less critical post.

The first batch of division commanders deployed to Korea—Church, Dean, Gay, Kean, and Keiser—generally appreciated Walker and took his badgering in stride. Those who later served under Milburn enjoyed the experience and championed their new boss. Coulter's subordinates, on the other hand, never gave him the kind of loyalty and support that helped shield Milburn from Ridgway's ax. In the independent Tenth Corps, Barr and Smith had as little respect for Almond's generalship as they did for him personally. McClure later had the same problem. Soule, however, responded better to Almond's leadership and worked well with him. As for the division chiefs Ridgway selected, they had less traumatic experiences. For one thing, the fact that Ridgway had personally chosen most of them generated lots of goodwill and loyalty, making them more accepting of his sometimes brusque ways. Van Fleet maintained this positivity through his good-naturedness and kindness. Moreover, by early 1951 the Eighth Army was waging a systematic and methodical war that was less chaotic, if not necessarily any easier, than their predecessors faced. Because there were fewer battlefield surprises, and since the Eighth Army was now better trained and equipped than previously, these men made fewer mistakes that roiled the command structure. Put another way, Ridgway's personnel policies and strategy homogenized the Eighth Army's combat command leadership in a way that benefited its war effort.

Evaluating Commanders

Assessing commanders is an unscientific, subjective, and tricky task. Generalship, like beauty, is often in the eye of the beholder. There are inherent difficulties in all criteria. The easiest benchmark is to judge commanders according to their ability to fulfill their missions—whether or not they won their battles. Certainly a general who defeated the enemy is probably better than one who did not. Doing so, though, disregards factors that should be taken into account and over which a general may not have control. These include the opposing enemy, prevailing terrain, available resources, and guidance from superiors. The obstacles William Dean faced at the head of the Twenty-fourth Division at the beginning of the Korean War, for example, were much more daunting than those Babe Bryan confronted months later and should be considered in gauging both men. Weighing the estimations of contemporaries and historians is another evaluative tool, but is also problematic. Opinions are inherently personalized and are therefore subject to ax-grinding, bias, distortion, emotionalism, and incomplete information. The more controversial the officer, the more likely these hazards will manifest themselves, as evidenced by the polemic literature surrounding MacArthur. A final, and somewhat related, appraisal method is the fates of generals. By this technique, those generals who gained promotion and recognition were probably more successful than those who did not. Of course, there are plenty of reasons other than merit why an officer might get elevated above his peers, including connections, politicking, and seniority. Just because Breitling Coulter was promoted and appointed deputy commander of the Eighth Army does not mean he was a successful general—far from it. Fortunately, using all these yardsticks together to rate generalship provides a redundancy that promises more accuracy than any single measure.

Twenty-one men led the Eighth Army and its various corps and divisions during the Korean War's first vital year. Because of the army's institutionalized racism and sexism, all of them were white men, but other than that and their chosen profession, they had surprisingly little in common. There was no single type of officer who filled these positions. Almost all of them were in their fifties, with Walker the oldest at sixty and Ruffner the youngest at forty-eight. The average age was fifty-eight for the Eighth Army commanders, fifty-seven for the corps commanders, and fifty-two for the division commanders. The most obvious longitudinal change was a decline in the average age of division commanders from fifty-four for the original ones to a bit less than fifty for those Ridgway selected.

All twenty-one officers had at least some higher education. Twelve graduated from West Point, two (Almond and Ruffner) from the Virginia Military Institute, and three (Coulter, Dean, and Gay) from other institutions. Barr, Church, McClure, and Soule all started college but left—in McClure's case, not by his own accord—and secured commissions to fight in World War I. Unlike many of their similarly positioned World War II predecessors, none of them rose from the enlisted ranks. Once in the army, all received additional training. A startling percentage of these twenty-one officers did not attend both the Command and General Staff School and Army War College, even though graduating from both places was the preferred route to the top of the army's hierarchy. A big reason for this is that World War II prevented many of these men from putting their time in at the Army War College. So although all but two of them went to the Command and General Staff School, only nine darkened the doors of the Army War College. Gay and Van Fleet were unique because they did not graduate from either place, which was particularly ironic in Van Fleet's case because he ended up in charge of the entire Eighth Army. World War II offered midlevel officers a chance to command big units, but only three of the thirteen officers who led divisions in Korea in 1950–1951 had such experience when they first took their divisions into action. Considering the army's prewar policy of giving divisions to officers who had not had the opportunity to lead large outfits, these numbers are not shocking for the original division commanders. However, the percentage is just about the same for the division commanders Ridgway installed, even though he had pretty much the entire officer corps from which to choose. As for the field army and corps chiefs, all of them had led regiments, divisions, and corps during World War II, so they were thoroughly familiar with their Korean War responsibilities.

Of these twenty-one field commanders, more than half were removed from their posts before the war settled into a stalemate. This seems like good evidence for serious leadership difficulties in the conflict's first year. A closer look undermines some of this thesis, but not all of it. Two of these officers died there—Walker in his jeep accident and Moore by heart attack—and Dean was captured. Ridgway was eventually promoted to MacArthur's position as theater commander, and ten others were still running their units when Ridgway suspended offensive operations. Although only one, McClure, was relieved for outright failure, Keiser's removal, ostensibly for exhaustion, was pretty close. A number of others—Barr, Church, Coulter, Gay, and Kean—were kicked upstairs, sent home, or both because Ridgway was dissatisfied with their performances or concluded that they were too tired to continue in their posts. This meant that seven, or one third, fell short of the standards set for them by their superiors. Because World War II should have weeded out most of the army's substandard commanders, this percentage was surprisingly high, indicating that the army's prewar personnel policies did not always place the best-qualified men in the most important combat posts.

No review of Korean War leadership is complete without examining MacArthur's role in the conflict. His supporters point to Inchon as the biggest piece of evidence for MacArthur's superior generalship on the peninsula. Indeed, it is impossible to downplay his role in organizing and implementing this particular operation, which almost overnight terminated North Korean efforts to conquer South Korea unaided. Despite his brilliant victory at Inchon, though, MacArthur failed in the Korean War. In fact, he made one poor decision after another that contributed greatly to the Eighth Army's woes. MacArthur erred in initially underestimating North Korean potential, in removing the Tenth Corps from the strategic chessboard for several crucial weeks by dispatching it by sea to Wonsan, in distrusting Walker and dividing command in Korea between him and Almond, in manipulating JCS instructions, in discounting the possibility of sustained Chinese intervention, in failing to provide clear direction while the Chinese routed his armies, and in publicly disagreeing with Truman administration policies. Fortunately, American matériel superiority, the courage and skill of the officers and men in his theater, and Ridgway's performance enabled the Eighth Army to overcome these mistakes and defeat the enemy on the battlefield. MacArthur and his loyalists then and later defended his actions, but their justifications were often based on ex post facto rationales that did not always jibe with contemporary evidence. After his expulsion from the Philippines in 1942, MacArthur proved himself a great World War II general by repeatedly seizing the initiative, exhibiting great daring, acting unilaterally, and never taking counsel of his fears. Even his more questionable Pacific War tactics, such as playing his subordinates off against one another and undermining JCS strategy, seemed to pay off in the end. He behaved in the same way in Korea, but with tragic results. Like many other Americans, he never grasped that it was a different kind of conflict—politically, ideologically, geographically, and strategically—than anything he had previously experienced, and this proved his undoing.

Of the Eighth Army's three commanders during the war's first year, Ridgway was undoubtedly the most proficient. He took over a beaten and retreating army, and through sheer willpower, he got it fighting effectively in a matter of weeks. No doubt Ridgway possessed some advantages that Walker lacked: the confidence of his superiors and their support in overhauling the army's combat leadership, complete authority over all army forces on the peninsula, logisticians who succeeded in refitting beaten units quickly, and enemy exhaustion. However, he still confronted policy confusion in Washington and Tokyo, an ineffective South Korean army, and severe demoralization among his own men. He overcame them because he knew what he wanted to do and how he wanted to do it—and he got everyone to see things his way through the force of his personality. He used the Eighth Army's superior firepower, matériel, logistics, and mechanization to compel the enemy to fight the war on his terms. Indeed, by holding out in Korea, he provided a way for the Truman administration to end the war in an acceptable manner. It is rare in modern warfare for one man to almost single-handedly transform military fortunes, but Ridgway did so. For this reason he is one of the great combat commanders in modern American history.

Despite his problems with MacArthur, Walker also deserved credit for his performance during his six months in Korea. He took an unready army to the peninsula and managed, with substantial South Korean help, to stop the North Korean invasion. Observers praised his tactics along the Pusan Perimeter. Although Walker had little experience with or training in defensive warfare, he used his intelligence assets and mobility to shuffle his limited reserves from one threatened sector to another, thus maintaining the integrity of his lines. He later broke through North Korean defenses along the Pusan Perimeter and pushed northward to and beyond Pyongyang. After the Chinese intervened, Walker succeeded in extracting his army from along the Chongchon River and brought it back to South Korea without sustaining crippling losses.

On the other hand, there were plenty of sins on the other side of Walker's military ledger. After Inchon, he was more interested in seizing territory than in destroying enemy forces. A more methodical approach out of the Pusan Perimeter might have eliminated more North Korean troops and prevented them from escaping northward or melting into the countryside to wage guerrilla warfare later. Walker, however, worried that a slower advance would anger MacArthur, who believed that Inchon had pretty much ended the conflict and that all the Eighth Army needed to do was march straight to the Yalu River to win the war. Chinese intervention caught Walker flat-footed, and his initial response around Unsan was sluggish. After the Chinese launched their all-out offensive in late November, he could have tried harder to hold onto Pyongyang or to make a stand at Korea's narrow waist. He failed to recognize that the Chinese had suffered enormous casualties and were logistically unable to mount an aggressive pursuit. Instead, he retreated all the way back to the 38th Parallel. His actions supported Ridgway's subsequent claim that the Eighth Army was hurt more psychologically than physically. Walker was a solid combat commander who merited more understanding and better support from MacArthur. Had he gotten it, he might have avoided some of the mistakes he made.

Evaluating Van Fleet's generalship from April to June 1951 is difficult for a number of reasons. Most obviously, he operated in Ridgway's large shadow. When Van Fleet took over the Eighth Army, he inherited both Ridgway's subordinates and strategy. Moreover, Ridgway was often close at hand to keep an eye on Van Fleet. Fortunately, Van Fleet agreed with Ridgway's strategy of attrition and was if anything more gung-go about its implementation. Although Ridgway had successfully driven the Chinese and North Koreans out of South Korea, it was Van Fleet who inflicted on them the huge casualties necessary to bring them to the negotiating table by repelling their big spring offensive. Furthermore, with scarcely a pause, Van Fleet crossed the 38th Parallel and established the defensive line from which the Eighth Army fought for the remainder of the conflict. In doing so, he won Ridgway's respect and earned a reputation as a capable, confident, and aggressive combat commander.

Of the five American corps commanders in the Eighth Army during the war's first year, Ned Almond was the most capable. There was much to dislike about Almond—he was mean, racist, overbearing, and abusive—and these less admirable traits sometimes undermined his effectiveness as a general. He made mistakes as Tenth Corps commander, most obviously by dispersing his units across northeast Korea while the Chinese were massing against him, and later in placing American units under South Korean command during the fighting in the central corridor. However, Almond also possessed plenty of aggressiveness, energy, skill, and self-confidence. Harnessing and using these more positive attributes required a strong-willed and hands-on commander capable of putting Almond in his place. MacArthur failed to do so in late 1950, and the Tenth Corps was lucky to escape from North Korea with so little damage. Fortunately, both Ridgway and Van Fleet succeeded in channeling Almond's talents in a direction beneficial to the Eighth Army. Under their commands Almond stymied enemy efforts in the central corridor and later played a critical role in repelling the Chinese spring offensive. It was small wonder that Ridgway and Van Fleet both rated him highly. For all of Almond's undoubted flaws, he usually got the job done—and that was what the army paid him to do.

Shrimp Milburn's basic affability was certainly one of his great strengths as a corps commander, but there was more to his generalship than that. In Korea he proved himself a solid and skilled combat leader who committed few military sins. He oversaw the Pusan Perimeter breakout, seized Pyongyang, and later played a key role in Ridgway's and Van Fleet's offensives across the 38th Parallel. He was not infallible; his efforts to micromanage the fighting around Unsan during the initial Chinese intervention, for instance, contributed to the 8th Cav Regiment's discomfiture there. Milburn was in many ways the quintessential twentieth-century American army general: well educated, methodical, thoroughly professional, and proficient in his craft. Ridgway, however, was right in observing that Milburn, for all his admirable traits, lacked that little extra spark that separated ordinary from extraordinary generals. He was perfectly suitable for a conventional conflict in which the army could apply its usual advantages in matériel, firepower, logistics, and mechanization to overcome the enemy. In situations that required more unorthodox approaches, such as those the Eighth Army faced in the winter of 1950–1951, Milburn was out of his element. Fortunately, one of Ridgway's accomplishments was creating a battlefield environment in which officers such as Milburn could fulfill their missions. Milburn's Korean War record was therefore perfectly acceptable—no more and no less.

Of the three remaining corps commanders, Bryant Moore's tenure was too short to evaluate him fairly. Hoge was, like Milburn, a perfectly satisfactory general, but his more outgoing personality made him appear more aggressive. Hoge faced his share of challenges in Korea, most obviously during the Chinese spring offensive, but he was not tested as often or as strenuously as Milburn was. Even so, both Ridgway and Van Fleet approved of his actions, and his Ninth Corps overcame severe obstacles in both repelling the Chinese spring offensive and pushing across the 38th Parallel. As for Breitling Coulter, he should have performed well in Korea. After all, he had attended the Command and General Staff School and the Army War College, and he had successfully led a division in Italy during World War II. His impressive résumé, however, failed to prepare him for the chaotic conditions he confronted in Korea. He did not do as much as he should have to help the Second Division along the Chongchon, and he showed insufficient enthusiasm for fighting north of Seoul during the Chinese New Year's offensive. At the corps level, Coulter never demonstrated the kind of initiative, operational awareness, and poise that good generals possess.

Historians and contemporaries have criticized the army's first set of division commanders in Korea. They argue that these men were not top-drawer officers who rose to their posts through strict merit but were rather mediocrities selected for reasons other than their abilities. The Eighth Army's poor initial performance on the peninsula, as well as its panicky and confused response to Chinese intervention, seems like good evidence for these conclusions. In fact, there is some truth to these assertions, but they must be qualified and placed in context. For one thing, these officers went into battle with ill-trained and poorly equipped troops who were at first in no condition to stand up to the disciplined North Koreans. It is therefore unfair to compare their records with those of their successors who led veteran soldiers with plenty of weapons and matériel at their disposal.

Moreover, it is not right to tar them all with the same critical brush. Despite their lack of previous combat leadership experience, Gay, Kean, and Soule all developed into satisfactory division chiefs. Gay and Kean learned from their early mistakes and became increasingly effective in repulsing North Korean attacks on their positions within the Pusan Perimeter. Gay went on to spearhead the Pusan Perimeter breakout and the invasion of North Korea. Although the Chinese mauled part of Gay's First Cavalry Division around Unsan, Milburn was more responsible for the setback than Gay. Later Gay succeeded in protecting Pyongyang when the Eighth Army's flank collapsed east of Kunu-ri. As for Kean, his biggest accomplishments were thwarting the North Korean drives toward Masan and maintaining the Twenty-fifth Division positions along the Chongchon long enough to help the bulk of the Eighth Army escape. Finally, Soule met Almond's exacting standards in northeast Korea and then went on to serve Milburn equally well. Despite persistent reports of his excessive drinking, no one could point to evidence that this adversely affected his generalship.

Judging the remaining original division commanders is more problematic. William Dean was, on paper, the most capable of the lot because he had previous combat leadership experience, but he was in action for only a few short, eventful weeks. Although he made his share of mistakes, he succeeded in slowing the North Korean advance. His successor at the head of the Twenty-fourth Division, John Church, left much to be desired. He did not improve as quickly or as much as did Gay and Kean, and he failed to distinguish himself in the Pusan Perimeter breakout, the invasion of North Korea, and the Chinese intervention. His biggest accomplishment was twice extricating his division from its exposed position north of the Chongchon, but in each instance, he faced minimal enemy opposition and had the advantage of mechanization. Church had little previous combat leadership experience and suffered from poor health, both of which certainly contributed to his mediocre record. In fact, he probably would never have risen to division command except that he happened to be on hand in Korea when Dean went missing. Dutch Keiser's introduction to Korean War combat along the Naktong River was as traumatic and difficult as that of all his divisional colleagues. Unfortunately, he did not learn enough in the Pusan Perimeter to help him along the Chongchon. Despite his undoubted courage at Kunu-ri, he still lost the battle and a good bit of his division. Church's and Keiser's uninspiring performances, though, surpassed Dave Barr's. Barr lobbied hard to get the Seventh Division under the assumption that he would never have to take it into action. He fought credibly in front of Seoul, but serving under the demanding and overbearing Almond gradually sapped his energy and confidence. Almond increasingly distrusted him and hesitated to give him an opportunity to prove himself. In northeast Korea, Almond dispersed his division and stripped him of much of his authority, so that by the end of the campaign Barr felt helpless, bitter, exhausted, and distraught.

With the exception of Robert McClure, the records of those who replaced the original division commanders seem to indicate that they were a more capable group of combat officers. Although Ridgway and Van Fleet criticized some of them for their slowness, McClure was the only one who committed a serious military sin in the first half of 1951. However, these officers were in many ways like their predecessors. Most had no previous combat leadership experience, and they were on average only somewhat younger. Circumstances as much as skill enabled them to manage their divisions so effectively. By early 1951, the Eighth Army was a veteran, well-equipped force, not the ill-trained and poorly armed entity that Walker had taken to Korea six months earlier. In addition, Ridgway fought the war in a way conducive to his new division commanders' training and mind-sets. Ridgway deliberately played to the army's strengths by emphasizing firepower, logistics, and mechanization. Whether advancing or retreating, these officers were comfortable waging war under these circumstances, and they performed well enough to defeat the enemy.

Reflecting on the Korean War years later, one journalist observed that for many generals the conflict was a "strange and difficult world."[2] Indeed, American involvement in Korea caught almost everyone by complete surprise, and many officers never completely adjusted to the war's limited nature. The army's unpreparedness included its senior combat leadership in Japan. Because the army never expected to fight in East Asia, many of the generals leading the large combat formations there were not up-and-comers but rather mediocre placeholders. No one, for instance, envisioned a Barr or a Kean or even a Walker using his position as a stepping-stone to chief of staff. A number of them turned in creditable performances in Korea, but others did not, and this uneven leadership accounted for some, though certainly not all, of the army's difficulties in the first months of the war. Fortunately, the army's top leaders recognized this problem and made appropriate changes, though perhaps not as quickly or completely as they should have. Under this improved leadership, the Eighth Army went on to defeat the Chinese and North Koreans on the battlefield, thus laying the groundwork for a negotiated settlement that preserved South Korean independence.

Notes

INTRODUCTION

1. Dean, *General Dean's Story*, 5–13.
2. Quoted in Goulden, *Korea*, 3.

CHAPTER 1. A SUDDEN AND UNEXPECTED CONFLICT

1. MacArthur, *Reminiscences*, 332–333.
2. Joseph Swing, interview with D. Clayton James, 26 August 1971, Joseph Swing Papers, United States Army Heritage and Education Center (USAHEC), 27–28.
3. Barksdale Hamlett, interview with Jack Ridgway and Paul Walter, 10 March 1976, Senior Officers Debriefing Program, USAHEC, section 4, 48.
4. Robert B. Laundry, interview with Hugh Ahmann, 1–2 March 1983, United States Air Force Oral History Office in the Truman Library Oral Histories, 235.
5. For details of the more positive aspects of MacArthur's character, see Ridgway, *Korean War*, 81–83; J. Lawton Collins, interview with Charles Sperow, 1972, Senior Officers Debriefing Program, USAHEC, 1:337, 339–340; John Chiles, interview with D. Clayton James, 27 July 1977, Truman Library, 31–32, 48–49; Bruce Clarke, interview with Jerry Hess, 14 January 1970, Truman Library, 122–124; John Muccio, interview with Jerry Hess, 18 February 1971, Truman Library, 72; Maxwell Taylor, interview with Richard Minion, 19 October 1972, Senior Officers Debriefing Program, USAHEC, section 1, 16; John Walters, interview with William Parnell III, 1980, Senior Officers Debriefing Program, USAHEC, 699; Haig, *Inner Circles*, 20, 26; Edward Almond, interview with D. Clayton James, 4 August 1971, D. Clayton James Papers, Mitchell Memorial Library (MML), box 11, folder 17, 25–26; John Michaelis, interview with D. Clayton James, 1 June 1977, D. Clayton James Papers, MML, box 12, folder 28, 19; Edwin Wright, interview with D. Clayton James, 28 August 1971, D. Clayton James Papers, MML, box 13, folder 8, 43; Baillie, *High Tension*, 222–223; Sebald, *With MacArthur in Japan*, 231; Frank Pace, interview with D. Clayton James, 12 July 1977, D. Clayton James Papers, MML, box 11, folder 36, 17.
6. Quoted in Schaller, *Douglas MacArthur*, 74. For some negative evaluations of MacArthur, see Ridgway, *Korean War*, 142; J. Lawton Collins interview, USAHEC, 1:337, 339–340; Chiles interview, Truman Library, 23, 51; Bruce Clarke interview, 122–124; Edwin Wright interview, box 13, folder 8, 43; Baillie, *High Tension*, 222–223; Matthew Ridgway, interview with John Blair, 6 January 1972, Senior Officers Debriefing Program, USAHEC, section 3, 74, 78; Rinaldo Van Brunt, interview with Clay Blair, n.d., Clay and Joan Blair Collection, USAHEC, box 23, 63; Wade, *CSI Report No. 5*, 8.

7. Ridgway, *Korean War,* 142; J. Lawton Collins interview, USAHEC, 1:338, Chiles interview, Truman Library, 23; Haig, *Inner Circles,* 20, 22, 26; Almond interview, MML, box 11, folder 17, 33–34; Michaelis interview, MML, box 12, folder 28, 32; James Polk, interview with Roland Tausch, 20 January 1972, Senior Officers Debriefing Program, USAHEC, section 2, 26–27; Almond to John Wiltz, 5 May 1977, Edward Almond Papers, Douglas MacArthur Memorial Archives (DMMA), reel 1078, RG-38, box 4, folder 3; Alsop, *I've Seen the Best,* 323.

8. MacArthur, *Reminiscences,* 327.

9. For information on MacArthur's visit, see ibid., 327, 332–333; Haig, *Inner Circles,* 19–21, 26–27; Edwin Wright interview, box 13, folder 8, 21–22; Edward Almond interview, 28 March 1975, Senior Officers Debriefing Program, USAHEC, section 4, 13–14; Noble, *Embassy at War,* 85–91; David Douglas Duncan, "US Gets into Fight for Korea," *Life,* 10 July 1950, 26; Frank Gibney, *Time,* 10 July 1950, 13.

10. Michaelis interview, Mississippi State Library, box 12, folder 28, 32.

11. Robertson, *Counterattack,* 4; Heefner, *Patton's Bulldog,* 154–156; Collins, *War in Peacetime,* 5–6; Dean, *General Dean's Story,* 13–14; Edwin Wright interview, box 13, folder 8, 14–15; Almond interview, 28 March 1975, USAHEC, section 4, 15–16; Harold Martin, *Saturday Evening Post,* 9 September 1950, 33; Herbert Powell, interview with Philip Stevens, Robert McCue, Hubert Bartron, William Rhyan, and Jerry Novak, 26 April 1974, Senior Officers Debriefing Program, USAHEC, section 5, 28; Almond to Ward Maris, 9 March 1950, Almond Papers, DMMA, reel 1079, RG-38, box 8, folder 5; Charles B. Smith, interview with William Davies, 7–8 January 1992, Charles B. Smith Papers, USAHEC, box 1, 1; William Harris comments, n.d., Background Files for *South to Naktong,* National Archives and Records Administration, RG-319, box 11, folder External Review; Landrum to Roy Appleman, 18 November 1953, Background Files for *South to Naktong,* RG-319, box 11, Letters Used in Revision, folder Chapter 4, Part 2; John Dunn to Appleman, 17 June 1955, Background Files for *South to Naktong,* RG-319, box 11, Letters Used in Revision, folder Chapter 4, Part 3.

12. E. Michael Lynch, interview with Clay Blair, n.d., Clay and Joan Blair Collection, USAHEC, Senior Officers Debriefing Program, box 17, 78.

13. The quote is from Harold Johnson, interview with Richard Jenson and Rupert Glover, 7 February 1972, Senior Officers Debriefing Program, USAHEC, 52. See also Donnelly, "Bilko's Army"; Heefner, *Patton's Bulldog,* 157–158; Michaelis interview, MML, box 12, folder 28, 32; Edward Moore, interview with D. Clayton James, 21 June 1977, D. Clayton James Papers, MML, box 11, folder 30, 7.

CHAPTER 2. STAND OR DIE

1. Barth, *Tropic Lightning,* 1.

2. The quote is from Beech, *Tokyo and Points East,* 147. For views of Dean's thinking, background, and character as well as his mission, see Dean, *General Dean's Story,* 18–20, 22–24; Higgins, *War in Korea,* 77; Barth, *Tropic Lightning,* 1–2; E. Michael Lynch, interview with John Toland, 11 March 1987, John Toland Papers, Roosevelt Library, container 143,

part 2, 8; Almond interview, 28 March 1975, USAHEC, section 4, 21; Noble, *Embassy at War*, 127.

3. *Time*, 31 July 1950, 20.

4. The quote is from Dean, *Dean's Story*, 30. See also Collins, *War in Peacetime*, 84; Dean, *Dean's Story*, 3, 22–27; Barth, *Tropic Lightning*, 4–5; Dunn to Appleman, 17 June 1955, Roy Appleman Papers, USAHEC, box 21; J. Lawton Collins, Memo of Korea Trip, 17 July 1950, J. Lawton Collins Papers, Eisenhower Library, box 23; David Bisset Jr. to Appleman, 14 July 1952, Background Files for *South to Naktong*, RG-319, box 13, folder October 1950; Arthur Clarke to Appleman, 30 June 1952, Background Files for *South to Naktong*, box 13, folder October 1950.

5. Stanley Larsen, interview with Robert Holmes, 26 August 1976, Senior Officers Debriefing Program, USAHEC, section 3, 25–26; Moore interview, MML, box 11, folder 30, 10.

6. Landrum to Appleman, 18 November 1953, Background Files for *South to Naktong*, RG-319, box 11, folder Letters Used in Revision, Chapter 4.

7. Summation of the Remarks of General MacArthur, 13 July 1950, Collins Papers, Eisenhower Library, box 23; Forrest Kleinman to Roy Appleman (via Dean), n.d., Background Files for *South to Naktong*, RG-319, box 10, folder Outline, Vol. 2; Landrum to Appleman, early to mid-January 1954, Background Files for *South to Naktong*, RG-319, box 11, folder Letters Used in Revision, Chapter 4, Part 3.

8. Charles Beauchamp comments, 7 January 1953, Background Files for *South to Naktong*, RG-319, box 11, folder Revision, Chapter 4, Part 2; Bisset to Appleman, 14 July 1952, Background Files for *South to Naktong*, RG-319, box 13, Folder October 1950.

9. Dean, *Dean's Story*, 3.

10. The statistics are from Blair, *Forgotten War*, 141. See also Dean, *Dean's Story*, 30–32.

11. Higgins, *War in Korea*, 46–48; Barth, *Tropic Lightning*, 1; E. Michael Lynch interview, Roosevelt Library, container 143, part 2, 8; Almond interview, 28 March 1975, USAHEC, section 4, 12–13; Charles Beauchamp, interview with Clay Blair, n.d., Clay and John Blair Collection, USAHEC, box 9, 35; Van Brunt interview, box 23, 81, 119; Edward Moore, interview with Clay Blair, n.d., Clay and Joan Blair Collection, USAHEC, box 19, 59–60; Noble, *Embassy at War*, 52–56, 78–79; Maihafer, *From the Hudson*, 211; Moore interview, MML, box 11, folder 30, 25.

12. Harris, *Puerto Rico's Fighting 65th Infantry*, 56.

13. *Time*, 31 July 1950, 20.

14. For assessments of Walker's character and personality, see ibid., 18–20; Collins, *War in Peacetime*, 89–90, 92–93, 110; Edward Lasher, interview with D. R. Lasher, 27 October 1972, Senior Officers Debriefing Program, USAHEC, section 3, 78; Higgins, *War in Korea*, 113; Haig, *Inner Circles*, 27; Barth, *Tropic Lightning*, 50; James Lynch, interview with D. Clayton James, 24 May 1977, D. Clayton James Papers, MML, box 12, folder 21, 10; Michaelis interview, MML, box 12, folder 28, 12–13; Paik, *From Pusan*, 114; Edwin Wright interview, box 13, folder 8, 14, 15; Thompson, *Cry Korea*, 211; Sebald, *With MacArthur in Japan*, 192–193; Jack Anderson, *Washington Merry-Go-Round*, 25 August 1950; Voorhees,

Korean Tales, 55–56; Polk interview, 20 January 1972, section 2, 33–34; Powell interview, 26 April 1974, USAHEC, section 5, 30–31; Beauchamp interview, USAHEC, box 9, 36–37; E. Michael Lynch interview, USAHEC, box 17, 30; Frank Lowe to Harry Truman, 26 October 1950, Frank Lowe Papers, USAHEC, box 1; Heller, *Korean War,* 23–24; Wade, *CSI Report No. 5,* 8–9; Noble, *Embassy at War,* 140–143; Landrum comments, 28 June 1954, Background Files for *South to Naktong,* RG-319, box 11, folder Letters Used in Revision, Chapter 4; William Collier comments, 10 March 1958, Background Files for *South to Naktong,* RG-319, box 11, folder Letters Used in Revision; John Dabney to Richard Stephens, 26 November 1957, Background Files for *South to Naktong,* RG-319, box 11, folder Letters Used in Revision, Chapter 4, Part 2; Dabney to Appleman, 18 December 1953, Background Files for *South to Naktong,* RG-319, box 11, folder Letters Used in Revision, Chapter 4, Part 2; Dabney to Appleman, 19 January 1954, Background Files for *South to Naktong,* RG-319, box 13, folder Correspondence Relating to Critiques and Comments.

15. Michaelis interview, MML, box 12, folder 28, 12–13.

16. Ibid., 12–13, 35–36; Collins, *War in Peacetime,* 89–90; J. Lawton Collins interview, USAHEC, 1:334–336; MacArthur, *Reminiscences,* 383; Larsen interview, section 4, 4; Haig, *Inner Circles,* 27; Edwin Wright interview, box 13, folder 8, 15; E. Michael Lynch interview, Roosevelt Library, container 143, 9–10; Ridgway interview, 6 January 1972, USAHEC, section 3, 73; Dabney to Stephens, 26 November 1957, Background Files for *South to Naktong,* RG-319, box 11, folder Letters Used in Revision, 4, Part 2; J. Lawton Collins, interview with Alfred Goldberg, Roger Trask, Doris Condit, and Steve Rearden, 2 July 1981, interview with General J. Lawton Collins, Combined Arms Research Library, 28–29, 32.

17. Polk interview, 34.

18. Collins, *War in Peacetime,* 110; Michaelis interview, MML, box 12, folder 28, 14, 16–17; Paik, *From Pusan,* 114; Hobart Gay, interview with Willard Wallace, 4–5 October 1981, Senior Officers Debriefing Program, USAHEC, 57; Beauchamp interview, box 9, 36–37; Noble, *Embassy at War,* 142–143; Collier comments, 10 March 1958, Background Files for *South to Naktong,* RG-319, box 11, folder Letters Used in Revision, Chapter 4; Barth, *Tropic Lightning,* 50; Muccio interview, 70, 74–75; Heller, *Korean War,* 24.

19. *Time,* 31 July 1950, 18.

20. Dean, *Dean's Story,* 26.

21. Collins, *War in Peacetime,* 83–84; Higgins, *War in Korea,* 115; E. Michael Lynch interview, Roosevelt Library, container 143, part 1, 7–8; Landrum to Appleman, 11 November 1953, Background Files for *South to Naktong,* RG-319, box 11, folder Letters Used in Revision, Chapter 4; Landrum to Appleman, early to mid-January 1954, Background Files for *South to Naktong,* RG-319, box 11, folder Letters Used in Revision, Chapter 4, Part 3.

22. Collins, *War in Peacetime,* 90; Larsen interview, section 1, 7; Barth, *Tropic Lightning,* 59; E. Michael Lynch interview, Roosevelt Library, container 143, part 4, 1; Van Brunt interview, box 23, 119–122; Welborn Dolvin, interview with Clay Blair, n.d., Clay and Joan Blair Collection, USAHEC, box 13, 115–116; John Michaelis, interview with Clay Blair, n.d., Clay and Joan Blair Collection, USAHEC, box 18, 50–51; John Throckmorton, interview with Clay Blair, n.d., Clay and Joan Blair Collection, USAHEC, box 22, 22–23; Lan-

drum to Appleman early to mid-January 1954, Background Files for *South to Naktong*, RG-319, box 11, folder Letters Used in Revision, Chapter 4, Part 3.

23. Paik, *From Pusan*, 27.

24. The quote is from E. Michael Lynch interview, Roosevelt Library, container 143, part 4, 1. See also Collins, *War in Peacetime*, 91–92; James Lynch interview, box 12, folder 21, 8; E. Michael Lynch interview, Roosevelt Library, container 143, part 2, 8; *El Paso Times*, 4 April 1965; Almond to Edward Brooks, 30 July 1949, Almond Papers, DMMA, reel 1079, RG-38, box 7, folder 3; Peter Clainos, interview with Clay Blair, n.d., Clay and Joan Blair Collection, USAHEC, box 11, 33–34, 152; Hamlett Edson, interview with Clay Blair, n.d., Clay and Joan Blair Collection, USAHEC, box 13, 16; Moore interview, USAHEC, box 19, 45–46; Charles Palmer, interview with Clay Blair, n.d., Clay and Joan Blair Collection, US-AHEC, box 20, 36; Lowe to Truman, 7 February 1951, Lowe Papers, box 1; Hal Boyle, *Evening Independent*, 26 September 1950, 2; Landrum to Appleman, early to mid-January 1954, Background Files for *South to Naktong*, RG-319, box 11, folder Letters Used in Revision, Chapter 4, Part 3.

25. *Newsweek*, 31 July 1950, 13; Beech, *Tokyo and Points East*, 205; Johnson interview, USAHEC, 52; Charles Palmer interview, USAHEC, box 20, 71–72, 100; *Evening Day*, 27 July 1950, 26; Bigart, *Forward Positions*, 135; Hobart Gay to Appleman, 17 July and 24 August 1953, Background Files for *South to Naktong*, RG-319, box 11, folder Letters Used in Revision, Chapter 4, Part 2; Landrum to Appleman, early to mid-January 1954, Background Files for *South to Naktong*, RG-319, box 11, folder Letters Used in Revision, Chapter 4, Part 3.

26. Collins, *War in Peacetime*, 94–95.

27. The journalist identifies the speaker only as a general officer, but the context indicates it was probably Church. See W. H. Lawrence, *New York Times*, 1 August 1950, 1, 3. See also Moore interview, MML, box 11, folder 30, 12, 14.

28. Hal Boyle, *Tuscaloosa News*, 31 July 1950, 4.

29. Higgins, *War in Korea*, 115; Noble, *Embassy at War*, 140–141, 168–169; Landrum to Appleman, 18 November 1953, Background Files for *South to Naktong*, RG-319, box 11, folder Letters Used in Revision, Chapter 4; Landrum comments, 8 March 1954, Background Files for *South to Naktong*, RG-319, box 11, folder Letters Used in Revision, Chapter 4.

30. Almond interview, 28 March 1975, USAHEC, section 4, 21–22.

31. Ibid.; Collins, *War in Peacetime*, 92–93; Ridgway, *Korean War*, 163; Haig, *Inner Circles*, 27; E. Michael Lynch interview, Roosevelt Library, container 143, part 1, 2; Ridgway interview, 6 January 1972, USAHEC, section 3, 73; Heller, *Korean War*, 34; Landrum to Appleman, 18 November 1953, Background Files for *South to Naktong*, RG-319, box 11, folder Letters Used in Revision, Chapter 4.

32. Higgins, *War in Korea*, 115.

33. *Evening Day*, 29 July 1950, 1.

34. Frank Holeman, interview with Niel Johnson, 9 June 1987, Truman Library, 58; Barth, *Tropic Lightning*, 11; Edwin Elliot, interview with Arthur Kelly, 17 January 1986,

Louis B. Nunn Center for Oral History, University of Kentucky Libraries; Bigart, *Forward Positions*, 139; Landrum to Appleman, 18 November 1953, Background Files for *South to Naktong*, RG-319, box 11, folder Letters Used in Revision, Chapter 4.

35. The statistics are from Appleman, *South to the Naktong*, 262.

36. David Barr comments, n.d., Records of the General Staff, Office of the Chief of Military History, Background Files for *South to Naktong*, *North to Yalu*, National Archives and Records Administration, RG-319, box 13, folder October 1950.

37. Gay to Appleman, 24 August 1953, Background Files for *South to Naktong*, RG-319, box 11, folder Letters Used in Revision, Chapter 4, Part 2.

38. For the various views of these events, see Notes of Conference with MacArthur, 9 August 1950, Matthew Ridgway Papers, USAHEC, box 8, folder August 1950; Collins, *War in Peacetime*, 108–109; Stratemeyer, 7, 19, and 20 August, 1 September 1950, *Three Wars*, 97, 120, 128, 158; Matthew Ridgway, interview with Harold L. Hitchens and Frederick A. Hetzel, 5 March 1982, University Library System, University of Pittsburgh, 23–24; Ridgway interview, 6 January 1972, USAHEC, section 3, 73, 84; Edson interview, 9–10; Heller, *Korean War*, 23–24, 34–35; Blair, *Forgotten War*, 188–190; Averell Harriman, interview with D. Clayton James, 20 June 1977, D. Clayton James Papers, MML, box 12, folder 1, 8–10, 23.

39. James Bell, "US Counters Mass with Mobility," *Life*, 21 August 1950, 18.

40. Harold Martin, *Saturday Evening Post*, 9 September 1950, 187.

41. John Michaelis to Appleman, 24 January 1953, Background Files for *South to Naktong*, RG-319, box 14, folder External Review.

42. John Osborne, "US Counters Mass with Mobility," *Life*, 21 August 1950, 15.

43. For Michaelis's thinking and actions, see Higgins, *War in Korea*, 117, 126; Barth, *Tropic Lightning*, 12; Michaelis interview, MML, box 12, folder 28, 7–8; Martin, *Saturday Evening Post*, 9 September 1950, 33, 187; Michaelis interview, USAHEC, 50–51; Landrum to Appleman, 18 November 1953, Background Files for *South to Naktong*, RG-319, box 11, folder Letters Used in Revision, Chapter 4; Landrum comments, 8 March 1954, Background Files for *South to Naktong*, RG-319, box 11, folder Letters Used in Revision, Chapter 4; Michaelis to Appleman, 24 January 1953, Background Files for *South to Naktong*, RG-319, box 14, folder External Review; Stephens comments, n.d., Background Files for *South to Naktong*, RG-319, box 14, folder External Review; *Palm Beach Post*, 11 August 1950, 15; Charles Smith, 7–8 January 1992, Charles B. Smith Papers, USAHEC, box 1, 2.

44. Bell, "US Counters Mass with Mobility," 19.

45. Edward Craig, interview with L. E. Tatan, 27 May 1968, Marine Corps Oral History Collection, United States Marine Corps Historical Division (USMCHD), 96–97, 100–101; Edward Craig, interview with ———, 8 May 1951, Marine Corps Oral History Collection, USMCHD, 70; Edward Craig, interview with D. Clayton James, 3 September 1971, D. Clayton James Papers, MML, box 11, folder 38, 11–12, 33–34; Don Whitehead, *Lawrence Daily Journal-World*, 14 August 1950, 3.

46. Alsop, *I've Seen the Best*, 315–316.

47. William Kean to Appleman, 17 July 1953, Background Files for *South to Naktong*, RG-319, box 13, folder Correspondence Relating to Critiques and Comments.

48. In addition to Kean, other participants argued that the operation was a success.

For example, see George Barth comments, 17 March 1958, Background Files for *South to Naktong*, RG-319, box 11, folder Letters Used in Revision, Chapter 4, Part 2; Barth to Stephens, 14 April 1958, Background Files for *South to Naktong*, RG-319, box 13, folder Correspondence Relating to Critiques and Comments.

49. *Time*, 7 August 1950, 18–19.

50. Gay interview, 45; Clainos interview, box 11, 99–100.

51. *Time*, 28 August 1950, 23.

52. Collins, *War in Peacetime*, 108–109.

53. Ibid., 109; J. Lawton Collins memo, August 1950, J. Lawton Collins Papers, Eisenhower Library, box 23, folder Korea Trip; Stratemeyer, 19 and 22 August 1950, *Three Wars*, 120, 128; *New York Times*, 29 August 1950, 3; J. Lawton Collins interview, Combined Arms Research Library, 28–29.

54. Paul Freeman, interview with James Ellis, 29 November 1973, Senior Officers Debriefing Program, USAHEC, section 1, 7.

55. Ibid., 7, 99; Almond to Laurence Keiser, 18 February 1950, Almond Papers, DMMA, reel 1079, RG-38, box 8, folder 3; Van Brunt interview, box 23, 119; Gerald Epley, interview with Clay Blair, n.d., Clay and Joan Blair Collection, USAHEC, box 14, 21, 46; Michaelis interview, USAHEC, box 18, 66; Second Infantry Division Reports, 8 July to 30 August 1950, Korean War Project, http://www.kwp.org/, 1–10.

56. *Time*, 21 August 1950, 18; Robert Wadlington to Appleman, 1 April 1953, Background Files for *South to Naktong*, RG-319, box 14, folder External Review; Stephens comments, n.d., Background Files for *South to Naktong*, RG-319, box 14, folder External Review; Memo for the Assistant Chief of Staff, 8 September 1950 Collins Papers, Eisenhower Library, box 23, folder Korea File.

57. Stratemeyer, 1 September 1950, *Three Wars*, 158.

58. *Time*, 18 September 1950, 39; Garrison Davidson comments, 18 February 1954, Background Files for *South to Naktong*, RG-319, box 11, folder Letters Used in Revision, Chapter 4; Sam Walker, interview with John Toland, 29 March 1988, Toland Papers, Roosevelt Library, container 143, part 2, 7–8; Walton Walker to John Coulter, 7 September 1950, DMMA, reel 175, RG-9, 8th Army Incoming, 1–15 September 1950; Thomas Gillis, interview with Clay Blair, n.d., Clay and Joan Blair Collection, USAHEC, box 15, 33; *Pacific Stars and Stripes*, 12 October 1950, 1; Landrum comments, 28 June 1954, Background Files for *South to Naktong*, RG-319, box 11, folder Letters Used in Revision, Chapter 4; Landrum comments, 8 March 1954, Background Files for *South to Naktong*, RG-319, box 11, folder Letters Used in Revision, Chapter 4; Coulter to Stephens, 22 November 1957, Background Files for *South to Naktong*, RG-319, box 11, folder Letters Used in Revision, Chapter 4, Part 2; Coulter to Appleman, 7 July 1953, Background Files for *South to Naktong*, RG-319, box 11, folder Letters Used in Revision, Chapter 4, Part 2; Stephens to Appleman, 14 May 1953, Background Files for *South to Naktong*, RG-319, box 15, folder Correspondence Requesting or Receiving Information.

59. Sam Holliday to Roy Appleman, 18 April 1953, Background Files for *South to Naktong*, RG-319, box 10, folder 1st Battalion, 29th Infantry.

60. Appleman, *South to the Naktong*, 472.

61. Freeman interview, 30 November 1973, USAHEC, section 1, 99, 102–103; Epley interview, box 14, 31–32; Paul Freeman, interview with Clay Blair, n.d., Clay and Joan Blair Collection, USAHEC, 54–55; Paul Freeman to Stephens, 30 October 1957, Background Files for *South to Naktong*, RG-319, box 13, folder Correspondence Relating to Critiques and Comments.

62. Walker's pilot, E. Michael Lynch, told the same basic story to a couple different interviewers. See E. Michael Lynch interview, Roosevelt Library, container 143, part 1, 11–13, 15–19; E. Michael Lynch interview, Roosevelt Library, container 143, part 2, 1–5; E. Michael Lynch interview, Roosevelt Library, container 143, Questionnaire, 14; E. Michael Lynch, USAHEC, box 17, 17, 24–25, 26–27.

63. Chiles interview, Truman Library, 40; Stratemeyer, 1 September 1950, *Three Wars*, 158; E. Michael Lynch interview, USAHEC, box 17, 26–27.

64. The quote is from Landrum comments, 28 June 1954, Background Files for *South to Naktong*, RG-319, box 11, folder Letters Used in Revision, Chapter 4. Landrum did not identify the division commander, but it was almost certainly Gay.

65. Gay to Appleman, 17 July 1953, Background Files for *South to Naktong*, RG-319, box 11, folder Letters Used in Revision, Chapter 4, Part 2.

66. *Time*, 18 September 1950, 42.

67. Gay to Appleman, 17 July 1953, Background Files for *South to Naktong*, RG-319, box 11, folder Letters Used in Revision, Chapter 4, Part 2.

68. Appleman, *South to the Naktong*, 547.

69. Jack Anderson, *Washington Merry-Go-Round*, 25 August 1950.

CHAPTER 3. MACARTHUR'S LAST HURRAH

1. Lynn Smith, "A Nickel after a Dollar," *Army*, September 1970, 28.

2. For views of the Inchon landing, see also Collins, *War in Peacetime*, 125, 141–142; MacArthur, *Reminiscences*, 151–153; Almond interview, 28 March 1975, USAHEC, section 4, 39–40; Matthew Ridgway, interview with John Toland, 4 December 1986, Matthew Ridgway Papers, USAHEC, box 88, side 1, 4; Heller, *Korean War*, 24–25, 26; J. Lawton Collins, Memo of Korea Trip, 17 July 1950, Collins Papers, Eisenhower Library, box 23; Harriman interview, box 12, folder 1, 9–10.

3. There are several accounts of the meeting. See Collins, *War in Peacetime*, 75–76; Chiles interview, Truman Library, 41–42; MacArthur, *Reminiscences*, 349, 351–353; Haig, *Inner Circles*, 36; Smith, "Nickel," 25; Almond interview, 28 March 1975, USAHEC, section 4, 39–41; Heller, *Korean War*, 24–25; Quinn, *Buffalo Bill Remembers*, 274–275.

4. William Ennis Jr. interview with Miguel Monteverde, 6 April 1986, Senior Officers Debriefing Program, USAHEC, 144.

5. David Barr comments, Background Files for *South to Naktong*, RG-319, box 13, folder October 1950.

6. Haig, *Inner Circles*, 41–42; Smith, "Nickel," 29; Heinl, *Victory*, 55–56; *Time*, 23 October 1950, 29; Almond interview, 28 March 1975, USAHEC, section 4, 22.

7. Heinl, *Victory*, 36–37; Chester Allen, interview with L. E. Tatan and Benis Frank, 9 September 1969, Marine Corps Oral History Collection, USMCHD, session 5, 136–137;

Clifton Cates, interview with Benis Frank, 10 October 1967, Marine Corps Oral History Collection, USMCHD, session 5, 178; Edward Craig interview, 8 May 1951, Marine Corps Oral History Collection, USMCHD, 8–9.

8. Almond interview, MML, box 11, folder 17, 15–17.

9. Collins later claimed that he got along fine with Almond. See J. Lawton Collins interview, Combined Arms Research Library, 32. See also Collins, *War in Peacetime,* 121–122; John Chiles interview, Truman Library, 12, 39–40, 41–42; William Train, interview with Reginald Moore, 3 January 1983, Senior Officers Debriefing Program, USAHEC, 2:340; Almond interview, MML, box 11, folder 17, 15–18; Heinl, *Victory,* 52–54; Almond interview, 28 March 1975, USAHEC, section 4, 27–30, 42–43; Almond interview, 29 March 1975, US-AHEC, section 5, 63; Polk interview, section 2, 29–30; Almond, "How Inchon was Chosen for the X Corps Amphibious Landing There on 15 September 1950," Almond Papers, DMMA, reel 1077, RG-38, box 3, folder 5; John Chiles, interview with Clay Blair, n.d., Clay and Joan Blair Collection, USAHEC, box 11, 98–99; Frank Mildren, interview with D. Clayton James, 24 May 1977, D. Clayton James Papers, MML, box 11, folder 29, 11.

10. Haig, *Inner Circles,* 43; Almond interview, MML, box 11, folder 17, 2–8, 35; Almond to H. J. Brees, 16 October 1950, Almond Papers, DMMA, reel 1077, RG-38, box 2, folder 1; J. Lawton Collins interview, USAHEC, 1:342–343.

11. William McCaffrey to Appleman, 1 July 1979, Appleman Papers, box 29.

12. J. Lawton Collins interview, 1972, USAHEC, 1:336–337; Chiles interview, Truman Library, 17, 24; Almond interview, MML, box 11, folder 17, 35; *Time,* 23 October 1950, 29; Almond interview, 28 March 1975, USAHEC, section 3, 68.

13. Paul Freeman interview with Blair, box 14, 130.

14. Powell interview, 17 October 1974, USAHEC, section 6, 73.

15. The quote is from Chiles interview, USAHEC, box 11, 53. For characterizations of Almond, see J. Lawton Collins interview, USAHEC, 1:336–337; Chiles interview, Truman Library, 9–10, 17, 22; MacArthur, *Reminiscences,* 327; Haig, *Inner Circles,* 39–40, 43–45; Charles Palmer, interview with D. Clayton James, 14 June 1977, D. Clayton James Papers, MML, box 12, folder 37, 26; Alpha Bowser, interview with D. Clayton James, 3 September 1971, D. Clayton James Papers, MML, box 11, folder 25, 20–22, 34; Edwin Wright interview, box 13, folder 8, 17; Sebald, *With MacArthur in Japan,* 195–196; *Time,* 23 October 1950, 29; Polk interview, section 2, 30; Ridgway interview 6 January 1972, USAHEC, section 3, 75–77; Appleman to Almond, 15 October 1975, Almond Papers, DMMA, reel 1078, RG-38, box 4, folder 4; McCaffrey to Appleman, 14 June 1981, Appleman Papers, box 20; Smith, "Nickel," 26; E. Michael Lynch interview, Roosevelt Library, container 143, part 1, 2; Craig interview, MML, box 11, folder 38, 25–26; William Sebald, interview with D. Clayton James, 30 July 1977, MML, box 11, folder 45, 21–22; Mildren interview, MML, box 11, folder 29, 7–8.

16. Alpha Bowser, interview with Benis Frank, 16 June 1970, Marine Corps Oral History Collection, USMCHD, 142, 154–155; Bowser interview, MML, box 11, folder 25, 10; Almond interview, 28 March 1975, USAHEC, section 4, 34–35; McCaffrey to Appleman, 10 September 1978, Appleman Papers, box 20; William McCaffrey, interview with John Baggott, 1997, Senior Officer Oral History Program, William McCaffrey Papers, USAHEC,

134; Almond comments, 10 December 1953, Background Files for *South to Naktong,* RG-319, box 13, folder Correspondence Relating to Critiques and Comments; Oliver Smith comments, n.d., Background Files for *South to Naktong,* RG-319, box 14, folder External Review.

17. For discussion of these different doctrinal approaches, see Bowser interview, Marine Corps Oral History Collection, USMCHD, 163–164; Frank Mildren, interview with James Scott, 1980, Senior Officer Debriefing Program, USAHEC, 124–125; Almond comments, 10 December 1953, Background Files for *South to Naktong,* RG-319, box 13, folder Correspondence Relating to Critiques and Comments; David Barr comments, n.d., Background Files for *South to Naktong,* RG-319, box 13, folder October 1950.

18. Ridgway interview, 6 January 1972, USAHEC, section 3, 77.

19. Almond interview, 28 March 1975, USAHEC, section 4, 34–35.

20. The quote is from Chiles interview, USAHEC, box 11, 59. See also Chiles interview, Truman Library, 21–22; Craig interview, Marine Corps Oral History Collection, 52; Bowser interview, Marine Corps Oral History Collection, USMCHD, 158; Bowser interview, MML, box 11, folder 25, 36–37; Heinl, *Victory,* 36; Charles Banks, interview with Benis Frank, 10 June 1969, Marine Corps Oral History Collection, USMCHD, 38; Lowe to Truman, 28 February 1951, Lowe Papers, box 1; McCaffrey to Appleman, 10 September 1978, Appleman Papers, box 20; Craig interview, MML, box 11, folder 38, 29.

21. MacArthur, *Reminiscences,* 353.

22. Edwin Wright interview, box 13, folder 8, 61–62.

23. *Time,* 25 September 1950, 26.

24. Blair, *Forgotten War,* 278; Craig interview, MML, box 11, folder 38, 11–12.

25. Herbert Powell, interview with Clay Blair, n.d., Clay and Joan Blair Collection, USAHEC, box 21, 31.

26. The quote is from McCaffrey to Appleman, 2 March 1981, Appleman Papers, box 20. For impressions of Barr and the Seventh Division, see Bowser interview, Marine Corps Oral History Collection, USMCHD, 161; Heinl, *Victory,* 55–56; Klingon, *Soldier's General,* 167–169; Almond interview, 28 March 1975, USAHEC, section 4, 33; Powell interview, 26 April 1974, USAHEC, section 5, 65; Powell interview, 17 October 1974, USAHEC, section 6, 87; John Gavin, "Bear Facts," *Military Review,* February 1954, 23; Beauchamp interview, box 9, 7, 110; Joseph Gurfein, interview with Clay Blair, n.d., Clay and Joan Blair Collection, USAHEC, 56; Powell interview with Blair, USAHEC, box 21, 33; McCaffrey to Appleman, 2 and 6 March and 14 June 1981, Appleman Papers, box 20; Merrill Needham to Appleman, 16 October 1985, Appleman Papers, box 21; James Forrestal, 1 March 1948, *Forrestal Diaries,* 2:383; Moore interview, MML, box 11, folder 30, 24.

27. Bowser interview, Marine Corps Oral History Collection, USMCHD, 163–164.

28. The quote is from Oliver Smith comments, n.d., Background Files for *South to Naktong,* RG-319, box 14, folder External Review. See also Stanton, *America's Tenth Legion,* 113; Haig, *Inner Circles,* 41–42; Bowser interview, Marine Corps Oral History Collection, USMCHD, 163–164.

29. Chiles interview, Truman Library, 36–37; Haig, *Inner Circles,* 40–42, 47; *Time,* 23 October 1950, 29; Almond interview, 28 March 1975, USAHEC, section 4, 34–35, 51,

52–55; Almond to Chiles, 25 March 1968, Almond Papers, DMMA, reel 1078, RG-38, box 4, folder 5; Almond comments, 10 December 1953, Background Files for *South to Naktong,* RG-319, box 13, folder Correspondence Relating to Critiques and Comments; Almond to his wife, 24 September 1950, Edward Almond Papers, USAHEC, box 77, "Correspondence with His Wife."

30. Haig, *Inner Circles,* 41–42; Heinl, *Victory,* 212–213, 220; Almond interview, 28 March 1975, Almond Papers, USAHEC, section 4, 52–55; Beauchamp comments, 15 July 1953, Background Files for *South to Naktong,* RG-319, box 11, folder Letters Used in Revision, Chapter 4, Part 2; Almond comments, 10 December 1953, Background Files for *South to Naktong,* RG-319, box 13, folder Correspondence Relating to Critiques and Comments.

31. Beauchamp comments, 15 July 1953, Background Files for *South to Naktong,* RG-319, box 11, folder Letters Used in Revision, Chapter 4, Part 2; McCaffrey to Appleman, 14 June 1981, Appleman Papers, box 20.

32. Haig, *Inner Circles,* 45–46.

33. Edward Almond to Douglas MacArthur, 25 September 1950, Almond Papers, DMMA, reel 1077, RG-38, box 2, folder 6; Beauchamp comments, 15 July 1953, Background Files for *South to Naktong,* RG-319, box 11, folder Letters Used in Revision, Chapter 4, Part 2; Almond comments, 10 December 1953, Background Files for *South to Naktong,* RG-319, box 13, folder Correspondence Relating to Critiques and Comments; McCaffrey to Appleman, 14 June 1981, Appleman Papers, box 20.

34. Oliver Smith comments, n.d., Background Files for *South to Naktong,* RG-319, box 14, folder External Review.

35. For descriptions of the ceremony, see ibid.; Haig, *Inner Circles,* 47; Noble, *Embassy at War,* 203.

36. Frank Pace, interview with Lapsley Smith, 23 March 1975, Senior Officers Debriefing Program, USAHEC, section 2, 8.

37. The two Collins quotes are from Collins, *War in Peacetime,* 141–142.

38. Train interview, 2:326.

39. Collins, *War in Peacetime,* 122; Train interview, 2:326–327; E. Michael Lynch interview, Roosevelt Library, container 143, part 1, 4; Hal Boyle, *Tuscaloosa News,* 31 July 1953, 4; Maihafer, *From the Hudson,* 90; Edgar Conley to Appleman, 26 March 1956, Background Files for *South to Naktong,* RG-319, box 15, folder Correspondence Requesting and Receiving Information.

40. The quote is from J. Lawton Collins to MacArthur, 4 August 1950, DMMA, RG-5, box 3, folder 4. See also J. Lawton Collins to Frank Milburn, 1 August 1950, DMMA, RG-5, box 3, folder 3; MacArthur to the Department of the Army, 3 and 17 August 1950, DMMA, RG-9, box 26, folder 1.

41. Van Brunt interview, box 23, 31–32, 75–76; Gillis interview, box 15, 33; Landrum comments, 8 March 1954, Background Files for *South to Naktong,* RG-319, box 11, folder Letters Used in Revision, Chapter 4; Landrum to Appleman, early to mid-1954, Background Files for *South to Naktong,* RG-319, box 11, folder Letters Used in Revision, Chapter 4, Part 3; Sam Walker interview, container 143, part 2, 7–8.

42. Michaelis interview, MML, box 12, folder 28, 17–18.

43. James Lynch interview, MML, box 12, folder 21, 8–9.

44. Barth, *Tropic Lightning,* 58–59.

45. Dolvin interview with Blair, box 13, 113.

46. For characterizations of Milburn, see Oliver, *Tents,* 272; Johnson interview, USA-HEC, 47; Van Brunt interview, box 23, 59–60, 64–67, 105; William Quinn, interview with Clay Blair, n.d., Clay and Joan Blair Collection, USAHEC, box 21, 160–161; James Lynch interview, box 12, folder 21, 8–9; Harold Johnson, interview with D. Clayton James, 7 July 1971, D. Clayton James Papers, MML, box 12, folder 8, 37; Michaelis interview, MML, box 12, folder 28, 17–18; Paik, *From Pusan,* 49–50, 59; Thompson, *Cry Korea,* 210, 260; Matthew Ridgway interview, n.d., Clay and Joan Blair Collection, USAHEC, box 22, 66; Matthew Ridgway, interview with John Toland, 4 December 1986, Matthew Ridgway Papers, USAHEC, box 88, side 1, 11; Moore interview, MML, box 11, folder 30, 25.

47. Maihafer, *From the Hudson,* 90.

48. Paik, *From Pusan,* 51–52; Heinl, *Victory,* 147; Second Infantry Division Reports, 1 September to 31 October 1950, 28; Gay to Appleman, 30 September 1953, Background Files for *South to Naktong,* RG-319, box 11, folder Letters Used in Revision, Chapter 4, Part 3; Conley to Appleman, 26 March 1956, Background Files for *South to Naktong,* RG-319, box 15, folder Correspondence Requesting and Receiving Information.

49. Maihafer, *From the Hudson,* 121.

50. Robert Baker's After Action Report, n.d., Background Files for *South to Naktong,* RG-319, box 15, Correspondence Requesting and Receiving Information.

51. Michaelis interview, MML, box 12, folder 28, 22; Paik, *From Pusan,* 51–52; Second Infantry Division Reports, 1 September to 31 October 1950, 37; Moore interview, USA-HEC, box 19, 74–75; John Coulter to Stephens, 22 November 1957, Background Files for *South to Naktong,* RG-319, box 11, folder Letters Used in Revision, Chapter 4, Part 2; Gay to Appleman, 30 September 1953, Background Files for *South to Naktong,* RG-319, box 11, folder Letters Used in Revision, Chapter 4, Part 3; Conley to Appleman, 26 March 1956, Background Files for *South to Naktong,* RG-319, box 15, folder Correspondence Requesting and Receiving Information; Gay to Appleman, 31 December 1953, Background Files for *South to Naktong,* RG-319, box 15, folder Correspondence Requesting and Receiving Information; Harris to Appleman, 8 December 1953, Background Files for *South to Naktong,* RG-319, box 15, folder Correspondence Requesting and Receiving Information.

52. Epley interview, box 14, 56.

53. E. Michael Lynch interview, Roosevelt Library, container 143, part 1, 4; Train interview, USAHEC, 2:328–329; Van Brunt interview, box 23, 81; Gay to Appleman, 20 September 1953, Background Files for *South to Naktong,* RG-319, box 11, folder Letters Used in Revision, Chapter 4, Part 3.

54. John Dabney to Stephens, 26 November 1957, Background Files for *South to Naktong,* RG-319, box 11, folder Letters Used in Revision, Chapter 4, Part 2; David Barr comments, 25 May 1954, Background Files for *South to Naktong,* RG-319, box 13, folder October 1950; Oliver Smith comments, n.d., Background Files for *South to Naktong,* RG-319, box 14, folder External Review; Collins, *War in Peacetime,* 160–162.

55. Collins, *War in Peacetime,* 160–162, 170; Almond interview, 28 March 1975, USA-

HEC, section 4, 58–59; Dabney to Stephens, 26 November 1957, Background Files for *South to Naktong*, RG-319, box 11, folder Letters Used in Revision, Chapter 4, Part 2; Landrum to Stephens, 11 November 1957, Background Files for *South to Naktong*, RG-319, box 11, folder Letters Used in Revision, Chapter 4, Part 3; Haig, *Inner Circles*, 40–41.

56. MacArthur, *Reminiscences*, 359–360; MacArthur's testimony, 5 May 1951, United States Senate, *Hearings* (hereafter MacArthur Hearings), reel 1, part 6, 609; Haig, *Inner Circles*, 40–41; MacArthur comments, 15 November 1957, Background Files for *South to Naktong*, RG-319, box 12, folder MacArthur Comments; Appleman, *South to the Naktong*, 610–611.

57. Paik, *From Pusan*, 67; Thompson, *Cry Korea*, 173–175, 186–187; Van Brunt interview, box 23, 74; Dolvin interview with Blair, box 13, 163; *Sarasota Herald-Tribune*, 11 October 1950, 1; *Spokane Daily Chronicle*, 16 October 1950, 2; Gay to Appleman, early January 1954, Background Files for *South to Naktong*, RG-319, box 15, folder Correspondence Requesting and Receiving Information; *Time*, 23 October 1950, 27.

58. Harris to Appleman, 8 and 23 December 1953, Background Files for *South to Naktong*, RG-319, box 15, folder Correspondence Requesting and Receiving Information; Paik, *From Pusan*, 59, 73; Gay to Appleman, early January and 19 April 1954, Background Files for *South to Naktong*, RG-319, box 15, folder Correspondence Requesting and Receiving Information; James Webel statement, early 1954, Background Files for *South to Naktong*, RG-319, box 15, folder Correspondence Requesting and Receiving Information; Thompson, *Cry Korea*, 186–187.

59. Sams, *Medic*, 231; Thompson, *Cry Korea*, 210–211; *Time*, 30 October 1950, 32.

60. Heller, *Korean War*, 28; Gay to Appleman, early January 1954, Background Files for *South to Naktong*, RG-319, box 15, folder Correspondence Requesting and Receiving Information.

61. The quote and some of the information is from Throckmorton interview with Blair, box 22, 74–77. See also Appleman, *South to the Naktong*, 671.

62. *Time*, 25 September 1950, 26.

63. Almond to Walt Sheldon, 28 March 1967, Almond Papers, DMMA, reel 1079, RG-38, box 6, folder 9; Almond interview, 28 March 1975, USAHEC, section 4, 33.

CHAPTER 4. A POWERFUL NEW ENEMY

1. *News-Dispatch*, 31 October 1950, 1.

2. Ibid.; Michaelis interview, MML, box 12, folder 28, 13, 24; Gay interview, 50; Train interview, 2:337–338; Heller, *Korean War*, 29, 33; Gay to Appleman, 15 March 1954, Background Files for *South to Naktong*, RG-319, box 10, folder Letters and Maps; Johnson to Appleman, August 1954, Background Files for *South to Naktong*, RG-319, box 10, folder Letters and Maps; Gay to Appleman, 24 June 1954, Background Files for *South to Naktong*, RG-319, box 13, folder Correspondence Relating to Critiques and Comments; Percy Thompson, Situation on the Chongchon River, n.d., Background Files for *South to Naktong*, RG-319, box 15, folder Correspondence Requesting and Receiving Information; William Hennig, interview with Appleman, 23 March 1954, Background Files for *South to Naktong*, RG-319, box 15, folder Correspondence Requesting and Receiving Information.

3. Milburn comments, November 1957, Background Files for *South to Naktong*, RG-319, box 14, folder External Review.

4. Percy Thompson to Appleman, 9 April 1954, Background Files for *South to Naktong*, RG-319, box 15, folder Correspondence Requesting and Receiving Information.

5. For attitudes of members of the First Cavalry Division, see Charles Palmer interview, 14 June 1977, D. Clayton James Papers, MML, box 12, folder 37, 31; Gay interview, 50; Gillis interview, box 15, 47; Charles Palmer interview, USAHEC, box 20, 160; Gay to Appleman, 19 February and 15 March 1954, Background Files for *South to Naktong*, RG-319, box 10, folder Letter and Maps; Johnson to Appleman, August 1954, Background Files for *South to Naktong*, RG-319, box 10, folder Letters and Maps; John Millikin to Appleman, 6 May 1954, Background Files for *South to Naktong*, RG-319, box 10, folder Letters and Maps; Hennig interview, 23 March 1954, Background Files for *South to Naktong*, RG-319, box 15, folder Correspondence Requesting and Receiving Information.

6. Gay to Appleman, 19 February 1954, Background Files for *South to Naktong*, RG-319, box 10, folder Letters and Maps.

7. The quote is from Charles Palmer interview, USAHEC, box 20, 164. See also Gay to Appleman, 19 February 1954, Background Files for *South to Naktong*, RG-319, box 10, folder Letters and Maps.

8. Milburn comments, November 1957, Background Files for *South to Naktong*, RG-319, box 14, folder External Review.

9. Paik, *From Pusan*, 92–93; Gay to Appleman, 19 February 1954, Background Files for *South to Naktong*, RG-319, box 10, folder Letters and Maps.

10. Quoted in Paik, *From Pusan*, 95.

11. Gay to Appleman, 19 February 1954, Background Files for *South to Naktong*, RG-319, box 10, folder Letters and Maps; Milburn comments, November 1957, Background Files for *South to Naktong*, RG-319, box 14, folder External Review.

12. Maihafer, *From the Hudson*, 142–143.

13. Omar Bradley's testimony, 22 May 1951, MacArthur Hearings, reel 3, part 4, 2528, 2533.

14. MacArthur, *Reminiscences*, 371–372; Sebald, *With MacArthur in Japan*, 203; *Time*, 4 December 1950, 24; Landrum to Appleman, January 1954, Background Files for *South to Naktong*, RG-319, box 11, folder Letters Used in Revision, Chapter 4, Part 3; MacArthur's comments, 15 November 1957, Background Files for *South to Naktong*, RG-319, box 12, folder MacArthur Comments; MacArthur's testimony, 3 May 1951, MacArthur Hearings, reel 1, part 4, 52.

15. Dabney to Stephens, 26 November 1957, Background Files for *South to Naktong*, RG-319, box 11, folder Letters Used in Revision, Chapter 4, Part 2.

16. Ibid.; J. Lawton Collins interview, USAHEC, 1:334–336; MacArthur, *Reminiscences*, 372; Stratemeyer, 16 November 1950, *Three Wars*, 285; E. Michael Lynch interview, Roosevelt Library, container 143, part 2, 9; Ridgway interview, 6 January 1972, USAHEC, section 3, 76–77; Gurfein interview, box 16, 9–10; Landrum to Appleman, January 1954, Background Files for *South to Naktong*, RG-319, box 11, folder Letters Used in Revision, Chapter 4, Part 3; Landrum comments, 28 January 1954, Background Files for *South to*

Naktong, RG-319, box 11, folder Letters Used in Revision, Chapter 4; Henry Fisher comments, 7 November 1957, Background Files for *South to Naktong,* RG-319, box 14, folder External Review.

17. J. Lawton Collins to MacArthur, 4 August 1950, DMMA, RG-5, box 3, folder 3; Almond to Coulter, 10 December 1947, Almond Papers, DMMA, reel 1079, RG-38, box 7, folder 5; Chiles interview, USAHEC, box 11, 61–63; Wade Haislip letter, 12 November 1942, Coulter Papers, box 1; Coulter to Stephens, 22 November 1957, Background Files for *South to Naktong,* RG-319, box 11, folder Letters Used in Revision, Chapter 4, Part 2; Van Brunt interview, 75–76; J. Lawton Collins to Coulter, 24 May 1951, Ridgway Papers, box 9.

18. Second Infantry Division Reports, 1 November to 30 November 1950, Korean War Project, 19–21; Relman Morin, *Spokane Daily Chronicle,* 28 November 1950, 2; Fisher comments, 7 November 1957, Background Files for *South to Naktong,* RG-319, box 14, folder External Review.

19. Paik, *From Pusan,* 104; Stratemeyer, 24 November 1950, *Three Wars,* 299; Van Brunt interview, USAHEC, box 23, 68–70; Milburn comments, November 1957, Background Files for *South to Naktong,* RG-319, box 14, folder External Review.

20. The quote is from Michaelis interview, MML, box 12, folder 28, 25–26. See also Paul Freeman interview, 30 November 1973, USAHEC, section 1, 116; Sherman Pratt, in Tomedi, *No Bugles,* 63–64; Second Infantry Division Reports, 1 November to 30 November 1950, Korean War Project, 19–21, 26–30; Fisher comments, 7 November 1957, Background Files for *South to Naktong,* RG-319, box 14, folder External Review.

21. *Time,* 27 November 1950, 27.

22. Morin, *Spokane Daily Chronicle,* 28 November 1950, 2.

23. *Time,* 4 December 1950, 24.

24. For details of MacArthur's visit, see ibid.; MacArthur, *Reminiscences,* 372; Stratemeyer, 24 November 1950, *Three Wars,* 299; Thompson, *Cry Korea,* 275; Morin, *Spokane Daily Chronicle,* 28 November 1950, 2; Milburn comments, November 1957, Background Files for *South to Naktong,* RG-319, box 14, folder External Review.

25. The quote is from E. Michael Lynch interview, Roosevelt Library, container 143, 8. See also Landrum to Appleman, January 1954, Background Files for *South to Naktong,* RG-319, box 11, folder Letters Used in Revision, Chapter 4, Part 3.

26. Thompson, *Cry Korea,* 284.

27. Ibid., 278–279; Van Brunt interview, box 23, 42.

28. Appleman, *Disaster,* 85–86.

29. Stratemeyer, 27 November 1950, *Three Wars,* 309.

30. Marshall, *The River and the Gauntlet,* 169.

31. Ibid., 24.

32. Ibid., 88, 169–176; Second Infantry Division Reports, 1 November to 30 November 1950, Korean War Project, 26–32; Epley interview, box 14, 27–28, 50–51; Epley to Appleman, 26 October 1979, Appleman Papers, box 4; George Peploe to Appleman, 14 November 1979, Appleman Papers, box 4; Joseph Buys to Appleman, 13 March 1980, Appleman Papers, box 4; McCaffrey to Appleman, 6 March 1980, Appleman Papers, box 29.

33. Marshall, *The River and the Gauntlet,* 263.

34. Ibid., 263, 275; Second Infantry Division Reports, 1 November to 30 November 1950, Korean War Project, 34–37; Epley to Appleman, 26 October 1979, Appleman Papers, box 4.

35. Van Brunt interview, box 23, 95–96.

36. For details about Freeman's background, character, thinking, and actions, see Freeman interview, 30 November 1973, USAHEC, section 1, 117–119; Thompson, *Cry Korea,* 287; Marshall, *The River and the Gauntlet,* 327; Pratt, in Tomedi, *No Bugles,* 65; Second Infantry Division Reports, 1 November to 30 November 1950, Korean War Project, 36–37; Epley interview, box 14, 84; Freeman interview with Blair, box 14, 149; Michaelis interview, USAHEC, box 18, 63; Epley to Appleman, 26 October 1979, Appleman Papers, box 4; Sladen Bradley, interview with S. L. A. Marshall, 23 December 1950, S. L. A. Marshall Papers, USAHEC, box 4, 1–2; Freeman to S. L. A. Marshall, 9 December 1950, S. L. A. Marshall Papers, box 4.

37. Sladen Bradley interview, box 4, 6.

38. Stratemeyer, 26 December 1950, *Three Wars,* 363.

39. Marshall, *The River and the Gauntlet,* 275, 278, 318–320, 327; Second Infantry Division Reports, 1 November to 30 November 1950, Korean War Project, 6, 34–37; Epley interview, 73–74; Sladen Bradley interview, box 4, 2, 5; Sams, *Medic,* 239.

40. Stratemeyer, 26 December 1950, *Three Wars,* 363; Epley interview, box 14, 61–62, 84; Freeman interview with Blair, USAHEC, box 14, 155; Epley to Appleman, 26 October 1979 and 31 March 1980, Appleman Papers, box 4; Ridgway to Appleman, 29 September 1979, Appleman Papers, USAHEC, box 4; Peploe to Appleman, 14 November 1979, Appleman Papers, box 4; Buys to Appleman, 13 March 1980, Appleman Papers, box 4; Sladen Bradley and Lucian Truscott, interview with S. L. A. Marshall, 23 December 1950, S. L. A. Marshall Papers, USAHEC, box 4; Appleman, *Disaster,* 292–293.

41. The quote is from Van Brunt interview, box 23, 119. See also Freeman interview, 30 November 1973, USAHEC, section 1, 121; Michaelis interview, USAHEC, box 18, 66; Ridgway interview with Blair, box 22, 94; Epley to Appleman, 26 October 1979 and 31 March 1980, Appleman Papers, box 4; S. L. A. Marshall comments, n.d., S. L. A. Marshall Papers, box 4, 1–3; Marshall, *Bringing Up the Rear,* 181–182; Appleman, *Disaster,* 257, 291; *New York Times,* 12 December 1950, 7; Chiles interview, USAHEC, box 11, 93; Epley interview, box 14, 67–68; E. Michael Lynch interview, USAHEC, box 17, 80; S. L. A. Marshall, "A Soldier Remembered," n.d., Appleman Papers, box 4; Sams, *Medic,* 239.

42. MacArthur, *Reminiscences,* 377.

43. For MacArthur's mind-set, see ibid., 374; Stratemeyer, 30 November 1950, *Three Wars,* 314; MacArthur to Defense Department, 3 December 1950, DMMA, reel 186, RG-9; MacArthur testimony, 3 May 1951, MacArthur Hearings, reel 1, part 4, 52.

44. Ridgway, *Korean War,* 61–62.

45. Collins, *War in Peacetime,* 229–230, 234; J. Lawton Collins interview, 1:332, 341; Stratemeyer, 6 December 1950, *Three Wars,* 330–331; United States Delegation Minutes of the Sixth Meeting of President Truman and Prime Minister Atlee, 8 December 1950, *Foreign Relations of the United States, 1950,* 1468–1470; J. Lawton Collins testimony, 25 May

1951, MacArthur Hearings, reel 4, part 1, 3228; Edward Almond, 6 December 1950, Almond Papers, USAHEC, box 80, "Personal Notes."

46. Muccio to Dean Acheson, 11 December 1950, *Foreign Relations of the United States, 1950,* 1521; Collins, *War in Peacetime,* 229–230; Stratemeyer, 6 December 1950, *Three Wars,* 333–334.

47. The quote is from Hal Boyle, *Tuscaloosa News,* 31 July 1953, 4. See also J. Lawton Collins interview, USAHEC, 1:334–336; E. Michael Lynch interview, Roosevelt Library, container 143, part 2, 9; E. Michael Lynch interview, Roosevelt Library, container 143, part 3, 9; Coulter to Stephens, 22 November 1957, Background Files for *South to Naktong,* RG-319, box 11, folder Letters Used in Revision, Chapter 4, Part 2; Landrum to Appleman, January 1954, Background Files for *South to Naktong,* RG-319, box 11, folder Letters Used in Revision, Chapter 4, Part 3.

48. Andy Barr, in Tomedi, *No Bugles,* 77.

49. Harry Summers, in Tomedi, *No Bugles,* 105.

50. Barth, *Tropic Lightning,* 47–48; Johnson interview, USAHEC, 53; Second Infantry Division Reports, 1 December to 31 December 1950, Korean War Project, 3–4; Michaelis interview, MML, box 12, folder 28, 13–14; Sams, *Medic,* 240.

51. The quote is from Collins, *War in Peacetime,* 236. See also Goulden, *Korea,* 424–425; Appleman, *Disaster,* 390–393; MacArthur, *Reminiscences,* 383; Barth, *Tropic Lightning,* 50; Sebald, *With MacArthur in Japan,* 206; Noble, *Embassy at War,* 143; Coulter to Stephens, 22 November 1957, Background Files for *South to Naktong,* RG-319, box 11, folder Letters Used in Revision, Chapter 4, Part 2; Almond to his wife, 25 December 1950, Almond Papers, USAHEC, box 77, "Correspondence with His Wife."

52. The quote is from Paik, *From Pusan,* 111. See also Lasher interview, part 4, 6–7; Barth, *Tropic Lightning,* 48, 50; Stratemeyer, 26 December 1950, *Three Wars,* 363; Sams, *Medic,* 239; David, *Battleground Korea.*

53. Barth, *Tropic Lightning,* 50.

54. Rollins Emmerich, 12 December 1957, Background Files for *South to Naktong,* RG-319, box 11, folder Letters Used in Revision, Chapter 4; Frank Tremaine, *Greensburg Daily Tribune,* 26 October 1950, 16; Hope, *Have Tux, Will Travel,* 195.

55. Stanton, *America's Tenth Legion,* 147; Hamlett interview, section 4, 41; MacArthur, *Reminiscences,* 359–360; Craig interview, 8 May 1951, Marine Corps Oral History Collection, 61; Haig, *Inner Circles,* 52–53; Klingon, *Soldier's General,* 139; Almond interview, 28 March 1975, USAHEC, section 4, 62, 70; Almond to Willis Crittenberger, 24 October 1950, Almond Papers, DMMA, reel 1077, RG-38, box 2, folder 1; Almond to MacArthur, 7 October 1950, Almond Papers, DMMA, reel 1077, RG-38, box 2, folder 5; Almond to Kelly Parsons, 3 November 1950, Almond Papers, DMMA, reel 1077, RG-38, box 2, folder 2; Mildren interview, MML, box 11, folder 29, 14.

56. The quote is from Oliver Smith, interview, MML, box 12, folder 48, 2. See also Oliver Smith comments, Background Files for *South to Naktong,* RG-319, box 14, folder External Review; Craig interview, 8 May 1951, Marine Corps Oral History Collection, 61, 66; Edward Almond interview, interview with Thomas Fergusson, 29 March 1975, "Inter-

view with Lt. General Edward M. Almond," http://www.chosinreservoir.com/almondinter view.htm, 4; Oliver Smith interview, MML, box 12, folder 48, 6; Almond, 20 February 1969, review of "Policy and Direction: The First Year," Almond Papers, DMMA, reel 1078, RG-38, box 4, folder 3, 12–13; McCaffrey to Appleman, 11 March 1978, Appleman Papers, box 20; Mildren interview, USAHEC, 124–125.

57. Stanton, *America's Tenth Legion,* 135, 144; Ennis interview, USAHEC, 144; Almond to T. St. J. Arnold, 16 October 1950, Almond Papers, DMMA, reel 1077, RG-38, box 2, folder 1; Almond to MacArthur, 7 October 1950, Almond Papers, DMMA, reel 1077, RG-38, box 2, folder 5; Almond to Walt Sheldon, 28 March 1967, Almond Papers, DMMA, reel 1079, RG-38, box 6, folder 9; McCaffrey to Appleman, 5 March 1981, Appleman Papers, box 20.

58. *Time,* 20 November 1950, 27; Craig interview, 8 May 1951, Marine Corps Marine Corps Oral History Collection, 61; Powell interview, 26 April 1974, USAHEC, section 5, 65; Powell interview, 17 October 1974, USAHEC, section 6, 21; Dabney to Stephens, 26 November 1957, Background Files for *South to Naktong,* RG-319, box 11, folder Letters Used in Revision, Chapter 4, Part 2; David Barr comments, 25 May 1954, Background Files for *South to Naktong,* RG-319, box 13, folder October 1950.

59. McCaffrey to Appleman, July 1979, Appleman Papers, box 20.

60. Ibid.; Dolcater, *3d Infantry Division,* 19, 57–61, 68–73; Almond to Alfred Gruenther, 15 November 1950, Almond Papers, DMMA, reel 1077, RG-38, box 2, folder 2; James Boswell interview, n.d., Clay and Joan Blair Collection, USAHEC, box 10, 117; William Harris, interview with Clay Blair, n.d., Clay and Joan Blair Collection, USAHEC, box 16, 97; Ridgway interview with Blair, box 22, 53; Stanton, *America's Tenth Legion,* 170; Harris, *Puerto Rico's Fighting 65th Infantry,* 104; Almond, 16 December 1950, Almond Papers, USAHEC, box 80, "Personal Notes."

61. Raymond Davis interview, 2–3 February 1977, Marine Corps Oral History Collection, USMCHD, part 2, 157–158.

62. Haig, *Inner Circles,* 55–56; Oliver Smith interview, MML, box 12, folder 48, 3–4; Bowser interview, MML, box 11, folder 25, 14; Almond interview, 28 March 1975, USAHEC, section 4, 65–66, 67–68; Mildren interview, USAHEC, 117–118; Almond to Parsons, 3 November 1950, Almond Papers, DMMA, reel 1077, RG-38, box 2, folder 2; Davis interview, part 2, 157–158; Emmerich comments, 12 December 1957, Background Files for *South to Naktong,* RG-319, box 11, folder Letters Used in Revision, Chapter 4; Craig interview, MML, box 11, folder 38, 14–15; Mildren interview, MML, box 11, folder 29, 15, 17; Almond, 30 October 1950, Almond Papers, USAHEC, box 80, "Personal Notes."

63. Almond to P. H. Vadan, 18 November 1950, Almond Papers, DMMA, reel 1077, RG-38, box 2, folder 2.

64. Almond to John Weckerling, 6 November 1950, Almond Papers, DMMA, reel 1077, RG-38, box 2, folder 2.

65. Klingon, *Soldier's General,* 140.

66. Ibid., 167.

67. For Powell's thinking, see ibid., 139, 140, 141, 144, 147, 149; Craig interview, 8 May 1951, Marine Corps Oral History Collection, 61, 66; Powell interview, 17 October 1974, USAHEC, section 6, 10, 21, 55, 66.

68. The quote is from Almond to David Barr, 21 November 1950, DMMA, reel 243, RG-9, X Corps Incoming. See also Almond interview with Fergusson, 1; Haig, *Inner Circles,* 57–58; Klingon, *Soldier's General,* 146, 151–153; Powell interview, 17 October 1974, USA-HEC, section 6, 55; Almond to Manton Eddy, 26 November 1950, Almond Papers, DMMA, reel 1077, RG-38, box 2, folder 2; *Pittsburgh Post-Gazette,* 22 November 1950, 4.

69. Oliver Smith comments, Background Files for *South to Naktong,* RG-319, box 14, folder External Review.

70. Almond later claimed that building the Hagaru-ri airfield was his idea, but the evidence disputes this. See Almond to Appleman, 29 October 1975, "Correspondence with Historians," Almond Papers, DMMA, reel 1078, RG-38, box 4, folder 3. See also Almond interview with Fergusson, 3–5; Craig interview, 8 May 1951, Marine Corps Oral History Collection, 49, 61–62, 66; Oliver Smith interview, MML, box 12, folder 48, 4–5, 6; Almond, 20 February 1969, review of *Policy and Direction: The First Year,* Almond Papers, DMMA, reel 1078, RG-38, box 4, folder 3, 12–13; Oliver Smith comments, Background Files for *South to Naktong,* RG-319, box 14, folder External Review.

71. Almond interview with Fergusson, 2; Beech, *Tokyo and Points East,* 195; Oliver Smith, interview with S. L. A. Marshall, n.d., S. L. A. Marshall Papers, USAHEC, box 4, 2; Craig interview, MML, box 11, folder 38, 37; Mildren interview, MML, box 11, folder 29, 27–28.

72. J. Lawton Collins interview, USAHEC, 1:336.

73. McCaffrey to Appleman, 5 March 1981, Appleman Papers, box 20.

74. For Almond's reaction to the Chinese attack, see Almond interview with Fergusson, 3–4, 5–6; Haig, *Inner Circles,* 60–61, 62; Stratemeyer, 30 November 1950, *Three Wars,* 314; Almond to MacArthur, 30 November 1950, DMMA, reel 243, RG-9, X Corps Incoming, 15–30 November 1950; X Corps War Diary, Monthly Summary, Almond Papers, DMMA, reel 1077, RG-38, box 1, folder 1, 9, 16.

75. Bowser interview, Marine Corps Oral History Collection, USMCHD, 178–179.

76. Pat Scully, in Tomedi, *No Bugles,* 77.

77. Banks interview, 38; Bowser interview, Marine Corps Oral History Collection, USMCHD, 178–179; Beech, *Tokyo and Points East,* 185–186; Almond to MacArthur, 2 and 4 December 1950, DMMA, RG-9, reel 243, X Corps Incoming, December 1950.

78. Almond interview with Fergusson, 2; Almond to MacArthur, 30 November 1950, DMMA, reel 243, RG-9, X Corps Incoming, 15–30 November 1950; Klingon, *Soldier's General,* 156; Almond to Mrs. Allan MacLean, 27 December 1950, Almond Papers, DMMA, reel 1077, RG-38, box 2, folder 3; Appleman to Almond, 3 March 1977, Almond Papers, DMMA, reel 1078, RG-38, box 4, folder 4; Beauchamp interview, box 9, 47; John Paddock to Appleman, 22 June 1981, Appleman Papers, box 8; McCaffrey to Appleman, 6 March 1981, Appleman Papers, box 20.

79. McCaffrey to Appleman, 5 June 1981, Appleman Papers, box 20.

80. Powell interview, 17 October 1974, USAHEC, section 6, 59; Gavin, "Bear Facts," 18–19; McCaffrey to Appleman, 6 and 30 March 1981, Appleman Papers, box 20.

81. Collins, *War in Peacetime,* 229–230; Almond interview with Fergusson, 6–8; Bowser interview, Marine Corps Oral History Collection, USMCHD, 174; Almond to

MacArthur, 2 and 4 December 1950, DMMA, reel 243, RG-9, X Corps Incoming, December 1950; X Corps War Diary, Monthly Summary, 1–30 November 1950, Almond Papers, DMMA, reel 1077, RG-38, box 1, folder 1, 8; Almond to his wife, 30 November 1950, Almond Papers, USAHEC, box 77, "Correspondence with His Wife."

82. Oliver Smith interview with S. L. A. Marshall, box 4, 7.

83. Jack Wright, in Tomedi, *No Bugles,* 606–607.

84. The quote is from *Time,* 8 January 1951, 16. See also Beech, *Tokyo and Points East,* 185–186; Almond to MacArthur, 2 and 4 December 1950, DMMA, reel 243, RG-9, X Corps Incoming, December 1950; Almond to MacArthur, 24 December 1950, Almond Papers, DMMA, Correspondence and Radios to Higher Headquarters, 22 September 1950–12 July 1951, reel 1077, RG-38 box 2, folder 6; Oliver Smith interview with S. L. A. Marshall, box 4, 8; Pratt, in Tomedi, *No Bugles,* 63–64.

85. Klingon, *Soldier's General,* 158.

86. Ibid., 157; Almond interview with Fergusson, 7; Powell interview, 17 October 1974, USAHEC, section 6, 47, 60.

87. Rutherford Poats, *Pittsburgh Press,* 17 December 1950, 10.

88. Almond interview, 29 March 1975, USAHEC, section 5, 20.

89. Ibid.; Almond interview with Fergusson, 8; Klingon, *Soldier's General,* 157; Dolcater, *3d Infantry Division,* 104; Almond to Charles Willoughby, 23 December 1950, Almond Papers, DMMA, reel 1077, RG-38, box 2, folder 3; Almond to MacArthur, 24 December 1950, Almond Papers, DMMA, reel 1077, RG-38, box 2, folder 6; United States Delegation Minutes of the Sixth Meeting of President Truman and Prime Minister Atlee, 8 December 1950, *Foreign Relations of the United States, 1950,* 1470; Mildren interview, MML, box 11, folder 29, 6.

90. McCaffrey to Appleman, 5 December 1975, Appleman Papers, box 29.

91. Haig, *Inner Circles,* 65; Zonge, in Tomedi, *No Bugles,* 101; MacArthur to Defense Department, 25 December 1950, DMMA, reel 186, RG-9; Mildren interview, USAHEC, 131–132; Gavin, "Bear Facts," 24; Harris, *Puerto Rico's Fighting 65th Infantry,* 132.

92. Klingon, *Soldier's General,* 163.

93. The quote is from Almond to MacArthur, 25 December 1950, DMMA, reel 243, RG-9, X Corps Incoming, December 1950. See also Almond interview, 29 March 1975, USAHEC, section 5, 30–31; Almond to Edward Brooks, 27 December 1950, Almond Papers, DMMA, reel 1077, RG-38, box 2, folder 3; Sams, *Medic,* 240.

94. For criticisms of Coulter during and after the Second Chinese Offensive, see Matthew Ridgway, 9 May 1984, interview with Winton, Matthew B. Ridgway, "Troop Leadership at the Operational Level: The Eighth Army in Korea," *Military Review,* April 1990, 62–63; Van Brunt interview, box 23, 75–76; Chiles interview, USAHEC, box 11, 61–63; Freeman interview with Blair, box 14, 155; Ridgway to Appleman, 29 September 1979, Appleman Papers, box 4; Peploe to Appleman, 14 November 1979, Appleman Papers, box 4; Buys to Appleman, 13 March 1980, Appleman Papers, box 4; Landrum comments, 8 March 1954, Background Files for *South to Naktong,* RG-319, box 11, folder Letters Used in Revision, Chapter 4.

95. See, for instance, Almond interview with Fergusson, 6, 7; Almond to MacArthur, 24 December 1950, Almond Papers, DMMA, reel 1077, RG-38, box 2, folder 6.

96. Ridgway interview, 6 January 1972, USAHEC, section 3, 77. See also Collins, *War in Peacetime,* 196; MacArthur, *Reminiscences,* 374.

CHAPTER 5. RIDGWAY TO THE RESCUE

1. Collins, *War in Peacetime,* 237; Ridgway, *Soldier,* 193–198; interview with Winton in Ridgway, "Troop Leadership," 58.

2. Quoted in Taaffe, *Marshall and His Generals,* 270.

3. Melvin Zais, interview by William Golden and Richard Price, 1977, Senior Officers Debriefing Program, USAHEC, 1:229.

4. Quoted in Blair, *Forgotten War,* 559.

5. For positive views of Ridgway, see *Time,* 5 March 1951, 27; Collins, *War in Peacetime,* 238; Freeman interview, 18 April 1974, USAHEC, section 2, 2–3; Hamlett interview, section 7, 11–12; MacArthur, *Reminiscences,* 383; Barth, *Tropic Lightning,* 58; Almond interview, MML, box 11, folder 17, 22; James Lynch interview, box 12, folder 21, 10; Michaelis interview, MML, box 12, folder 28, 12, 16; Paik, *From Pusan,* 114; Edwin Wright interview, box 13, folder 8, 31–32; Sebald, *With MacArthur in Japan,* 231; Davis interview, part 2, 185; Beauchamp interview, box 9, 101.

6. Sebald, *With MacArthur in Japan,* 232.

7. For negative perspectives of Ridgway, see Hamlett interview, section 7, 11–12; Edmund Lasher interview, section 3, 78–79; James Lynch interview, box 12, folder 21, 10; Michaelis interview, MML, box 12, folder 28, 16; Edwin Wright interview, box 13, folder 8, 31–32; Chiles interview, USAHEC, box 11, 89; Moore interview, MML, box 11, folder 30, 24; Mildren interview, MML, box 11, folder 29, 21.

8. The quote is from J. Lawton Collins to Ridgway, 23 December 1950, Collins Papers, series 1, box 17. See also Collins, *War in Peacetime,* 236–238; Ridgway interview, University of Pittsburgh, 23–24; Ridgway interview, 6 January 1972, USAHEC, section 3, 84; Ridgway to Appleman, 8 March 1980, Appleman Papers, box 20; Heller, *Korean War,* 34–35.

9. Ridgway, *Soldier,* 201.

10. Ibid., 198–201; Ridgway, *Korean War,* 81–83; MacArthur, *Reminiscences,* 383; Ridgway interview, University of Pittsburgh, 4–5.

11. Quoted in James F. Schnabel, "Ridgway in Korea," *Military Review,* March 1964, 9.

12. Interview with Winton in Ridgway, "Troop Leadership," 67.

13. The quote is from Ridgway, *Korean War,* 86. See also Summers, in Tomedi, *No Bugles,* 105–106; Johnson interview, USAHEC, 53; Almond, 20 February 1969, review of "Policy and Direction: The First Year," Almond Papers, DMMA, reel 1078, RG-38, box 4, folder 3, 16; McCaffrey to Appleman, 13 March 1981, Appleman Papers, box 20; Heller, *Korean War,* 29–30; Ridgway, *Korean War,* 86–90; Paik, *From Pusan,* 129; Ridgway, *Soldier,* 202–204.

14. Interview with Winton in Ridgway, "Troop Leadership," 58.

15. Lasher interview, section 3, 75.

16. Dolvin interview with Blair, 4.

17. See, for example, Paik, *From Pusan,* 129; interview with Winton in Ridgway,

"Troop Leadership," 62, 67; Polk interview, section 2, 37–38; Ridgway, *Korean War,* 89–90; Thompson, *Cry Korea,* 325; Summers, in Tomedi, *No Bugles,* 105–106; Voorhees, *Korean Tales,* 55; Johnson interview, USAHEC, 53; Charles Palmer interview, USAHEC, 175; Ridgway interview with Toland, Ridgway Papers, box 88, side 1, 10.

18. Interview with Winton in Ridgway, "Troop Leadership," 57–58.

19. Ridgway to J. Lawton Collins, 8 January 1951, Collins Papers, series 1, box 17.

20. Ridgway, *Korean War,* 85–86, 90–91, 95, 98–99; interview with Winton in Ridgway, "Troop Leadership," 61–62, 64–65; Hoge, *Engineer Memoirs,* 175–176.

21. *Time,* 15 January 1951, 23.

22. Ridgway, *Soldier,* 214.

23. Ibid., 204–205, 210; Ridgway, *Korean War,* 91, 95; Barth, *Tropic Lightning,* 51; Ridgway interview, 6 January 1972, USAHEC, section 4, 64–66; Sams, *Medic,* 242; Maihafer, *From the Hudson,* 202–203; Appleman, *Ridgway Duels,* 58.

24. Collins, *War in Peacetime,* 257; Ridgway, *Korean War,* 85–86; 88–89, 90, 91; J. Lawton Collins to MacArthur, 9 February 1951, DMMA, RG-16a, box 4, folder 9; interview with Winton in Ridgway, "Troop Leadership," 61–62; Ridgway, "Aide Memoire for General J. Lawton Collins," 16 January 1951, Ridgway Papers, box 68, folder 1; Ridgway to Haislip, 24 February 1951, Ridgway Papers, box 68, folder 2; Haislip to Ridgway, 14 February 1951, Ridgway Papers, box 68, folder 2; Memo for Record of Conference, 24 January 1951, Ridgway Papers, box 10; Ridgway to Alexander Bolling and Haislip, 11 January 1951, Collins Papers, box 23.

25. Collins, *War in Peacetime,* 244, 257; J. Lawton Collins to MacArthur, 9 February 1951, DMMA, RG-16a, box 4, folder 9; J. Lawton Collins to Ridgway, 26 January 1951, Collins Papers, series 1, box 17; Ridgway to J. Lawton Collins, 8 January 1951, Collins Papers, series 1, box 17; Charles Bolte, interview by Clay Blair, n.d., Clay and Joan Blair Collection, USAHEC, box 10; Ridgway to Coulter, 30 January 1951, Ridgway Papers, box 9; Ridgway to Appleman, 29 September 1979, Appleman Papers, box 4.

26. *Time,* 5 March 1951, 29; Ridgway interview, 6 January 1972, USAHEC, section 3, 11–14; Bolte interview, box 10, 83; Throckmorton interview with Blair, box 22, 67.

27. Ridgway interview with Toland, Ridgway Papers, box 88, side 1, 11. Ridgway did not name names, but it is clear that he was referring to Milburn.

28. Ridgway, *Korean War,* 89–90, 95; J. Lawton Collins to MacArthur, 9 February 1951, DMMA, RG-16a, box 4, folder 9; interview with Winton in Ridgway, "Troop Leadership," 62–63; Ridgway to J. Lawton Collins, 8 January 1951, Collins Papers, series 1, box 17; Van Brunt interview, box 23, 96–97; J. Lawton Collins to Ridgway, 24 May 1951, Ridgway Papers, box 9.

29. Almond to his wife, 25 December 1950, Almond Papers, USAHEC, box 77, "Correspondence with His Wife."

30. Almond, 20 February 1969, review of "Policy and Direction: The First Year," Almond Papers, DMMA, reel 1078, RG-38, box 4, folder 3, 16.

31. For Ridgway's relationship with Almond and Almond's thinking, see Bowser interview, MML, box 11, folder 25, 22; Almond interview, 29 March 1975, USAHEC, section 5,

32–33; Ridgway interview, 6 January 1972, USAHEC, section 3, 75–76; Chiles interview, USAHEC, box 11, 88; Ridgway to Appleman, 6 March 1978, Appleman Papers, box 20; Notes on Conversation with McCaffrey, 4 February 1976, Appleman Papers, box 29; Ridgway interview with Toland, Ridgway Papers, box 88, side 1, 5; Mildren interview, MML, box 11, folder 29, 22.

32. Conference Notes, 8 January 1951, Ridgway Papers, box 68, folder 1; Ridgway to Haislip, 24 February 1951, Ridgway Papers, box 68, folder 2; Ridgway to John Church, 25 January 1951, Ridgway Papers, box 9; MacArthur to Ridgway, 16 January 1951, Ridgway Papers, box 10; Ridgway interview with Toland, Ridgway Papers, box 88, side 1, 11; Maihafer, *From the Hudson,* 217.

33. Klingon, *Soldier's General,* 167; Beauchamp interview, box 9, 110; Gurfein interview, box 16, 56; Ridgway interview with Toland, Ridgway Papers, box 88, side 1, 11; Almond to David Barr, 9 January 1951, Almond Papers, DMMA, reel 1078, RG-38, box 5, folder 3.

34. Stratemeyer, 13 February 1951, *Three Wars,* 417; Ridgway to Haislip, 24 February 1951, Ridgway Papers, box 68, folder 2.

35. J. Lawton Collins to Ridgway, 26 January 1951, Collins Papers, series 1, box 17; Ridgway interview, 6 January 1972, USAHEC, section 3, 69–70; Ridgway to J. Lawton Collins, 7 February 1951, Ridgway Papers, box 9.

36. *New York Times,* 22 January 1951, 3.

37. Ridgway interview with Blair, box 22, 53.

38. Craig interview, Marine Corps Oral History Collection, 67–68; Bowser interview, Marine Corps Oral History Collection, USMCHD, 185; Oliver Smith interview, 25 August 1971, D. Clayton James Papers, MML, box 12, folder 48; E. Michael Lynch interview, Roosevelt Library, container 143, part 5, 11–12; E. Michael Lynch interview, Roosevelt Library, container 143, part 1, 2; Davis interview, part 2, 185; Ridgway to Appleman, 11 May 1984, Appleman Papers, box 20.

39. *Time,* 5 March 1951, 32; Ridgway interview with Blair, box 22, 56; Throckmorton interview with Blair, box 22, 10, 65–66; Maihafer, *From the Hudson,* 217; James Van Fleet to Ridgway, 9 January 1952, James Van Fleet Papers, George C. Marshall Foundation, part 5, box 77.

40. Gurfein interview, box 16, 56.

41. Quinn, *Buffalo Bill Remembers,* 281–282.

42. The quote is from McCaffrey to Appleman, 9 March 1981, Appleman Papers, box 20. For details about Ferenbaugh and his efforts to overhaul the Seventh Division, see Klingon, *Soldier's General,* 165–166, 167, 168, 169, 170, 173, 176, 179; Powell interview, 17 October 1974, USAHEC, section 6, 80–81; Public Information Office, Seventh Infantry Division, *Bayonet;* Almond to Ridgway, 16 February 1951, Almond Papers, DMMA, reel 1077, RG-38, box 2, folder 5; Almond's Personal Notes, 19 January 1951, Almond Papers, DMMA, reel 1077, RG-38, box 3, folder 6; Quinn interview, box 21, 53–54.

43. Ridgway interview, 6 January 1972, USAHEC, section 3, 64–66.

44. Edson interview, box 13, 58.

45. Bolte interview, box 10, 90; J. Lawton Collins to MacArthur, 9 February 1951,

DMMA, RG-16a, box 4, folder 9; Army Commander Notes, 13 April 1951, Almond Papers, DMMA, reel 1077, RG-38, box 1, folder 15, 3; Conference Notes, 8 January 1951, Ridgway Papers, box 68, folder 1; *Time,* 21 August 1950, 19.

46. Marshall, *Bringing Up the Rear,* 181.

47. Freeman interview, 10 November 1973, USAHEC, section 1, 99; Barth, *Tropic Lightning,* 22, 88–99; Stratemeyer, 26 December 1950, *Three Wars,* 363–364; David, *Battleground Korea;* Sladen Bradley to Almond, 7 January 1948, Almond Papers, DMMA, reel 1079, RG-38, box 7, folder 3; Dolvin interview with Blair, box 13, 178–182; Dolvin interview with Blair, box 14, 24; Freeman interview with Blair, box 14, 56; Michaelis interview, USAHEC, box 18, 81; McCaffrey to Appleman, 6 March 1980, Appleman Papers, box 29; Sams, *Medic,* 239.

48. *Time,* 5 March 1951, 32.

49. *Newsweek,* 19 February 1951, 27.

50. Ridgway, *Korean War,* 88–89.

51. *Time,* 5 March 1951, 28.

52. Ibid.; Ridgway, *Korean War,* 81–83, 89–90; Bowser interview, Marine Corps Oral History Collection, USMCHD, 179; Ridgway to J. Lawton Collins, 8 January 1951, Collins Papers, series 1, box 17; Ridgway interview, 6 January 1972, USAHEC, section 3, 61; Craig interview, MML, box 11, folder 38, 35–36; Mildren interview, MML, box 11, folder 29, 22; Almond, 27 December 1950, Almond Papers, USAHEC, box 80, "Personal Notes."

53. Collins, *War in Peacetime,* 253.

54. Memorandum by Lucius D. Battle, 19 January 1951, *Foreign Relations of the United States, 1951,* 102–103; J. Lawton Collins, Memo for Secretary of Defense, 19 January 1951, Collins Papers, box 23.

55. *Time,* 22 January 1951, 26.

56. Marshall, *Bringing Up the Rear,* 188.

57. *Time,* 22 January 1951, 26; Epley interview, box 14, 68–70; Freeman interview with Blair, box 14, 125–128; *New York Times,* 16 January 1951, 4; Ridgway to MacArthur, 17 January 1951, Ridgway Papers, box 68, folder 1; Notes on Conversation with McCaffrey, 4 February 1976, Appleman Papers, box 29; McCaffrey interview, 159, 162–163.

58. McCaffrey to Appleman, 6 March 1980, Appleman Papers, box 29; Notes on Conversation with McCaffrey, 4 February 1976, Appleman Papers, box 29.

59. Freeman interview, 30 November 1973, USAHEC, section 1, 122–124; Second Infantry Division Reports, vol. 5, Reports, 1 January to 31 January 1951, Korean War Project, 7–9; Almond, 9 January 1951, DMMA, reel 1078, RG-38, box 6, folder 5; Freeman interview with Blair, box 14, 125–128.

60. Almond interview, 29 March 1975, USAHEC, section 5, 35; X Corps Headquarters: Command Report, 1–31 January 1951, Almond Papers, DMMA, reel 1077, GG-38, box 1, folder 3; Almond to Ridgway, 14 January 1951, Almond Papers, DMMA, reel 1077, RG-38, box 2, folder 5; Almond to Appleman, 29 October 1975, Almond Papers, DMMA, reel 1078, RG-38, box 4, folder 3; Almond, 20 February 1969, review of "Policy and Direction: The First Year," Almond Papers, DMMA, reel 1078, RG-38, box 4, folder 3, 16; Almond, 13 January 1951, Almond Papers, DMMA, reel 1078, RG-38, box 6, folder 5;

Ridgway to MacArthur, 17 January 1951, Ridgway Papers, box 68, folder 1; Notes on Conversation with McCaffrey, 4 February 1976, Appleman Papers, box 29; McCaffrey interview, USAHEC, 159, 162–163; Mossman, *Ebb and Flow,* 222; Almond to Ridgway, 14 January 1951, USAHEC, box 86, "McClure File."

61. Almond interview, MML, box 11, folder 17, 16–17; Almond interview, 28 March 1975, USAHEC, section 4, 27–28; Almond to Brees, 16 October 1950, Almond Papers, DMMA, reel 1077, RG-38, box 2, folder 1; Almond to Clark Ruffner, 16 July 1951, Almond Papers, DMMA, reel 1078, RG-38, box 5, folder 5; Quinn interview, box 21, 166; Conference Notes, 8 January 1951, Ridgway Papers, box 68, folder 1; Memo of Record of Conference, 24 January 1951, Ridgway Papers, box 10; Ridgway to Appleman, 11 May 1984, Appleman Papers, box 20; Almond to Ruffner, 15 January 1951, Almond Papers, USAHEC, box 86, "McClure File"; Almond to his wife, 14 January 1951, Almond Papers, USAHEC, box 77.

62. Almond interview, 29 March 1975, USAHEC, section 5, 36.

63. Edward Rowney, interview by Clay Blair, n.d., Clay and Joan Blair Collection, USAHEC, box 22, 17.

64. *New York Times,* 16 January 1951, 4; Almond to Ruffner, 16 July 1951, Almond Papers, DMMA, reel 1078, RG-38, box 5, folder 5; Epley interview, box 14, 47; Freeman interview with Blair, box 14, 134–135; Quinn interview, box 21, 166; McCaffrey interview, 139; Mildren interview, MML, box 11, folder 29, 32–33; Powell interview, 17 October 1974, USAHEC, section 6, 69–70.

65. Almond to Ridgway, 15 January 1951, Almond Papers, DMMA, reel 1077, RG-38, box 2, folder 5.

66. Freeman interview, 30 November 1973, USAHEC, section 1, 127–128.

67. Ridgway to Almond, 20 January 1951, DMMA, reel 175, RG-9, Eighth Army Incoming; Ridgway interview, 6 January 1972, USAHEC, section 3, 76–77.

68. Chiles interview, USAHEC, box 11, 18–19.

69. Almond to Ridgway, 14 February 1951, Almond Papers, DMMA, reel 1077, RG-38, box 2, folder 5; Mossman, *Ebb and Flow,* 264.

70. *Time,* 26 February 1951, 23.

71. Freeman interview, 16 April 1974, USAHEC, section 2, 1–5; Second Infantry Division Reports, vol. 6, 1 February to 28 February 1951, Korean War Project, 13; Almond to Appleman, 29 October 1975, Almond Papers, DMMA, reel 1078, RG-38, box 4, folder 3.

72. Harold H. Martin, *Saturday Evening Post,* 19 May 1951, 157.

73. Freeman interview, 16 April 1974, USAHEC, section 2, 1–5; E. Michael Lynch interview, Roosevelt Library, container 143, 18–19; Almond's Personal Notes, 14 February 1951, Almond Papers, DMMA, reel 1077, RG-38, box 3, folder 6; Chiles interview, USAHEC, box 11, 117–118; Freeman interview with Blair, box 14, 123.

74. Almond to his wife, 18 January 1951, Almond Papers, USAHEC, box 77, "Correspondence with His Wife."

75. Michaelis interview, MML, box 12, folder 28, 14.

76. Frederick Weyand, interview by Lewis Sorley, 9–15 November 1999, Senior Officers Debriefing Program, USAHEC, 53.

77. The story of MacArthur's reprimand of Ridgway is from Edwin Wright interview, box 13, folder 8, 33–37.

78. Ridgway, *Korean War,* 109.

79. Ridgway interview, 6 January 1972, USAHEC, section 3, 79.

80. Ridgway interview, University of Pittsburgh, 5–6.

81. James Lynch interview, box 12, folder 21, 8–9; Paik, *From Pusan,* 131; Ridgway interview, 6 January 1972, USAHEC, section 3, 75–77; Almond memo, 8 February 1951, Almond Papers, DMMA, reel 1078, RG-38, box 6, folder 3; Ridgway to Milburn, 3 April 1951, Ridgway Papers, box 10; Ridgway interview with Toland, Ridgway Papers, box 88, side 1, 5; Blair, *Forgotten War,* 721.

82. Appleman, *Ridgway Duels,* 311; Throckmorton interview with Blair, box 22, 67; Ridgway to Milburn, 25 February 1951, Ridgway Papers, box 10.

83. The quote is from Ridgway to J. Lawton Collins, 3 April 1951, Ridgway Papers, box 9. See also Appleman, *Ridgway Duels,* 357–358; Oliver Smith interview, MML, box 12, folder 48, 16–17; Bowers and Greenwood, *Passing the Test,* 362; Haislip to Ridgway, 25 February 1951, Ridgway Papers, box 68, folder 2; Blair, *Forgotten War,* 727; Hoge, *Engineer Memoirs,* 151–152, 174, 175–176, 177, 180, 206, 223–224; Haislip to Ridgway, 25 February 1951, Ridgway Papers, box 68, folder 2.

84. *New York Times,* 16 January 1951, 4; Second Infantry Division Reports, vol. 7, Reports, 1 March to 31 March 1951, Korean War Project, 6, 9, 11, 13, 17; Second Infantry Division Reports, vol. 8, Reports, 1 April to 30 April 1951, Korean War Project, 15–16; Almond to Ruffner, 16 July 1951, Almond Papers, DMMA, reel 1078, RG-38, box 5, folder 5.

85. Klingon, *Soldier's General,* 165–166, 170, 176, 178, 179, 181; Powell interview, 17 October 1974, USAHEC, section 6, 81, 83–84; Almond memo, 19 January 1951, Almond Papers, DMMA, reel 1077, RG-38, box 3, folder 6.

86. *New York Times,* 22 January 1951, 3.

87. The quote is from James Boswell, interview by Clay Blair, n.d., Clay and Joan Blair Collection, USAHEC, box 10, 99–100. See also Dolcater, *3d Infantry Division,* 127; *Reading Eagle,* 27 January 1951, 1; David, *Battleground Korea.*

88. Oliver Smith interview, MML, box 12, folder 48, 10.

89. Bowser interview, Marine Corps Oral History Collection, USMCHD, 185; Lowe to Truman, 28 February 1951, Lowe Papers, box 1; Blair, *Forgotten War,* 728; Ridgway to Appleman, 11 May 1984, Appleman Papers, box 20.

90. Frank Pace Jr. interview by Jerry Hess, 17 February 1972, Truman Library, 104–105.

91. The story of Pace giving Ridgway the news is from Maihafer, *From the Hudson,* 228–229; Pace interview, USAHEC, section 2, 13–14; Ridgway, *Korean War,* 157–158; Pace interview, MML, box 11, folder 36, 3.

92. Pace interview, MML, box 11, folder 36, 17.

93. Quoted in Goulden, *Korea,* 484–485.

94. J. Lawton Collins interview, Combined Arms Research Library, 31.

95. For explanations of the Joint Chiefs' thinking, see Omar Bradley testimony, 15 May 1951, MacArthur Hearings, reel 2, part 7, 1936–1939; Omar Bradley testimony, 21

May 1951, MacArthur Hearings, reel 3, part 3, 2275–2278; J. Lawton Collins testimony, 25 May 1951, MacArthur Hearings, reel 4, part 7, 3120.

96. Stratemeyer, 11 May 1951, *Three Wars,* 477; Sebald, *With MacArthur in Japan,* 229; Almond interview, 29 March 1975, USAHEC, section 5, 43; MacArthur testimony, 3 May 1951, MacArthur Hearings, reel 1, part 4, 67.

97. Ridgway, *Korean War,* 159.

98. Collins, *War in Peacetime,* 283; Sebald, *With MacArthur in Japan,* 231; Ridgway, interview by Maurice Matloff, 18 April 1984, Oral History Interview with General M. B. Ridgway, Combined Arms Research Library, 5.

99. Collins, *War in Peacetime,* 284, 294–295; J. Lawton Collins interview, USAHEC, 1:153–155; Appleman, *Ridgway Duels,* 437–438; George Marshall testimony, 11 May 1951, MacArthur Hearings, reel 2, part 4, 1320; George Marshall testimony, 11 May 1951, MacArthur Hearings, reel 2, part 5, 1534–1536; J. Lawton Collins testimony, 25 May 1951, MacArthur Hearings, reel 4, part 1, 3213–3214; George Marshall testimony, 11 May 1951, MacArthur Hearings, reel 4, part 1, 3213–3214.

100. Collins, *War in Peacetime,* 294–295; Ridgway, *Korean War,* 163–164; Lasher interview, section 3, 79–80; Bruce Palmer Jr., interview by James Shelton and Edward Smith, 5 January 1976, Senior Officers Debriefing Program, USAHEC, interview 2, 121; Taylor interview, section 3, 25; Walters interview, 695–696; Barth, *Tropic Lightning,* 83; E. Michael Lynch interview, Roosevelt Library, container 143, part 4, 2; Voorhees, *Korean Tales,* 59, 60, 61, 63–64; Mildren interview, USAHEC, 152–153, 154–155; Chiles interview, USAHEC, box 11, 89; Frank Mildren interview with Blair, box 18, 139; Mildren interview, MML, box 11, folder 29, 25–26.

101. Ridgway, *Korean War,* 162.

102. James Van Fleet, interview by Bruce Williams, 3 March 1973, Senior Officers Debriefing Program, USAHEC, 3:7–9; *Time,* 23 April 1951, 36.

103. Ridgway interview with Blair, section 3, 86.

104. Ridgway, *Korean War,* 162; Ridgway interview, 6 January 1972, USAHEC, section 3, 85; Army Commander Notes, 13 April 1951, Almond Papers, DMMA, reel 1077, box 1, folder 15, 3; George Marshall testimony, 11 May 1951, MacArthur Hearings, reel 2, part 4, 1320; Blair, *Forgotten War,* 800.

105. Mildren interview, USAHEC, 152–153.

106. Van Fleet interview, 3:16.

107. Almond to his wife, 15 April 1951, Almond Papers, USAHEC, box 77, "Correspondence with His Wife."

108. Ibid., 16–17.

109. Ibid., 15, 16–17; Appleman to Almond, 15 October 1975, Almond Papers, DMMA, reel 1078, RG-38, box 4, folder 4; Almond to Van Fleet, 10 December 1947, Almond Papers, DMMA, reel 1080, RG-38, box 9, folder 4; Vorhees, *Korean Tales,* 60; Muccio interview, 74–75; Hoge, *Engineer Memoirs,* 174, 184.

110. Army Commander Notes, 13 April 1951, Almond Papers, DMMA, reel 1077, RG-38, folder 15, 3.

111. Klingon, *Soldier's General,* 181.

112. Bryan's quote is from Maihafer, *From the Hudson,* 229. See also Almond interview, 29 March 1975, USAHEC, section 5, 53; Aid, *Secret Sentry,* 37–38; Second Infantry Division Reports, vol. 8, Reports, 1 April to 30 April 1951, Korean War Project, 19–20, 22; Army Commander Notes, 13 April 1951, Almond Papers, DMMA, reel 1077, RG-38, box 1, folder 15, 3; Wilburt Brown, interview by Benis Frank, 24 August 1987, Marine Corps Oral History Collection, USMCHD, session 3, 171–172; Van Fleet interview, 3:23; Omar Bradley testimony, 22 May 1951, MacArthur Hearings, reel 3, part 4, 2389.

113. Van Fleet interview, 3:19–20.

114. Ibid., 18.

115. Ibid., 14, 23.

116. Hoge, *Engineer Memoirs,* 183.

117. Army Commander Notes, 1 May 1951, Almond Papers, DMMA, reel 1077, RG-38, box 1, folder 15, 3.

118. *Time,* 7 May 1951, 29.

119. Appleman, *Ridgway Duels,* 501; Mossman, *Ebb and Flow,* 428–429.

120. Almond interview, 29 March 1975, USAHEC, section 5, 58; Mildren interview, USAHEC, 123–124; Almond to Gerald Thomas, 15 July 1951, Almond Papers, DMMA, reel 1078, RG-38, box 5, folder 5; Bowser interview, Marine Corps Oral History Collection, USMCHD, 184–185; Blair, *Forgotten War,* 842.

121. Blair, *Forgotten War,* 861.

122. Bowers and Greenwood, *Passing the Test,* 374; Appleman, *Ridgway Duels,* 499.

123. Almond interview, 29 March 1975, USAHEC, section 5, 45; Mildren interview, USAHEC, 137–138; Tenth Corps Command Report, 1–31 May 1951, Almond Papers, DMMA, reel 1077, RG-38, folder 7, 6.

124. Almond interview, 29 March 1975, USAHEC, section 5, 46; Mildren interview, USAHEC, 145–146; Second Infantry Division Reports, vol. 9, Reports, 1 May to 31 May 1951, Korean War Project, 19–20, 29–30, 45; Bowers and Greenwood, *Passing the Test,* 379; *Tri City Herald,* 11 June 1951, 1; Almond to his wife, 27 May 1951, Almond Papers, USA-HEC, box 77, "Correspondence with His Wife."

125. Almond interview, MML, box 11, folder 17, 20–22; Paik, *From Pusan,* 151; Almond interview, 29 March 1975, USAHEC, section 5, 46–50; Bowers and Greenwood, *Passing the Test,* 379; Almond to Appleman, 29 October 1975, Almond Papers, DMMA, reel 1078, RG-38, box 4, folder 3.

126. *Newsweek,* 4 June 1951, 32.

127. Paik, *From Pusan,* 155.

128. Almond interview, MML, box 11, folder 17, 21–22; Almond interview, 29 March 1975, USAHEC, section 5, 49–52; Mildren interview, USAHEC, 142–143; Bowers and Greenwood, *Passing the Test,* 307–308; Almond to Appleman, 29 October 1975, Almond Papers, DMMA, reel 1078, RG-38, box 4, folder 3; Appleman to Almond, 15 October 1975, Almond Papers, DMMA, reel 1078, RG-38, box 4, folder 4; Mildren interview, MML, box 11, folder 29, 38.

129. Bowers and Greenwood, *Passing the Test,* 355–360, 362, 374; Tenth Corps Command Report, 1–30 June 1951, Almond Papers, DMMA, reel 1077, RG-38, box 1, folder 8,

2, 4; Appleman to Almond, 15 October 1975, Almond Papers, DMMA, reel 1078, RG-38, box 4, folder 4; Quinn, *Buffalo Bill Remembers,* 281–282; Blair, *Forgotten War,* 889; Hoge, *Engineer Memoirs,* 183.

130. Ridgway, *Soldier,* 219–220.

131. Omar Bradley testimony, 22 May 1951, MacArthur Hearings, reel 3, part 4, 2430–2432, 2517; Blair, *Forgotten War,* 902; Hoge, *Engineer Memoirs,* 174.

132. Almond interview, MML, box 11, folder 17, 22.

133. Ridgway, *Korean War,* 181; Taylor interview, USAHEC, section 3, 31; Almond interview, 29 March 1975, USAHEC, section 5, 52; Ridgway interview, 6 January 1972, USAHEC, section 3, 86; Sams, *Medic,* 259.

CONCLUSION

1. *Time,* 31 July 1950, 55; *El Paso Times,* 4 August 1965; Almond interview, 28 March 1975, USAHEC, section 4, 33; Powell interview with Blair, box 21, 33; Merrill Needham to Appleman, 16 October 1985, Appleman Papers, box 21.

2. Holeman interview, 58.

Bibliography

ARCHIVAL SOURCES

Abraham Lincoln Presidential Library and Museum, Springfield, Illinois
  Oral History of James Perry
Combined Arms Research Library, Fort Leavenworth, Kansas
  Oral Histories of J. Lawton Collins and Matthew Ridgway
Douglas MacArthur Memorial Archives (DMMA), Norfolk, Virginia
  Edward M. Almond Papers
Dwight D. Eisenhower Presidential Library and Museum, Abilene, Kansas
  J. Lawton Collins Papers
Franklin D. Roosevelt Presidential Library and Museum, Hyde Park, New York
  Oral Histories of E. Michael Lynch, Sam Walker
George C. Marshall Foundation, Lexington, Virginia
  James Van Fleet Papers
Harry S. Truman Library and Museum, Independence, Missouri
  Oral Histories of John Chiles, Bruce Clarke, Frank Holeman, Robert Laundry, John
  Muccio, Frank Pace Jr.
Hoover Institution Archives, Stanford University, Stanford, California
  Wade Haislip Papers
Mitchell Memorial Library (MML), Mississippi State University
  D. Clayton James' Oral Histories of Edward Almond, Alpha Bowser, Edward Craig,
  Averell Harriman, Harold Johnson, James Lynch, John Michaelis, Frank Mildren, Ed-
  ward Moore, Frank Pace Jr., Charles Palmer, Gines Perez, William Sebald, Oliver Smith,
  Edwin Wright
National Archives and Records Administration, College Park, Maryland
  Records of the Army Staff, Office of the Chief Military Historian, Background Files for
  South to Naktong, North to Yalu
United States Army Heritage and Education Center (USAHEC), Carlisle, Pennsylvania
  Senior Officers Debriefing Program interviews of Edward Almond, J. Lawton Collins,
  Richard Collins, Welborn Dolvin, Henry Emerson, William Ennis Jr., Alva Fitch, Paul
  Freeman, Hobart Gay, Barksdale Hamlett, Hamilton Howze, Harold Johnson, Stanley
  Larsen, Edmund Lasher, William McCaffrey, Frank Mildren, Frank Pace, Bruce Palmer
  Jr., James Polk, Herbert Powell, Matthew Ridgway, Maxwell Taylor, John Throckmor-
  ton, William Train, James Van Fleet, John Walters, Frederick Weyand, Melvin Zais

  Clay Blair interviews with James Adams, Charles Beauchamp, Charles Bolte, James

Boswell, William Caldwell, John Chiles, Peter Clainos, Frank Culley, Chester DeGavre, Welborn Dolvin, Hamlett Edson, Gerald Epley, Paul Freeman, Thomas Gillis, Joseph Gurfein, William Harris, E. Michael Lynch, John Michaelis, Frank Mildren, Edward Moore, Charles O'Neil, Charles Palmer, Herbert Powell, William Quinn, Matthew Ridgway, Edward Rowney, John Throckmorton, Rinaldo Van Brunt, Arthur Wilson

Papers of Edward Almond, Roy Appleman, Clay Blair, John Coulter, Paul Freeman, William Hoge, Frank Lowe, S. L. A. Marshall, William McCaffrey, Matthew Ridgway, Charles B. Smith, Joseph Swing

United States Marine Corps Historical Division (USMCHD), Quantico, Virginia
Oral Histories of Chester Allen, Charles Banks, Alpha Bowser, Wilburt Brown, Austin Brunelli, Clifton Cates, Edward Craig, Raymond Davis
University of Kentucky Libraries, Louie B. Nunn Center for Oral History, Colonel Arthur L. Kelly American Veterans Oral History Collection, Lexington, Kentucky
Oral History of Edwin Elliott
University of Pittsburgh, Pittsburgh, Pennsylvania
Interview with General Matthew B. Ridgway

NEWSPAPERS AND JOURNALS

Army
Combat Forces Journal
Deseret News
Dubuque Telegraph-Herald
El Paso Times
Eugene Register-Guard
Evening Day. The Evening Independent
Grape Belt Greensburg Daily Tribune
Journal of Military History
Lawrence Daily Journal-World
Life Magazine
Ludington Daily News
Military History
Military Review
Milwaukee Sentinel
Modesto Bee and News Herald
News-Dispatch
News-Sentinel
New York Times
Pacific Stars and Stripes
Palm Beach Post
Pittsburgh Post-Gazette
Pittsburgh Press
Reader's Digest
Reading Eagle

Sarasota Herald-Tribune
Saturday Evening Post
Spokane Daily Chronicle
Time
Tri City Herald
Tuscaloosa News
Windsor Daily Star
Youngstown Vindicator

WORKS CITED AND CONSULTED

Aid, Matthew M. *The Secret Sentry: The Untold Story of the National Security Agency.* New York: Bloomsbury Press, 2009.

Alexander, Bevin. *Korea: The First War We Lost.* New York: Hippocrene Books, 1986.

Alsop, Joseph W., with Adam Platt. *"I've Seen the Best of It": Memoirs.* New York: Norton, 1992.

Appleman, Roy E. *Disaster in Korea: The Chinese Confront MacArthur.* College Station: Texas A&M Press, 1989.

———. *Ridgway Duels for Korea.* College Station: Texas A&M Press, 1990.

———. *South to the Naktong, North to the Yalu.* Washington, DC: Center of Military History, 1992.

Baillie, Hugh. *High Tension: The Recollections of Hugh Baillie.* Freeport, NY: Books for Libraries Press, 1959.

Barth, George B. "The First Day in Korea." *Antiaircraft Journal* 95, no. 2 (March–April 1952): 26–29.

———. *Tropic Lightning and Taro Leaf in Korea, July '50–May '51.* Washington, DC: Department of the Army, 1955.

Beech, Keyes. *Tokyo and Points East.* New York: Doubleday, 1954.

Bigart, Homer. *Forward Positions: The War Correspondence of Homer Bigart.* Edited by Betsy Wade. Fayetteville: University of Arkansas Press, 1992.

Blair, Clay. *The Forgotten War: America in Korea, 1950–1953.* New York: Times Books, 1987.

Boose, Donald W., Jr. *US Army Forces in the Korean War, 1950–53.* New York: Osprey, 2006.

Bowers, William T., ed. *The Line: Combat Operations in Korea, January–February 1951.* Lexington: University Press of Kentucky, 2008.

Bowers, William T., and John T. Greenwood, eds. *Passing the Test: Combat in Korea, April–June 1951.* Lexington: University Press of Kentucky, 2011.

Braim, Paul F. *The Will to Win: The Life of General James A. Van Fleet.* Annapolis, MD: Naval Institute Press, 2001.

Busch, George B. *Duty: The Story of the 21st Infantry Regiment.* Sendai, Japan: Hyappan, 1953.

Clark, Mark W. *From the Danube to the Yalu.* New York: Harper, 1968.

Cohen, Eliot A., and John Gooch. *Military Misfortunes: The Anatomy of Failure in War.* New York: Free Press, 1990.

Coleman, J. D. *Wonju: The Gettysburg of the Korean War.* Washington, DC: Brassey's, 2000.

Collins, J. Lawton. *War in Peacetime: The History and Lessons of Korea.* Boston: Houghton Mifflin, 1969.

Conway-Lanz, Sahr. *Collateral Damage: Americans, Noncombatant Immunity and Atrocity after World War II.* New York: Routledge, 2006.

Cummings, Bruce. *The Origins of the Korean War.* Volume 2, *The Roaring of the Cataract, 1947–1950.* Princeton, NJ: Princeton University Press, 1990.

David, Allan A., ed. *Battleground Korea: The Story of the 25th Infantry Division.* 25th Infantry Division History Council, 1951.

Dean, William, as told to William L. Worden. *General Dean's Story.* New York: Viking, 1954.

Dolcater, Max W., ed. *3d Infantry Division in Korea.* Tokyo, Japan: 3d Infantry Division, 1953.

Donnelly, William M. "Bilko's Army: A Crisis in Command?" *Journal of Military History,* October 2011, 1183–1215.

Ent, Uzal W. *Fighting on the Brink: Defense of the Pusan Perimeter.* Paducah, KY: Turner, 1996.

Epley, William W. *America's First Cold War Army, 1945–1950.* Arlington, VA: Institute of Land Warfare, Association of the United States Army, 1993.

Fantua, David T. "The 'Long Pull' Army: NSC 68, the Korean War, and the Creation of the Cold War US Army." *Journal of Military History,* January 1997, 93–120.

Fehrenbach, T. R. *This Kind of War: A Study in Unpreparedness.* New York: Macmillan, 1963.

Foreign Relations of the United States, 1950: Korea. Volume 7. Washington, DC: Government Printing Office, 1976.

Foreign Relations of the United States, 1951: Korea and China. Volume 6, 2 parts. Washington, DC: Government Printing Office, 1977.

Forrestal, James. *The Forrestal Diaries.* Edited by Walter Millis with the collaboration of E. S. Duffield. New York: Viking, 1951.

Goulden, Joseph C. *Korea: The Untold Story of the War.* New York: McGraw-Hill, 1982.

Haig, Alexander M., Jr., with Charles McCarry. *Inner Circles: How America Changed the World.* New York: Warner Books, 1992.

Halberstam, David. *The Coldest Winter: America and the Korean War.* New York: Hyperion, 2007.

Hamburger, Kenneth E. *Leadership in the Crucible: The Korean War Battles of Twin Tunnels and Chipyong-ni.* College Station: Texas A&M University Press, 2003.

Hanson, Thomas E. *Combat Ready? The Eighth US Army on the Eve of the Korean War.* College Station: Texas A&M University Press, 2010.

Harris, W. W. *Puerto Rico's Fighting 65th US Infantry: From San Juan to Chorwan.* Novato, CA: Presidio, 2001.

Hastings, Max. *The Korean War.* New York: Simon & Schuster, 1987.

Heefner, Wilson A. *Patton's Bulldog: The Life and Service of General Walton H. Walker.* Shippensburg, PA: White Mane Books, 2001.

Heinl, Robert Debs, Jr. *Victory at High Tide: The Inchon-Seoul Campaign.* New York: Lippincott, 1968.

Heller, Francis H., ed. *The Korean War: A 25-Year Perspective.* Lawrence: Regents Press of Kansas, 1977.

Higgins, Marguerite. *War in Korea: The Report of a Woman Combat Correspondent.* Garden City, NY: Doubleday, 1951.

Hinshaw, Arned L. *Heartbreak Ridge: Korea, 1951.* New York: Praeger, 1989.

Hoge, William. *Engineer Memoirs: General William M. Hoge.* Washington, DC: Office of History, US Army Corps of Engineers, 1993.

Hope, Bob, as told to Pete Martin. *Have Tux, Will Travel.* New York: Simon & Schuster, 1954.

Hoyt, Edwin P. *The Bloody Road to Panmunjom.* New York: Stein & Day, 1985.

———. *The Pusan Perimeter: Korea, 1950.* New York: Stein & Day, 1984.

Huston, James A. *Guns and Butter, Powder and Rice: US Army Logistics in the Korean War.* London: Associated University Presses, 1989.

James, D. Clayton. *The Years of MacArthur.* Volume 3, *Triumph and Disaster, 1945–1964.* Boston: Houghton Mifflin, 1985.

James, D. Clayton, with Anne Sharp Wells. *Refighting the Last War: Command and Crisis in Korea, 1950–1953.* New York: Free Press, 1993.

Jian, Chen. *China's Road to the Korean War: The Making of the Sino-American Confrontation.* New York: Columbia University Press, 1994.

Kaufman, Burton J. *The Korean War: Challenges in Crisis, Credibility, and Command.* New York: Knopf, 1986.

Klingon, Greta Rouse. *The Soldier's General: Herbert Butler Powell.* Greta Rouse Klingon, 2002.

Knox, Donald, ed. *The Korean War, Pusan to Chosin: An Oral History.* New York: Harcourt Brace Jovanovich, 1985.

Knox, Donald, ed., with Alfred Coppel. *The Korean War: Uncertain Victory.* New York: Harcourt Brace Jovanovich, 1988.

Kretchik, Walter E. *US Army Doctrine: From the American Revolution to the War on Terror.* Lawrence: University Press of Kansas, 2011.

Leckie, Robert. *Conflict: The History of the Korean War, 1950–53.* New York: G. P. Putnam's Sons, 1962.

Leffler, Melvyn P. *A Preponderance of Power: National Security, The Truman Administration, and the Cold War.* Stanford, CA: Stanford University Press, 1992.

Li, Xiaobing, Allan R. Millett, and Bin Yu, ed. and trans. *Mao's Generals Remember Korea.* Lawrence: University Press of Kansas, 2001.

MacArthur, Douglas. *Reminiscences.* New York: McGraw-Hill, 1964.

Maihafer, Harry J. *From the Hudson to the Yalu: West Point '49 in the Korean War.* College Station: Texas A&M Press, 1993.

Malkasian, Carter. "Toward a Better Understanding of Attrition: The Korean and Vietnam Wars." *Journal of Military History,* July 2004, 911–942.

Marshall, S. L. A. *Bringing Up the Rear: A Memoir.* Edited by Cate Marshall. San Rafael, CA: Presidio, 1970.

———. *The River and the Gauntlet: Defeat of the Eighth Army by the Chinese Communist*

Forces, November, 1950, in the Battle of the Chongchon River, Korea. Westwood, CT: Greenwood Press, 1953.

Matray, James I., and Donald W. Boose Jr., eds. *The Ashgate Research Companion to the Korean War.* Burlington, VT: Ashgate, 2014.

Millett, Allan R. *The War for Korea, 1950–1951: They Came from the North.* Lawrence: University Press of Kansas, 2010.

Mitchell, George C. *Matthew B. Ridgway: Soldier, Statesman, Scholar, Citizen.* Mechanicsburg, PA: Stackpole Books, 2002.

Mossman, Billy C. *Ebb and Flow: November 1950–July 1951.* Washington, DC: Center of Military History, United States Army, 1990.

Nenninger, Timothy K. "Leavenworth and Its Critics: The US Army Command and General Staff School, 1920–1940." *Journal of Military History,* April 1974, 199–231.

Noble, Harold Joyce. *Embassy at War.* Edited by Frank Baldwin. Seattle: University of Washington Press, 1975.

Oliver, George S. *The Tents.* Spokane, WA: George S. Oliver, 2002.

Paik, Sun Yup. *From Pusan to Panmunjom.* Washington, DC: Potomac Books, 1992.

Public Information Office, Seventh Infantry Division. *The Bayonet: The History of the 7th Infantry Division in Korea.* Air Line Service, 1953.

Quinn, William W. *Buffalo Bill Remembers: Truth and Courage.* Fowlerville, MI: Wilderness Adventure Books, 1991.

Rice, Douglas, ed. *Voices from the Korean War: Personal Accounts of Those Who Served.* Bloomington, IL: iUniverse, 2011.

Ricks, Thomas E. *The Generals: American Military Command from World War II to Today.* New York: Penguin, 2012.

Ridgway, Matthew B. *The Korean War.* Garden City, NY: Doubleday, 1967.

Ridgway, Matthew B., as told to Harold H. Martin. *Soldier: The Memoirs of Matthew B. Ridgway.* Westport, CT: Greenwood Press, 1956.

Robertson, William Glann. *Counterattack on the Naktong, 1950.* Leavenworth, KS: Combat Studies Institute, 1985.

Sams, Crawford F. *"Medic": The Mission of an American Military Doctor in Occupied Japan and Wartorn Korea.* Edited by Zabelle Zakarian. London: East Gate Book, 1998.

Sandler, Stanley. *The Korean War: No Victors, No Vanquished.* Lexington: University Press of Kentucky, 1999.

Schaller, Michael. *Douglas MacArthur: The Far Eastern General.* New York: Oxford University Press, 1989.

Sebald, William J., with Russell Brines. *With MacArthur in Japan: A Personal History of the Occupation.* New York: Norton, 1965.

Shisler, Gail B. *For Country and Corps: The Life of General Oliver P. Smith.* Annapolis, MD: Naval Institute Press, 2009.

Skaggs, David C. "The KATUSA Experiment: The Integration of Korean Nationals into the US Army, 1950–1965." *Military Affairs,* April 1974, 53–58.

Spiller, Roger J., ed. *Combined Arms in Battle since 1939.* Leavenworth, KS: US Command and General Staff College Press, 1992.

Spurr, Russell. *Enter the Dragon: China's Undeclared War against the US in Korea, 1950–1951.* New York: Newmarket Press, 1988.

Stanton, Shelby L. *America's Tenth Legion: X Corps in Korea, 1950.* Novato, CA: Presidio, 1989.

Stratemeyer, George E. *The Three Wars of Lt. Gen. George E. Stratemeyer: His Korean War Diary.* Edited by William T. Y'Blood. Washington, DC: Air Force History and Museums Program, 1999.

Taaffe, Stephen R. *Marshall and His Generals: US Army Commanders in World War II.* Lawrence: University Press of Kansas, 2011.

Thompson, Reginald. *Cry Korea: The Korean War: A Reporter's Notebook.* London: Reportage Press, 2009.

Toland, John. *In Mortal Combat: Korea, 1950–1953.* New York: William Morrow, 1991.

Tomedi, Rudy, ed. *No Bugles, No Drums: An Oral History of the Korean War.* New York: Wiley, 1993.

Tucker, Spencer C., ed. *Encyclopedia of the Korean War: A Political, Social, and Military History.* Volume 1. Santa Barbara, CA: ABC-CLIO, 2000.

United States Senate. *Hearings before the Committee on Armed Services and the Committee on Foreign Relations, Eighty-second Congress, first session, to Conduct an Inquiry into the Military Situation in the Far East and the Facts Surrounding the Relief of General of the Army Douglas MacArthur from His Assignment in that Area. 82nd Cong.* Washington, DC: University Publications of America, 1951.

Voorhees, Melvin B. *Korean Tales.* New York: Simon & Schuster, 1952.

Wade, Gary. *CSI Report No. 5: Conversations with General J. Lawton Collins.* Fort Leavenworth, KS: Combat Studies Institute, 1983.

Weintraub, Stanley. *MacArthur's War: Korea and the Undoing of an American Hero.* New York: Free Press, 2000.

Wiersema, Richard. *No More Bad Force Myths: A Tactical Study of Regimental Combat in Korea, July 1950.* Fort Leavenworth, KS: School of Advanced Military Studies, United States Army Command and General Staff College, 1997.

Wiltz, John E. "The MacArthur Hearings of 1951: The Secret Testimony." *Military Affairs,* December 1975, 167–172.

Winton, Harold R. "Toward an American Philosophy of Command." *Journal of Military History,* October 2000, 1035–1060.

Index

Bowen, Frank, 195
Bowling Alley, South Korea, 45
Bradley, Omar, 27, 28, 30, 33, 40, 65, 160, 184, 185, 186, 187
Bradley, Sladen
    appointed Twenty-fifth Division commander, 161–162
    background and character, 161–162
    and Chinese spring offensive, 190, 191
    evaluation of, 201
    exhaustion of, 122
    and Kunu-ri, 113, 115
    and Kunu-ri/Gauntlet controversy, 116
    and retreat through Gauntlet, 116
Bryan, Blackshear
    appointed Twenty-fourth Division commander, 159–160
    background and character, 159–160
    and Chinese spring offensive, 190, 191
    and counterattack across 38th Parallel, 196
    evaluation of, 201

Cairo Conference, 5
Cates, Clifton, 72, 193
central corridor, 164–172
Champeny, Art, 43, 49
Chiles, John, 172, 194
Chinese intervention, 96–98
Chinese New Year's offensive, 151–153
Chinese spring offensive, 189–196
Chinhung, North Korea, 134
Chinju, South Korea, 34, 35, 42, 43, 85
Chipyong, Battle of, 171–172
Chochiwon, South Korea, 20
Chonan, South Korea, 20, 26, 85
Chongchon River, 91, 99, 100, 101, 102, 103, 104, 105, 112, 113, 114
Chonju, South Korea, 85
Chosan, North Korea, 91, 98
Chosin Reservoir, North Korea, 125, 128, 129–135
Chromite, Operation, 60–74, 91–93
Chumunjin, South Korea, 153
Church, John
    appointed Twenty-fourth Division commander, 24
    background and character, 24–25
    and Chinese New Year's offensive, 152
    and defense of Pohang, 49

deployed to Masan area, 34–35, 41
and drive to Pyongyang, 89
and Eighth Army advance to the Yalu, 91, 94
and end of the year offensive, 109, 110, 111
evaluation of, 57–58, 141, 200, 212, 214, 215, 219
and first Chinese offensive, 98, 99, 101, 102, 103
leads survey group to Korea, 13, 19
and Naktong Bulge, 44
and Pusan Perimeter breakout, 80
relieved of command, 156
and second Chinese offensive, 113, 141
and Twenty-fourth Division overhaul, 47–48
Cloverleaf Hill, South Korea, 44
Collins, J. Lawton
    and Chosin Reservoir, 131
    and decision to overhaul combat commanders, 151, 153, 156, 159, 162
    and division of Eighth Army and Tenth Corps, 88
    and Inchon landing, 61, 63–64, 79
    opinion of Almond, 66
    opinion of Coulter, 80
    opinion of Ferenbaugh, 160
    opinion of Hoge, 160
    opinion of MacArthur, 79, 184
    opinion of McClure, 165, 168
    opinion of Michaelis, 46
    opinion of Milburn, 81–82, 155
    opinion of Ridgway, 40, 145, 147, 148, 185
    opinion of Smith, 180
    opinion of Van Fleet, 40, 185–188
    opinion of Walker, 40, 46, 56, 122
    and second Chinese offensive, 119–120
    and selection of high-ranking combat commanders, 205–207, 210
    trip to Korea in August 1950, 46, 63–64
    trip to Korea in December 1950, 119–120
    trip to Korea in January 1951, 164
    trip to Korea in July 1950, 22
Corley, John, 112
Coughlin, John, 194
Coulter, John
    appointed Eighth Army deputy commander, 153–154